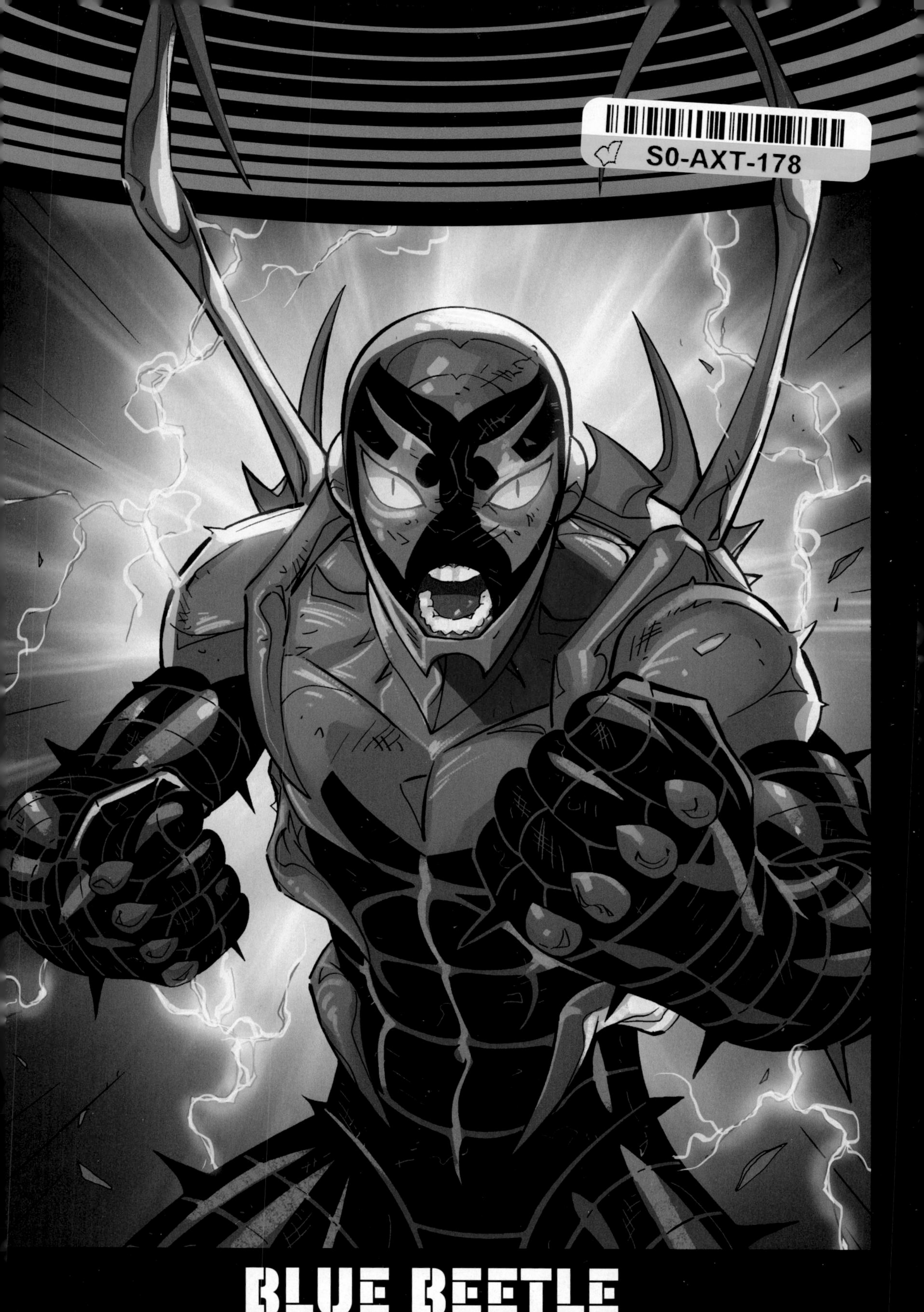

BLUE BEETLE

VOL.2 HARD CHOICES

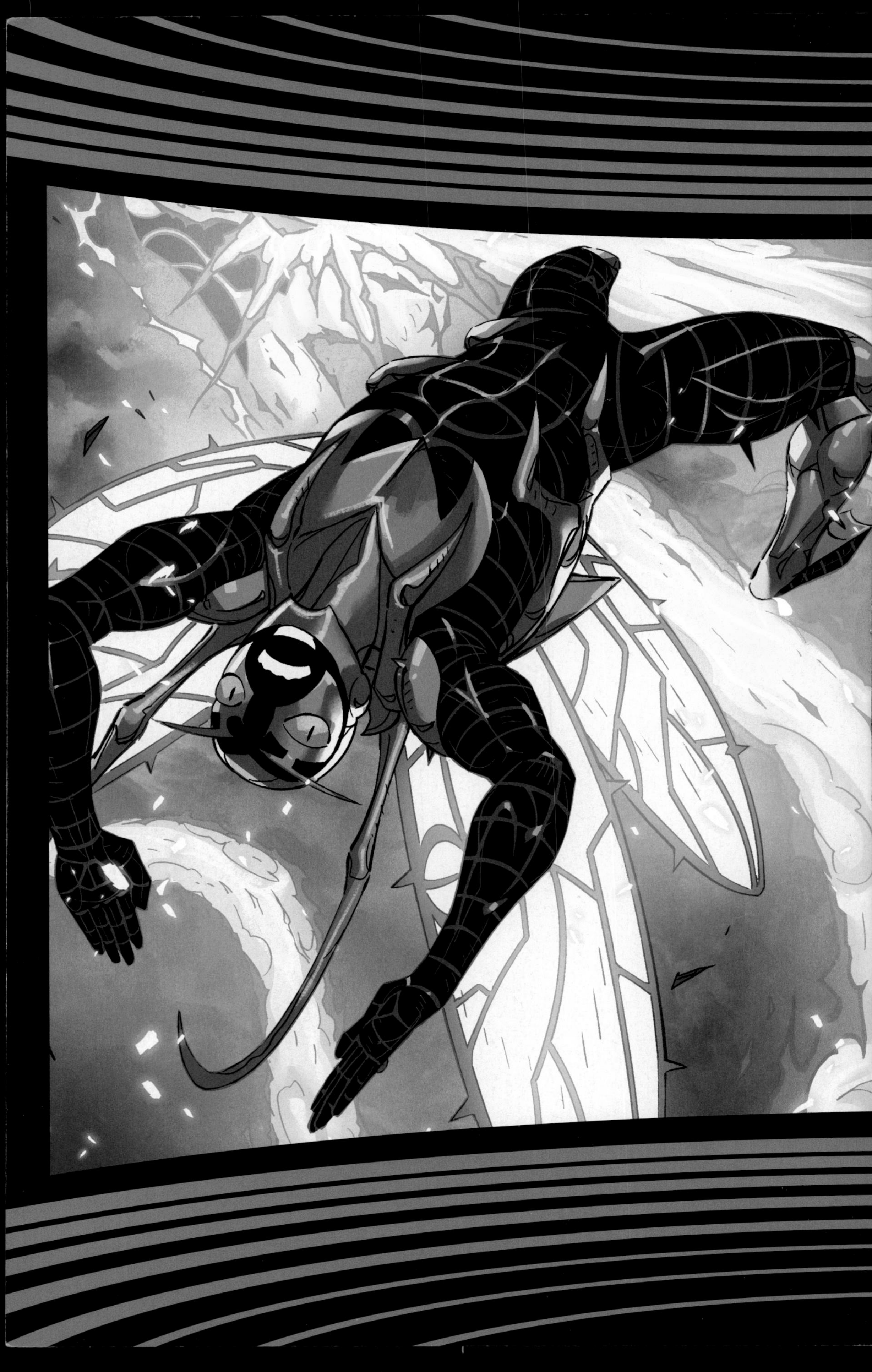

BLUE BEETLE
VOL.2 HARD CHOICES

KEITH GIFFEN
J.M. DeMATTEIS
SCOTT KOLINS
writers

SCOTT KOLINS
artist

ROMULO FAJARDO JR.
colorist

JOSH REED
letterer

SCOTT KOLINS
collection cover artist

BATMAN created by BOB KANE with BILL FINGER

JIM CHADWICK Editor – Original Series ✳ **ROB LEVIN** Assistant Editor – Original Series
JEB WOODARD Group Editor – Collected Editions ✳ **ERIKA ROTHBERG** Editor – Collected Edition
STEVE COOK Design Director – Books ✳ **SHANNON STEWART** Publication Design

BOB HARRAS Senior VP – Editor-in-Chief, DC Comics
PAT McCALLUM Executive Editor, DC Comics

DIANE NELSON President ✳ **DAN DiDIO** Publisher ✳ **JIM LEE** Publisher ✳ **GEOFF JOHNS** President & Chief Creative Officer
AMIT DESAI Executive VP – Business & Marketing Strategy, Direct to Consumer & Global Franchise Management
SAM ADES Senior VP & General Manager, Digital Services ✳ **BOBBIE CHASE** VP & Executive Editor, Young Reader & Talent Development
MARK CHIARELLO Senior VP – Art, Design & Collected Editions ✳ **JOHN CUNNINGHAM** Senior VP – Sales & Trade Marketing
ANNE DePIES Senior VP – Business Strategy, Finance & Administration ✳ **DON FALLETTI** VP – Manufacturing Operations
LAWRENCE GANEM VP – Editorial Administration & Talent Relations ✳ **ALISON GILL** Senior VP – Manufacturing & Operations
HANK KANALZ Senior VP – Editorial Strategy & Administration ✳ **JAY KOGAN** VP – Legal Affairs ✳ **JACK MAHAN** VP – Business Affairs
NICK J. NAPOLITANO VP – Manufacturing Administration ✳ **EDDIE SCANNELL** VP – Consumer Marketing
COURTNEY SIMMONS Senior VP – Publicity & Communications ✳ **JIM (SKI) SOKOLOWSKI** VP – Comic Book Specialty Sales & Trade Marketing
NANCY SPEARS VP – Mass, Book, Digital Sales & Trade Marketing ✳ **MICHELE R. WELLS** VP – Content Strategy

BLUE BEETLE VOL. 2: HARD CHOICES

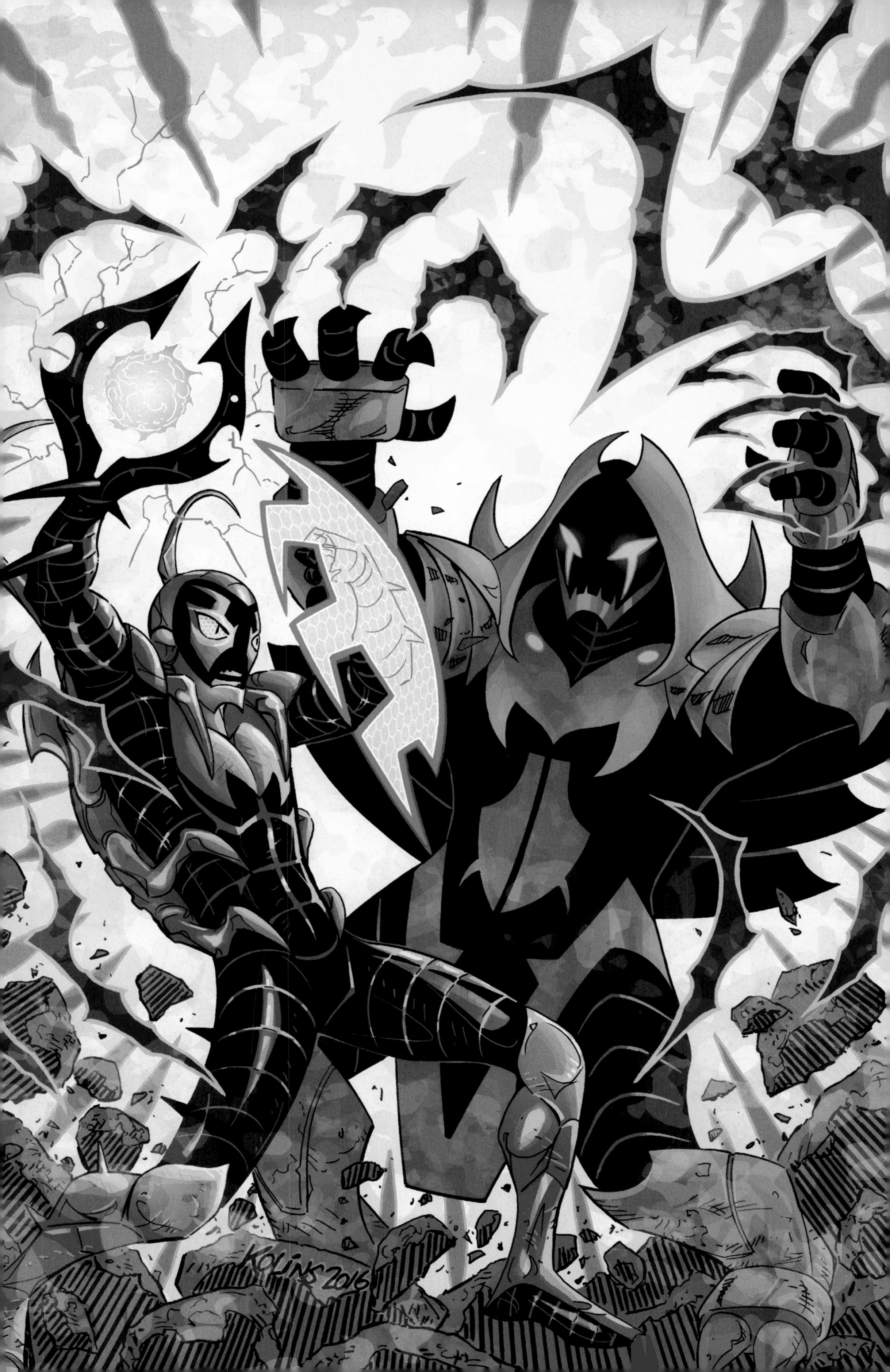
KOLINS 2016

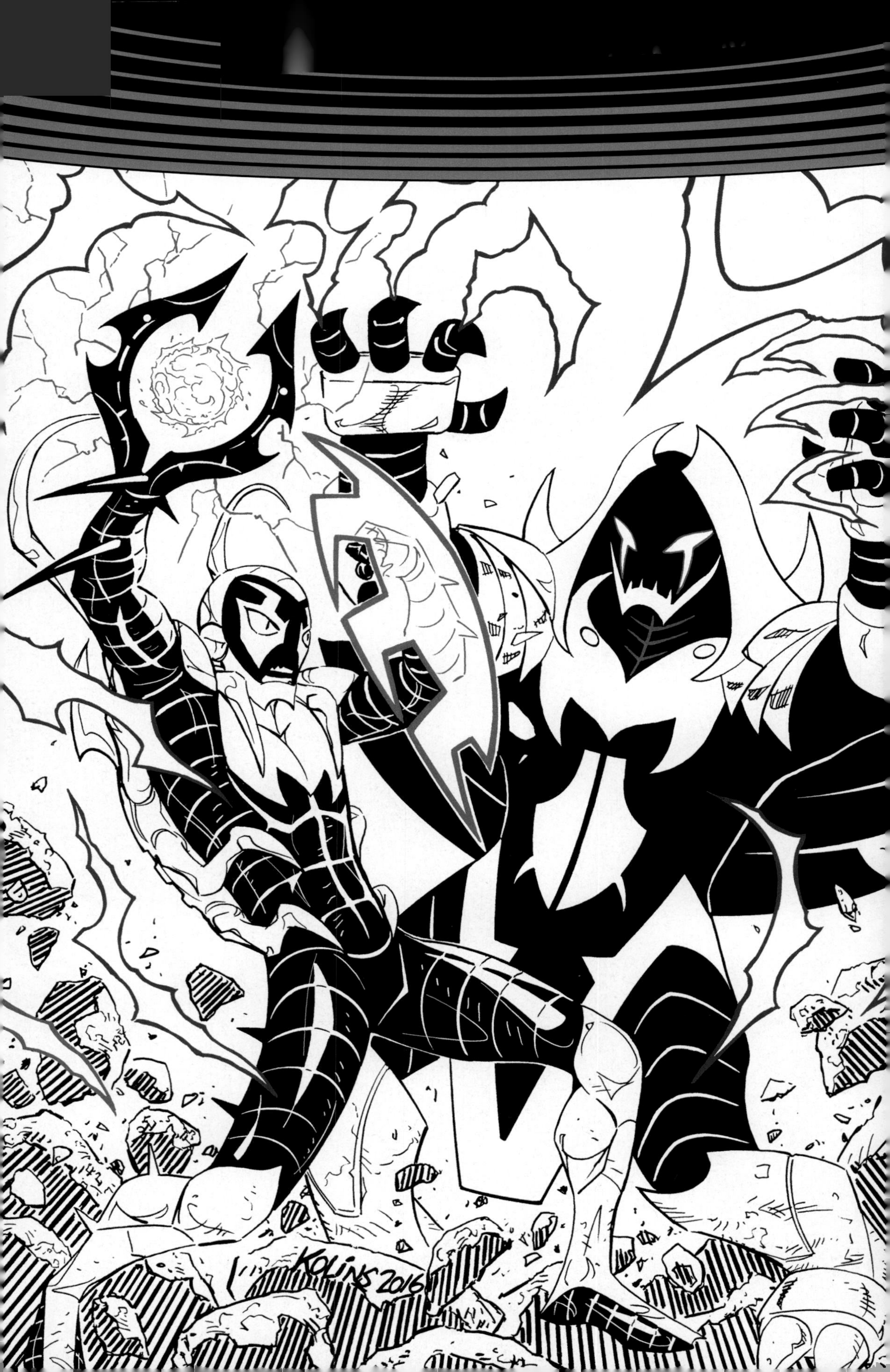
KOLINS 2016

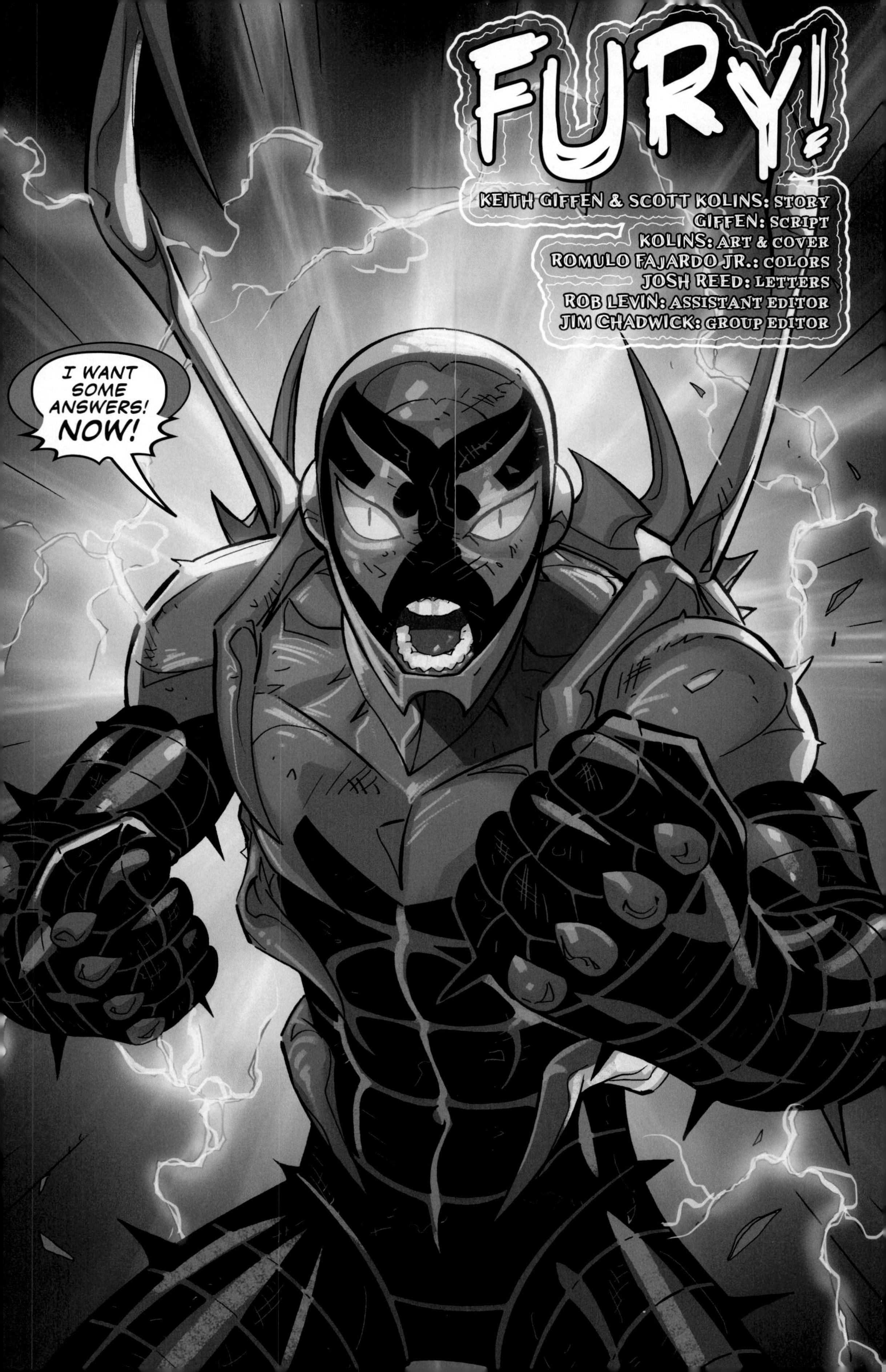
FURY!
KEITH GIFFEN & SCOTT KOLINS: STORY
GIFFEN: SCRIPT
KOLINS: ART & COVER
ROMULO FAJARDO JR.: COLORS
JOSH REED: LETTERS
ROB LEVIN: ASSISTANT EDITOR
JIM CHADWICK: GROUP EDITOR
I WANT SOME ANSWERS! NOW!

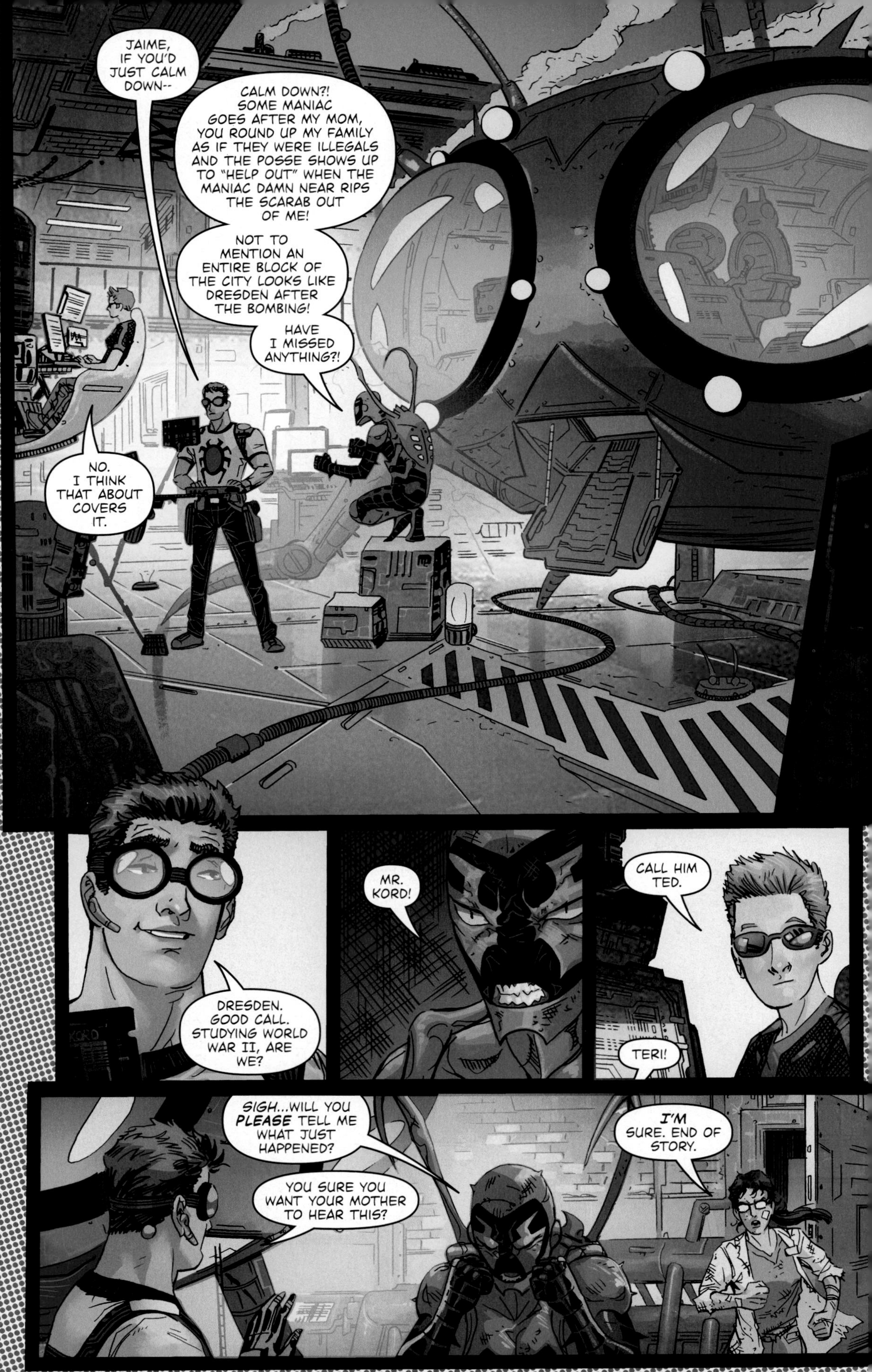
JAIME, IF YOU'D JUST CALM DOWN--
CALM DOWN?! SOME MANIAC GOES AFTER MY MOM, YOU ROUND UP MY FAMILY AS IF THEY WERE ILLEGALS AND THE POSSE SHOWS UP TO "HELP OUT" WHEN THE MANIAC DAMN NEAR RIPS THE SCARAB OUT OF ME!
NOT TO MENTION AN ENTIRE BLOCK OF THE CITY LOOKS LIKE DRESDEN AFTER THE BOMBING!
HAVE I MISSED ANYTHING?!
NO. I THINK THAT ABOUT COVERS IT.
DRESDEN. GOOD CALL. STUDYING WORLD WAR II, ARE WE?
MR. KORD!
CALL HIM TED.
TERI!
SIGH...WILL YOU *PLEASE* TELL ME WHAT JUST HAPPENED?
YOU SURE YOU WANT YOUR MOTHER TO HEAR THIS?
I'M SURE. END OF STORY.

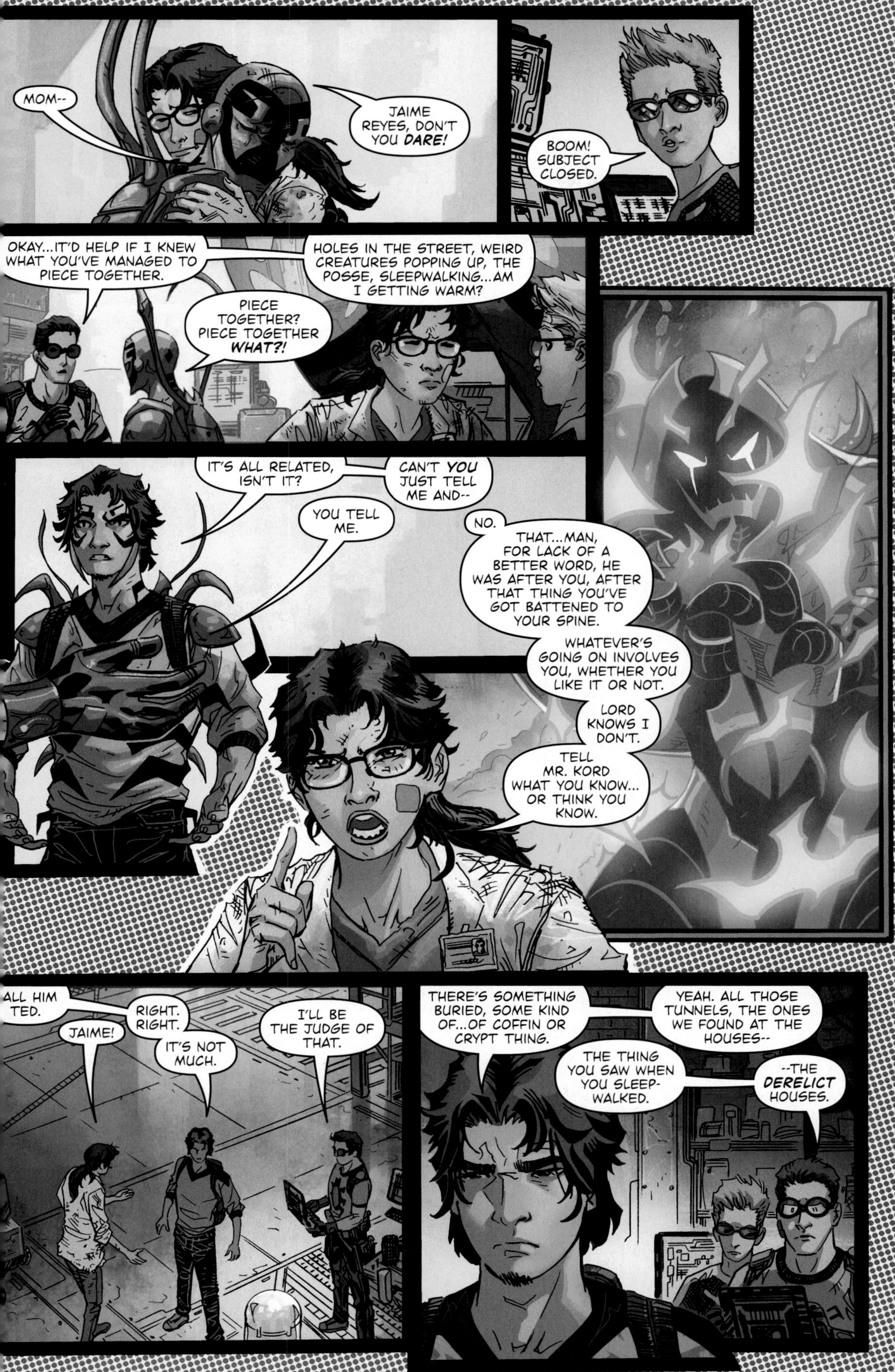
MOM--
JAIME REYES, DON'T YOU *DARE!*
BOOM! SUBJECT CLOSED.
OKAY...IT'D HELP IF I KNEW WHAT YOU'VE MANAGED TO PIECE TOGETHER.
HOLES IN THE STREET, WEIRD CREATURES POPPING UP, THE POSSE, SLEEPWALKING...AM I GETTING WARM?
PIECE TOGETHER? PIECE TOGETHER *WHAT?!*
IT'S ALL RELATED, ISN'T IT?
CAN'T *YOU* JUST TELL ME AND--
YOU TELL ME.
NO.
THAT...MAN, FOR LACK OF A BETTER WORD, HE WAS AFTER YOU, AFTER THAT THING YOU'VE GOT BATTENED TO YOUR SPINE.
WHATEVER'S GOING ON INVOLVES YOU, WHETHER YOU LIKE IT OR NOT.
LORD KNOWS I DON'T.
TELL MR. KORD WHAT YOU KNOW... OR THINK YOU KNOW.
ALL HIM TED.
JAIME!
RIGHT. RIGHT.
IT'S NOT MUCH.
I'LL BE THE JUDGE OF THAT.
THERE'S SOMETHING BURIED, SOME KIND OF...OF COFFIN OR CRYPT THING.
YEAH. ALL THOSE TUNNELS, THE ONES WE FOUND AT THE HOUSES--
THE THING YOU SAW WHEN YOU SLEEP-WALKED.
--THE *DERELICT* HOUSES.

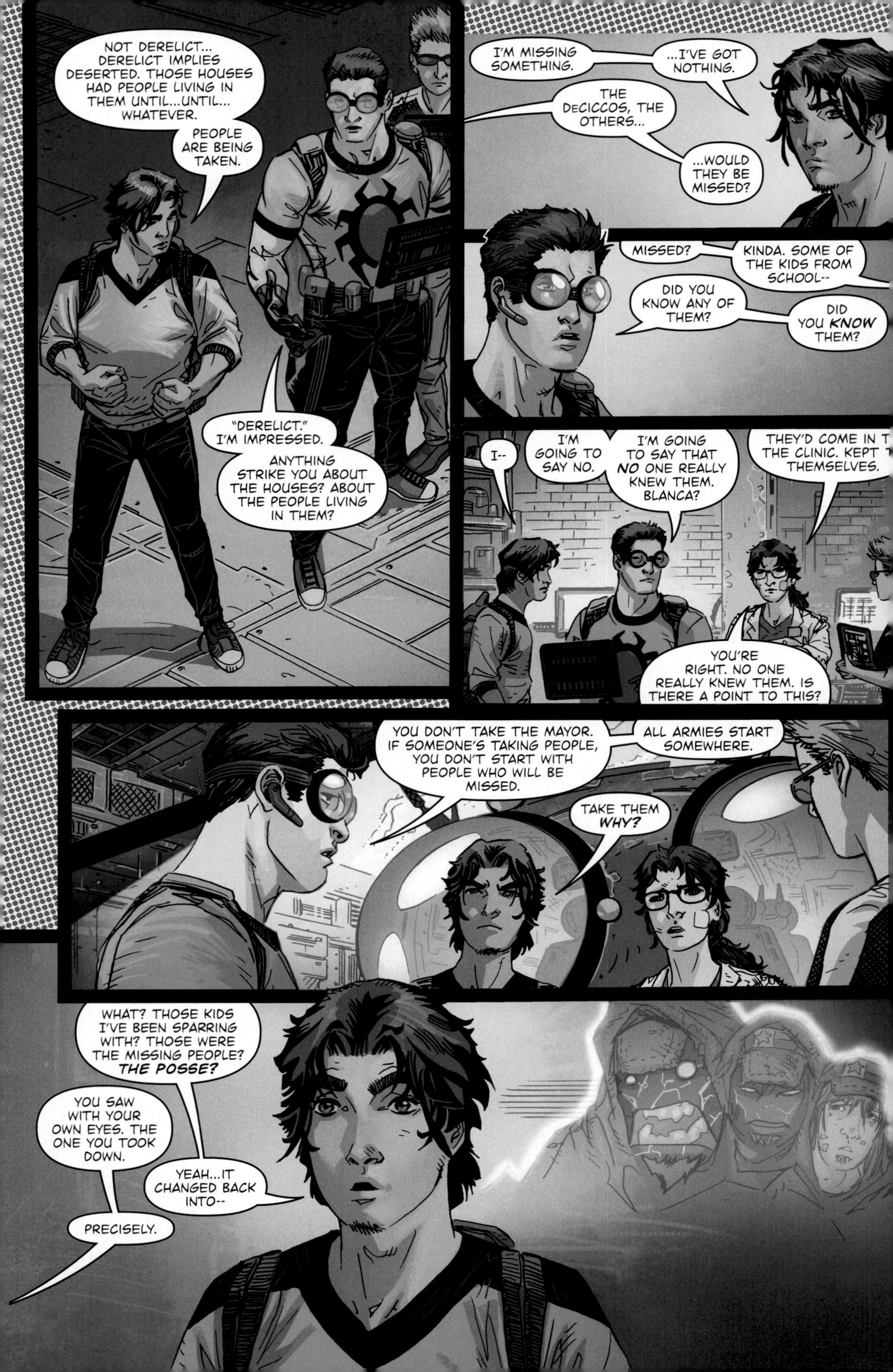

NOT DERELICT... DERELICT IMPLIES DESERTED. THOSE HOUSES HAD PEOPLE LIVING IN THEM UNTIL...UNTIL... WHATEVER.
PEOPLE ARE BEING TAKEN.
"DERELICT." I'M IMPRESSED.
ANYTHING STRIKE YOU ABOUT THE HOUSES? ABOUT THE PEOPLE LIVING IN THEM?
I'M MISSING SOMETHING.
...I'VE GOT NOTHING.
THE DECICCOS, THE OTHERS...
...WOULD THEY BE MISSED?
MISSED?
KINDA. SOME OF THE KIDS FROM SCHOOL--
DID YOU KNOW ANY OF THEM?
DID YOU *KNOW* THEM?
I--
I'M GOING TO SAY NO.
I'M GOING TO SAY THAT *NO* ONE REALLY KNEW THEM. BLANCA?
THEY'D COME IN T THE CLINIC. KEPT T THEMSELVES.
YOU'RE RIGHT. NO ONE REALLY KNEW THEM. IS THERE A POINT TO THIS?
YOU DON'T TAKE THE MAYOR. IF SOMEONE'S TAKING PEOPLE, YOU DON'T START WITH PEOPLE WHO WILL BE MISSED.
ALL ARMIES START SOMEWHERE.
TAKE THEM *WHY?*
WHAT? THOSE KIDS I'VE BEEN SPARRING WITH? THOSE WERE THE MISSING PEOPLE? *THE POSSE?*
YOU SAW WITH YOUR OWN EYES. THE ONE YOU TOOK DOWN.
YEAH...IT CHANGED BACK INTO--
PRECISELY.

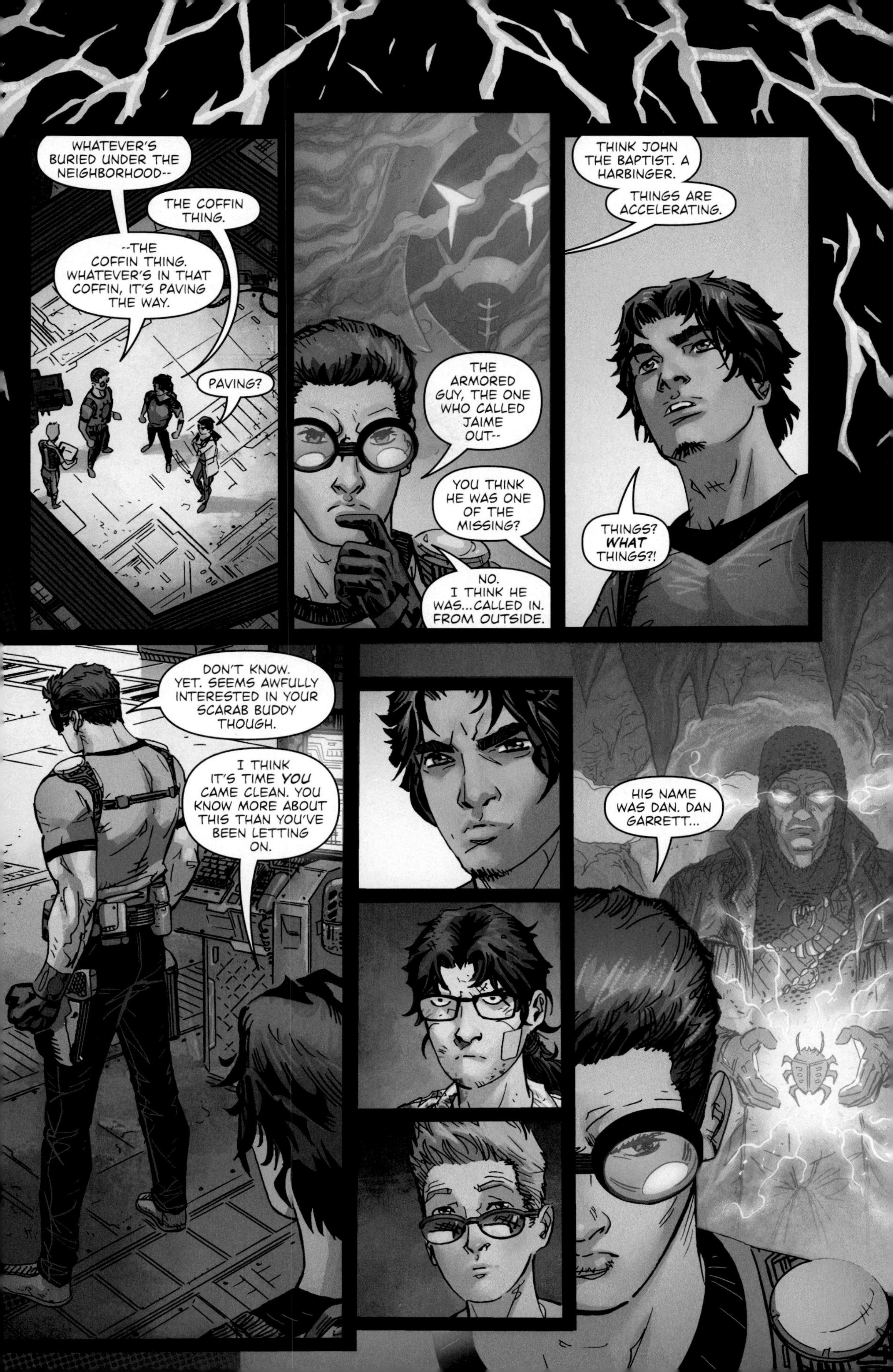
WHATEVER'S BURIED UNDER THE NEIGHBORHOOD--
THE COFFIN THING.
--THE COFFIN THING. WHATEVER'S IN THAT COFFIN, IT'S PAVING THE WAY.
PAVING?
THE ARMORED GUY, THE ONE WHO CALLED JAIME OUT--
YOU THINK HE WAS ONE OF THE MISSING?
NO. I THINK HE WAS...CALLED IN. FROM OUTSIDE.
THINK JOHN THE BAPTIST. A HARBINGER.
THINGS ARE ACCELERATING.
THINGS? **WHAT** THINGS?!
DON'T KNOW. YET. SEEMS AWFULLY INTERESTED IN YOUR SCARAB BUDDY THOUGH.
I THINK IT'S TIME **YOU** CAME CLEAN. YOU KNOW MORE ABOUT THIS THAN YOU'VE BEEN LETTING ON.
HIS NAME WAS DAN. DAN GARRETT...

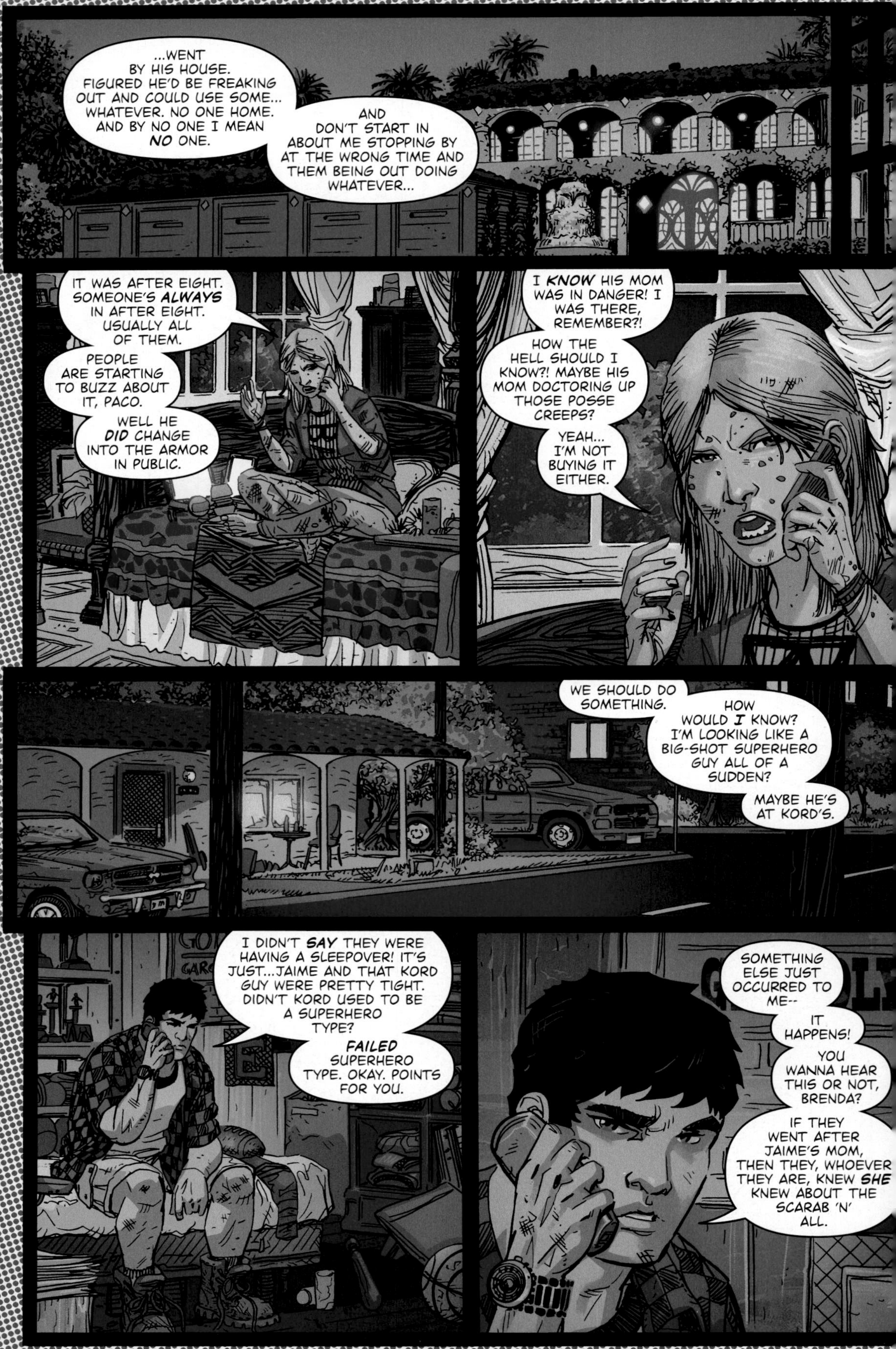
...WENT BY HIS HOUSE. FIGURED HE'D BE FREAKING OUT AND COULD USE SOME... WHATEVER. NO ONE HOME. AND BY NO ONE I MEAN **NO** ONE.
AND DON'T START IN ABOUT ME STOPPING BY AT THE WRONG TIME AND THEM BEING OUT DOING WHATEVER...
IT WAS AFTER EIGHT. SOMEONE'S **ALWAYS** IN AFTER EIGHT. USUALLY ALL OF THEM.
PEOPLE ARE STARTING TO BUZZ ABOUT IT, PACO.
WELL HE **DID** CHANGE INTO THE ARMOR IN PUBLIC.
I **KNOW** HIS MOM WAS IN DANGER! I WAS THERE, REMEMBER?!
HOW THE HELL SHOULD I KNOW?! MAYBE HIS MOM DOCTORING UP THOSE POSSE CREEPS?
YEAH... I'M NOT BUYING IT EITHER.
WE SHOULD DO SOMETHING.
HOW WOULD **I** KNOW? I'M LOOKING LIKE A BIG-SHOT SUPERHERO GUY ALL OF A SUDDEN?
MAYBE HE'S AT KORD'S.
I DIDN'T **SAY** THEY WERE HAVING A SLEEPOVER! IT'S JUST...JAIME AND THAT KORD GUY WERE PRETTY TIGHT. DIDN'T KORD USED TO BE A SUPERHERO TYPE?
FAILED SUPERHERO TYPE. OKAY. POINTS FOR YOU.
SOMETHING ELSE JUST OCCURRED TO ME--
IT HAPPENS!
YOU WANNA HEAR THIS OR NOT, BRENDA?
IF THEY WENT AFTER JAIME'S MOM, THEN THEY, WHOEVER THEY ARE, KNEW **SHE** KNEW ABOUT THE SCARAB 'N' ALL.

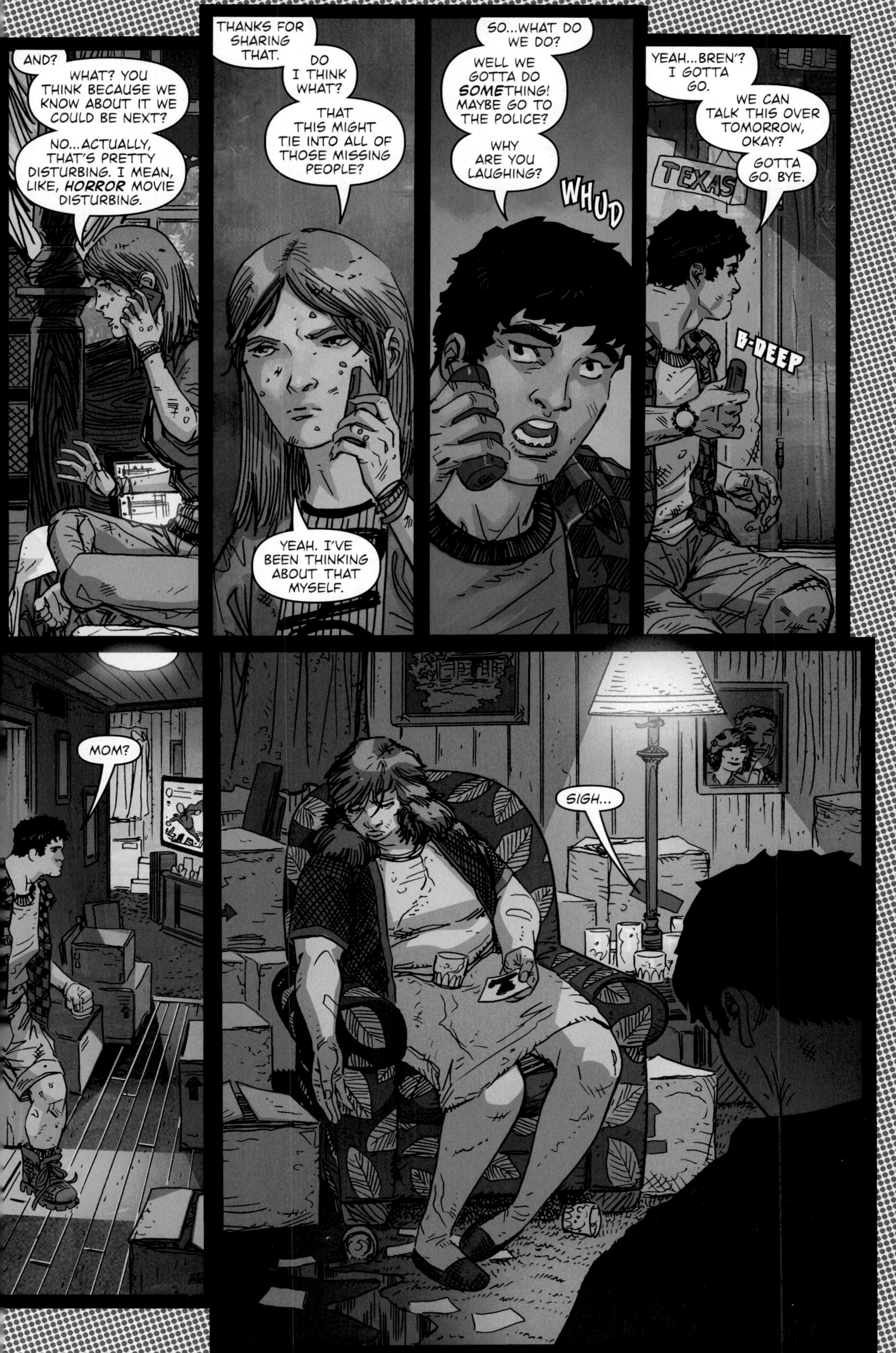
AND?
WHAT? YOU THINK BECAUSE WE KNOW ABOUT IT WE COULD BE NEXT?
NO...ACTUALLY, THAT'S PRETTY DISTURBING. I MEAN, LIKE, **HORROR** MOVIE DISTURBING.
THANKS FOR SHARING THAT.
DO I THINK WHAT?
THAT THIS MIGHT TIE INTO ALL OF THOSE MISSING PEOPLE?
YEAH. I'VE BEEN THINKING ABOUT THAT MYSELF.
SO...WHAT DO WE DO?
WELL WE GOTTA DO **SOME**THING! MAYBE GO TO THE POLICE?
WHY ARE YOU LAUGHING?
WHUD
YEAH...BREN'? I GOTTA GO.
WE CAN TALK THIS OVER TOMORROW, OKAY?
GOTTA GO. BYE.
TEXAS
B-DEEP
MOM?
SIGH...

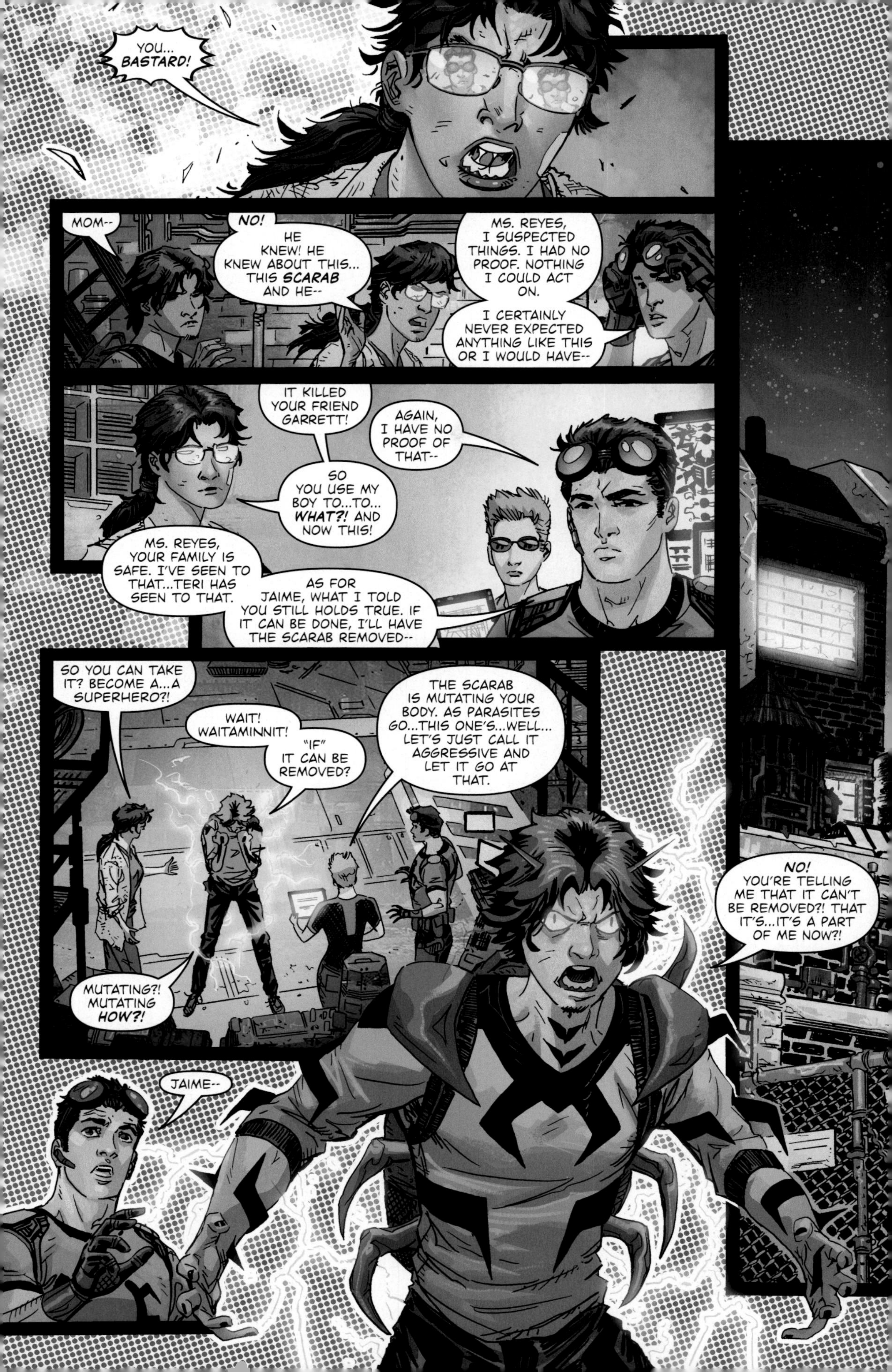
YOU... BASTARD!
MOM--
NO! HE KNEW! HE KNEW ABOUT THIS... THIS SCARAB AND HE--
MS. REYES, I SUSPECTED THINGS. I HAD NO PROOF. NOTHING I COULD ACT ON.
I CERTAINLY NEVER EXPECTED ANYTHING LIKE THIS OR I WOULD HAVE--
IT KILLED YOUR FRIEND GARRETT!
AGAIN, I HAVE NO PROOF OF THAT--
SO YOU USE MY BOY TO...TO... WHAT?! AND NOW THIS!
MS. REYES, YOUR FAMILY IS SAFE. I'VE SEEN TO THAT...TERI HAS SEEN TO THAT.
AS FOR JAIME, WHAT I TOLD YOU STILL HOLDS TRUE. IF IT CAN BE DONE, I'LL HAVE THE SCARAB REMOVED--
SO YOU CAN TAKE IT? BECOME A...A SUPERHERO?!
WAIT! WAITAMINNIT!
"IF" IT CAN BE REMOVED?
THE SCARAB IS MUTATING YOUR BODY. AS PARASITES GO...THIS ONE'S...WELL... LET'S JUST CALL IT AGGRESSIVE AND LET IT GO AT THAT.
MUTATING?! MUTATING HOW?!
NO! YOU'RE TELLING ME THAT IT CAN'T BE REMOVED?! THAT IT'S...IT'S A PART OF ME NOW?!
JAIME--

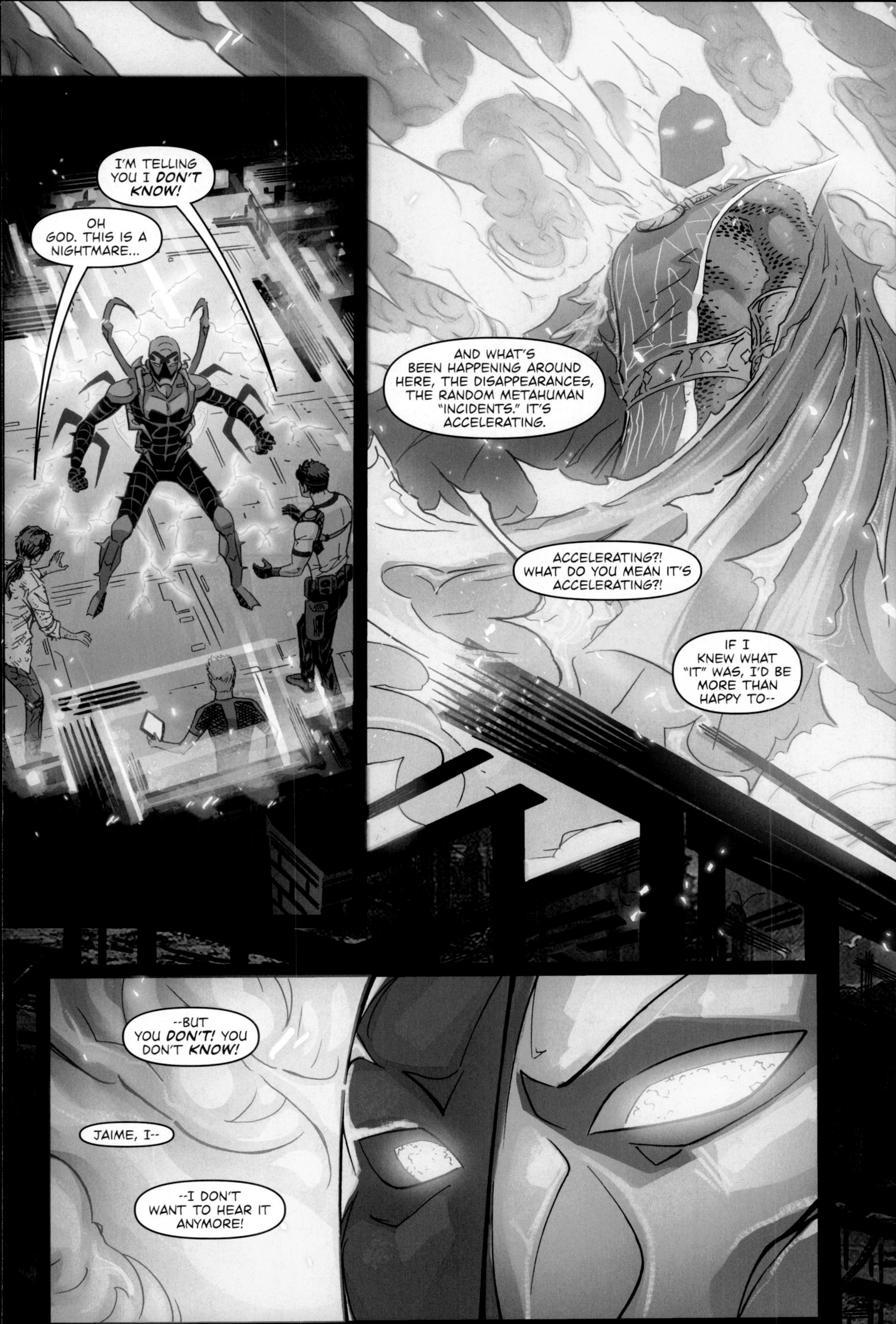
I'M TELLING YOU I **DON'T KNOW!**
OH GOD. THIS IS A NIGHTMARE...
AND WHAT'S BEEN HAPPENING AROUND HERE, THE DISAPPEARANCES, THE RANDOM METAHUMAN "INCIDENTS." IT'S ACCELERATING.
ACCELERATING?! WHAT DO YOU MEAN IT'S ACCELERATING?!
IF I KNEW WHAT "IT" WAS, I'D BE MORE THAN HAPPY TO--
--BUT YOU **DON'T!** YOU DON'T **KNOW!**
JAIME, I--
--I DON'T WANT TO HEAR IT ANYMORE!

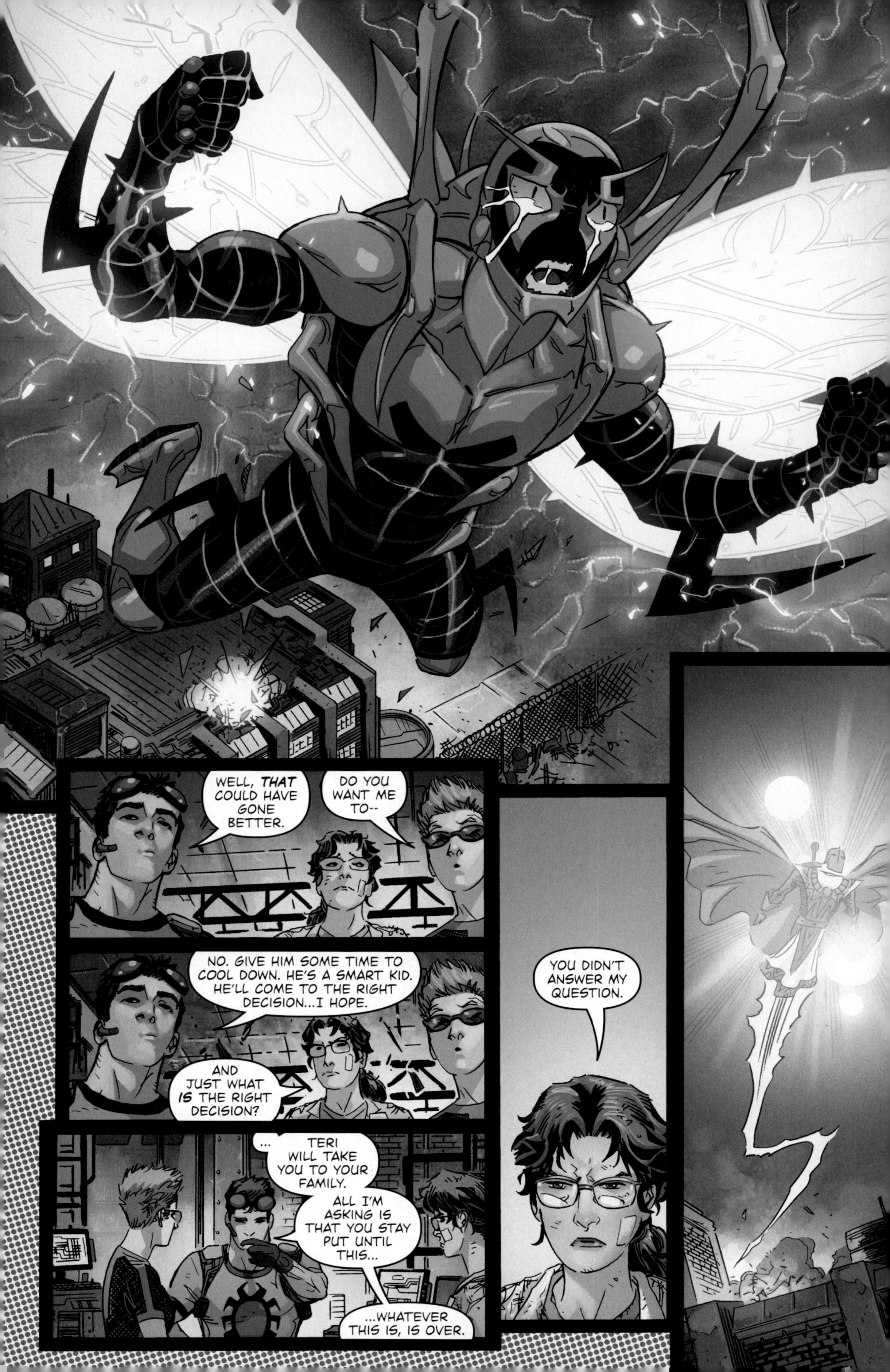
WELL, THAT COULD HAVE GONE BETTER.
DO YOU WANT ME TO--
NO. GIVE HIM SOME TIME TO COOL DOWN. HE'S A SMART KID. HE'LL COME TO THE RIGHT DECISION...I HOPE.
AND JUST WHAT IS THE RIGHT DECISION?
...
TERI WILL TAKE YOU TO YOUR FAMILY.
ALL I'M ASKING IS THAT YOU STAY PUT UNTIL THIS...
...WHATEVER THIS IS, IS OVER.
YOU DIDN'T ANSWER MY QUESTION.

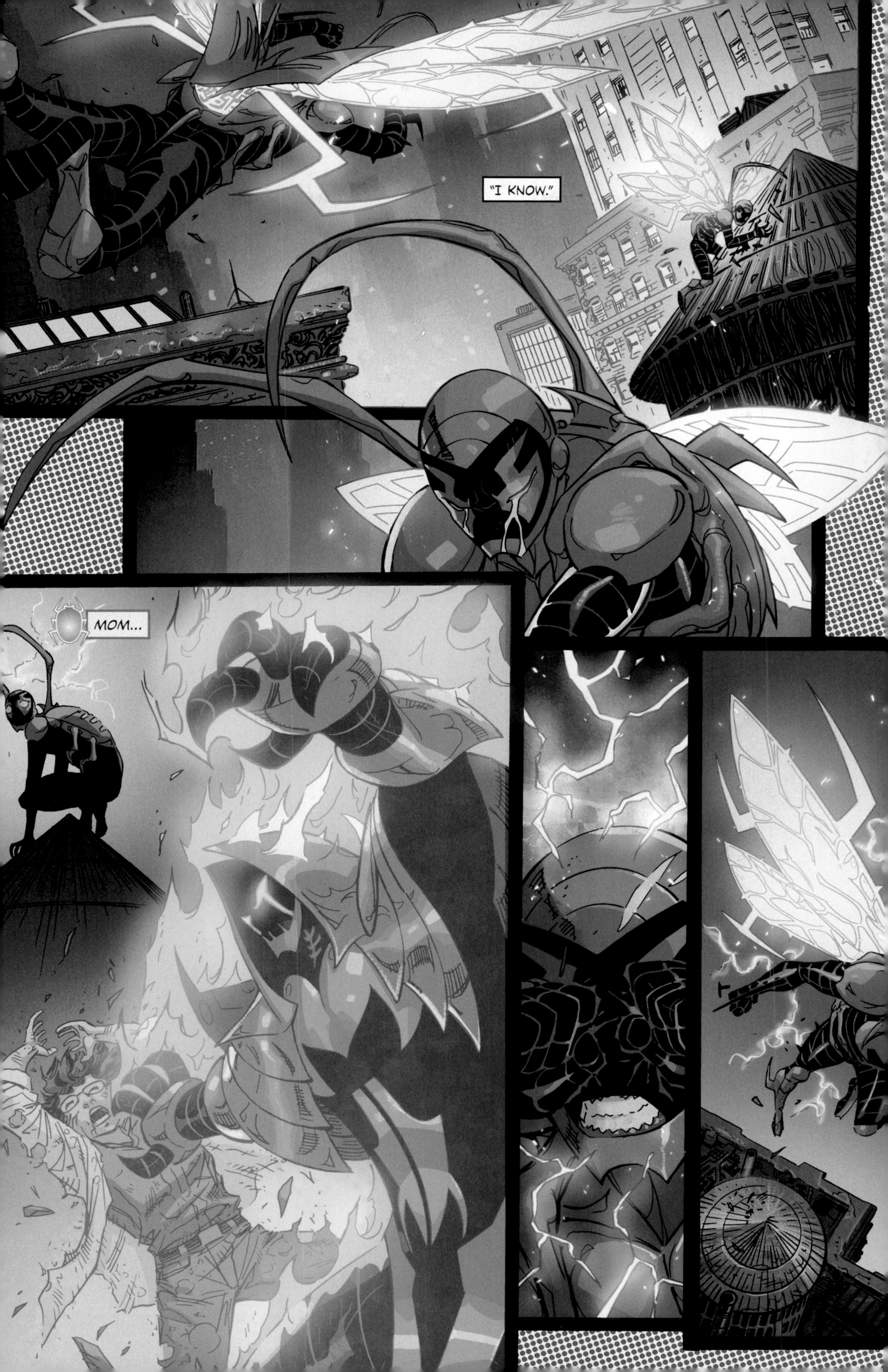
"I KNOW."
MOM...

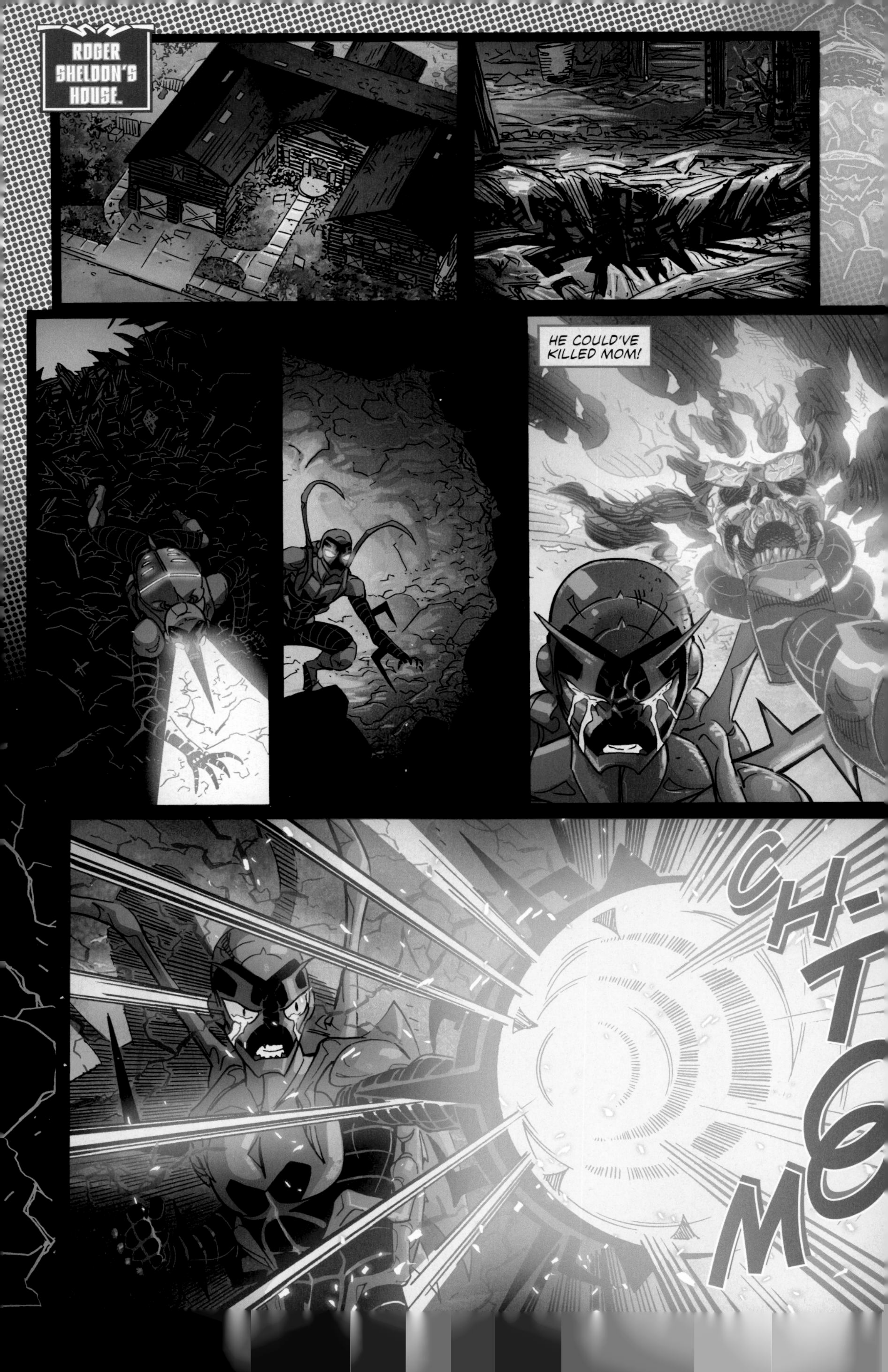
ROGER SHELDON'S HOUSE.
HE COULD'VE KILLED MOM!
CH-T-O-O-M

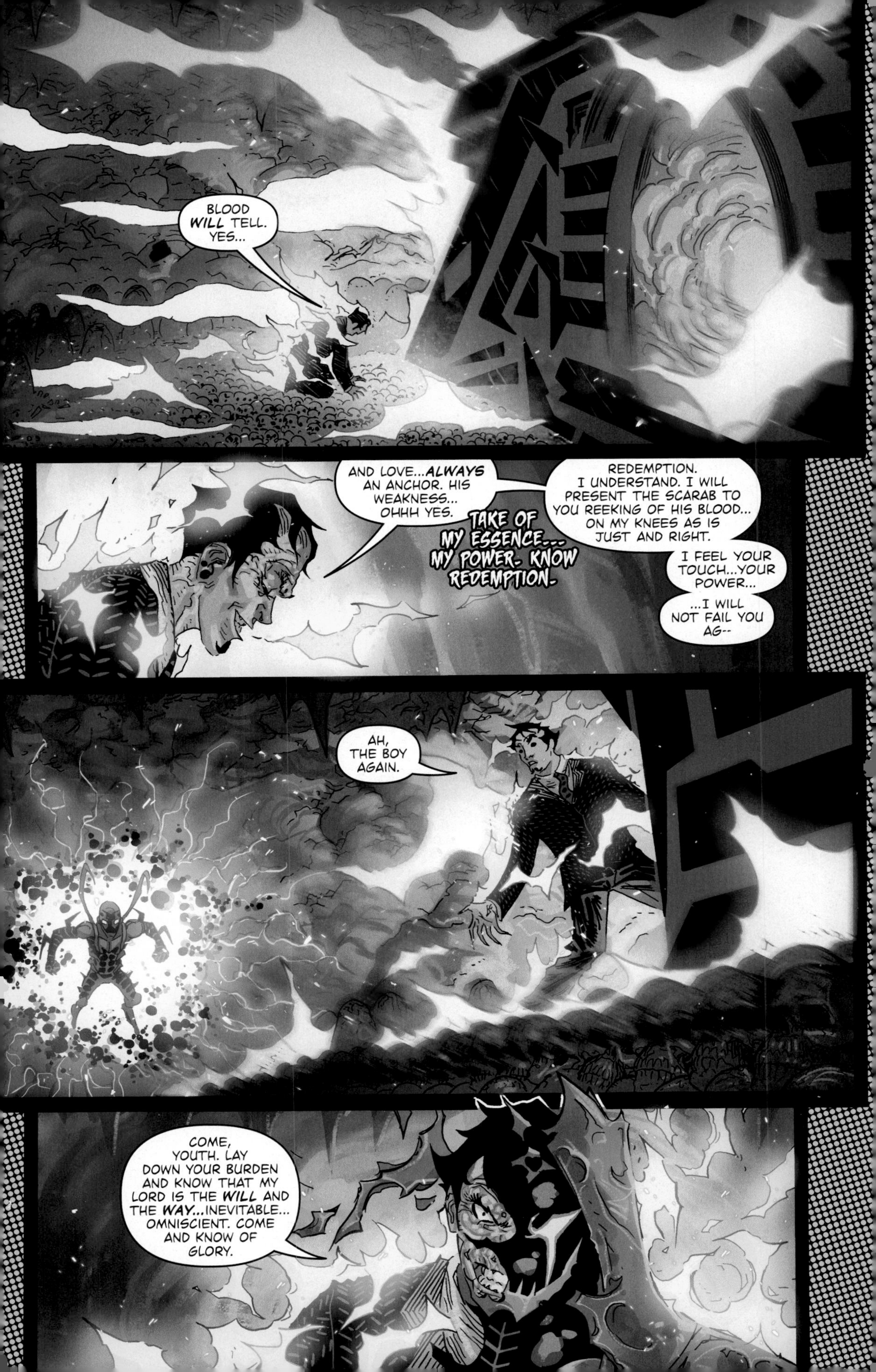
BLOOD WILL TELL. YES...
AND LOVE...ALWAYS AN ANCHOR. HIS WEAKNESS... OHHH YES.
TAKE OF MY ESSENCE... MY POWER. KNOW REDEMPTION.
REDEMPTION. I UNDERSTAND. I WILL PRESENT THE SCARAB TO YOU REEKING OF HIS BLOOD... ON MY KNEES AS IS JUST AND RIGHT.
I FEEL YOUR TOUCH...YOUR POWER...
...I WILL NOT FAIL YOU AG--
AH, THE BOY AGAIN.
COME, YOUTH. LAY DOWN YOUR BURDEN AND KNOW THAT MY LORD IS THE WILL AND THE WAY...INEVITABLE... OMNISCIENT. COME AND KNOW OF GLORY.

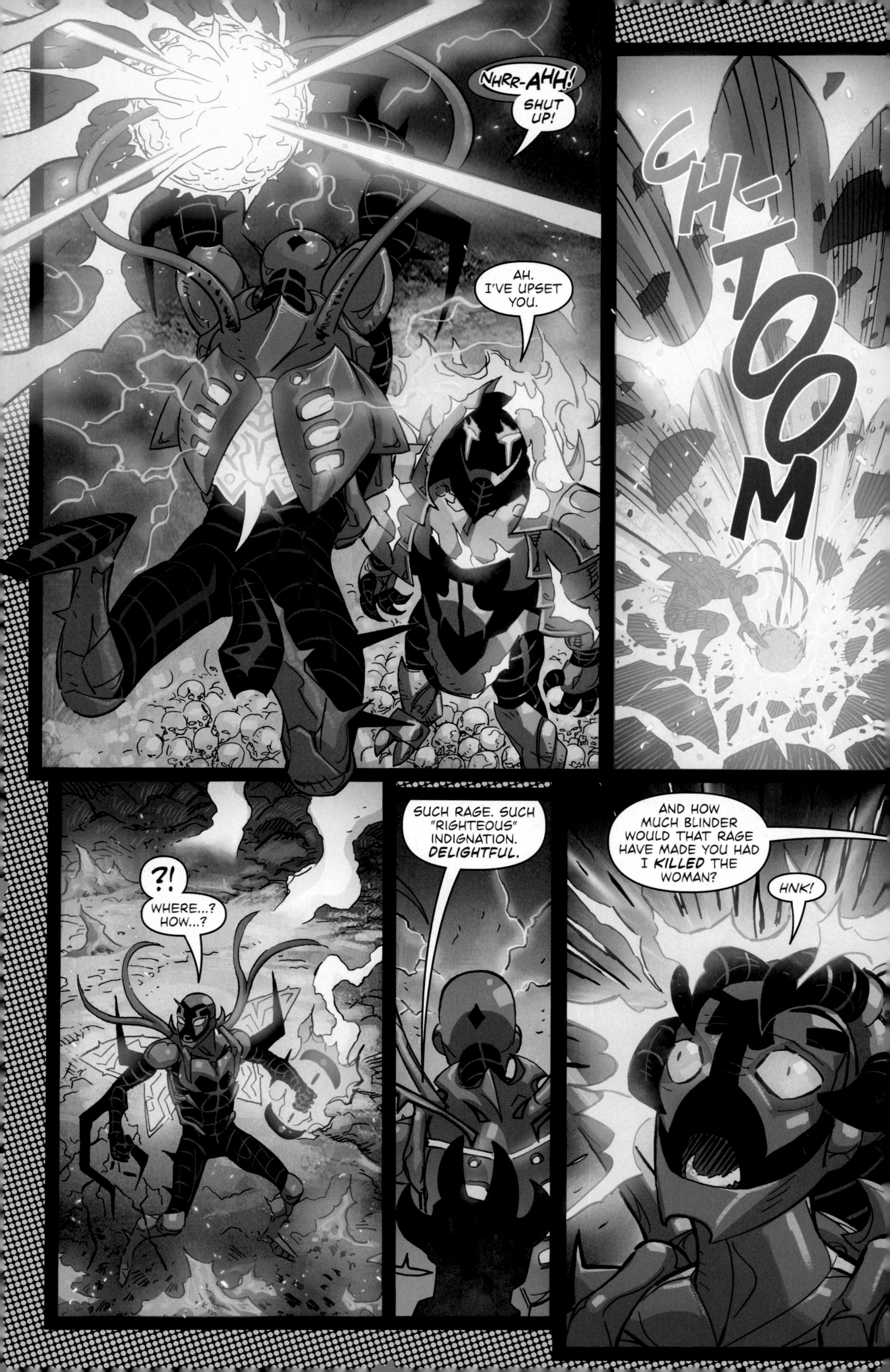
NHRR-AHH! SHUT UP!
AH. I'VE UPSET YOU.
CH-TOOM
?! WHERE...? HOW...?
SUCH RAGE. SUCH "RIGHTEOUS" INDIGNATION. DELIGHTFUL.
AND HOW MUCH BLINDER WOULD THAT RAGE HAVE MADE YOU HAD I KILLED THE WOMAN?
HNK!

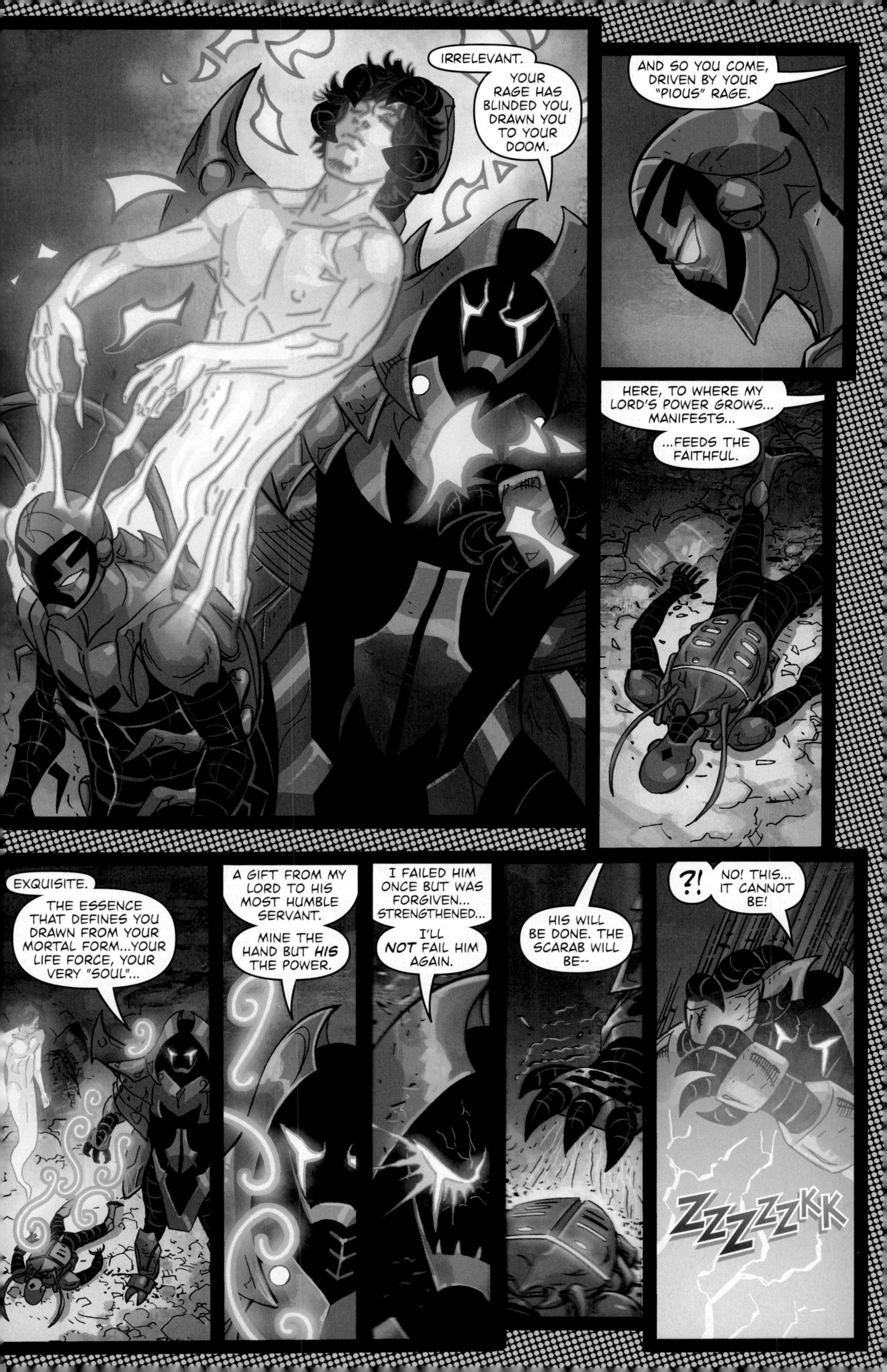
IRRELEVANT.
YOUR RAGE HAS BLINDED YOU, DRAWN YOU TO YOUR DOOM.
AND SO YOU COME, DRIVEN BY YOUR "PIOUS" RAGE.
HERE, TO WHERE MY LORD'S POWER GROWS... MANIFESTS...
...FEEDS THE FAITHFUL.
EXQUISITE.
THE ESSENCE THAT DEFINES YOU DRAWN FROM YOUR MORTAL FORM...YOUR LIFE FORCE, YOUR VERY "SOUL"...
A GIFT FROM MY LORD TO HIS MOST HUMBLE SERVANT.
MINE THE HAND BUT HIS THE POWER.
I FAILED HIM ONCE BUT WAS FORGIVEN... STRENGTHENED...
I'LL NOT FAIL HIM AGAIN.
HIS WILL BE DONE. THE SCARAB WILL BE--
?!
NO! THIS... IT CANNOT BE!
ZZZZZKK

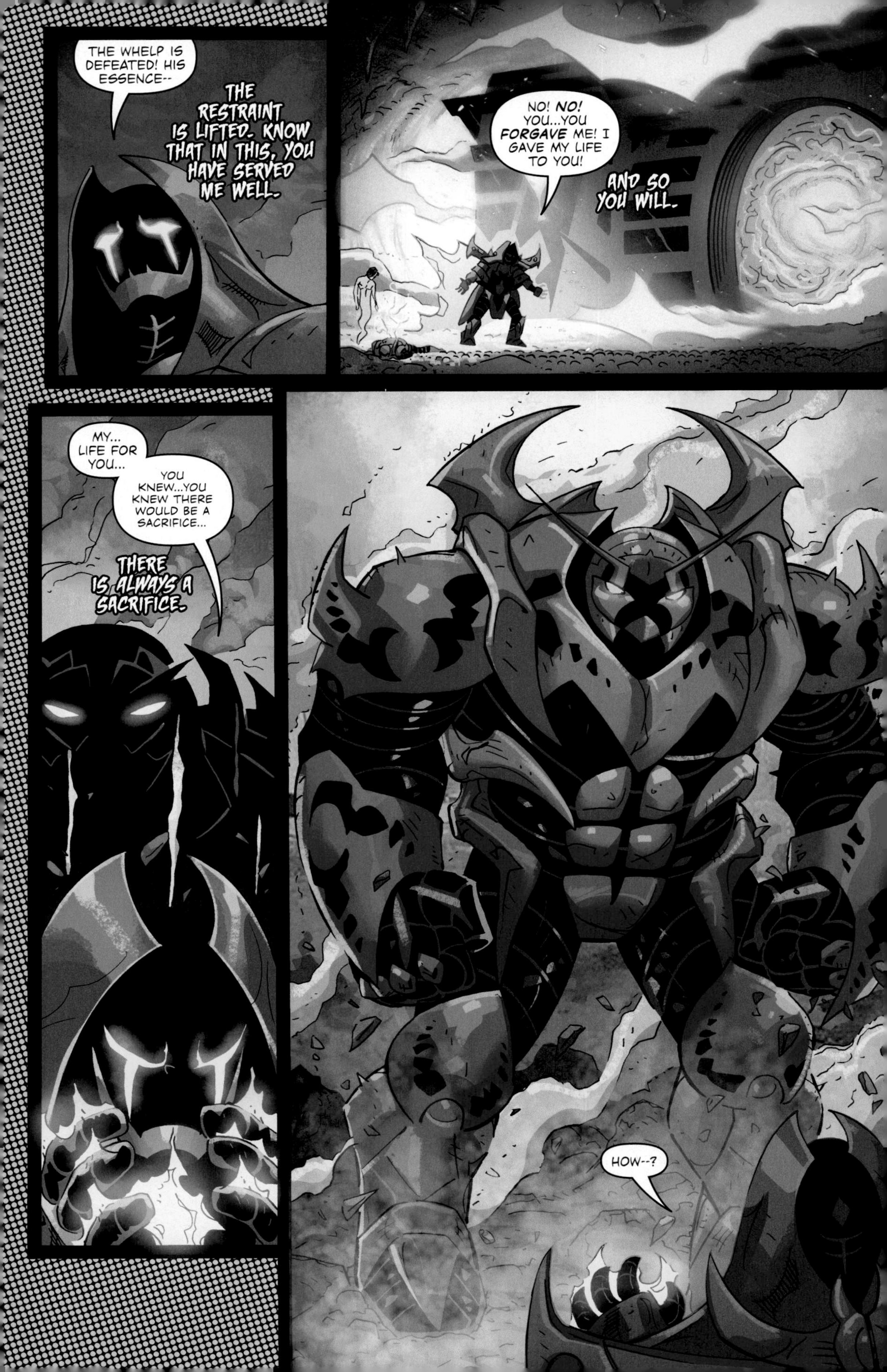
THE WHELP IS DEFEATED! HIS ESSENCE--
THE RESTRAINT IS LIFTED. KNOW THAT IN THIS, YOU HAVE SERVED ME WELL.
NO! NO! YOU...YOU FORGAVE ME! I GAVE MY LIFE TO YOU!
AND SO YOU WILL.
MY... LIFE FOR YOU...
YOU KNEW...YOU KNEW THERE WOULD BE A SACRIFICE...
THERE IS ALWAYS A SACRIFICE.
HOW--?

SH-TOOM-

THRAK

CHOOM

SKRAKKTCHT

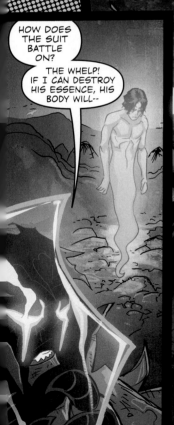

HOW DOES THE SUIT BATTLE ON?

THE WHELP! IF I CAN DESTROY HIS ESSENCE, HIS BODY WILL--

UNNGH!

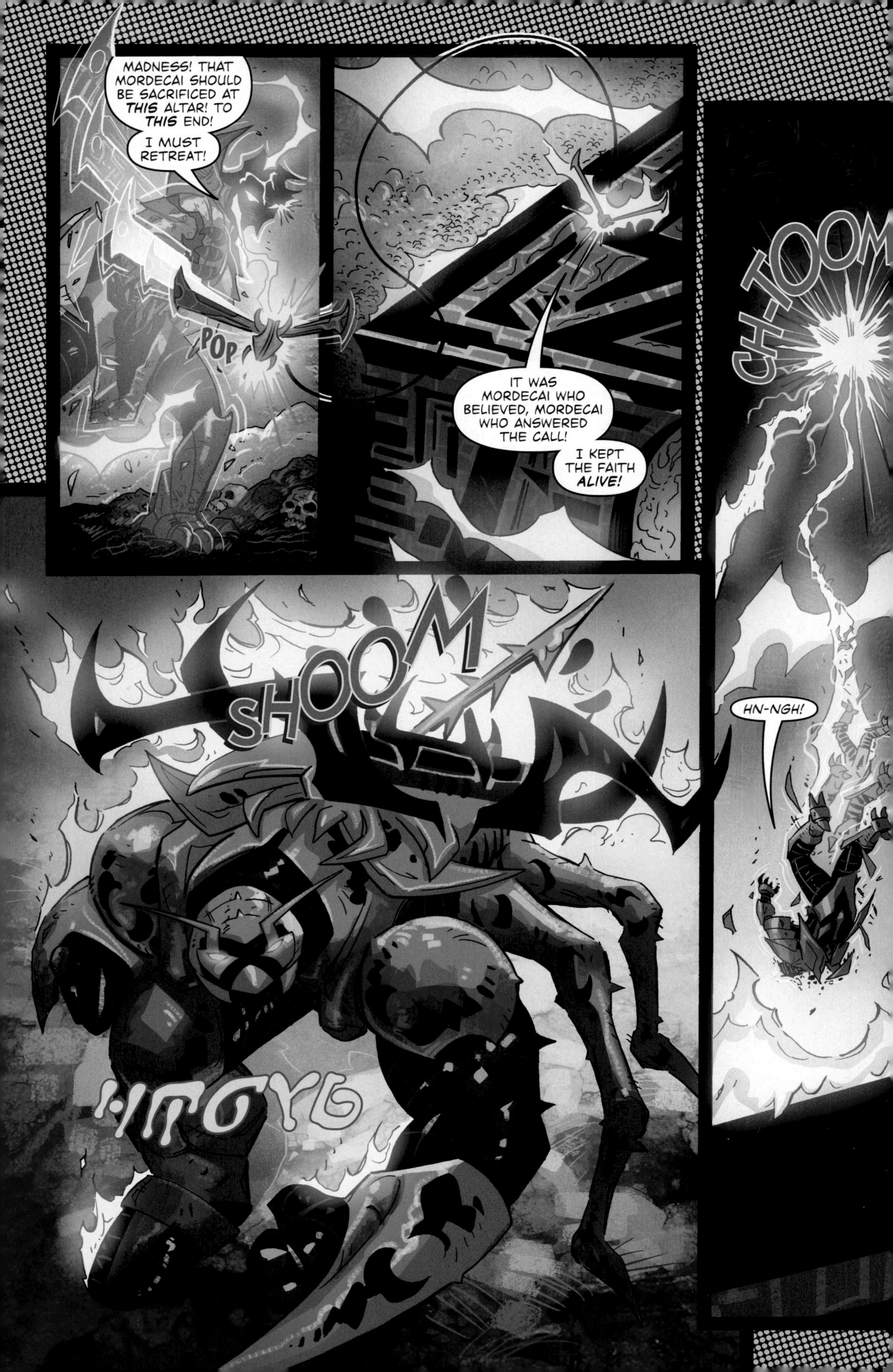
MADNESS! THAT MORDECAI SHOULD BE SACRIFICED AT THIS ALTAR! TO THIS END!
I MUST RETREAT!
POP
IT WAS MORDECAI WHO BELIEVED, MORDECAI WHO ANSWERED THE CALL!
I KEPT THE FAITH ALIVE!
CH-TOOM
SHOOM
HN-NGH!

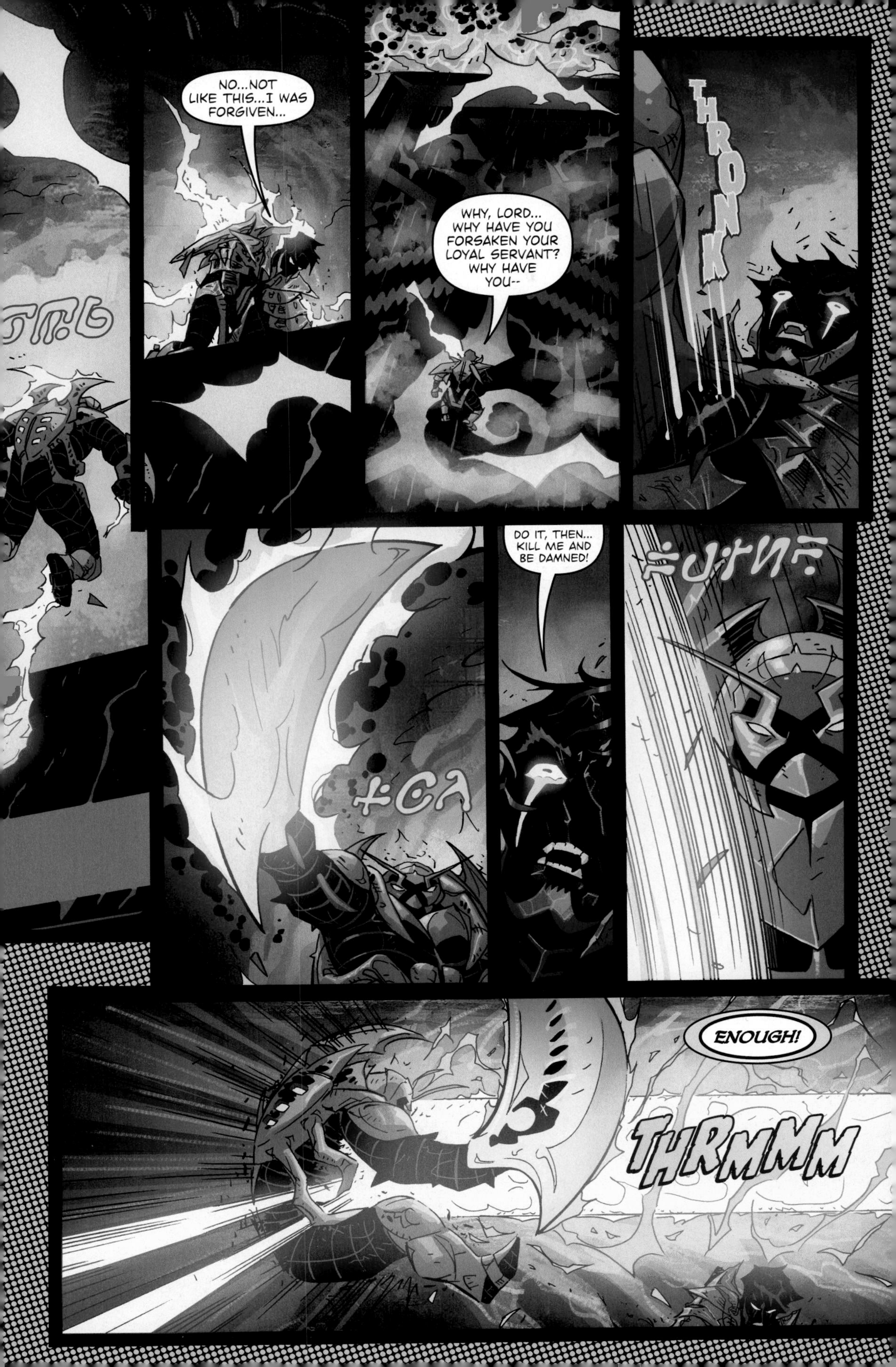
NO...NOT LIKE THIS...I WAS FORGIVEN...
WHY, LORD... WHY HAVE YOU FORSAKEN YOUR LOYAL SERVANT? WHY HAVE YOU--
THRONK
DO IT, THEN... KILL ME AND BE DAMNED!
ENOUGH!
THRMMM

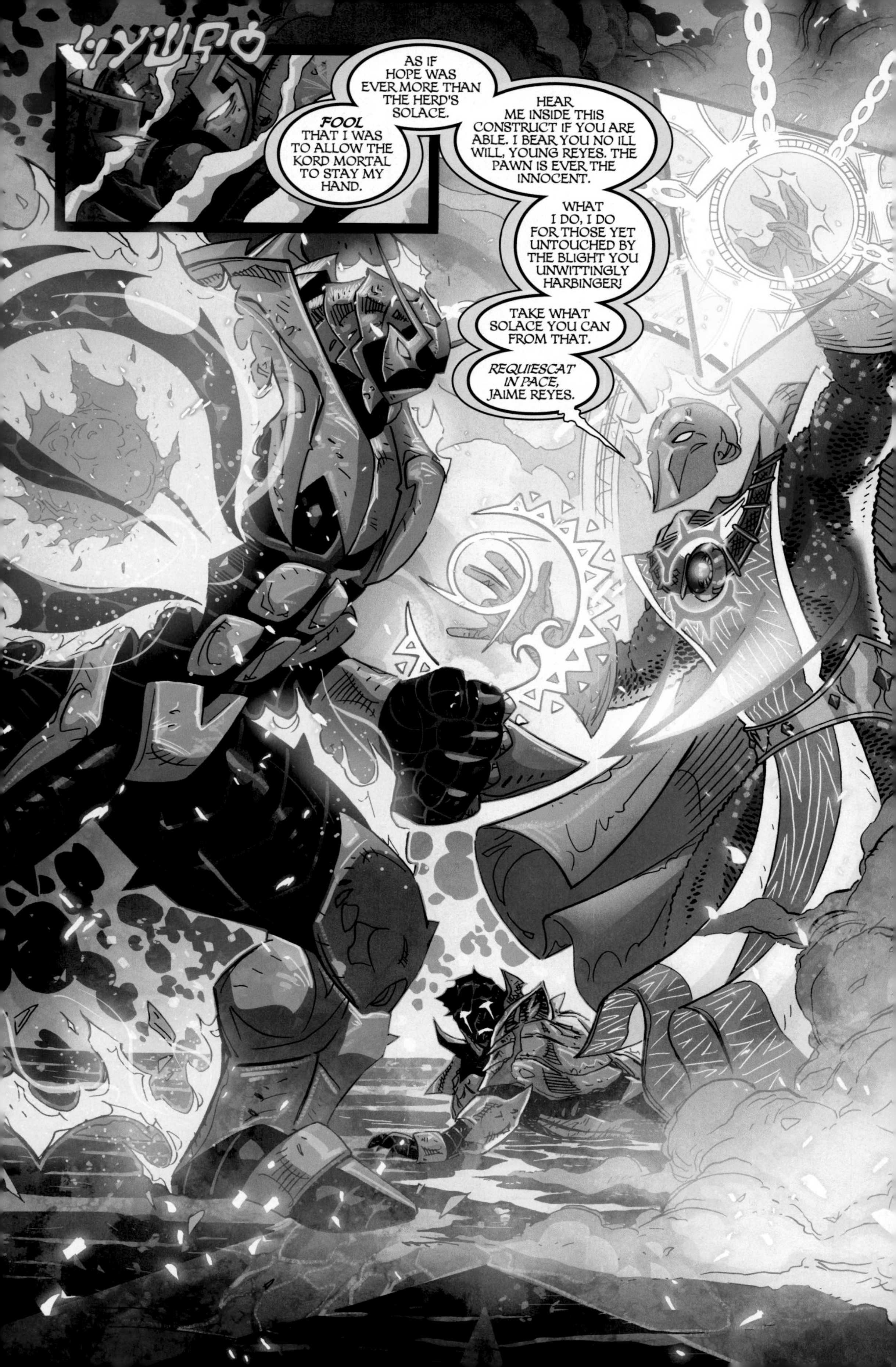
FOOL THAT I WAS TO ALLOW THE KORD MORTAL TO STAY MY HAND.
AS IF HOPE WAS EVER MORE THAN THE HERD'S SOLACE.
HEAR ME INSIDE THIS CONSTRUCT IF YOU ARE ABLE. I BEAR YOU NO ILL WILL, YOUNG REYES. THE PAWN IS EVER THE INNOCENT.
WHAT I DO, I DO FOR THOSE YET UNTOUCHED BY THE BLIGHT YOU UNWITTINGLY HARBINGER!
TAKE WHAT SOLACE YOU CAN FROM THAT.
REQUIESCAT IN PACE, JAIME REYES.

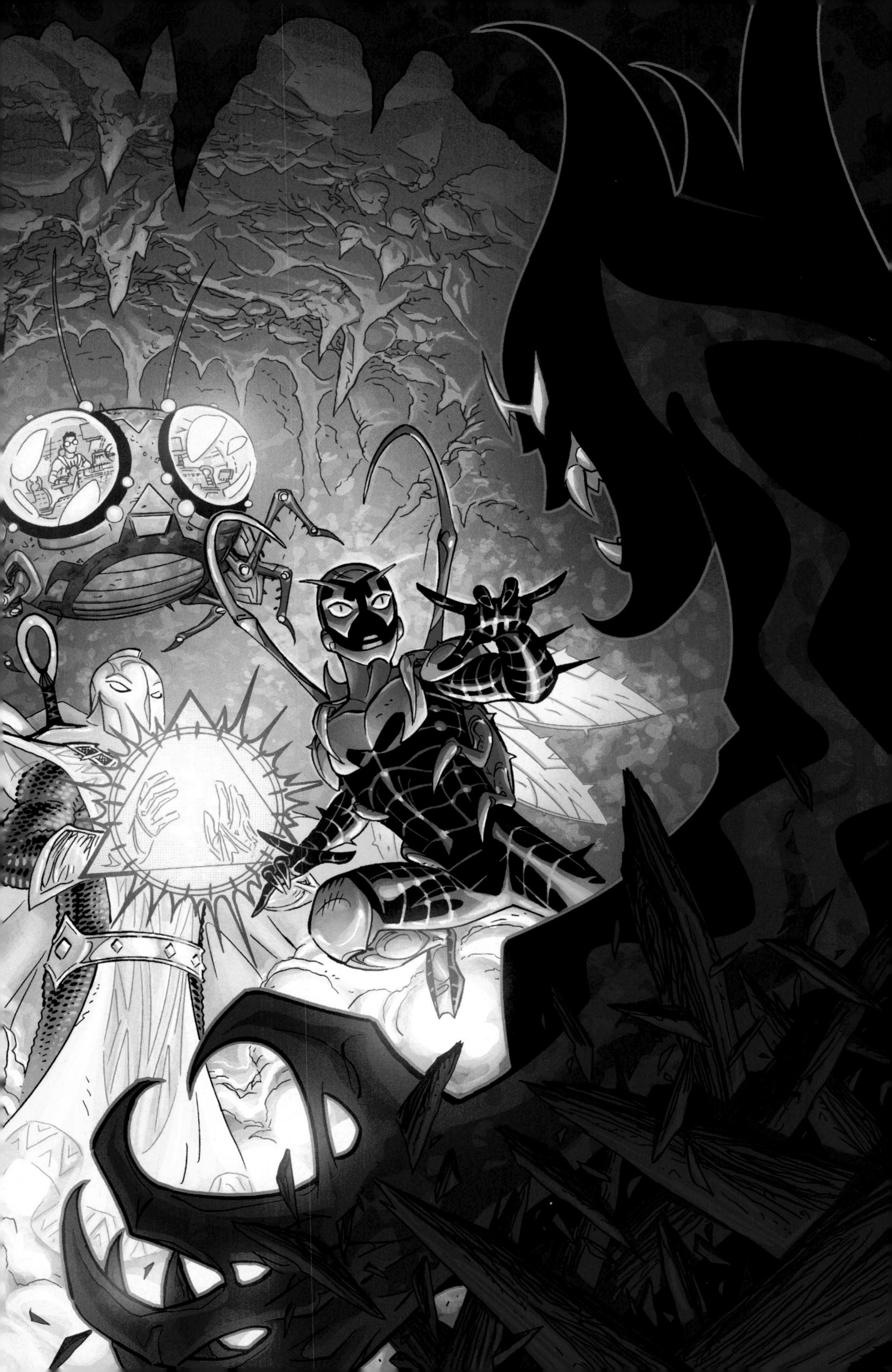

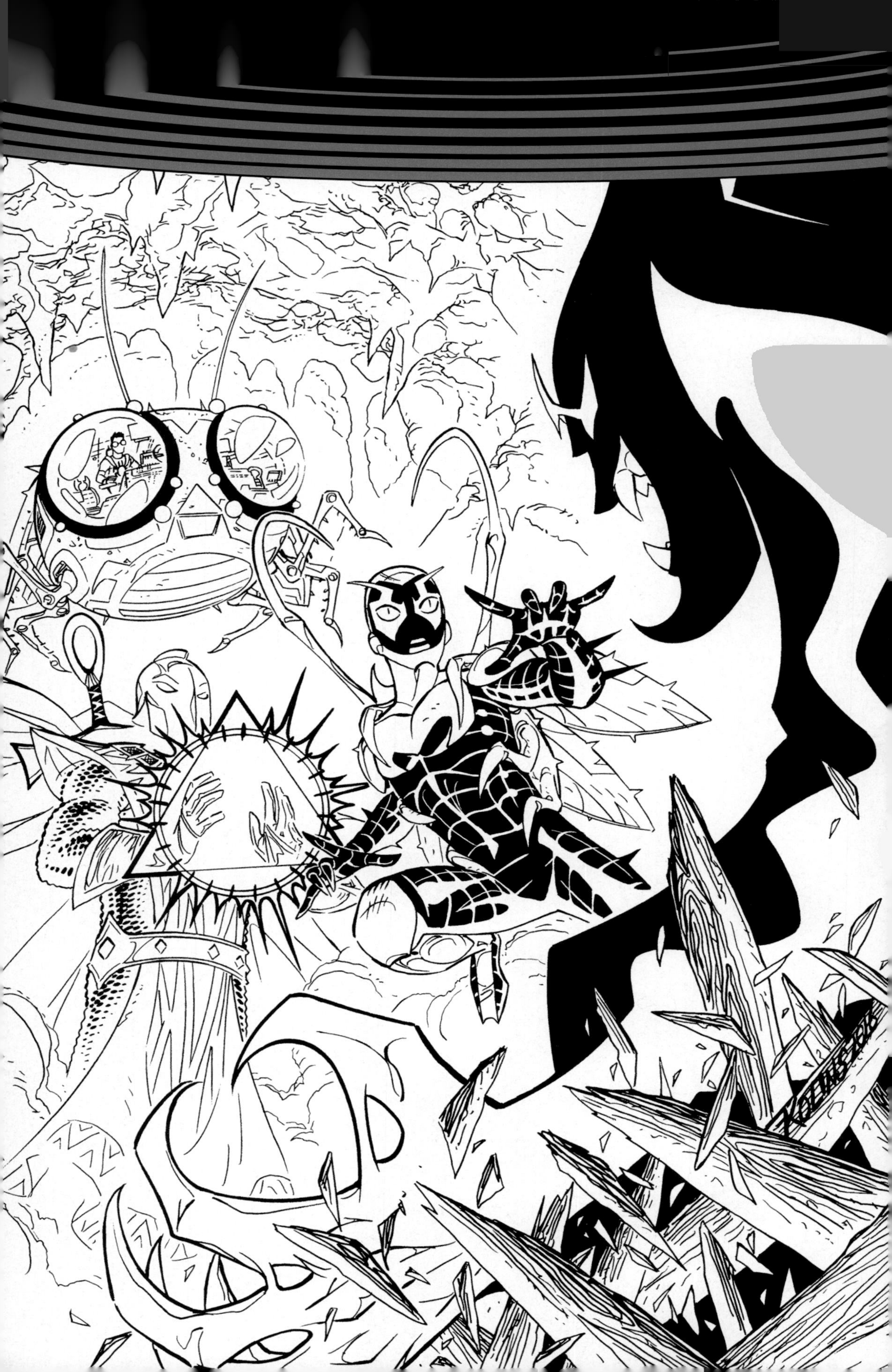

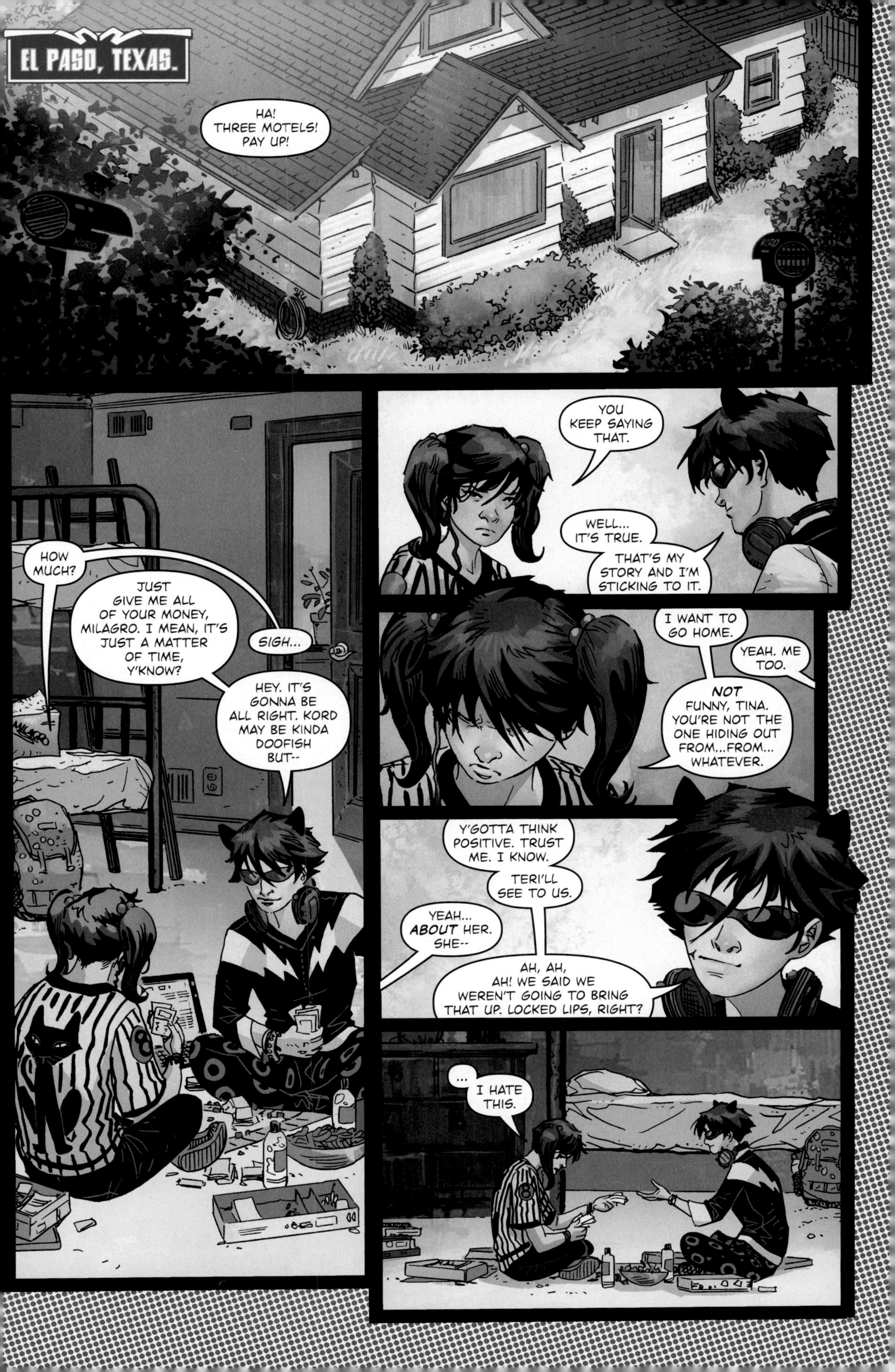
EL PASO, TEXAS.
HA! THREE MOTELS! PAY UP!
HOW MUCH?
JUST GIVE ME ALL OF YOUR MONEY, MILAGRO. I MEAN, IT'S JUST A MATTER OF TIME, Y'KNOW?
SIGH...
HEY. IT'S GONNA BE ALL RIGHT. KORD MAY BE KINDA DOOFISH BUT--
YOU KEEP SAYING THAT.
WELL... IT'S TRUE.
THAT'S MY STORY AND I'M STICKING TO IT.
I WANT TO GO HOME.
YEAH. ME TOO.
NOT FUNNY, TINA. YOU'RE NOT THE ONE HIDING OUT FROM...FROM... WHATEVER.
Y'GOTTA THINK POSITIVE. TRUST ME. I KNOW.
TERI'LL SEE TO US.
YEAH... ABOUT HER. SHE--
AH, AH, AH! WE SAID WE WEREN'T GOING TO BRING THAT UP. LOCKED LIPS, RIGHT?
... I HATE THIS.

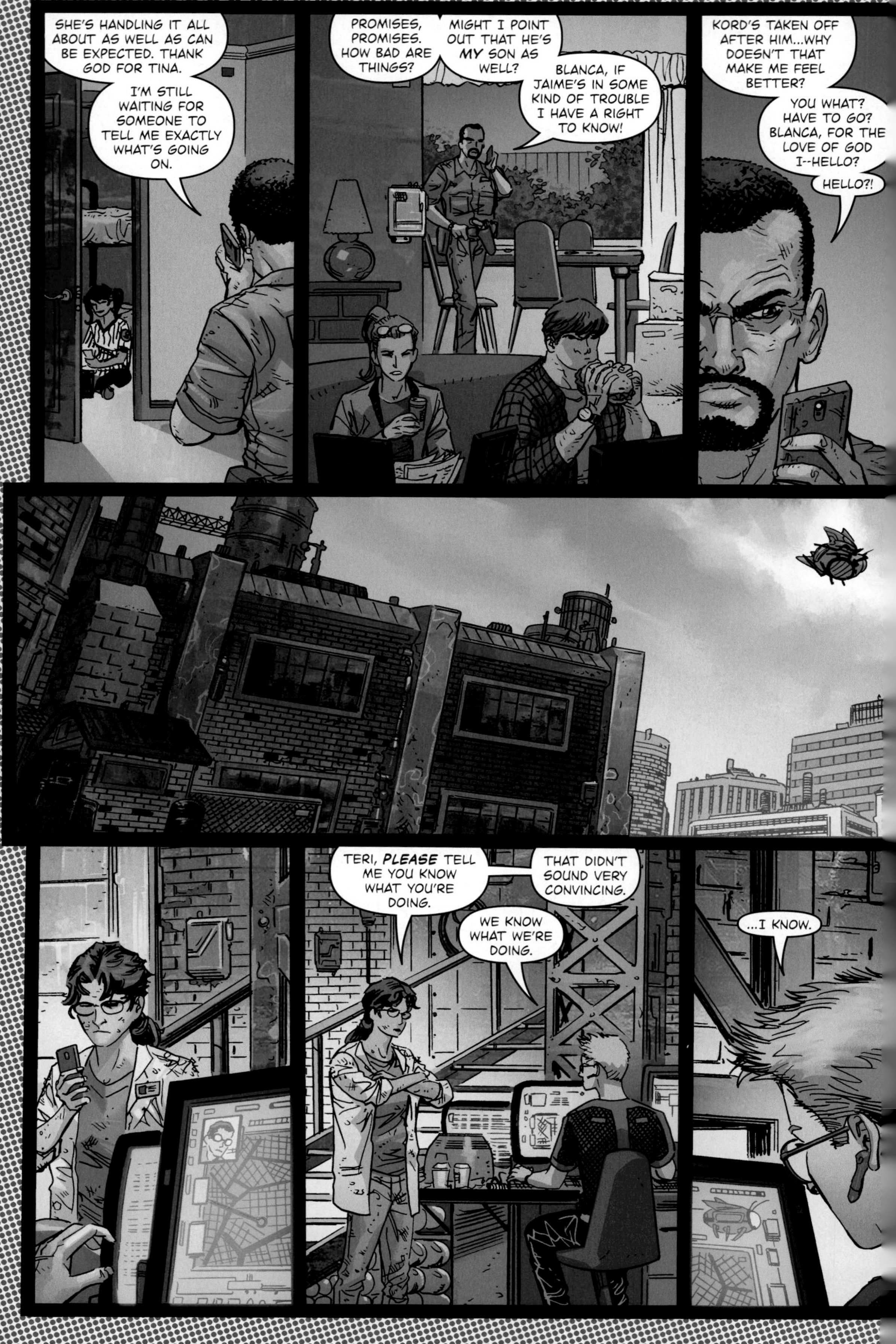
SHE'S HANDLING IT ALL ABOUT AS WELL AS CAN BE EXPECTED. THANK GOD FOR TINA.
I'M STILL WAITING FOR SOMEONE TO TELL ME EXACTLY WHAT'S GOING ON.
PROMISES, PROMISES. HOW BAD ARE THINGS?
MIGHT I POINT OUT THAT HE'S MY SON AS WELL?
BLANCA, IF JAIME'S IN SOME KIND OF TROUBLE I HAVE A RIGHT TO KNOW!
KORD'S TAKEN OFF AFTER HIM...WHY DOESN'T THAT MAKE ME FEEL BETTER?
YOU WHAT? HAVE TO GO? BLANCA, FOR THE LOVE OF GOD I--HELLO?
HELLO?!
TERI, PLEASE TELL ME YOU KNOW WHAT YOU'RE DOING.
THAT DIDN'T SOUND VERY CONVINCING.
WE KNOW WHAT WE'RE DOING.
...I KNOW.

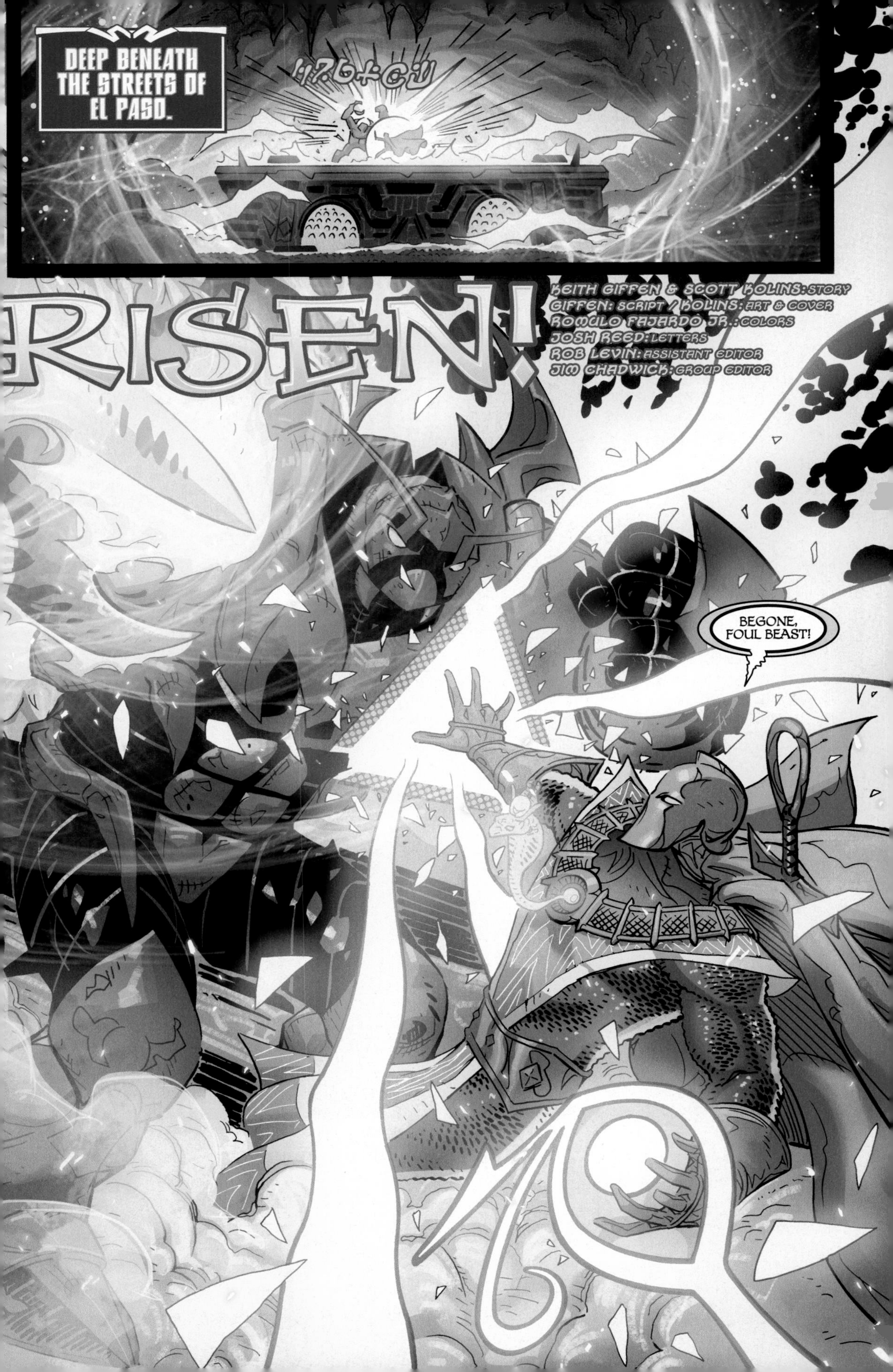
DEEP BENEATH THE STREETS OF EL PASO...
RISEN!
KEITH GIFFEN & SCOTT KOLINS: STORY
GIFFEN: SCRIPT / KOLINS: ART & COVER
ROMULO FAJARDO JR.: COLORS
JOSH REED: LETTERS
ROB LEVIN: ASSISTANT EDITOR
JIM CHADWICK: GROUP EDITOR
BEGONE, FOUL BEAST!

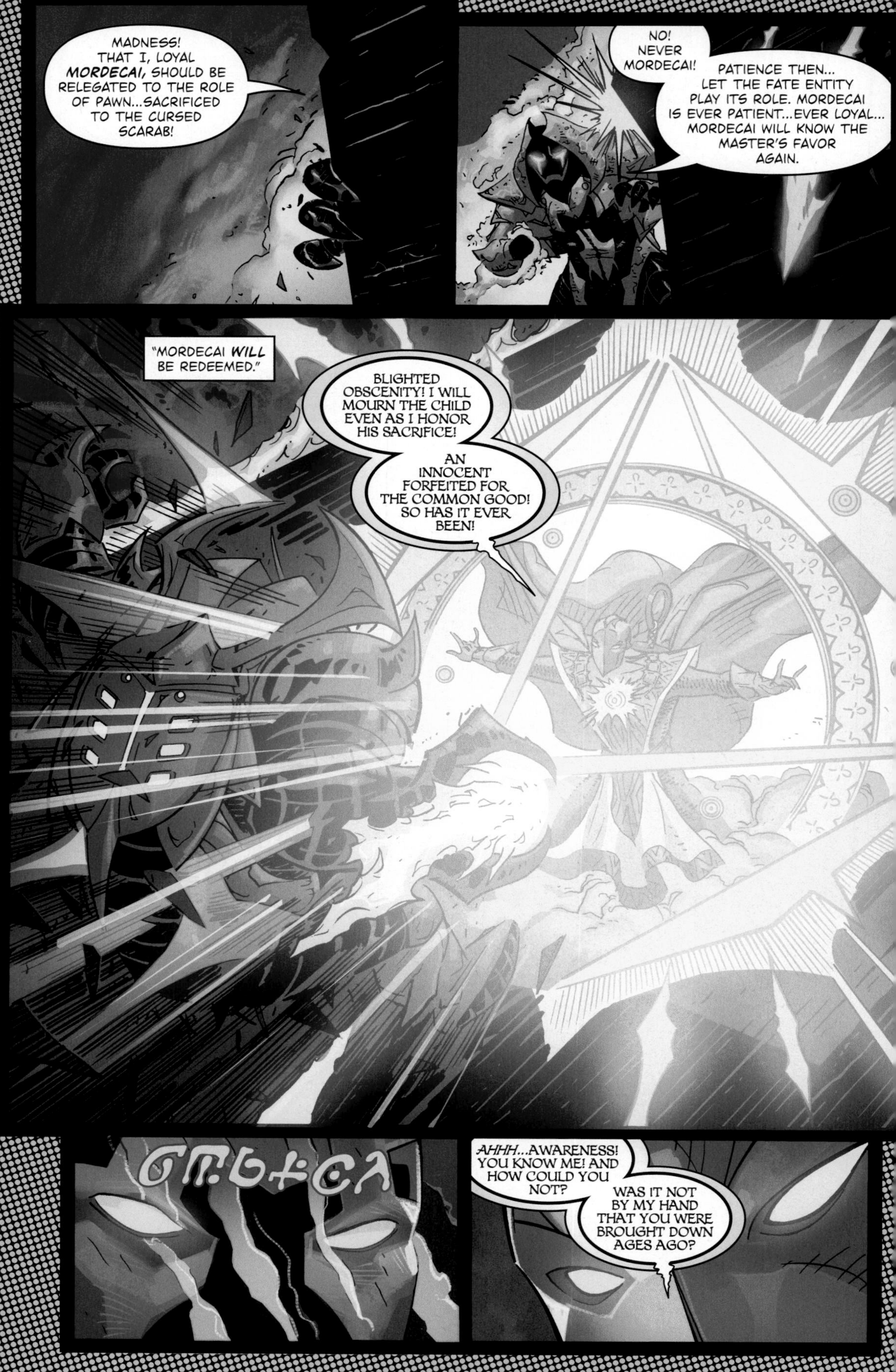
MADNESS! THAT I, LOYAL MORDECAI, SHOULD BE RELEGATED TO THE ROLE OF PAWN...SACRIFICED TO THE CURSED SCARAB!
NO! NEVER MORDECAI!
PATIENCE THEN... LET THE FATE ENTITY PLAY ITS ROLE. MORDECAI IS EVER PATIENT...EVER LOYAL... MORDECAI WILL KNOW THE MASTER'S FAVOR AGAIN.
"MORDECAI WILL BE REDEEMED."
BLIGHTED OBSCENITY! I WILL MOURN THE CHILD EVEN AS I HONOR HIS SACRIFICE!
AN INNOCENT FORFEITED FOR THE COMMON GOOD! SO HAS IT EVER BEEN!
AHHH...AWARENESS! YOU KNOW ME! AND HOW COULD YOU NOT?
WAS IT NOT BY MY HAND THAT YOU WERE BROUGHT DOWN AGES AGO?

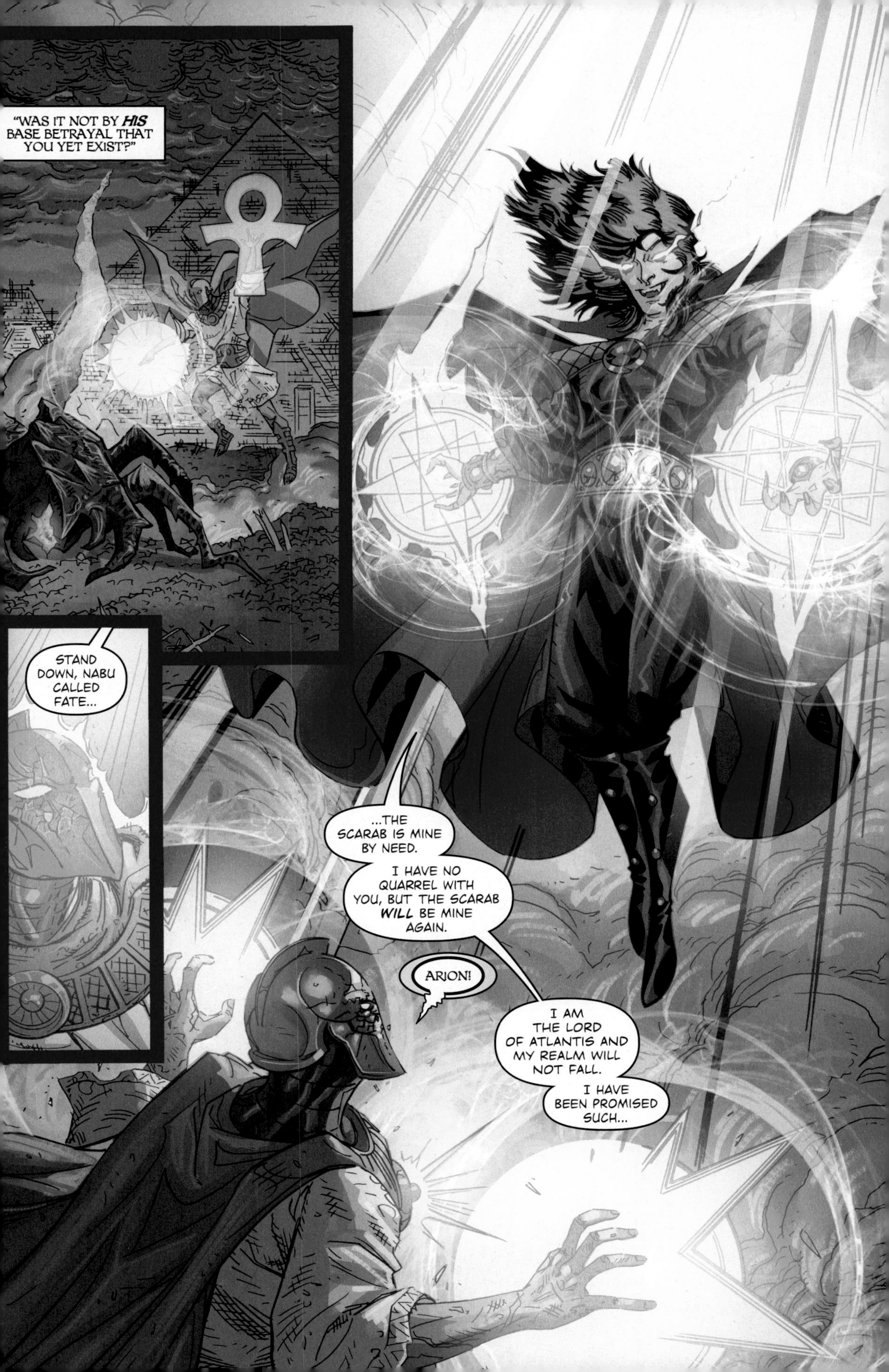
"WAS IT NOT BY HIS BASE BETRAYAL THAT YOU YET EXIST?"
STAND DOWN, NABU CALLED FATE...
...THE SCARAB IS MINE BY NEED.
I HAVE NO QUARREL WITH YOU, BUT THE SCARAB WILL BE MINE AGAIN.
ARION!
I AM THE LORD OF ATLANTIS AND MY REALM WILL NOT FALL.
I HAVE BEEN PROMISED SUCH...

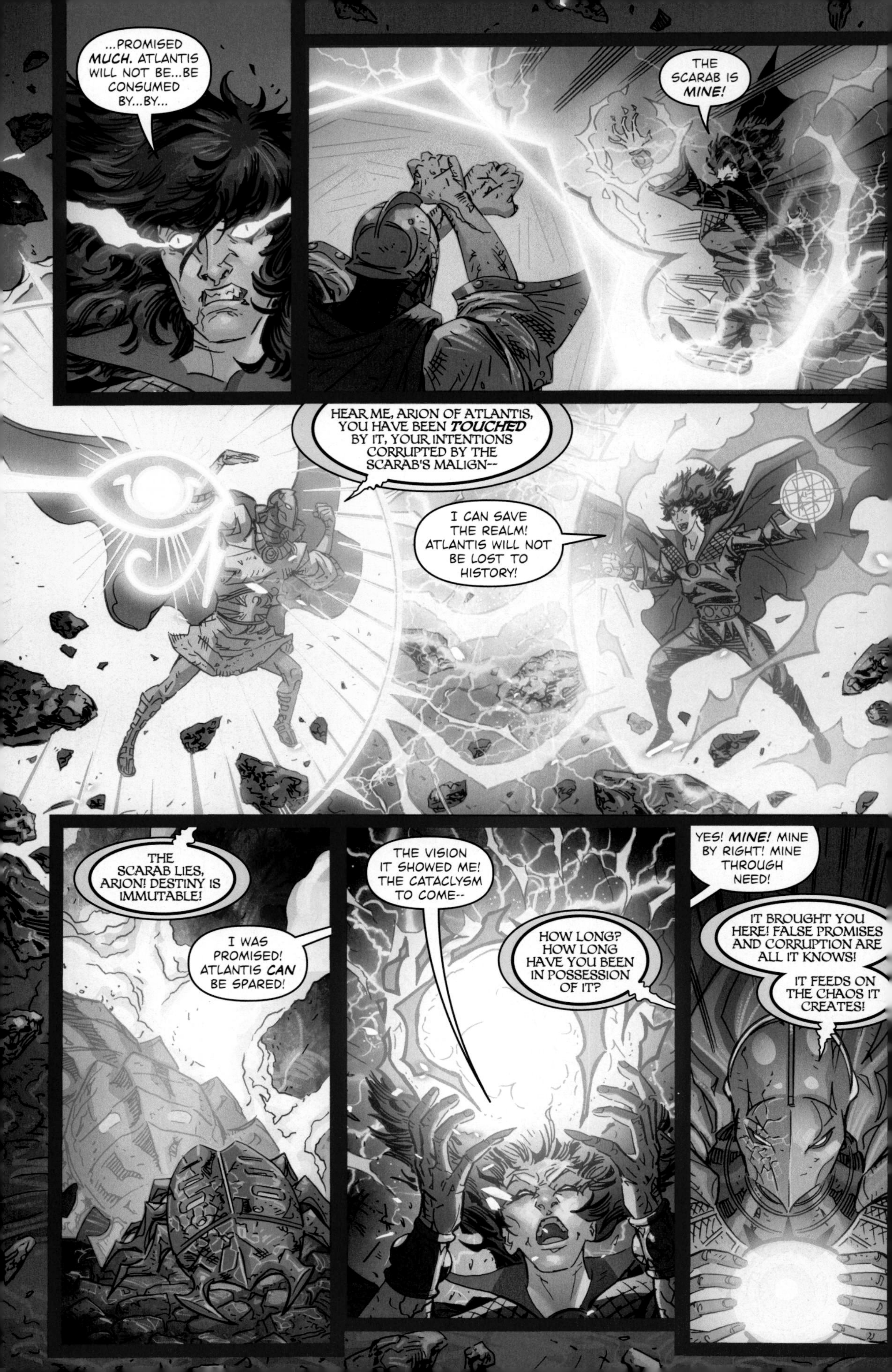
...PROMISED MUCH. ATLANTIS WILL NOT BE...BE CONSUMED BY...BY...
THE SCARAB IS MINE!
HEAR ME, ARION OF ATLANTIS, YOU HAVE BEEN TOUCHED BY IT, YOUR INTENTIONS CORRUPTED BY THE SCARAB'S MALIGN--
I CAN SAVE THE REALM! ATLANTIS WILL NOT BE LOST TO HISTORY!
THE SCARAB LIES, ARION! DESTINY IS IMMUTABLE!
I WAS PROMISED! ATLANTIS CAN BE SPARED!
THE VISION IT SHOWED ME! THE CATACLYSM TO COME--
HOW LONG? HOW LONG HAVE YOU BEEN IN POSSESSION OF IT?
YES! MINE! MINE BY RIGHT! MINE THROUGH NEED!
IT BROUGHT YOU HERE! FALSE PROMISES AND CORRUPTION ARE ALL IT KNOWS!
IT FEEDS ON THE CHAOS IT CREATES!

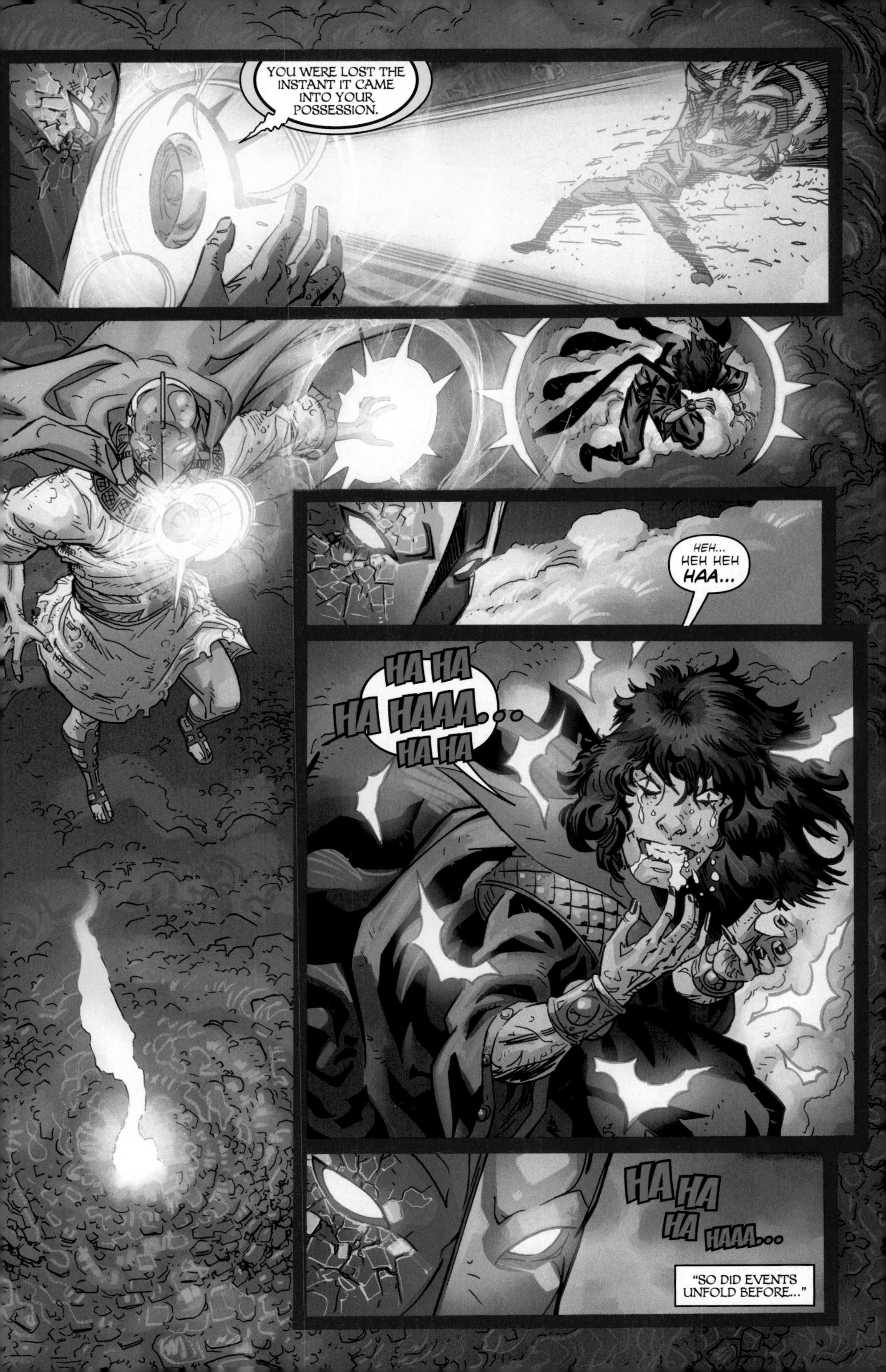
YOU WERE LOST THE INSTANT IT CAME INTO YOUR POSSESSION.
HEH... HEH HEH HAA...
HA HA HA HAAA... HA HA
HA HA HA HAAA...
"SO DID EVENTS UNFOLD BEFORE..."

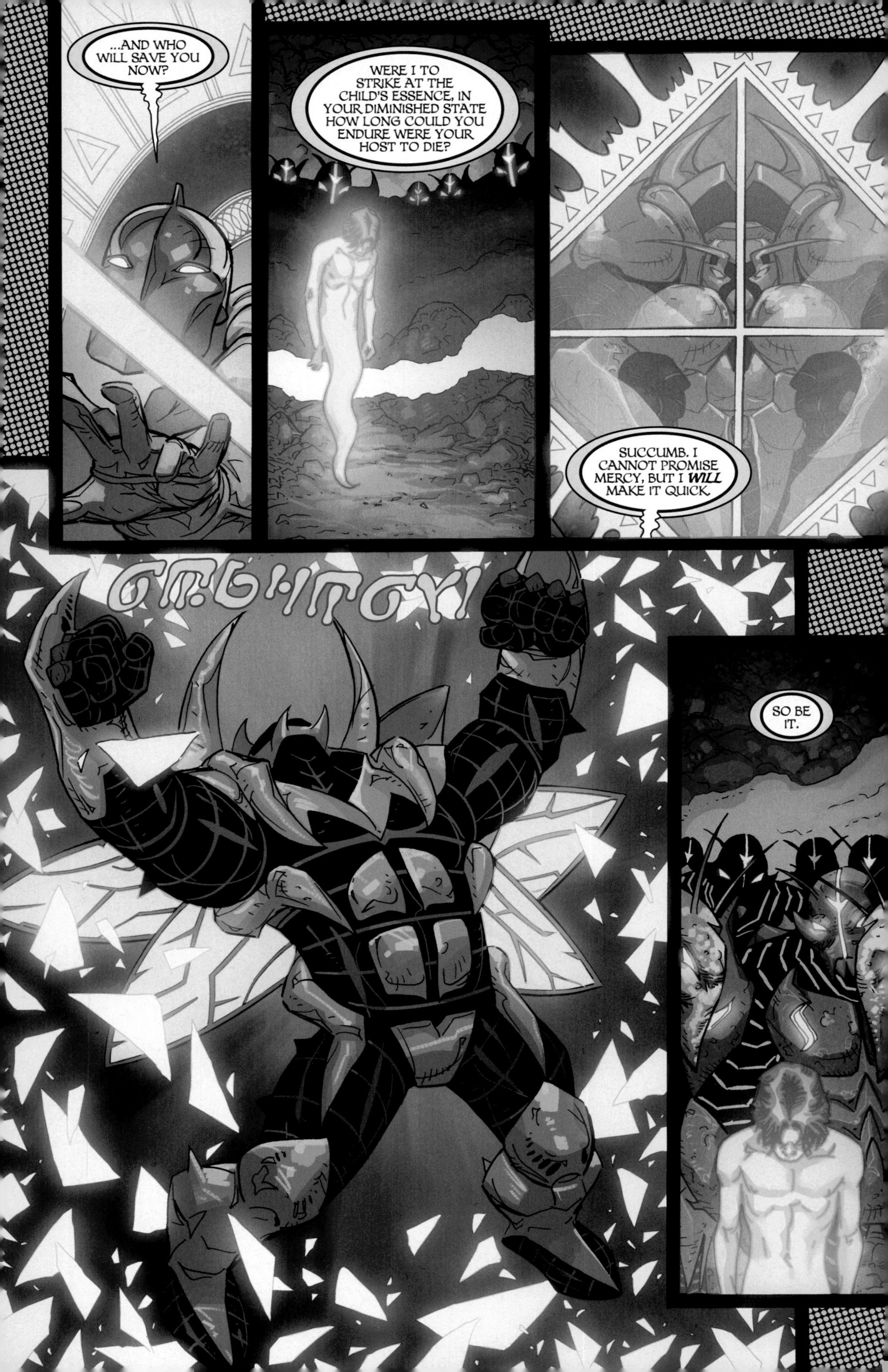
...AND WHO WILL SAVE YOU NOW?
WERE I TO STRIKE AT THE CHILD'S ESSENCE, IN YOUR DIMINISHED STATE HOW LONG COULD YOU ENDURE WERE YOUR HOST TO DIE?
SUCCUMB. I CANNOT PROMISE MERCY, BUT I *WILL* MAKE IT QUICK.
SO BE IT.

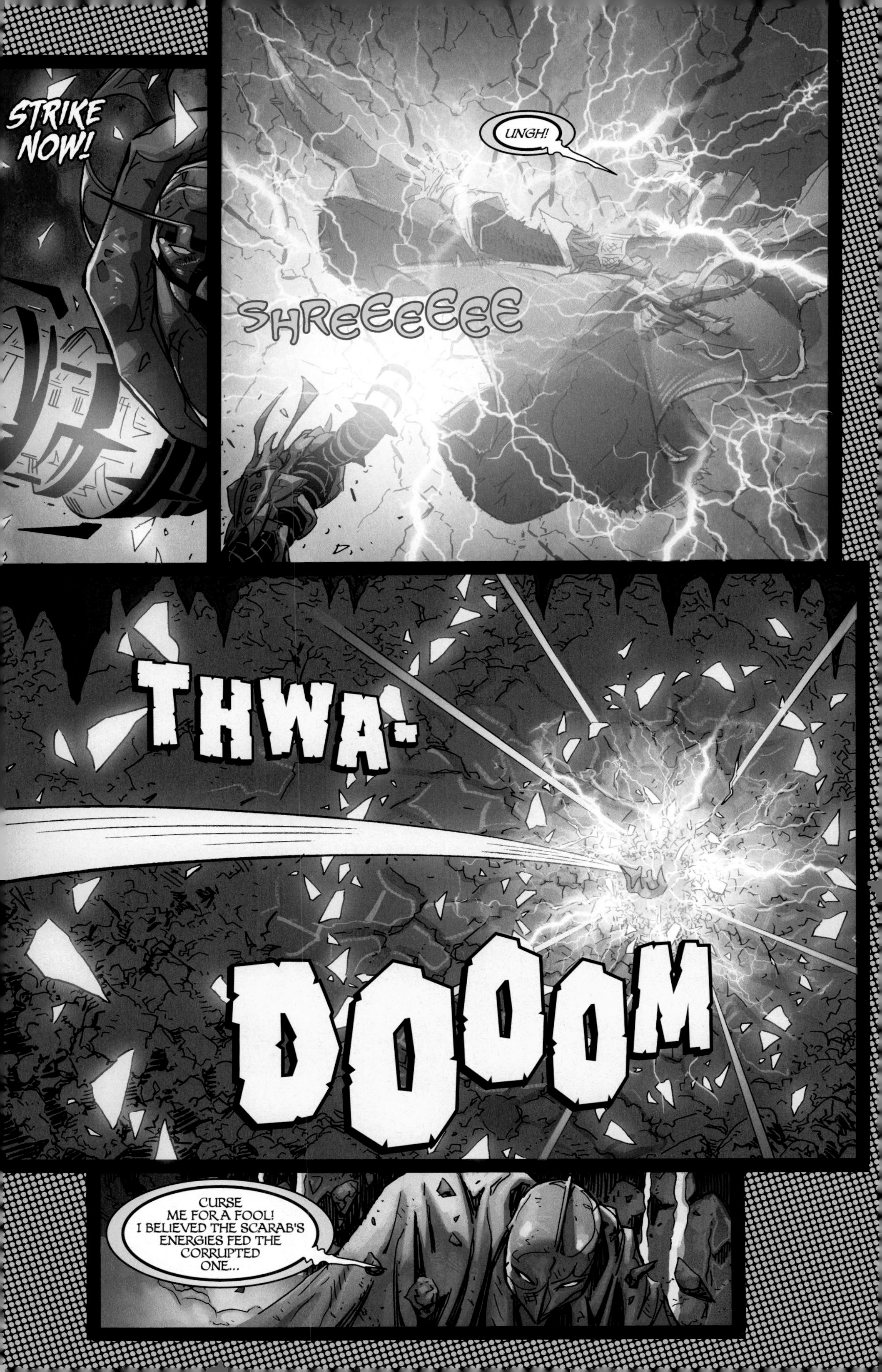
STRIKE NOW!
UNGH!
SHREEEEEEE
THWA-
DOOOM
CURSE ME FOR A FOOL! I BELIEVED THE SCARAB'S ENERGIES FED THE CORRUPTED ONE...

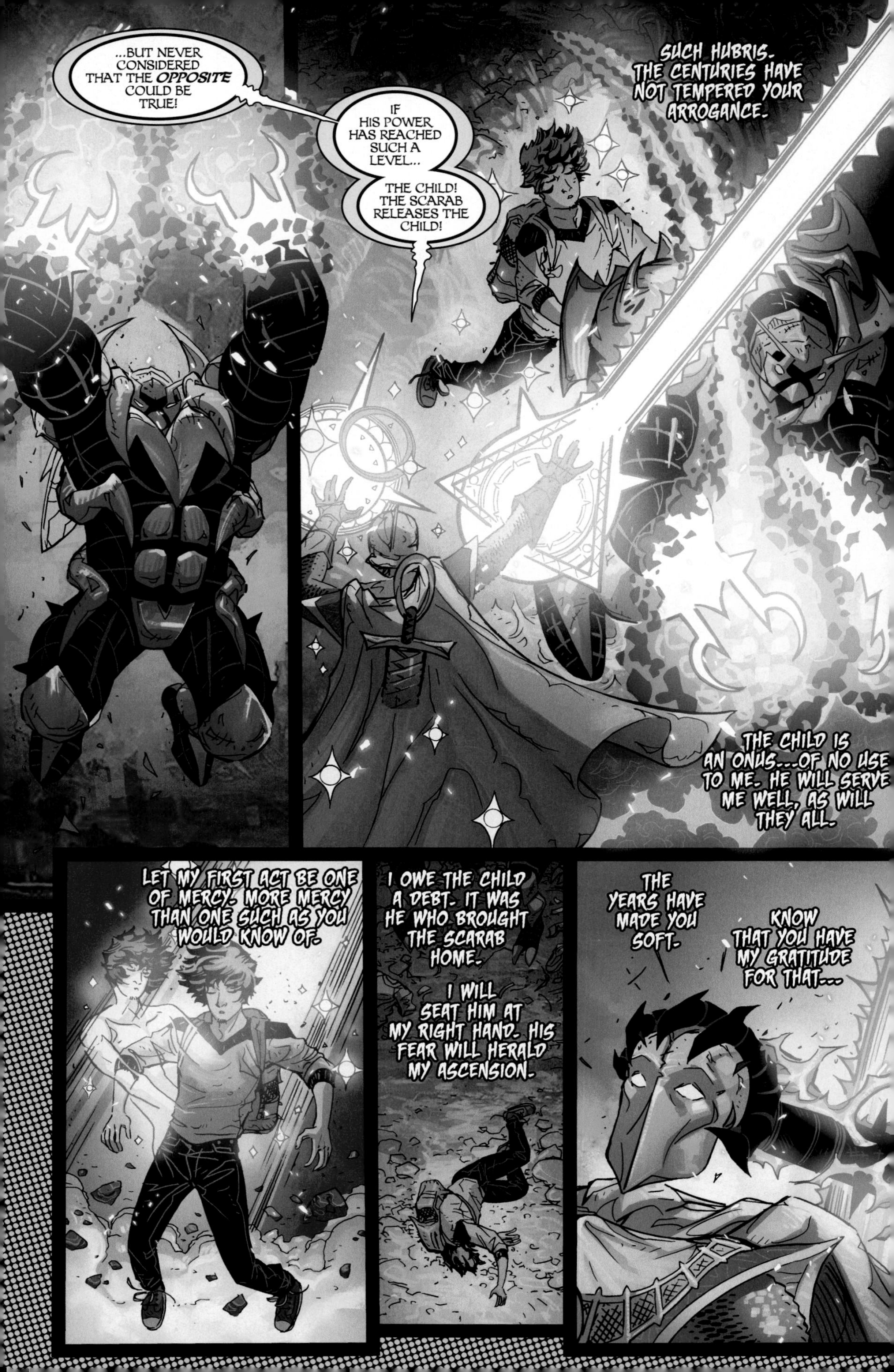

...BUT NEVER CONSIDERED THAT THE *OPPOSITE* COULD BE TRUE!
IF HIS POWER HAS REACHED SUCH A LEVEL...
THE CHILD! THE SCARAB RELEASES THE CHILD!
SUCH HUBRIS. THE CENTURIES HAVE NOT TEMPERED YOUR ARROGANCE.
THE CHILD IS AN ONUS...OF NO USE TO ME. HE WILL SERVE ME WELL, AS WILL THEY ALL.
LET MY FIRST ACT BE ONE OF MERCY. MORE MERCY THAN ONE SUCH AS YOU WOULD KNOW OF.
I OWE THE CHILD A DEBT. IT WAS HE WHO BROUGHT THE SCARAB HOME.
I WILL SEAT HIM AT MY RIGHT HAND. HIS FEAR WILL HERALD MY ASCENSION.
THE YEARS HAVE MADE YOU SOFT.
KNOW THAT YOU HAVE MY GRATITUDE FOR THAT...

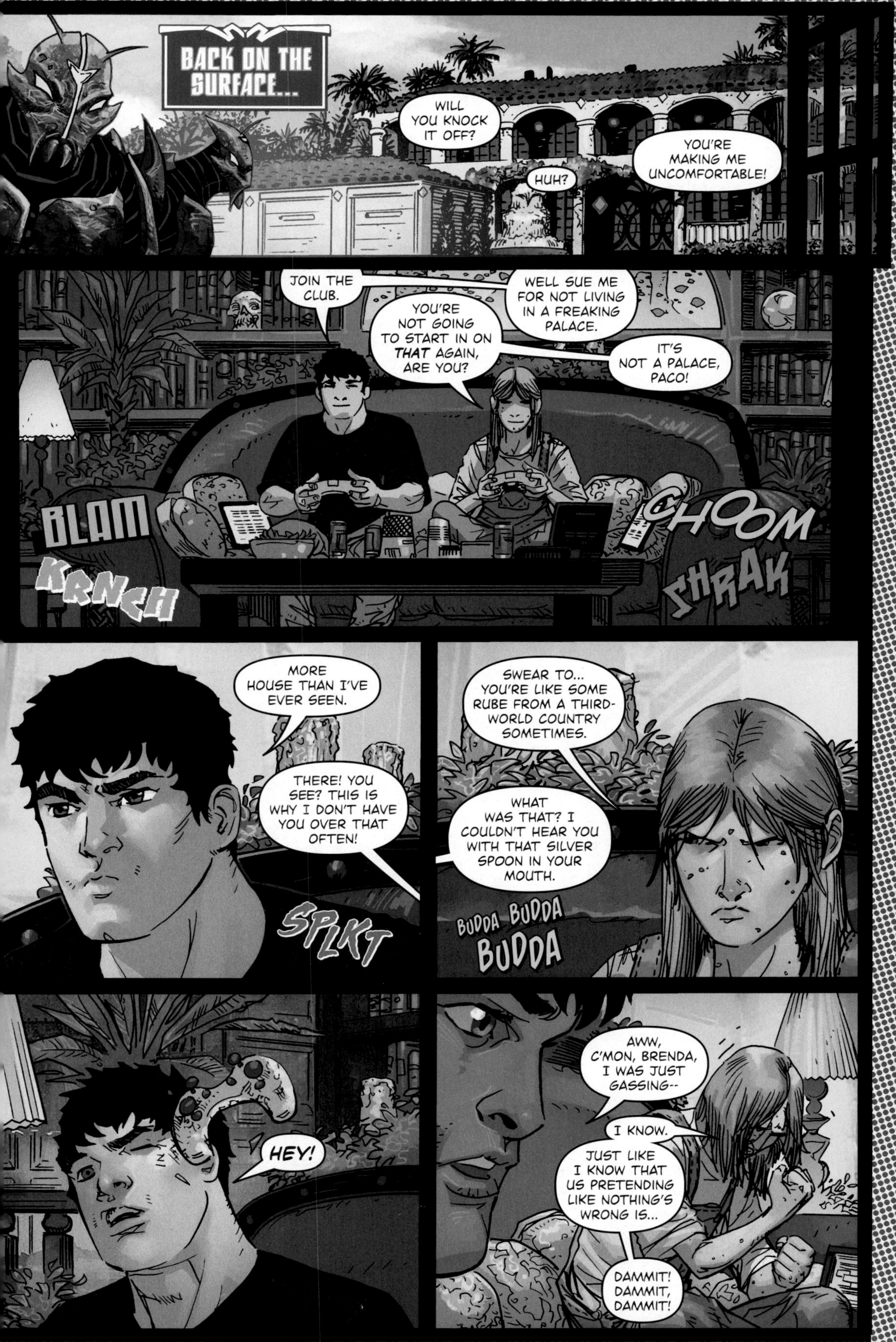
BACK ON THE SURFACE...
WILL YOU KNOCK IT OFF?
HUH?
YOU'RE MAKING ME UNCOMFORTABLE!
JOIN THE CLUB.
WELL SUE ME FOR NOT LIVING IN A FREAKING PALACE.
YOU'RE NOT GOING TO START IN ON THAT AGAIN, ARE YOU?
IT'S NOT A PALACE, PACO!
BLAM
KRNCH
CHOOM
SHRAK
MORE HOUSE THAN I'VE EVER SEEN.
THERE! YOU SEE? THIS IS WHY I DON'T HAVE YOU OVER THAT OFTEN!
SPLKT
SWEAR TO... YOU'RE LIKE SOME RUBE FROM A THIRD-WORLD COUNTRY SOMETIMES.
WHAT WAS THAT? I COULDN'T HEAR YOU WITH THAT SILVER SPOON IN YOUR MOUTH.
BUDDA BUDDA BUDDA
HEY!
AWW, C'MON, BRENDA, I WAS JUST GASSING--
I KNOW.
JUST LIKE I KNOW THAT US PRETENDING LIKE NOTHING'S WRONG IS...
DAMMIT! DAMMIT, DAMMIT!

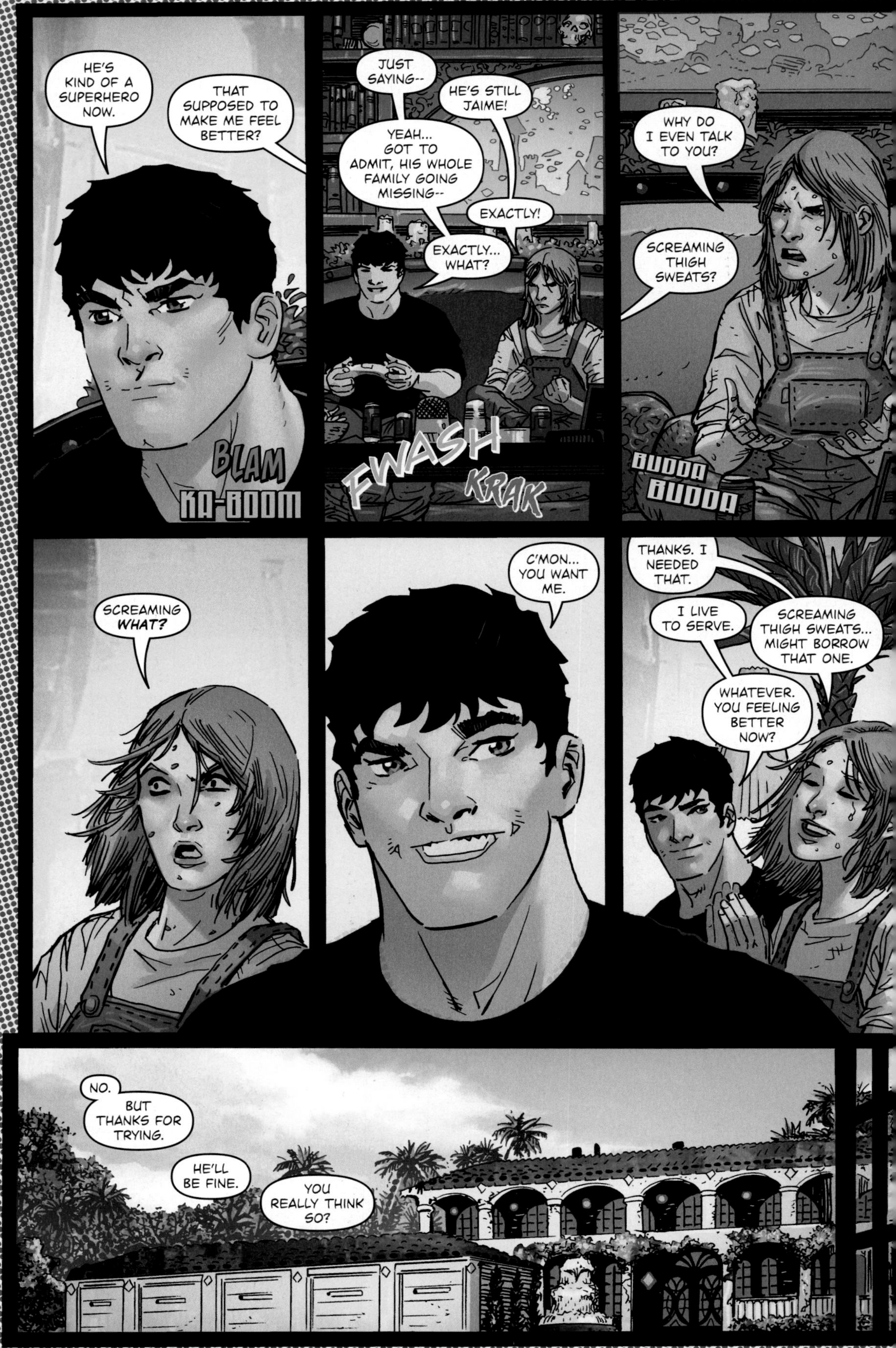
HE'S KIND OF A SUPERHERO NOW.
THAT SUPPOSED TO MAKE ME FEEL BETTER?
BLAM
KA-BOOM
JUST SAYING--
HE'S STILL JAIME!
YEAH... GOT TO ADMIT, HIS WHOLE FAMILY GOING MISSING--
EXACTLY!
EXACTLY... WHAT?
FWASH
KRAK
WHY DO I EVEN TALK TO YOU?
SCREAMING THIGH SWEATS?
BUDDA BUDDA
SCREAMING WHAT?
C'MON... YOU WANT ME.
THANKS. I NEEDED THAT.
I LIVE TO SERVE.
SCREAMING THIGH SWEATS... MIGHT BORROW THAT ONE.
WHATEVER. YOU FEELING BETTER NOW?
NO.
BUT THANKS FOR TRYING.
HE'LL BE FINE.
YOU REALLY THINK SO?

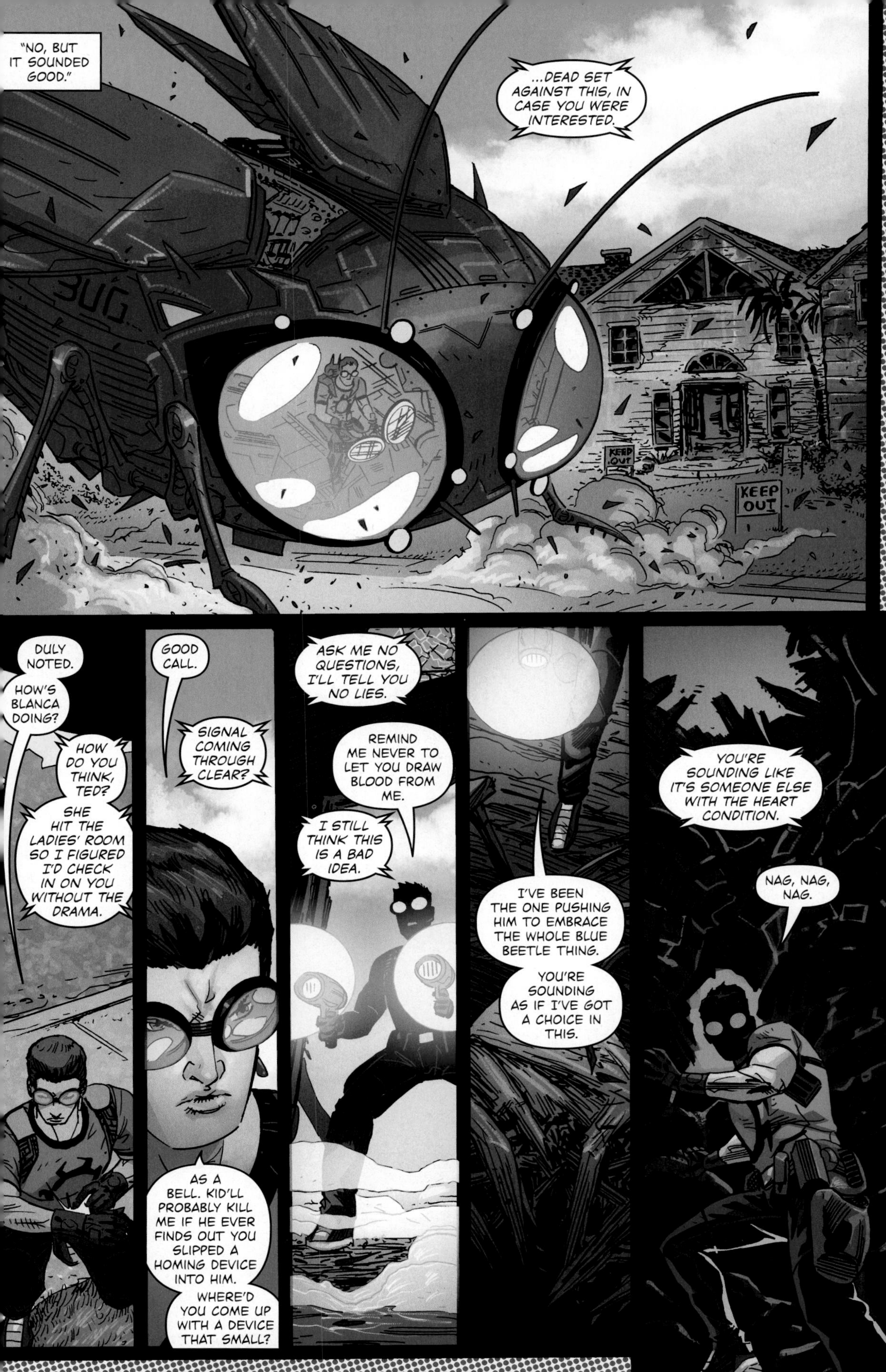
"NO, BUT IT SOUNDED GOOD."
...DEAD SET AGAINST THIS, IN CASE YOU WERE INTERESTED.
BUG
KEEP OUT
KEEP OUT
DULY NOTED.
HOW'S BLANCA DOING?
HOW DO YOU THINK, TED?
SHE HIT THE LADIES' ROOM SO I FIGURED I'D CHECK IN ON YOU WITHOUT THE DRAMA.
GOOD CALL.
SIGNAL COMING THROUGH CLEAR?
AS A BELL. KID'LL PROBABLY KILL ME IF HE EVER FINDS OUT YOU SLIPPED A HOMING DEVICE INTO HIM.
WHERE'D YOU COME UP WITH A DEVICE THAT SMALL?
ASK ME NO QUESTIONS, I'LL TELL YOU NO LIES.
REMIND ME NEVER TO LET YOU DRAW BLOOD FROM ME.
I STILL THINK THIS IS A BAD IDEA.
I'VE BEEN THE ONE PUSHING HIM TO EMBRACE THE WHOLE BLUE BEETLE THING.
YOU'RE SOUNDING AS IF I'VE GOT A CHOICE IN THIS.
YOU'RE SOUNDING LIKE IT'S SOMEONE ELSE WITH THE HEART CONDITION.
NAG, NAG, NAG.

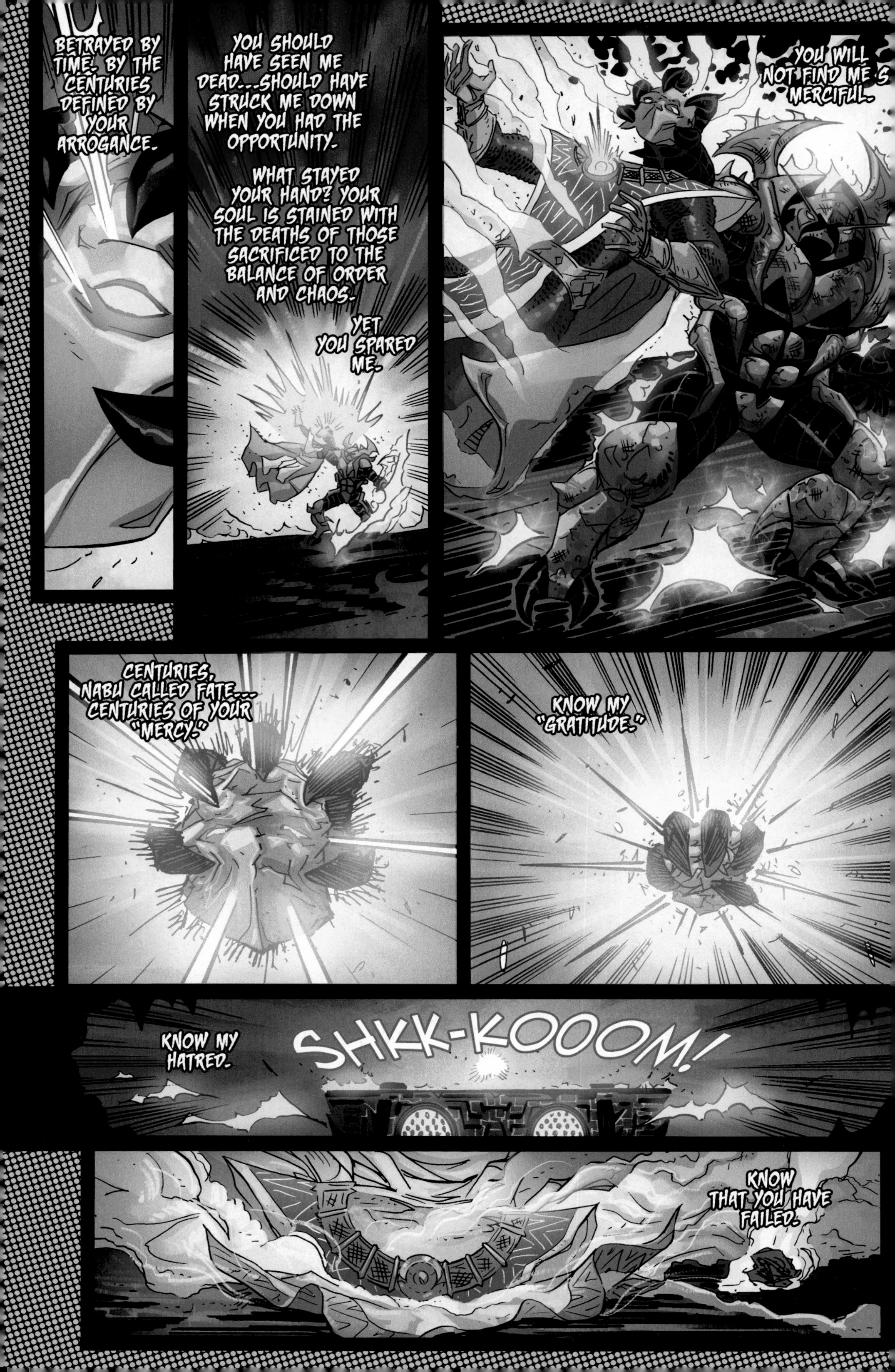
BETRAYED BY TIME. BY THE CENTURIES DEFINED BY YOUR ARROGANCE.
YOU SHOULD HAVE SEEN ME DEAD...SHOULD HAVE STRUCK ME DOWN WHEN YOU HAD THE OPPORTUNITY.
WHAT STAYED YOUR HAND? YOUR SOUL IS STAINED WITH THE DEATHS OF THOSE SACRIFICED TO THE BALANCE OF ORDER AND CHAOS.
YET YOU SPARED ME.
YOU WILL NOT FIND ME S MERCIFUL.
CENTURIES, NABU CALLED FATE...CENTURIES OF YOUR "MERCY."
KNOW MY "GRATITUDE."
KNOW MY HATRED.
SHKK-KOOOM!
KNOW THAT YOU HAVE FAILED.

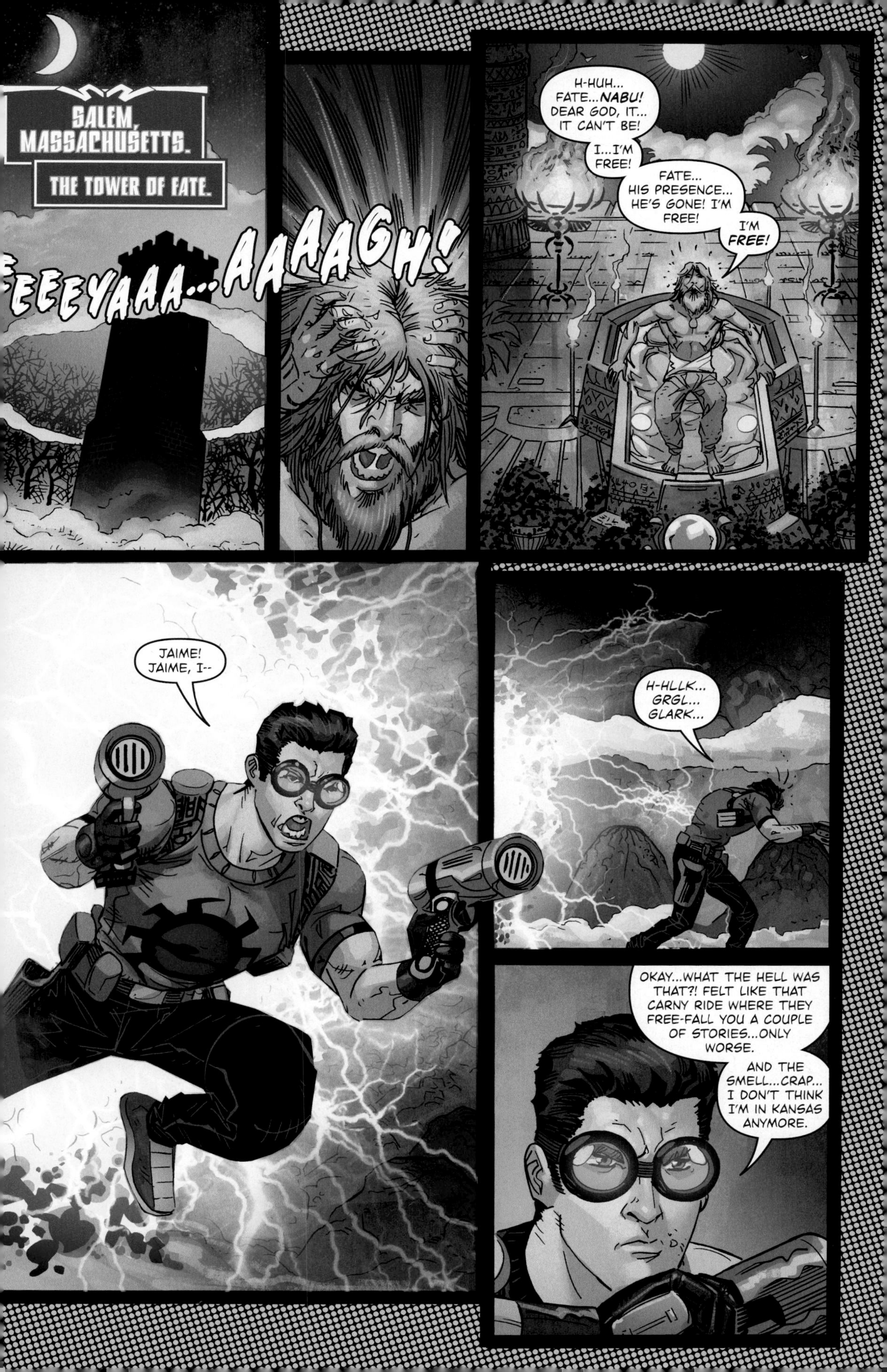
SALEM, MASSACHUSETTS.
THE TOWER OF FATE.
EEEYAAA...AAAAAGH!
H-HUH... FATE...NABU! DEAR GOD, IT... IT CAN'T BE!
I...I'M FREE!
FATE... HIS PRESENCE... HE'S GONE! I'M FREE!
I'M FREE!
JAIME! JAIME, I--
H-HLLK... GRGL... GLARK...
OKAY...WHAT THE HELL WAS THAT?! FELT LIKE THAT CARNY RIDE WHERE THEY FREE-FALL YOU A COUPLE OF STORIES...ONLY WORSE.
AND THE SMELL...CRAP... I DON'T THINK I'M IN KANSAS ANYMORE.

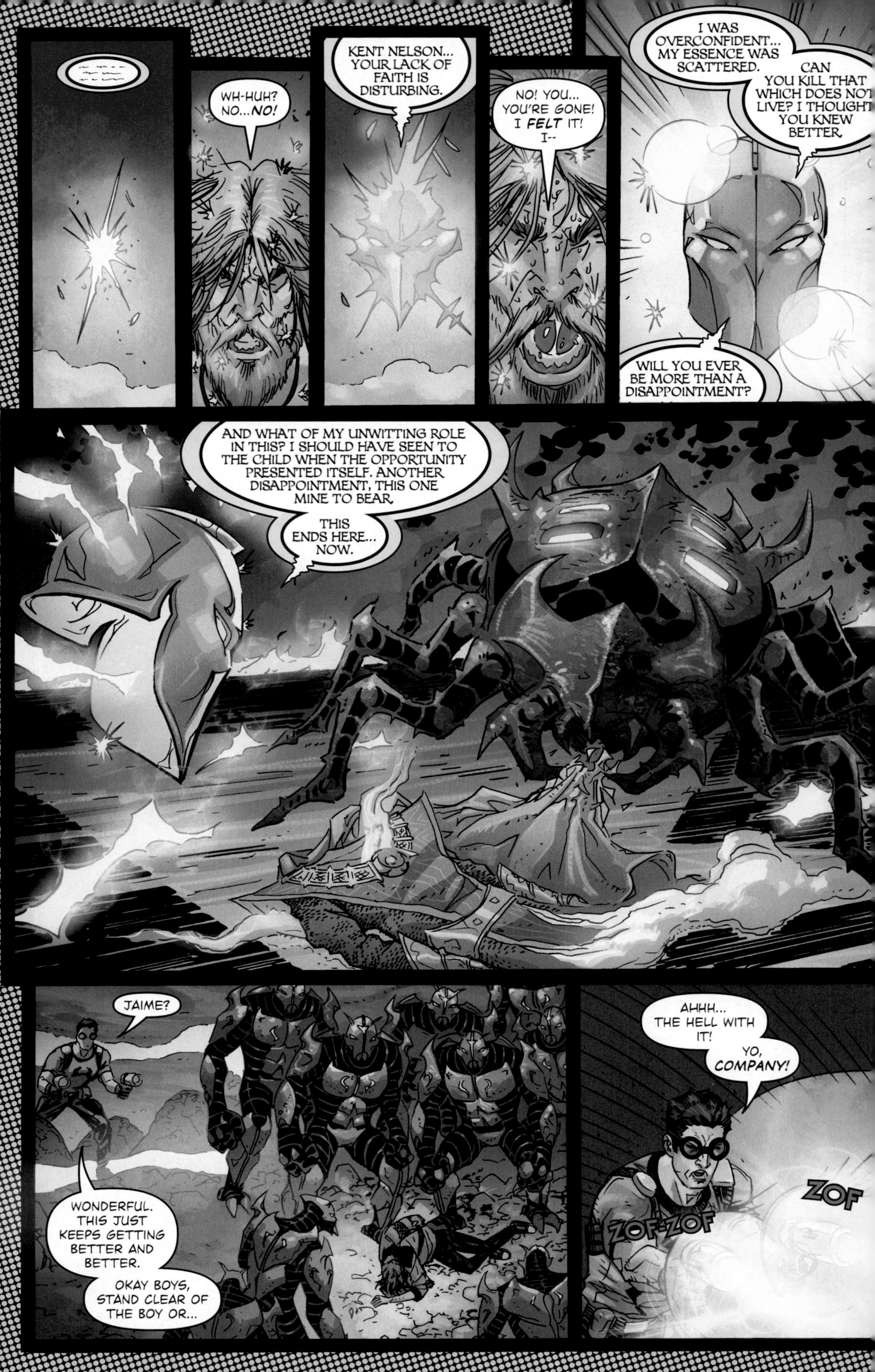
WH-HUH? NO...NO!
KENT NELSON... YOUR LACK OF FAITH IS DISTURBING.
NO! YOU... YOU'RE GONE! I FELT IT! I--
I WAS OVERCONFIDENT... MY ESSENCE WAS SCATTERED.
CAN YOU KILL THAT WHICH DOES NOT LIVE? I THOUGHT YOU KNEW BETTER.
WILL YOU EVER BE MORE THAN A DISAPPOINTMENT?
AND WHAT OF MY UNWITTING ROLE IN THIS? I SHOULD HAVE SEEN TO THE CHILD WHEN THE OPPORTUNITY PRESENTED ITSELF. ANOTHER DISAPPOINTMENT, THIS ONE MINE TO BEAR.
THIS ENDS HERE... NOW.
JAIME?
WONDERFUL. THIS JUST KEEPS GETTING BETTER AND BETTER.
OKAY BOYS, STAND CLEAR OF THE BOY OR...
AHHH... THE HELL WITH IT!
YO, COMPANY!
ZOF
ZOF-ZOF

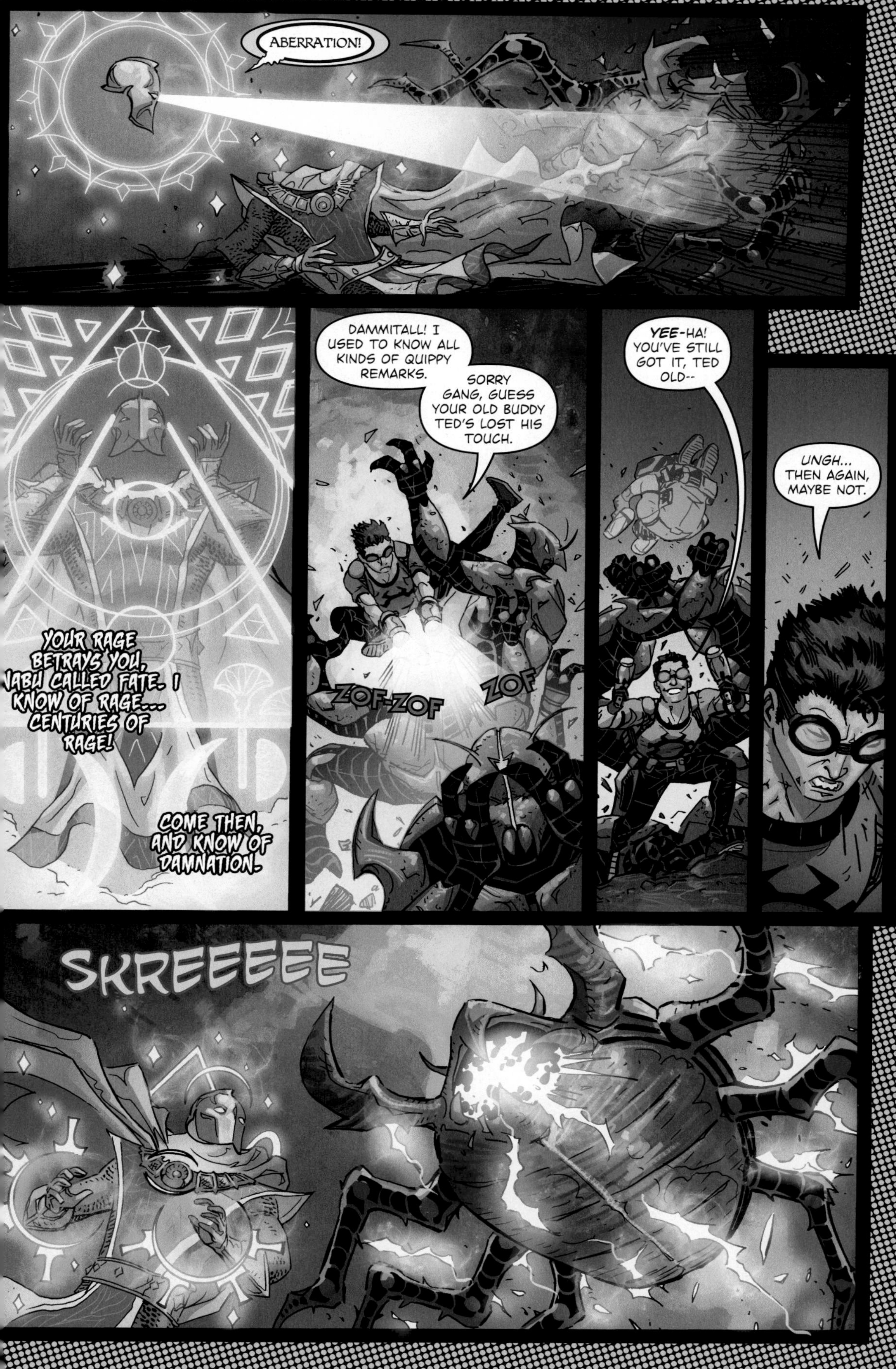
ABERRATION!
YOUR RAGE BETRAYS YOU, NABU CALLED FATE. I KNOW OF RAGE... CENTURIES OF RAGE!
COME THEN, AND KNOW OF DAMNATION.
DAMMITALL! I USED TO KNOW ALL KINDS OF QUIPPY REMARKS.
SORRY GANG, GUESS YOUR OLD BUDDY TED'S LOST HIS TOUCH.
ZOF-ZOF
ZOF
YEE-HA! YOU'VE STILL GOT IT, TED OLD--
UNGH... THEN AGAIN, MAYBE NOT.
SKREEEEEE

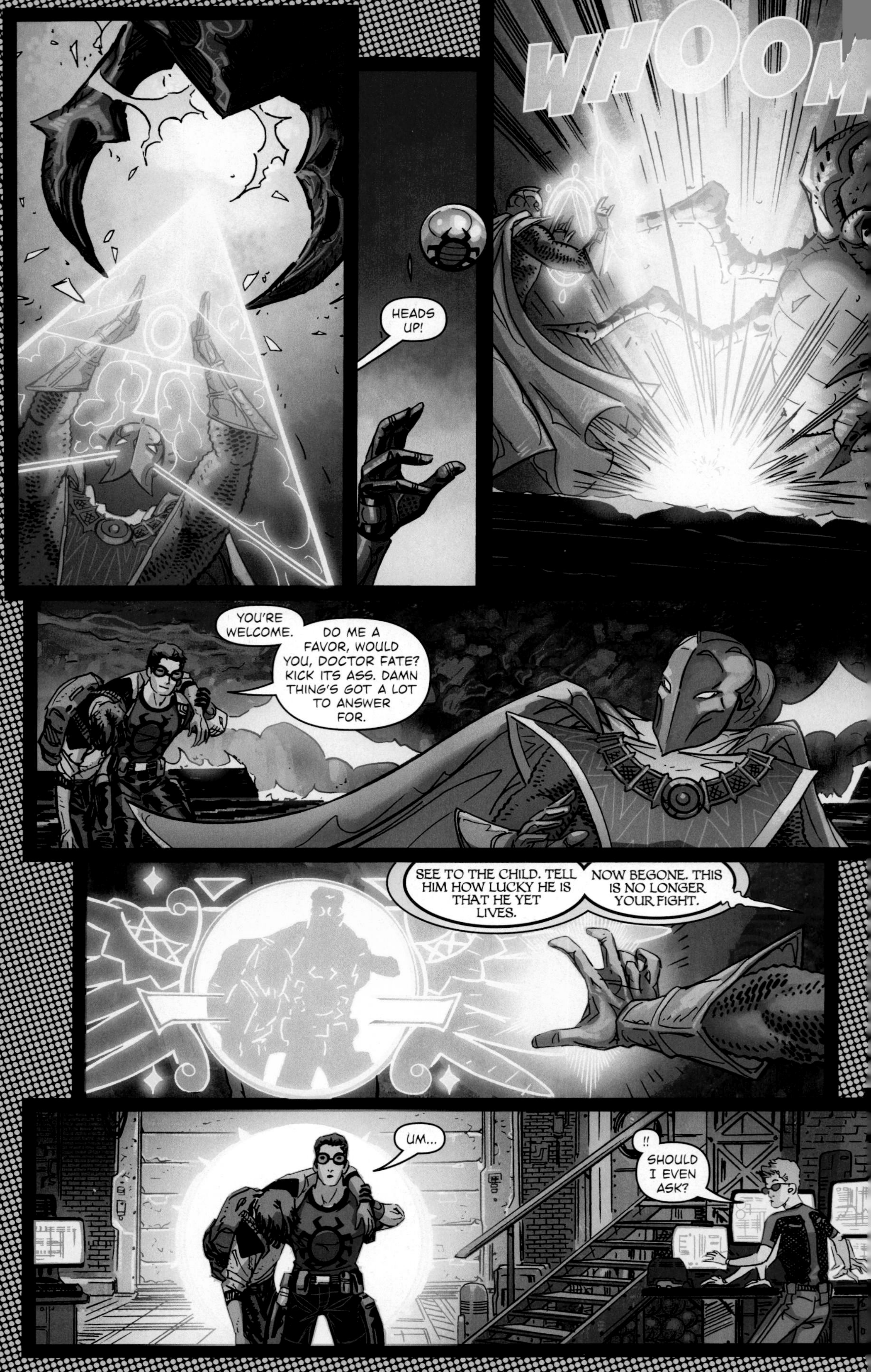
WHOOM
HEADS UP!
YOU'RE WELCOME.
DO ME A FAVOR, WOULD YOU, DOCTOR FATE? KICK ITS ASS. DAMN THING'S GOT A LOT TO ANSWER FOR.
SEE TO THE CHILD. TELL HIM HOW LUCKY HE IS THAT HE YET LIVES.
NOW BEGONE. THIS IS NO LONGER YOUR FIGHT.
UM...
!!
SHOULD I EVEN ASK?

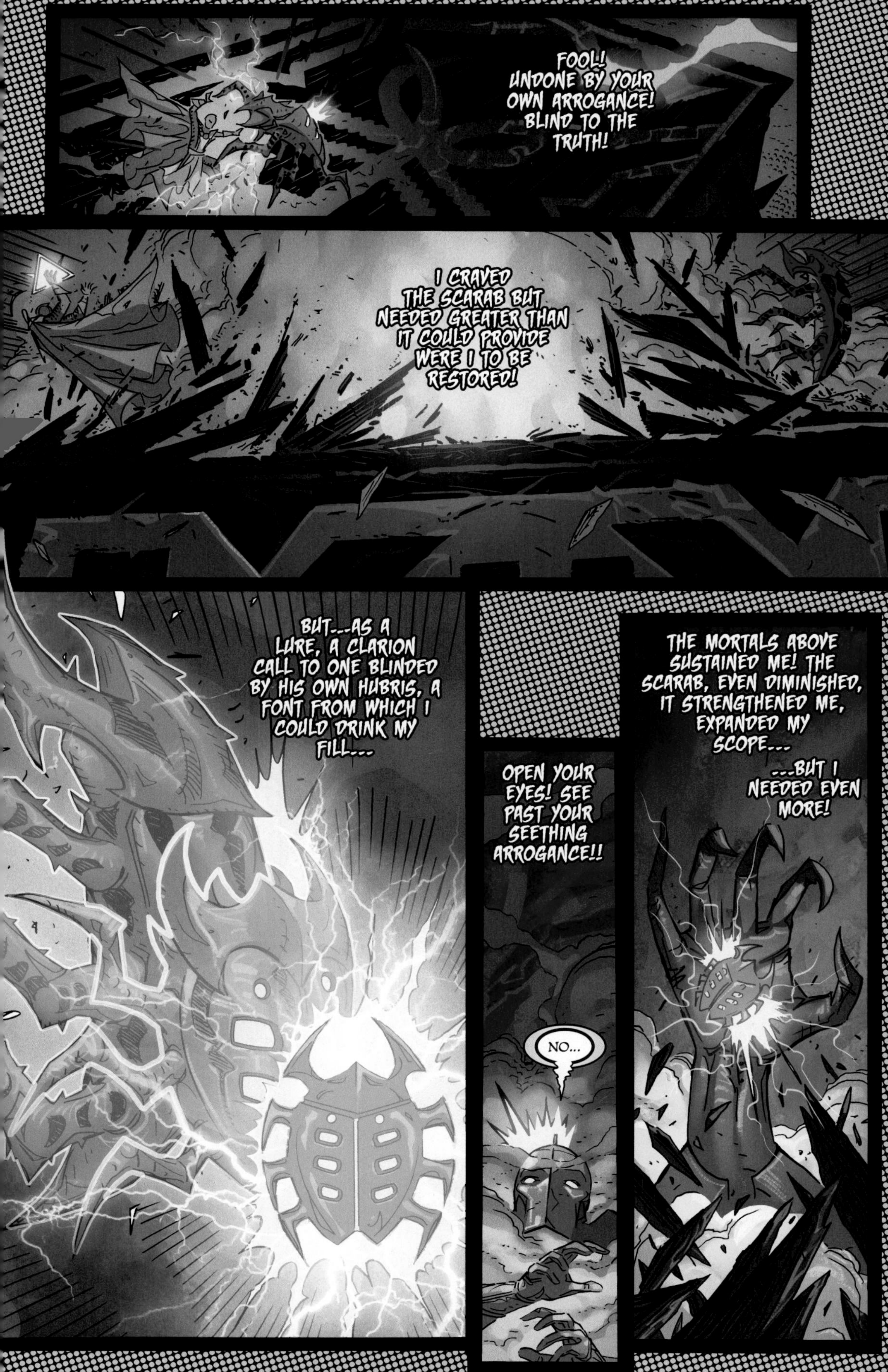
FOOL! UNDONE BY YOUR OWN ARROGANCE! BLIND TO THE TRUTH!
I CRAVED THE SCARAB BUT NEEDED GREATER THAN IT COULD PROVIDE WERE I TO BE RESTORED!
BUT...AS A LURE, A CLARION CALL TO ONE BLINDED BY HIS OWN HUBRIS, A FONT FROM WHICH I COULD DRINK MY FILL...
OPEN YOUR EYES! SEE PAST YOUR SEETHING ARROGANCE!!
NO...
THE MORTALS ABOVE SUSTAINED ME! THE SCARAB, EVEN DIMINISHED, IT STRENGTHENED ME, EXPANDED MY SCOPE...
...BUT I NEEDED EVEN MORE!

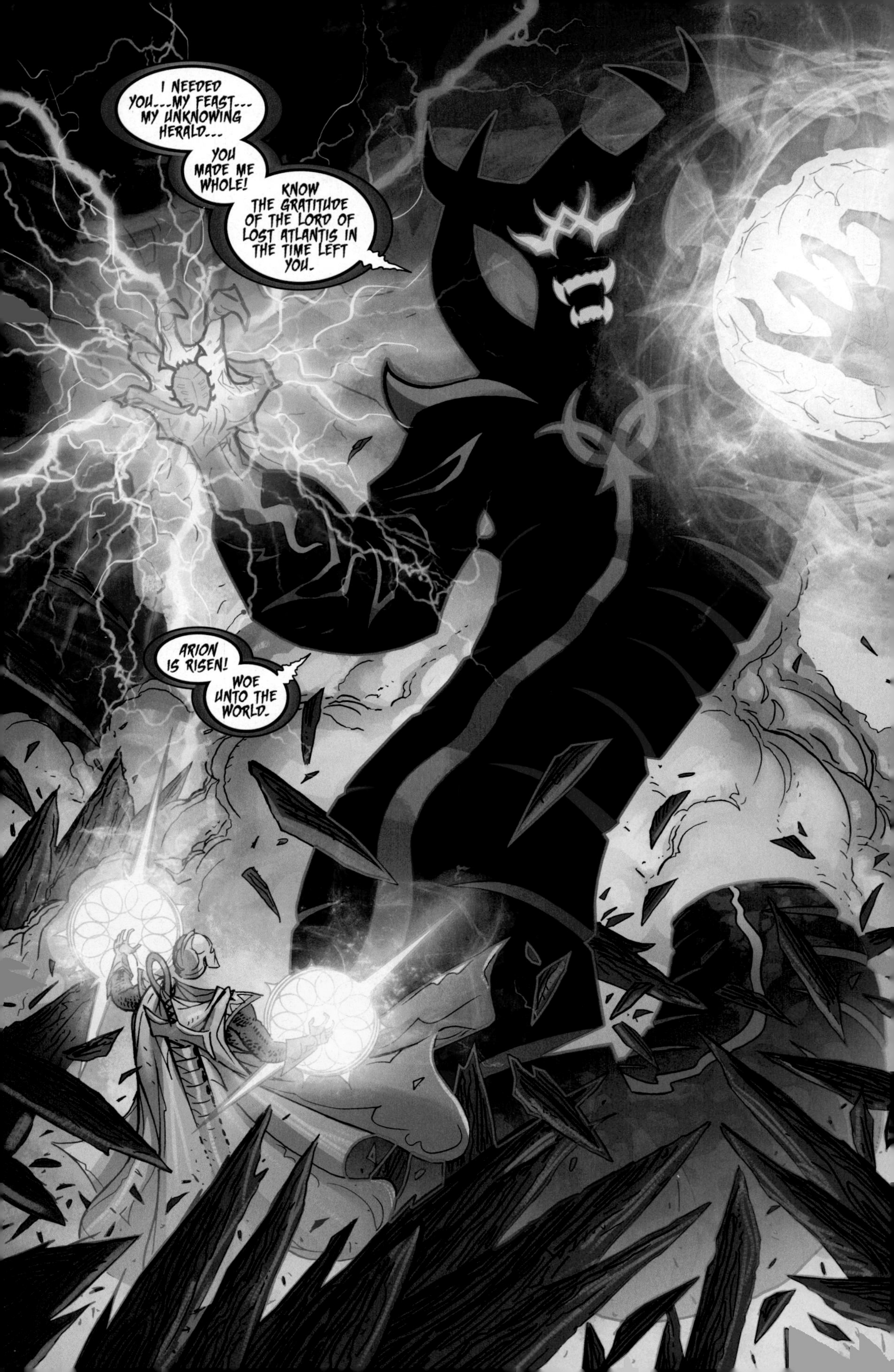

I NEEDED YOU...MY FEAST... MY UNKNOWING HERALD...
YOU MADE ME WHOLE!
KNOW THE GRATITUDE OF THE LORD OF LOST ATLANTIS IN THE TIME LEFT YOU.
ARION IS RISEN!
WOE UNTO THE WORLD.

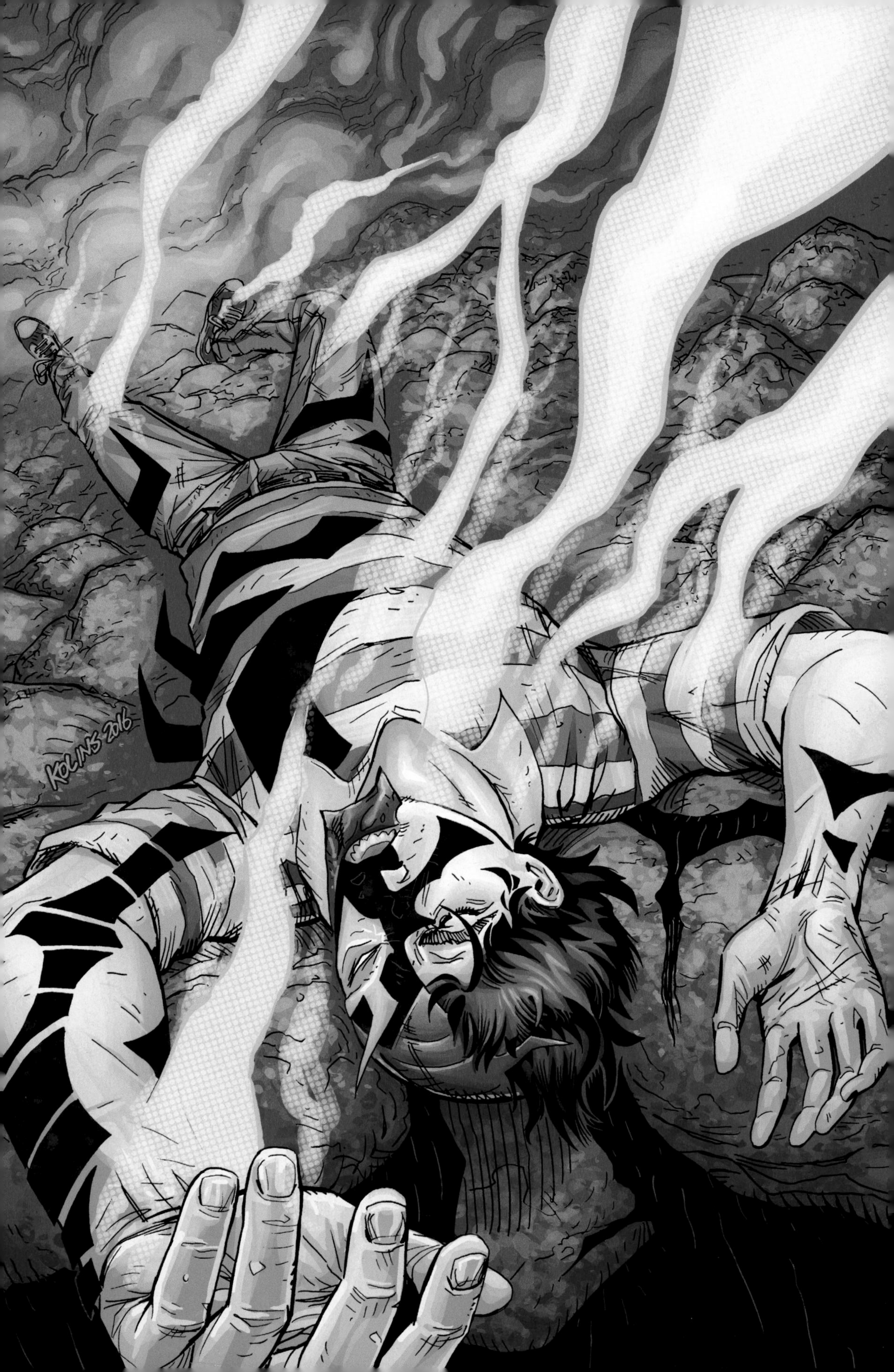
KOLINS 2016

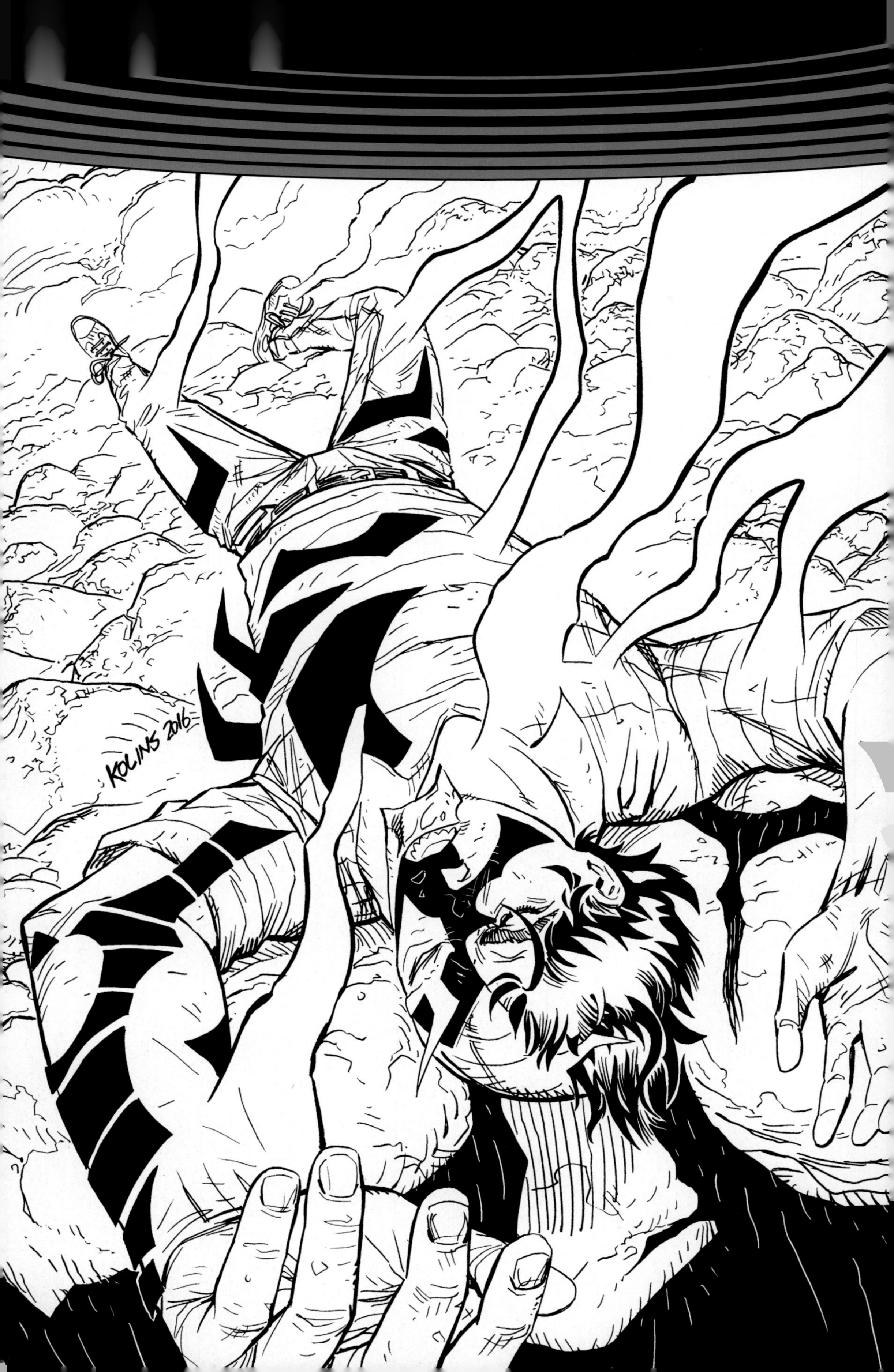
KOLINS 2016

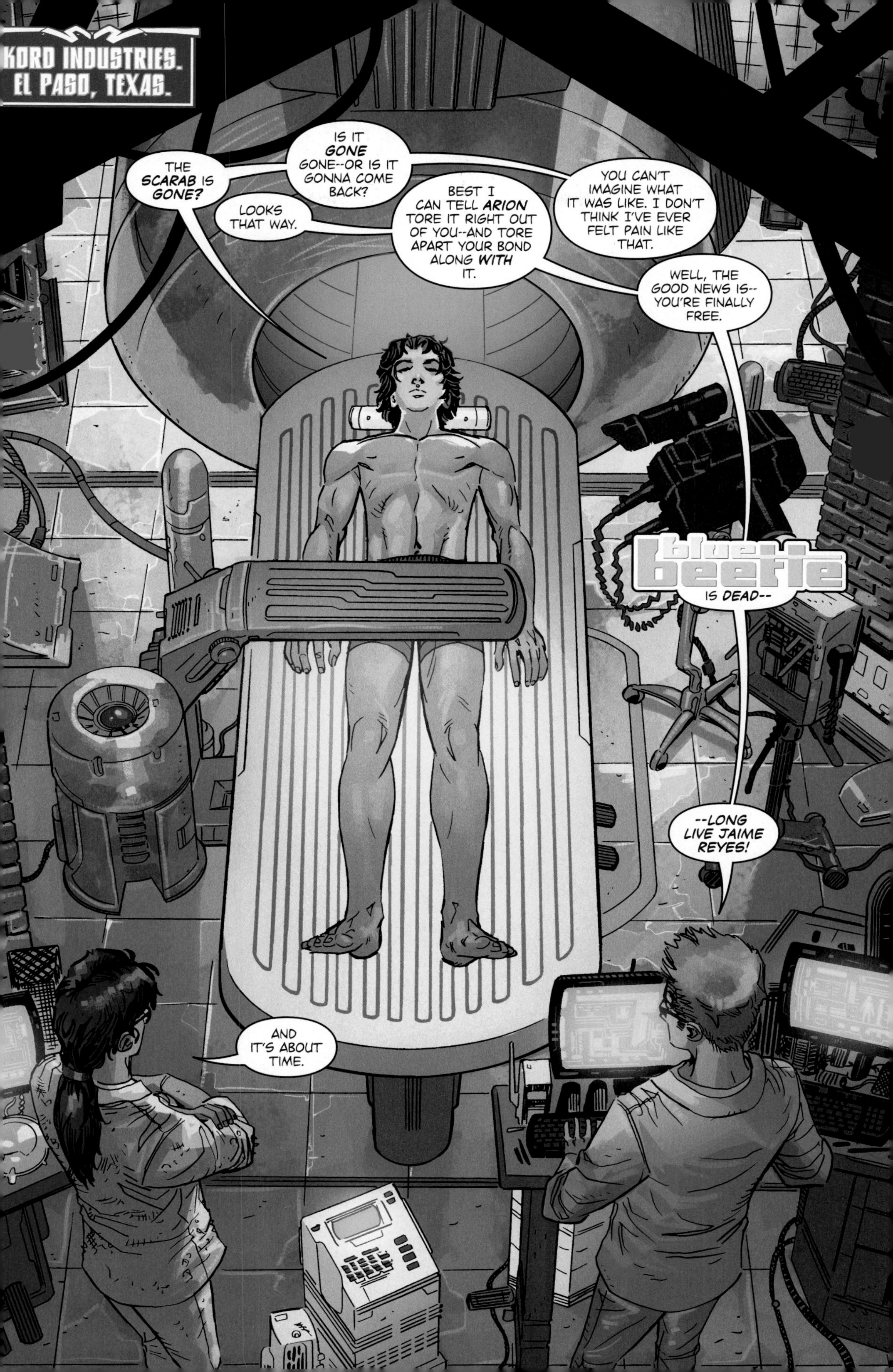
KORD INDUSTRIES. EL PASO, TEXAS.
THE SCARAB IS GONE?
IS IT GONE GONE--OR IS IT GONNA COME BACK?
LOOKS THAT WAY.
BEST I CAN TELL ARION TORE IT RIGHT OUT OF YOU--AND TORE APART YOUR BOND ALONG WITH IT.
YOU CAN'T IMAGINE WHAT IT WAS LIKE. I DON'T THINK I'VE EVER FELT PAIN LIKE THAT.
WELL, THE GOOD NEWS IS--YOU'RE FINALLY FREE.
blue beetle
IS DEAD--
--LONG LIVE JAIME REYES!
AND IT'S ABOUT TIME.

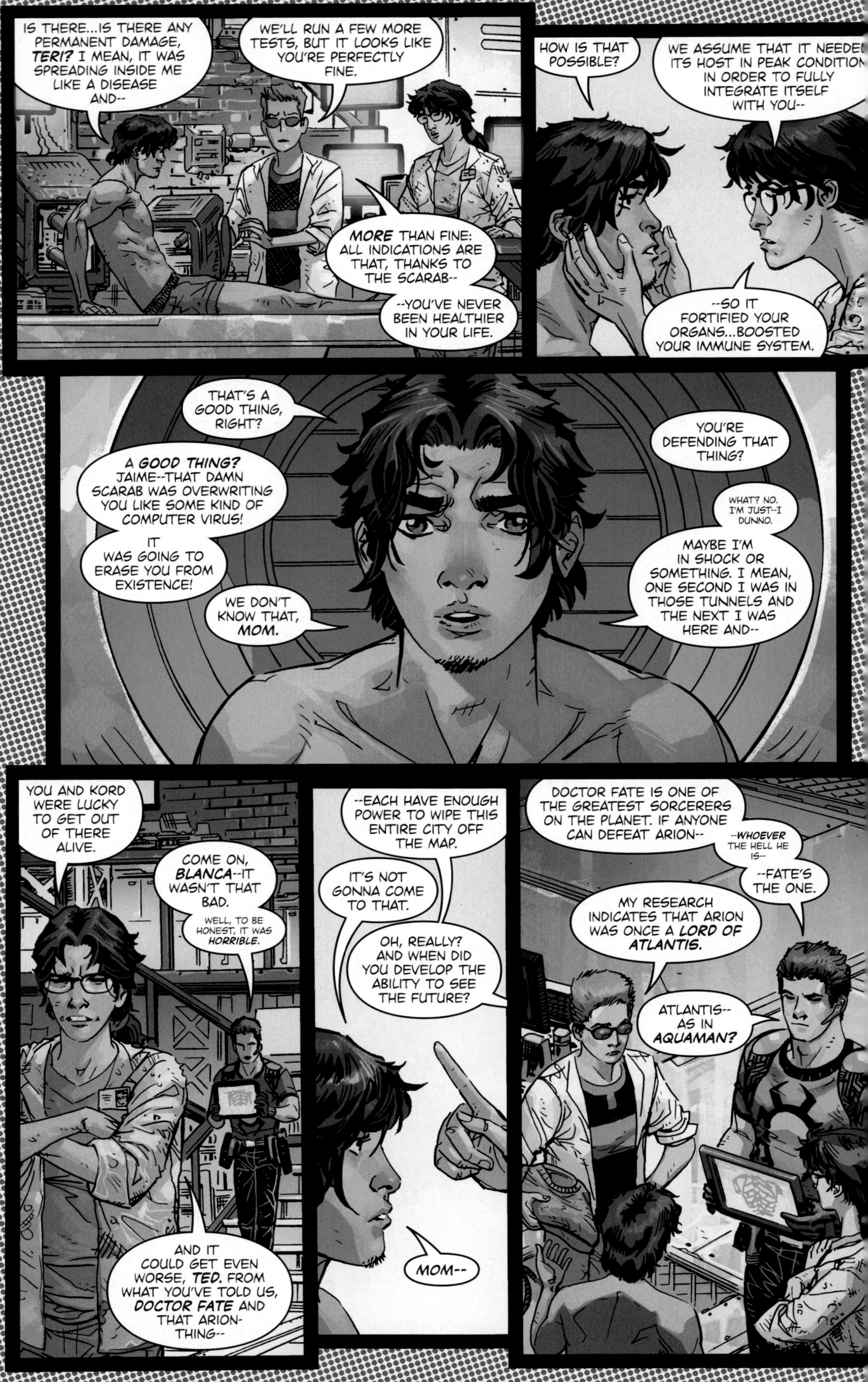
IS THERE...IS THERE ANY PERMANENT DAMAGE, TERI? I MEAN, IT WAS SPREADING INSIDE ME LIKE A DISEASE AND--
WE'LL RUN A FEW MORE TESTS, BUT IT LOOKS LIKE YOU'RE PERFECTLY FINE.
MORE THAN FINE: ALL INDICATIONS ARE THAT, THANKS TO THE SCARAB--
--YOU'VE NEVER BEEN HEALTHIER IN YOUR LIFE.
HOW IS THAT POSSIBLE?
WE ASSUME THAT IT NEEDED ITS HOST IN PEAK CONDITION IN ORDER TO FULLY INTEGRATE ITSELF WITH YOU--
--SO IT FORTIFIED YOUR ORGANS...BOOSTED YOUR IMMUNE SYSTEM.
THAT'S A GOOD THING, RIGHT?
A GOOD THING? JAIME--THAT DAMN SCARAB WAS OVERWRITING YOU LIKE SOME KIND OF COMPUTER VIRUS!
IT WAS GOING TO ERASE YOU FROM EXISTENCE!
WE DON'T KNOW THAT, MOM.
YOU'RE DEFENDING THAT THING?
WHAT? NO. I'M JUST--I DUNNO.
MAYBE I'M IN SHOCK OR SOMETHING. I MEAN, ONE SECOND I WAS IN THOSE TUNNELS AND THE NEXT I WAS HERE AND--
YOU AND KORD WERE LUCKY TO GET OUT OF THERE ALIVE.
COME ON, BLANCA--IT WASN'T THAT BAD.
WELL, TO BE HONEST, IT WAS HORRIBLE.
AND IT COULD GET EVEN WORSE, TED. FROM WHAT YOU'VE TOLD US, DOCTOR FATE AND THAT ARION-THING--
--EACH HAVE ENOUGH POWER TO WIPE THIS ENTIRE CITY OFF THE MAP.
IT'S NOT GONNA COME TO THAT.
OH, REALLY? AND WHEN DID YOU DEVELOP THE ABILITY TO SEE THE FUTURE?
MOM--
DOCTOR FATE IS ONE OF THE GREATEST SORCERERS ON THE PLANET. IF ANYONE CAN DEFEAT ARION--
--WHOEVER THE HELL HE IS--
--FATE'S THE ONE.
MY RESEARCH INDICATES THAT ARION WAS ONCE A LORD OF ATLANTIS.
ATLANTIS--AS IN AQUAMAN?

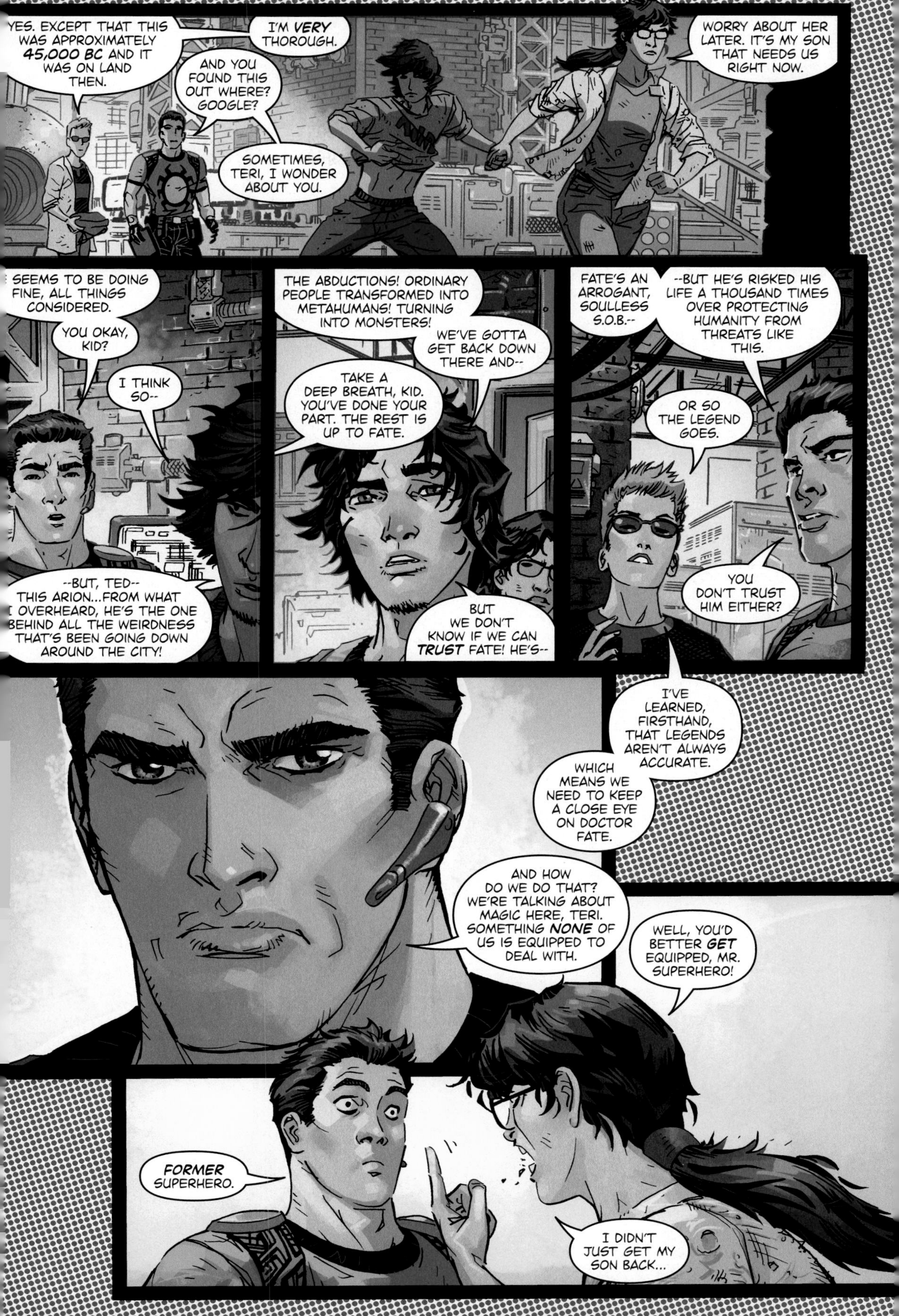
YES. EXCEPT THAT THIS WAS APPROXIMATELY **45,000 BC** AND IT WAS ON LAND THEN.
I'M ***VERY*** THOROUGH.
AND YOU FOUND THIS OUT WHERE? GOOGLE?
SOMETIMES, TERI, I WONDER ABOUT YOU.
WORRY ABOUT HER LATER. IT'S MY SON THAT NEEDS US RIGHT NOW.
SEEMS TO BE DOING FINE, ALL THINGS CONSIDERED.
YOU OKAY, KID?
I THINK SO--
--BUT, TED-- THIS ARION...FROM WHAT I OVERHEARD, HE'S THE ONE BEHIND ALL THE WEIRDNESS THAT'S BEEN GOING DOWN AROUND THE CITY!
THE ABDUCTIONS! ORDINARY PEOPLE TRANSFORMED INTO METAHUMANS! TURNING INTO MONSTERS!
WE'VE GOTTA GET BACK DOWN THERE AND--
TAKE A DEEP BREATH, KID. YOU'VE DONE YOUR PART. THE REST IS UP TO FATE.
BUT WE DON'T KNOW IF WE CAN ***TRUST*** FATE! HE'S--
FATE'S AN ARROGANT, SOULLESS S.O.B.--
--BUT HE'S RISKED HIS LIFE A THOUSAND TIMES OVER PROTECTING HUMANITY FROM THREATS LIKE THIS.
OR SO THE LEGEND GOES.
YOU DON'T TRUST HIM EITHER?
I'VE LEARNED, FIRSTHAND, THAT LEGENDS AREN'T ALWAYS ACCURATE.
WHICH MEANS WE NEED TO KEEP A CLOSE EYE ON DOCTOR FATE.
AND HOW DO WE DO THAT? WE'RE TALKING ABOUT MAGIC HERE, TERI. SOMETHING ***NONE*** OF US IS EQUIPPED TO DEAL WITH.
WELL, YOU'D BETTER ***GET*** EQUIPPED, MR. SUPERHERO!
FORMER SUPERHERO.
I DIDN'T JUST GET MY SON BACK...

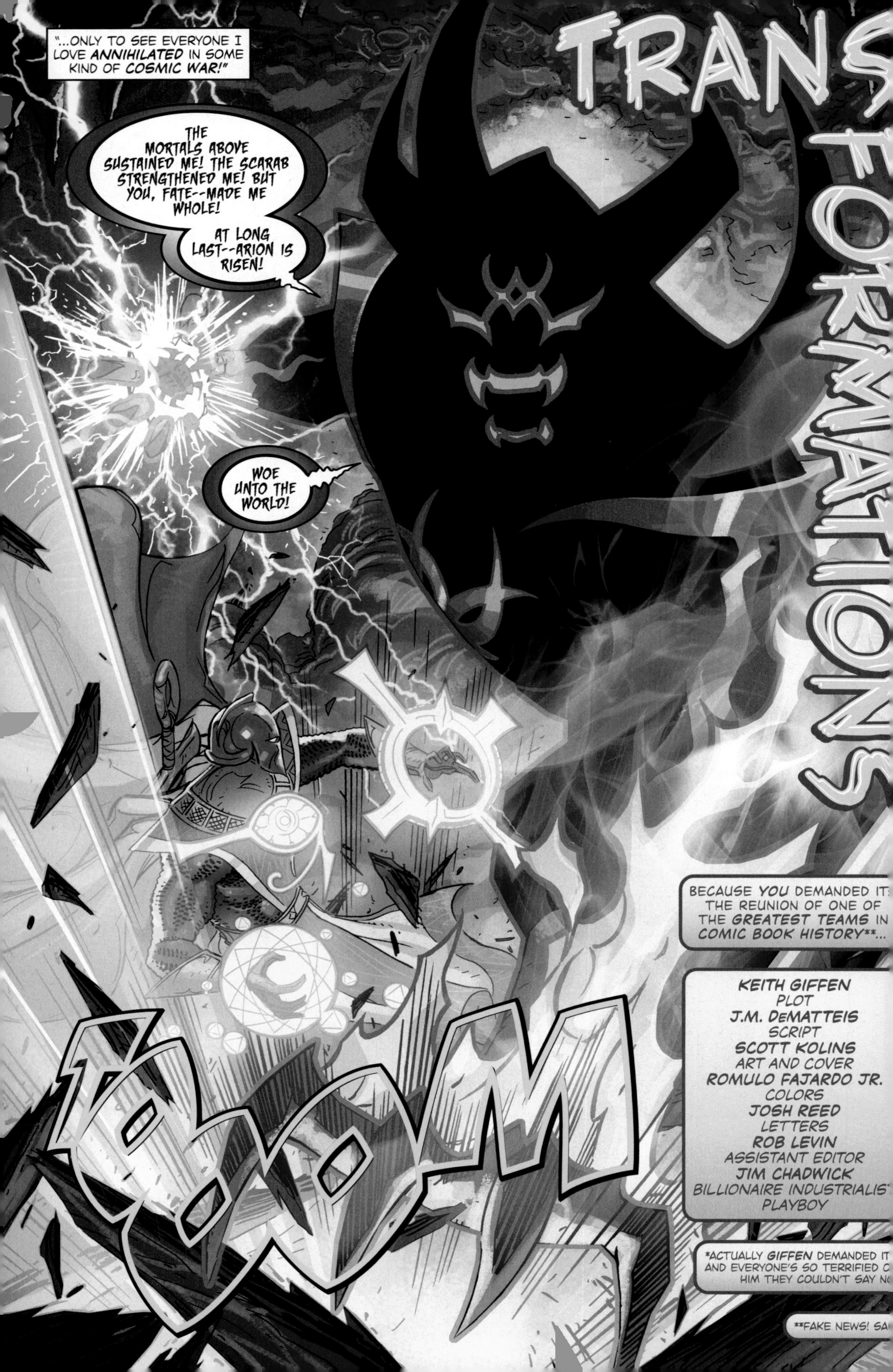
"...ONLY TO SEE EVERYONE I LOVE ANNIHILATED IN SOME KIND OF COSMIC WAR!"
THE MORTALS ABOVE SUSTAINED ME! THE SCARAB STRENGTHENED ME! BUT YOU, FATE--MADE ME WHOLE!
AT LONG LAST--ARION IS RISEN!
WOE UNTO THE WORLD!
TRANSFORMATIONS
BECAUSE YOU DEMANDED IT: THE REUNION OF ONE OF THE GREATEST TEAMS IN COMIC BOOK HISTORY**...
KEITH GIFFEN PLOT
J.M. DEMATTEIS SCRIPT
SCOTT KOLINS ART AND COVER
ROMULO FAJARDO JR. COLORS
JOSH REED LETTERS
ROB LEVIN ASSISTANT EDITOR
JIM CHADWICK BILLIONAIRE INDUSTRIALIST PLAYBOY
*ACTUALLY GIFFEN DEMANDED IT AND EVERYONE'S SO TERRIFIED OF HIM THEY COULDN'T SAY NO
**FAKE NEWS! SA
TOOM

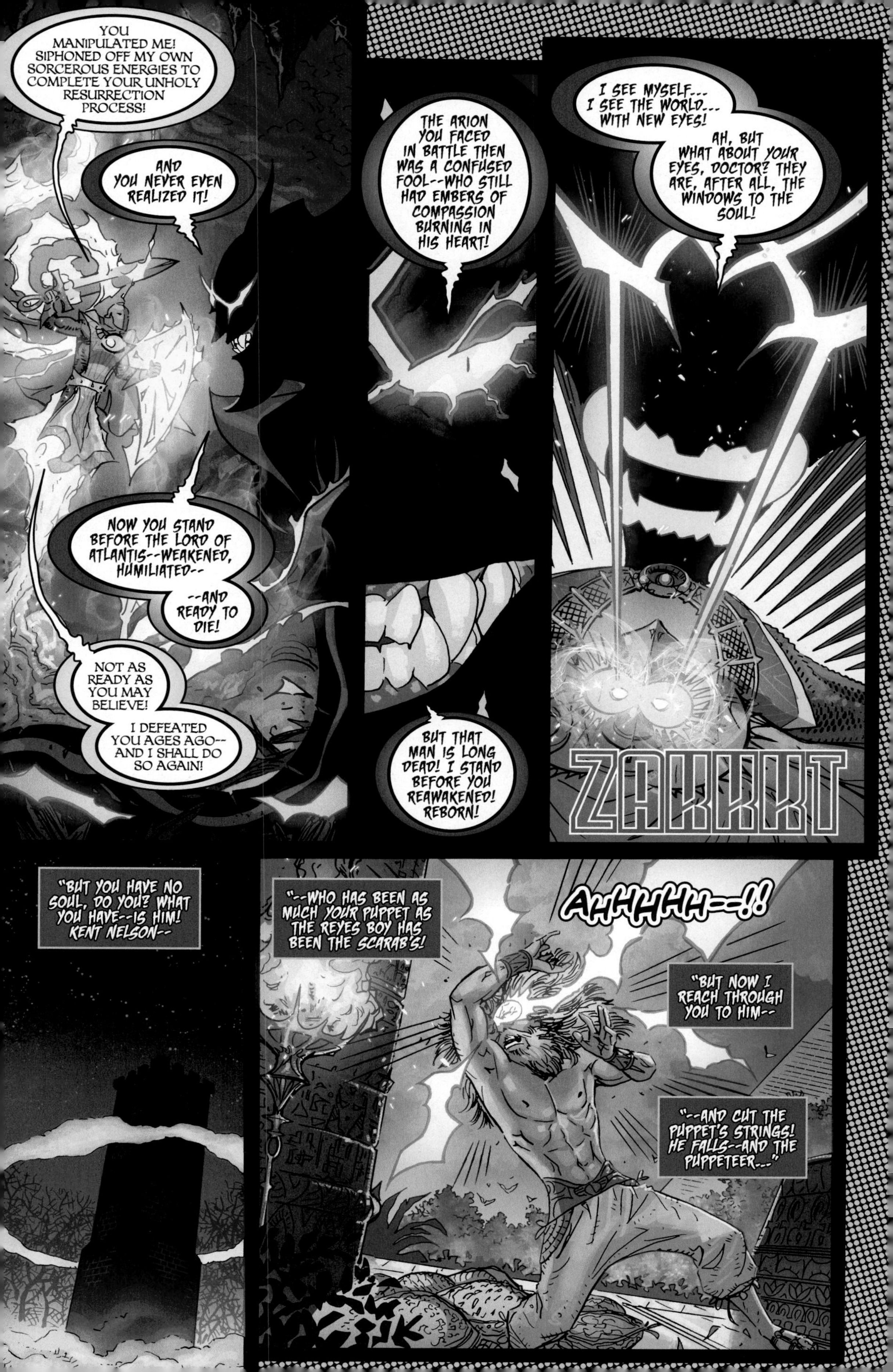
YOU MANIPULATED ME! SIPHONED OFF MY OWN SORCEROUS ENERGIES TO COMPLETE YOUR UNHOLY RESURRECTION PROCESS!
AND YOU NEVER EVEN REALIZED IT!
NOW YOU STAND BEFORE THE LORD OF ATLANTIS--WEAKENED, HUMILIATED--
--AND READY TO DIE!
NOT AS READY AS YOU MAY BELIEVE!
I DEFEATED YOU AGES AGO--AND I SHALL DO SO AGAIN!
THE ARION YOU FACED IN BATTLE THEN WAS A CONFUSED FOOL--WHO STILL HAD EMBERS OF COMPASSION BURNING IN HIS HEART!
BUT THAT MAN IS LONG DEAD! I STAND BEFORE YOU REAWAKENED! REBORN!
I SEE MYSELF... I SEE THE WORLD... WITH NEW EYES!
AH, BUT WHAT ABOUT YOUR EYES, DOCTOR? THEY ARE, AFTER ALL, THE WINDOWS TO THE SOUL!
ZAKKKT
"BUT YOU HAVE NO SOUL, DO YOU? WHAT YOU HAVE--IS HIM! KENT NELSON--
"--WHO HAS BEEN AS MUCH YOUR PUPPET AS THE REYES BOY HAS BEEN THE SCARAB'S!
AHHHHH--!!
"BUT NOW I REACH THROUGH YOU TO HIM--
"--AND CUT THE PUPPET'S STRINGS! HE FALLS--AND THE PUPPETEER..."

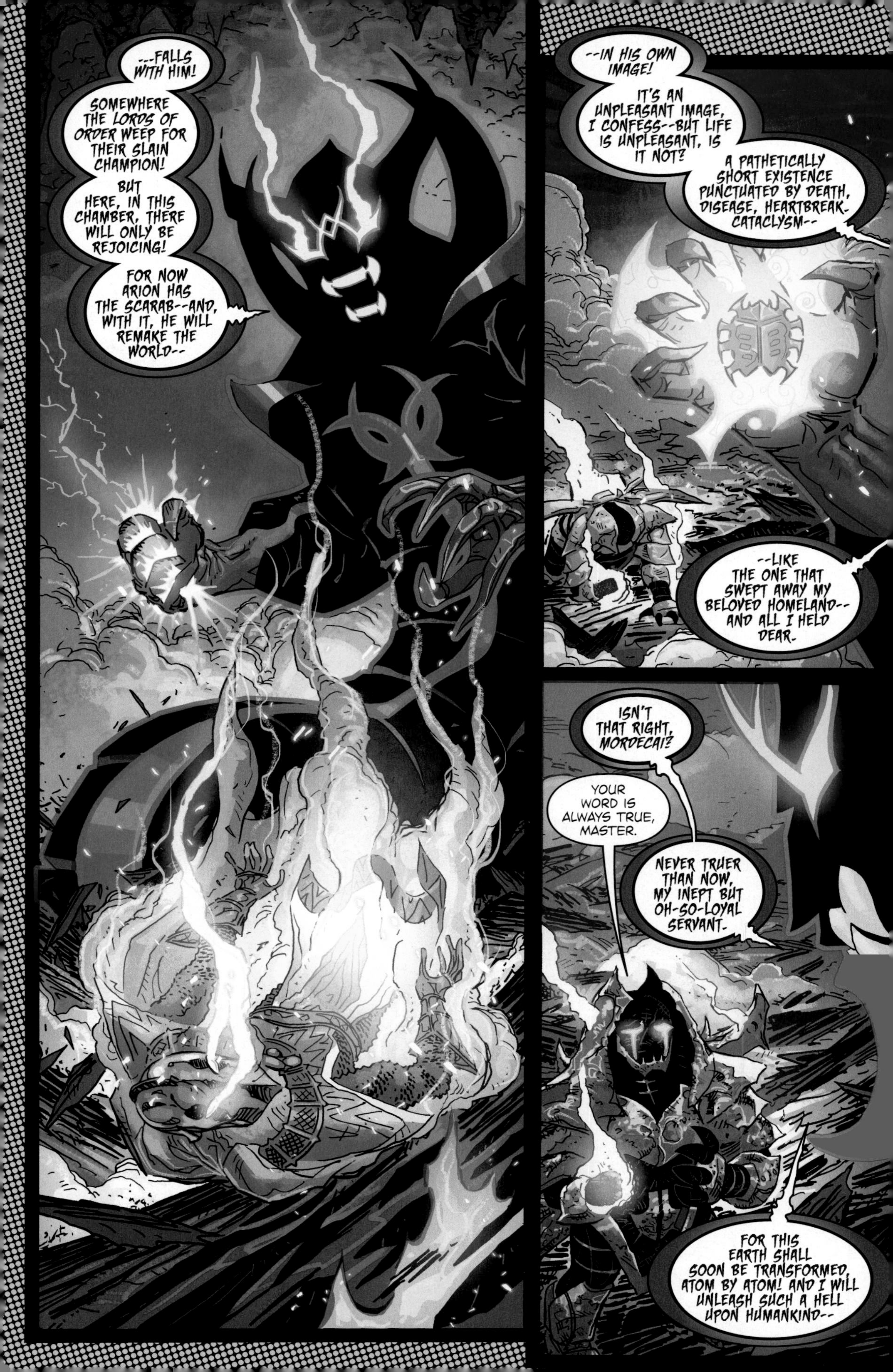
--FALLS WITH HIM!
SOMEWHERE THE LORDS OF ORDER WEEP FOR THEIR SLAIN CHAMPION!
BUT HERE, IN THIS CHAMBER, THERE WILL ONLY BE REJOICING!
FOR NOW ARION HAS THE SCARAB--AND, WITH IT, HE WILL REMAKE THE WORLD--
--IN HIS OWN IMAGE!
IT'S AN UNPLEASANT IMAGE, I CONFESS--BUT LIFE IS UNPLEASANT, IS IT NOT?
A PATHETICALLY SHORT EXISTENCE PUNCTUATED BY DEATH, DISEASE, HEARTBREAK. CATACLYSM--
--LIKE THE ONE THAT SWEPT AWAY MY BELOVED HOMELAND--AND ALL I HELD DEAR.
ISN'T THAT RIGHT, MORDECAI?
YOUR WORD IS ALWAYS TRUE, MASTER.
NEVER TRUER THAN NOW, MY INEPT BUT OH-SO-LOYAL SERVANT.
FOR THIS EARTH SHALL SOON BE TRANSFORMED, ATOM BY ATOM! AND I WILL UNLEASH SUCH A HELL UPON HUMANKIND--

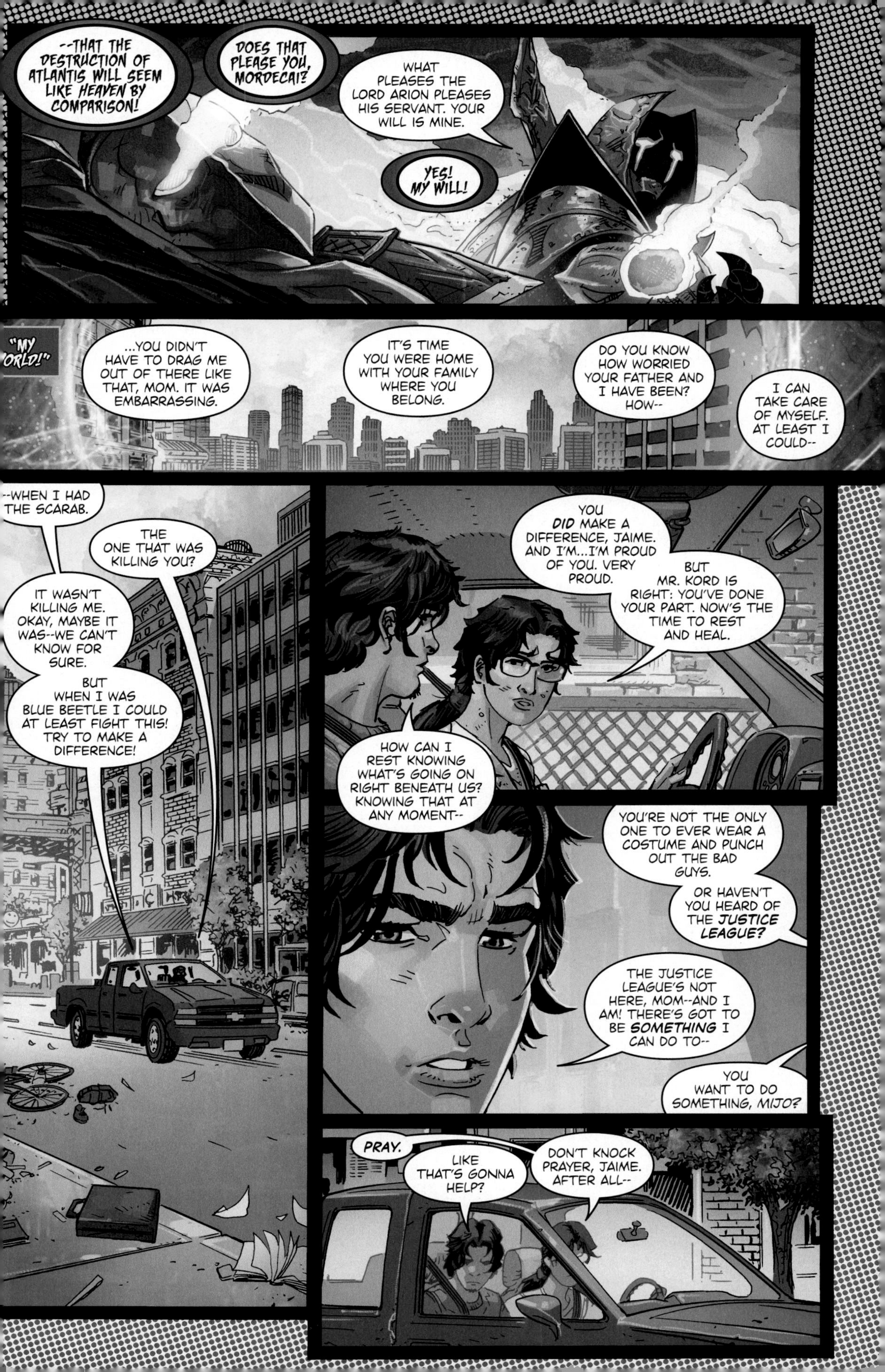
--THAT THE DESTRUCTION OF ATLANTIS WILL SEEM LIKE HEAVEN BY COMPARISON!
DOES THAT PLEASE YOU, MORDECAI?
WHAT PLEASES THE LORD ARION PLEASES HIS SERVANT. YOUR WILL IS MINE.
YES! MY WILL!
"MY ORLD!"
...YOU DIDN'T HAVE TO DRAG ME OUT OF THERE LIKE THAT, MOM. IT WAS EMBARRASSING.
IT'S TIME YOU WERE HOME WITH YOUR FAMILY WHERE YOU BELONG.
DO YOU KNOW HOW WORRIED YOUR FATHER AND I HAVE BEEN? HOW--
I CAN TAKE CARE OF MYSELF. AT LEAST I COULD--
--WHEN I HAD THE SCARAB.
THE ONE THAT WAS KILLING YOU?
IT WASN'T KILLING ME. OKAY, MAYBE IT WAS--WE CAN'T KNOW FOR SURE.
BUT WHEN I WAS BLUE BEETLE I COULD AT LEAST FIGHT THIS! TRY TO MAKE A DIFFERENCE!
YOU DID MAKE A DIFFERENCE, JAIME. AND I'M...I'M PROUD OF YOU. VERY PROUD.
BUT MR. KORD IS RIGHT: YOU'VE DONE YOUR PART. NOW'S THE TIME TO REST AND HEAL.
HOW CAN I REST KNOWING WHAT'S GOING ON RIGHT BENEATH US? KNOWING THAT AT ANY MOMENT--
YOU'RE NOT THE ONLY ONE TO EVER WEAR A COSTUME AND PUNCH OUT THE BAD GUYS.
OR HAVEN'T YOU HEARD OF THE JUSTICE LEAGUE?
THE JUSTICE LEAGUE'S NOT HERE, MOM--AND I AM! THERE'S GOT TO BE SOMETHING I CAN DO TO--
YOU WANT TO DO SOMETHING, MIJO?
PRAY.
LIKE THAT'S GONNA HELP?
DON'T KNOCK PRAYER, JAIME. AFTER ALL--

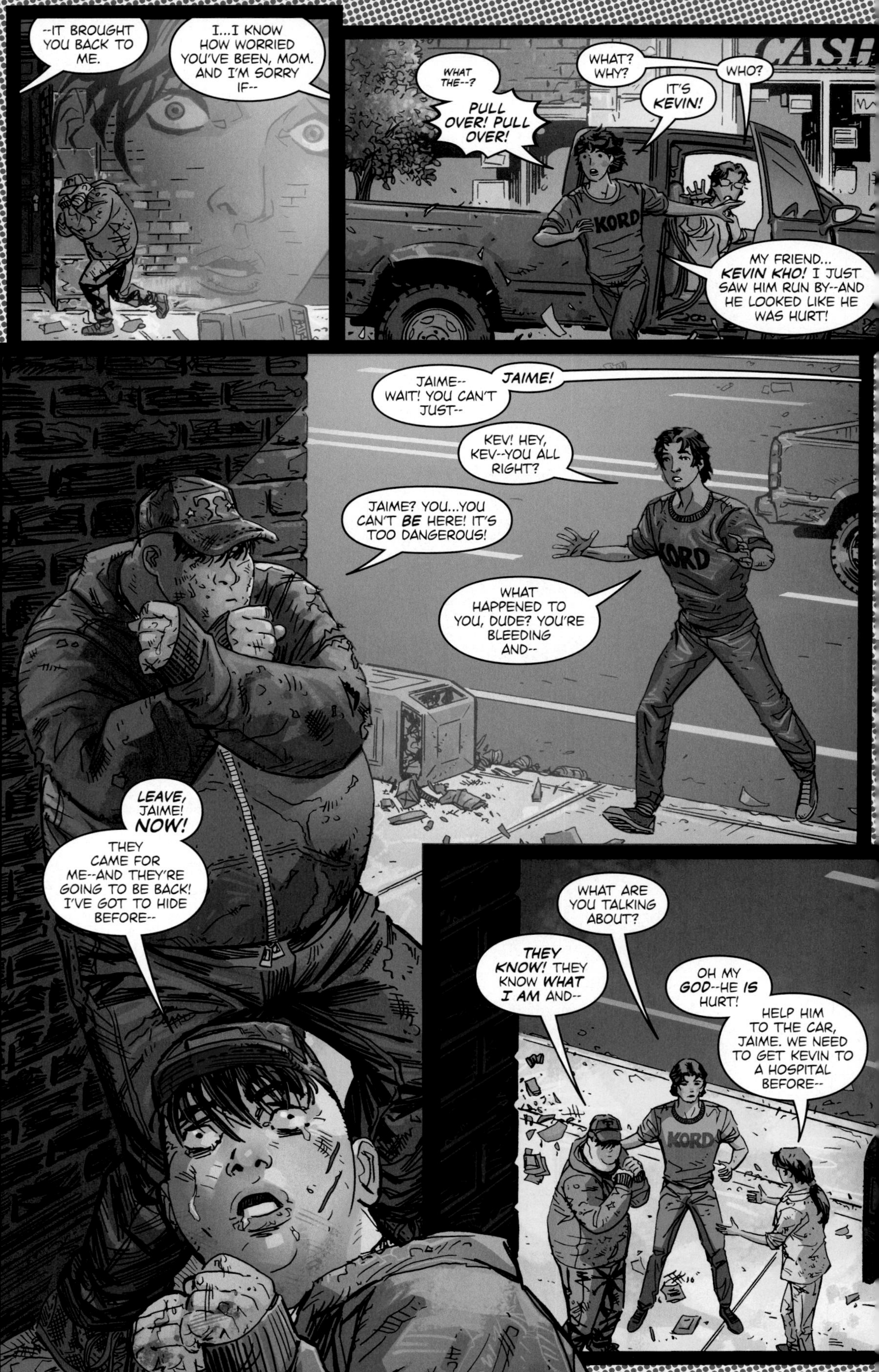
--IT BROUGHT YOU BACK TO ME.
I...I KNOW HOW WORRIED YOU'VE BEEN, MOM. AND I'M SORRY IF--
CASH
WHAT THE--?
PULL OVER! PULL OVER!
WHAT? WHY?
WHO?
IT'S KEVIN!
KORD
MY FRIEND... KEVIN KHO! I JUST SAW HIM RUN BY--AND HE LOOKED LIKE HE WAS HURT!
JAIME!
JAIME-- WAIT! YOU CAN'T JUST--
KEV! HEY, KEV--YOU ALL RIGHT?
JAIME? YOU...YOU CAN'T BE HERE! IT'S TOO DANGEROUS!
KORD
WHAT HAPPENED TO YOU, DUDE? YOU'RE BLEEDING AND--
LEAVE, JAIME! NOW!
THEY CAME FOR ME--AND THEY'RE GOING TO BE BACK! I'VE GOT TO HIDE BEFORE--
WHAT ARE YOU TALKING ABOUT?
THEY KNOW! THEY KNOW WHAT I AM AND--
OH MY GOD--HE IS HURT!
HELP HIM TO THE CAR, JAIME. WE NEED TO GET KEVIN TO A HOSPITAL BEFORE--
KORD

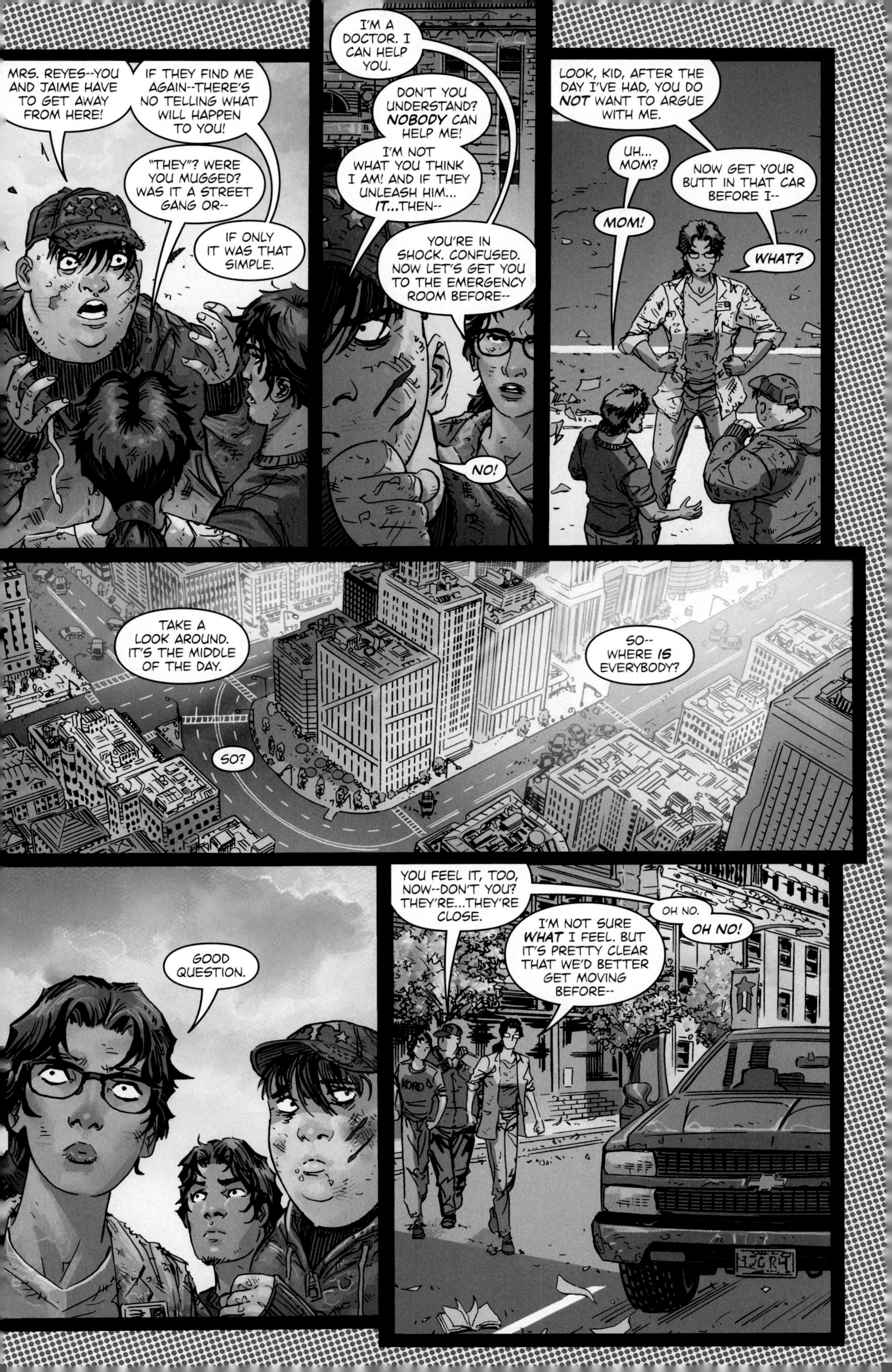
MRS. REYES--YOU AND JAIME HAVE TO GET AWAY FROM HERE!
IF THEY FIND ME AGAIN--THERE'S NO TELLING WHAT WILL HAPPEN TO YOU!
"THEY"? WERE YOU MUGGED? WAS IT A STREET GANG OR--
IF ONLY IT WAS THAT SIMPLE.
I'M A DOCTOR. I CAN HELP YOU.
DON'T YOU UNDERSTAND? **NOBODY** CAN HELP ME!
I'M NOT WHAT YOU THINK I AM! AND IF THEY UNLEASH HIM... **IT...**THEN--
YOU'RE IN SHOCK. CONFUSED. NOW LET'S GET YOU TO THE EMERGENCY ROOM BEFORE--
NO!
LOOK, KID, AFTER THE DAY I'VE HAD, YOU DO **NOT** WANT TO ARGUE WITH ME.
UH... MOM?
NOW GET YOUR BUTT IN THAT CAR BEFORE I--
MOM!
WHAT?
TAKE A LOOK AROUND. IT'S THE MIDDLE OF THE DAY.
SO?
SO--WHERE **IS** EVERYBODY?
GOOD QUESTION.
YOU FEEL IT, TOO, NOW--DON'T YOU? THEY'RE...THEY'RE CLOSE.
I'M NOT SURE **WHAT** I FEEL. BUT IT'S PRETTY CLEAR THAT WE'D BETTER GET MOVING BEFORE--
OH NO.
OH NO!

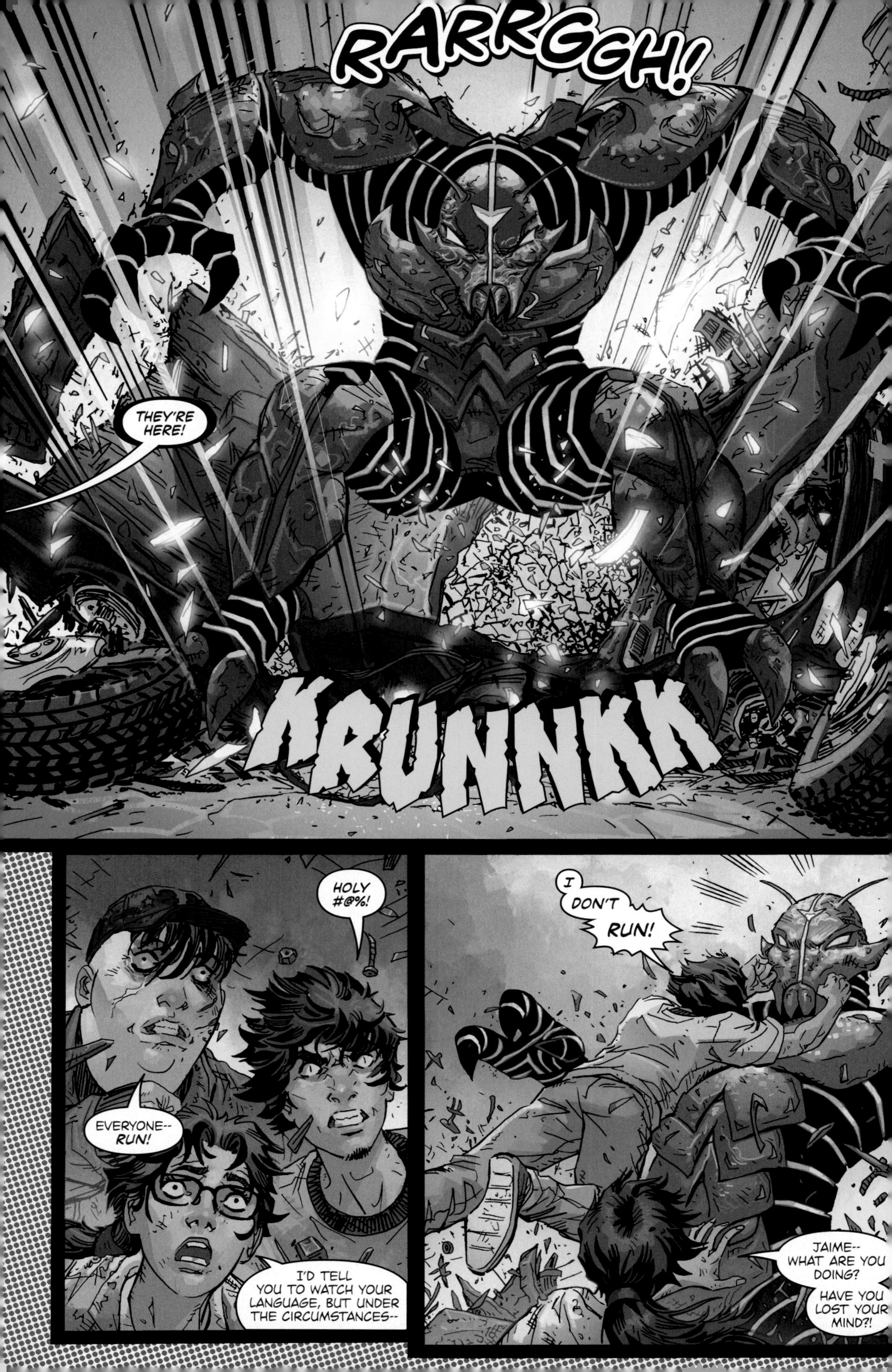
RARRGGH!
THEY'RE HERE!
KRUNNKK
HOLY #@%!
EVERYONE-- RUN!
I'D TELL YOU TO WATCH YOUR LANGUAGE, BUT UNDER THE CIRCUMSTANCES--
I DON'T RUN!
JAIME-- WHAT ARE YOU DOING?
HAVE YOU LOST YOUR MIND?!

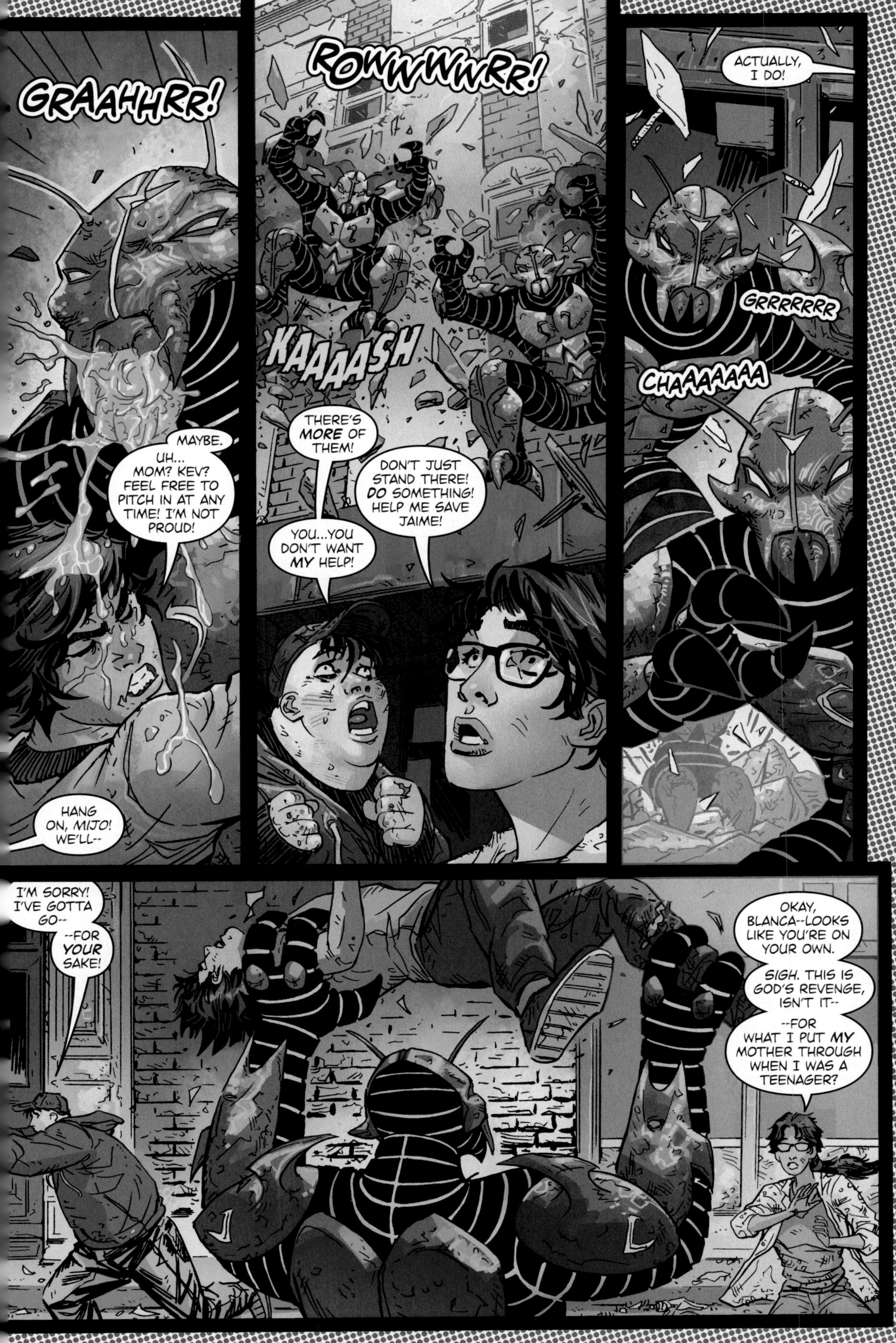
GRAAHHRR!
MAYBE.
UH... MOM? KEV? FEEL FREE TO PITCH IN AT ANY TIME! I'M NOT PROUD!
HANG ON, MIJO! WE'LL--
ROWWWWRR!
KAAAASH
THERE'S MORE OF THEM!
DON'T JUST STAND THERE! DO SOMETHING! HELP ME SAVE JAIME!
YOU...YOU DON'T WANT MY HELP!
ACTUALLY, I DO!
GRRRRRR
CHAAAAAA
I'M SORRY! I'VE GOTTA GO--
--FOR YOUR SAKE!
OKAY, BLANCA--LOOKS LIKE YOU'RE ON YOUR OWN.
SIGH. THIS IS GOD'S REVENGE, ISN'T IT--
--FOR WHAT I PUT MY MOTHER THROUGH WHEN I WAS A TEENAGER?

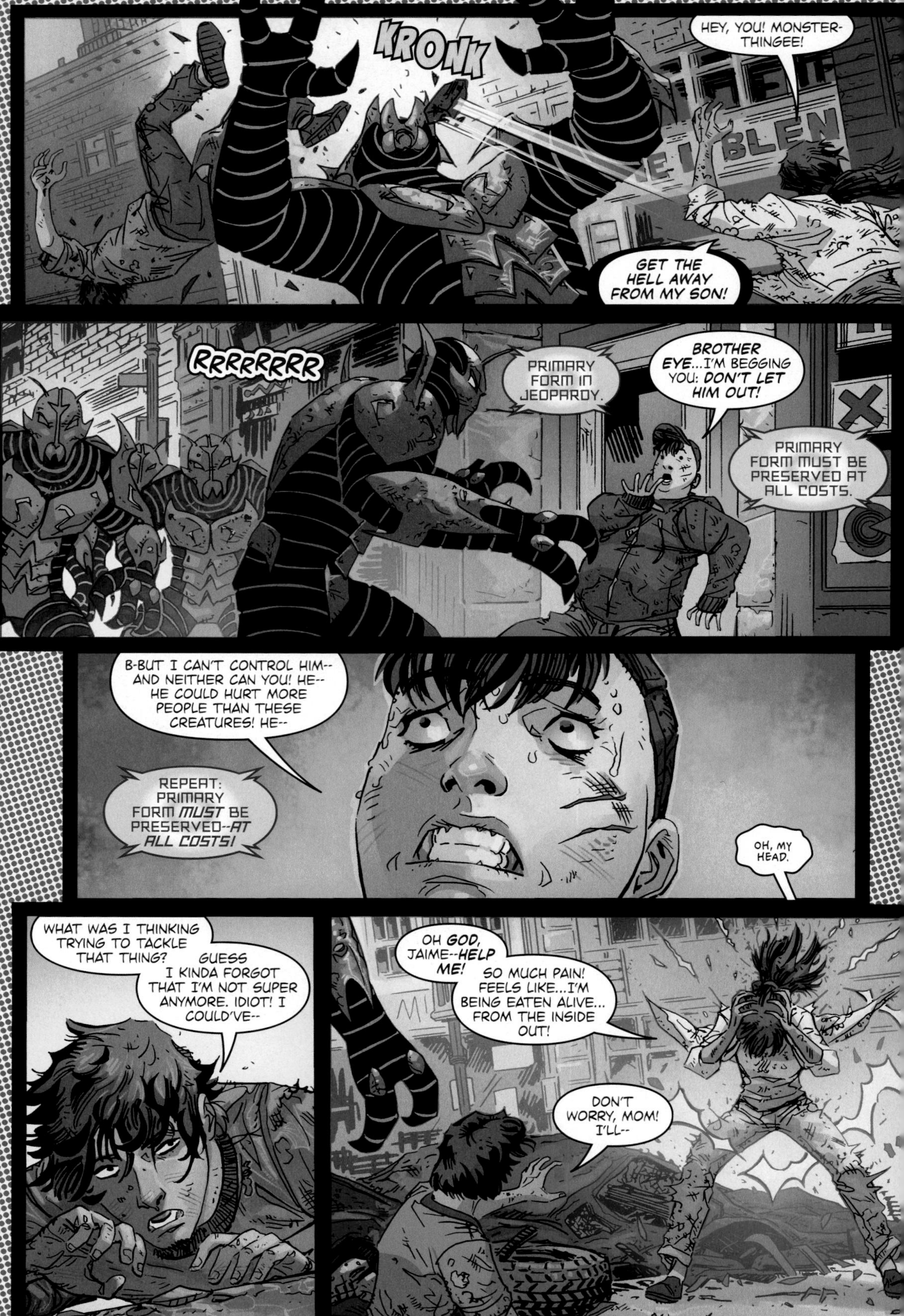
KRONK
HEY, YOU! MONSTER-THINGEE!
GET THE HELL AWAY FROM MY SON!
RRRRRRRR
PRIMARY FORM IN JEOPARDY.
BROTHER EYE...I'M BEGGING YOU: DON'T LET HIM OUT!
PRIMARY FORM MUST BE PRESERVED AT ALL COSTS.
B-BUT I CAN'T CONTROL HIM--AND NEITHER CAN YOU! HE--HE COULD HURT MORE PEOPLE THAN THESE CREATURES! HE--
REPEAT: PRIMARY FORM MUST BE PRESERVED--AT ALL COSTS!
OH, MY HEAD.
WHAT WAS I THINKING TRYING TO TACKLE THAT THING?
GUESS I KINDA FORGOT THAT I'M NOT SUPER ANYMORE. IDIOT! I COULD'VE--
JAIME!
OH GOD, JAIME--HELP ME!
SO MUCH PAIN! FEELS LIKE...I'M BEING EATEN ALIVE... FROM THE INSIDE OUT!
DON'T WORRY, MOM! I'LL--

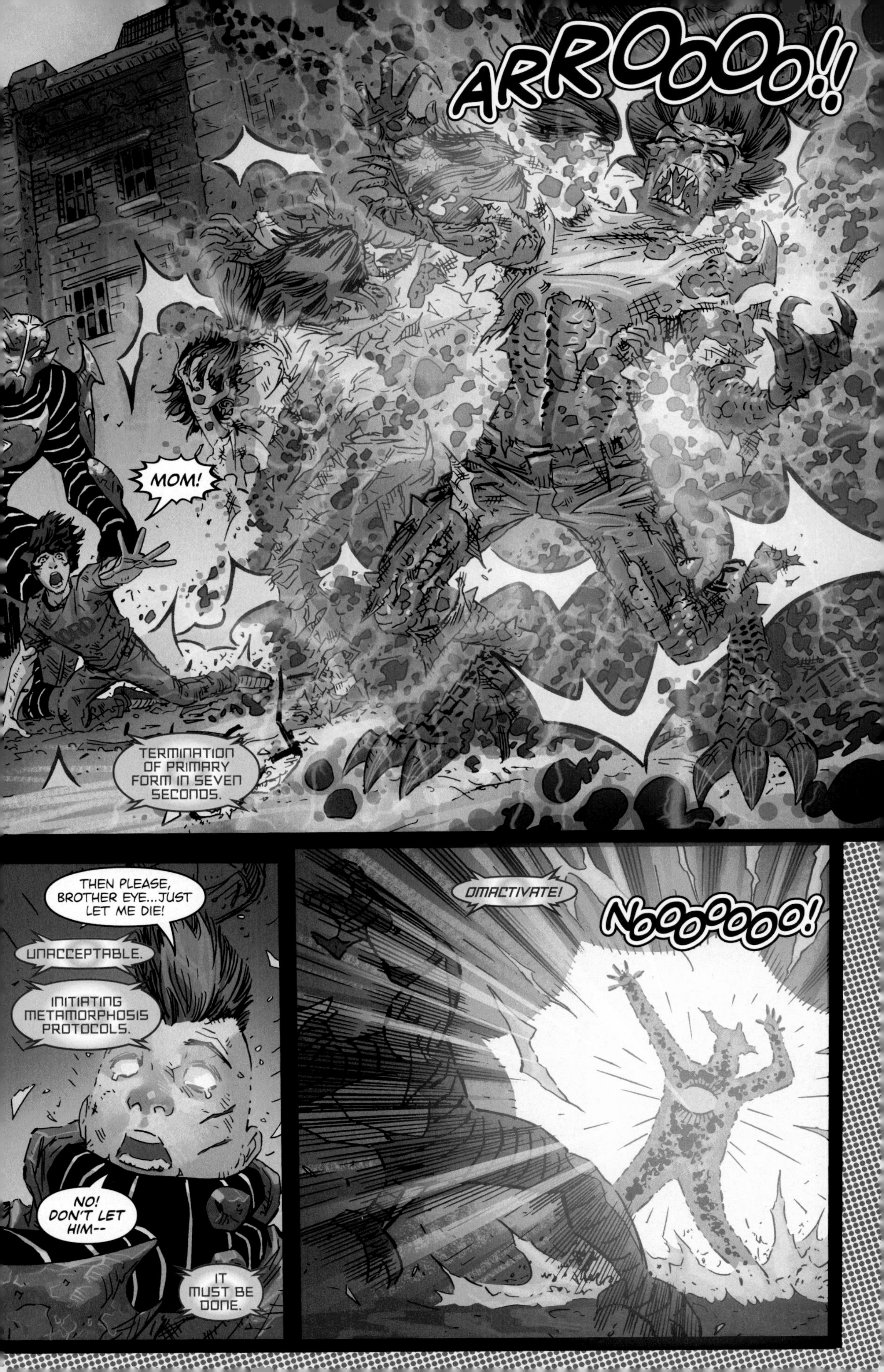
ARROOOO!!
MOM!
TERMINATION OF PRIMARY FORM IN SEVEN SECONDS.
THEN PLEASE, BROTHER EYE...JUST LET ME DIE!
UNACCEPTABLE.
INITIATING METAMORPHOSIS PROTOCOLS.
NO! DON'T LET HIM--
IT MUST BE DONE.
OMACTIVATE!
NOOOOOOO!

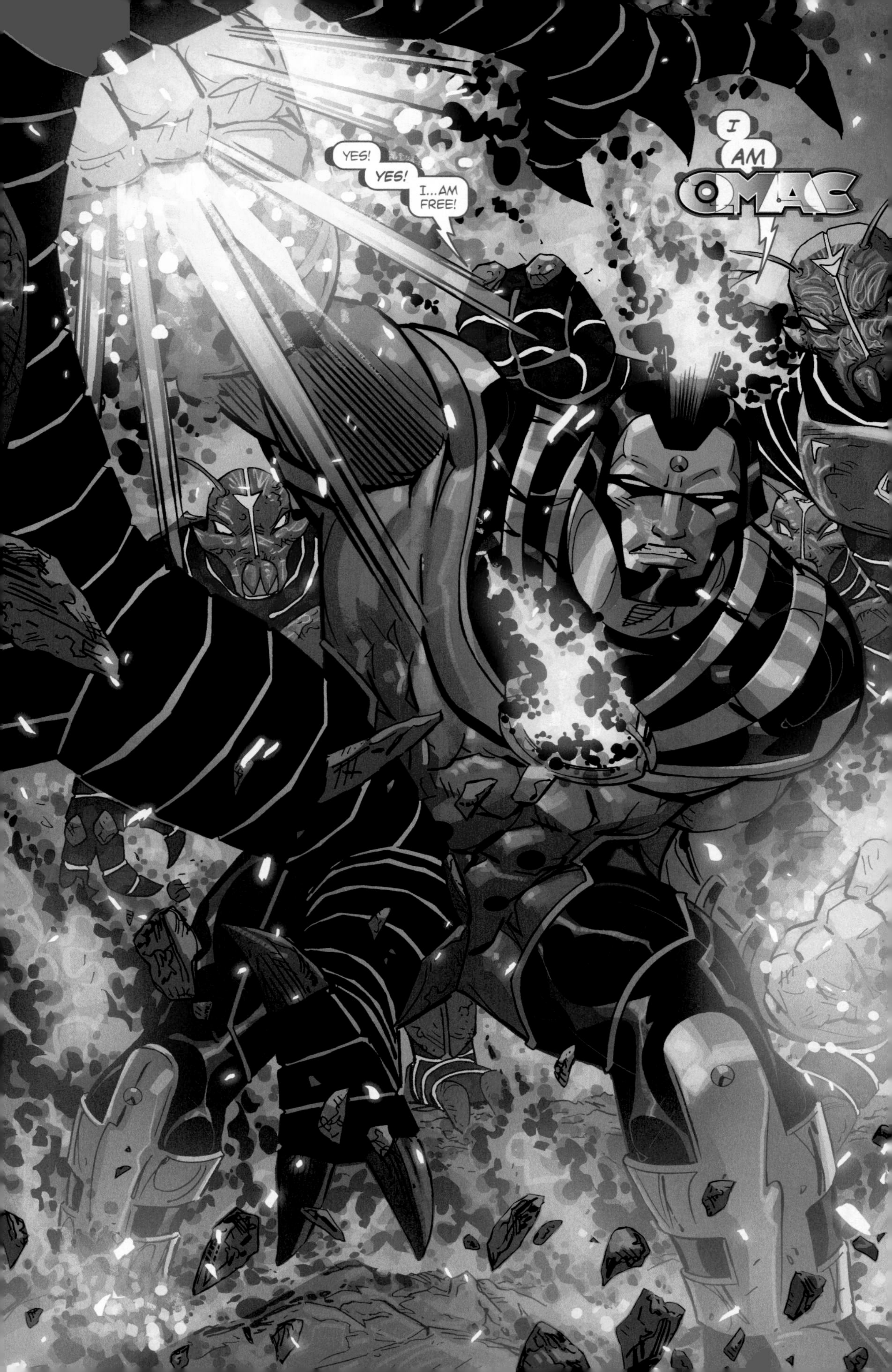

YES! YES! I...AM FREE!
I AM OMAC

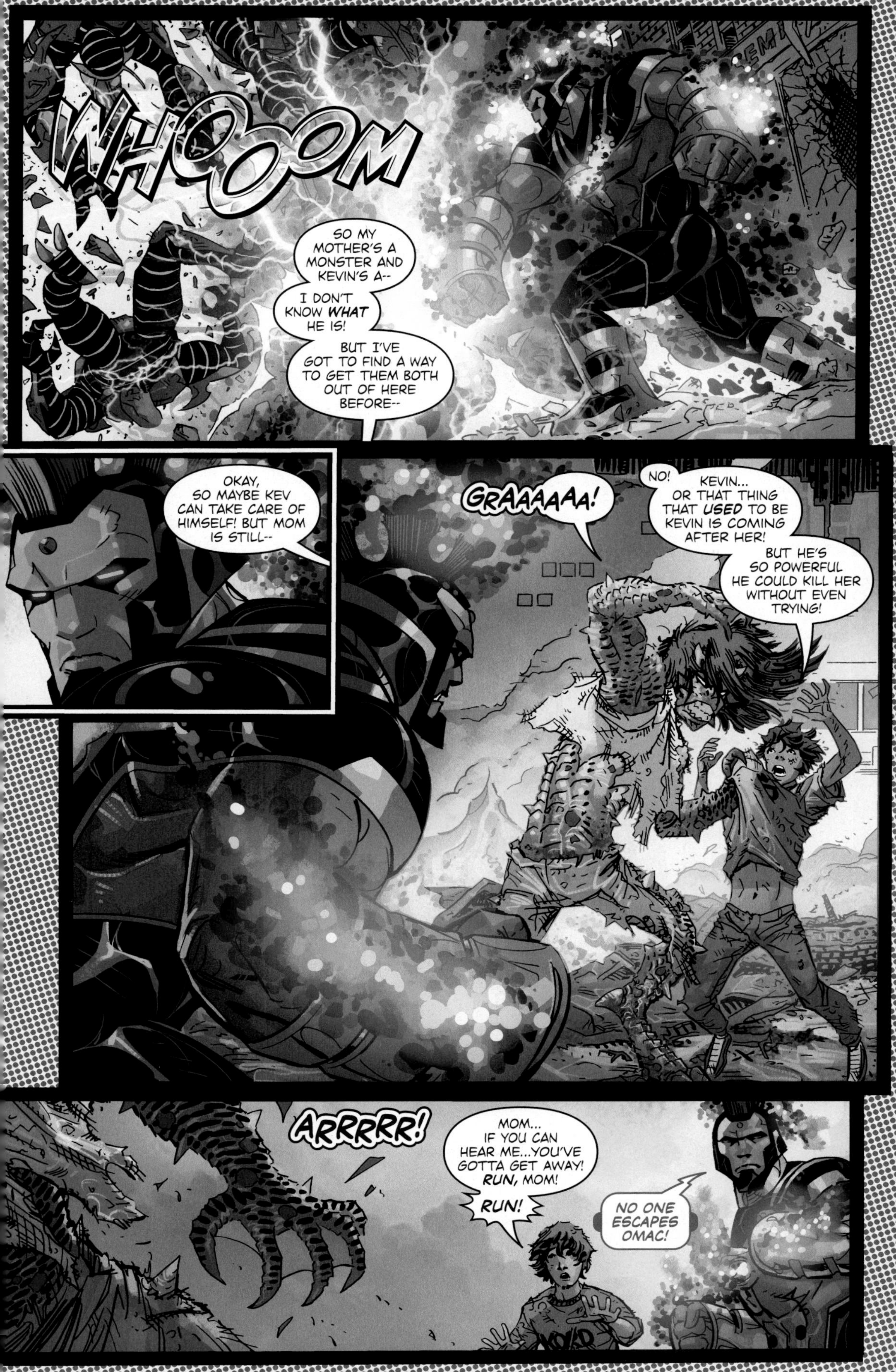
WHOOOOM
SO MY MOTHER'S A MONSTER AND KEVIN'S A--
I DON'T KNOW WHAT HE IS!
BUT I'VE GOT TO FIND A WAY TO GET THEM BOTH OUT OF HERE BEFORE--
OKAY, SO MAYBE KEV CAN TAKE CARE OF HIMSELF! BUT MOM IS STILL--
GRAAAAAA!
NO!
KEVIN... OR THAT THING THAT USED TO BE KEVIN IS COMING AFTER HER!
BUT HE'S SO POWERFUL HE COULD KILL HER WITHOUT EVEN TRYING!
ARRRRR!
MOM... IF YOU CAN HEAR ME...YOU'VE GOTTA GET AWAY! RUN, MOM!
RUN!
NO ONE ESCAPES OMAC!

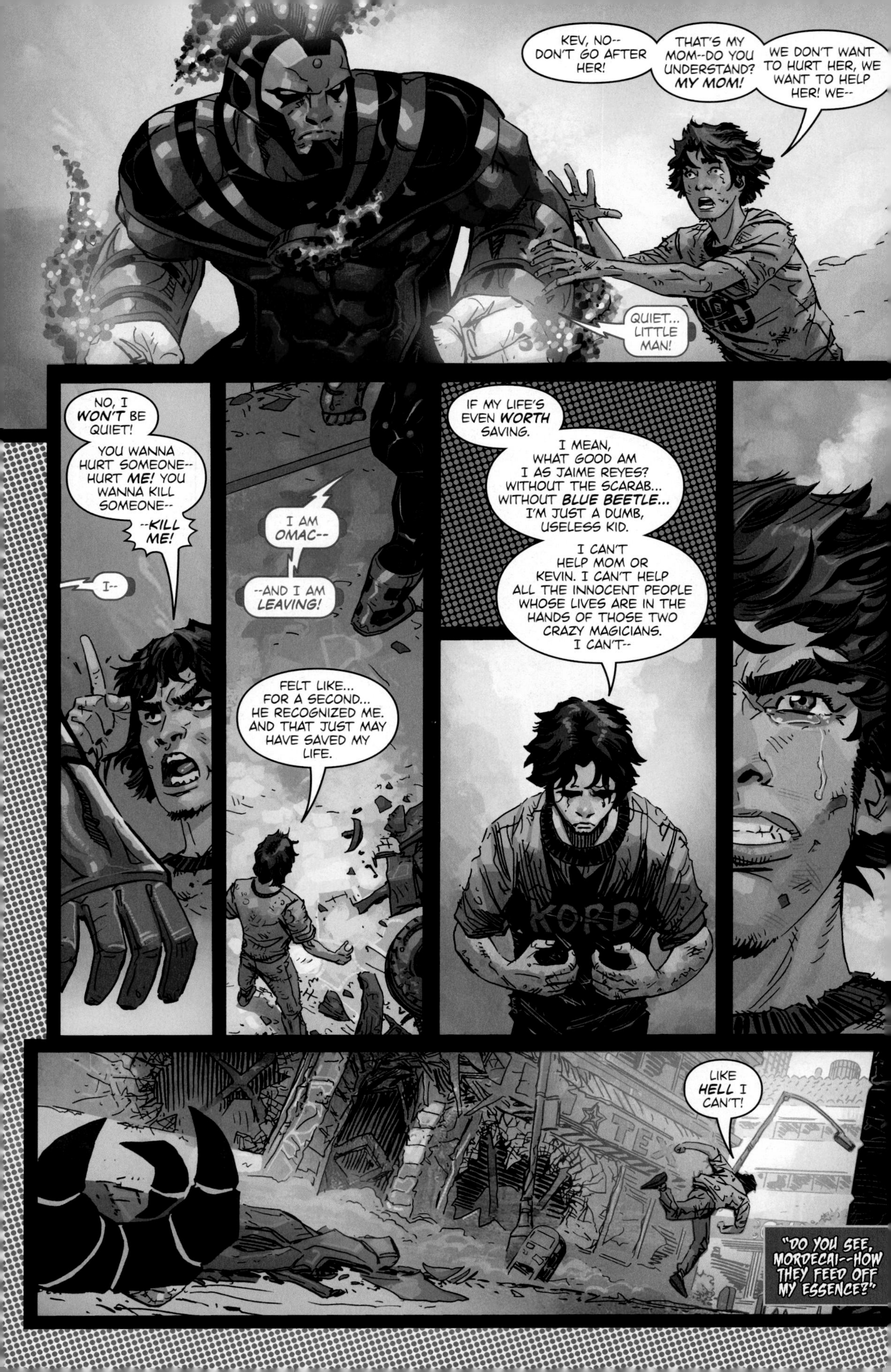
KEV, NO-- DON'T GO AFTER HER!
THAT'S MY MOM--DO YOU UNDERSTAND? MY MOM!
WE DON'T WANT TO HURT HER, WE WANT TO HELP HER! WE--
QUIET... LITTLE MAN!
NO, I WON'T BE QUIET!
YOU WANNA HURT SOMEONE-- HURT ME! YOU WANNA KILL SOMEONE--
--KILL ME!
I--
I AM OMAC--
--AND I AM LEAVING!
FELT LIKE... FOR A SECOND... HE RECOGNIZED ME. AND THAT JUST MAY HAVE SAVED MY LIFE.
IF MY LIFE'S EVEN WORTH SAVING.
I MEAN, WHAT GOOD AM I AS JAIME REYES? WITHOUT THE SCARAB... WITHOUT BLUE BEETLE... I'M JUST A DUMB, USELESS KID.
I CAN'T HELP MOM OR KEVIN. I CAN'T HELP ALL THE INNOCENT PEOPLE WHOSE LIVES ARE IN THE HANDS OF THOSE TWO CRAZY MAGICIANS. I CAN'T--
KORD
LIKE HELL I CAN'T!
"DO YOU SEE, MORDECAI--HOW THEY FEED OFF MY ESSENCE?"

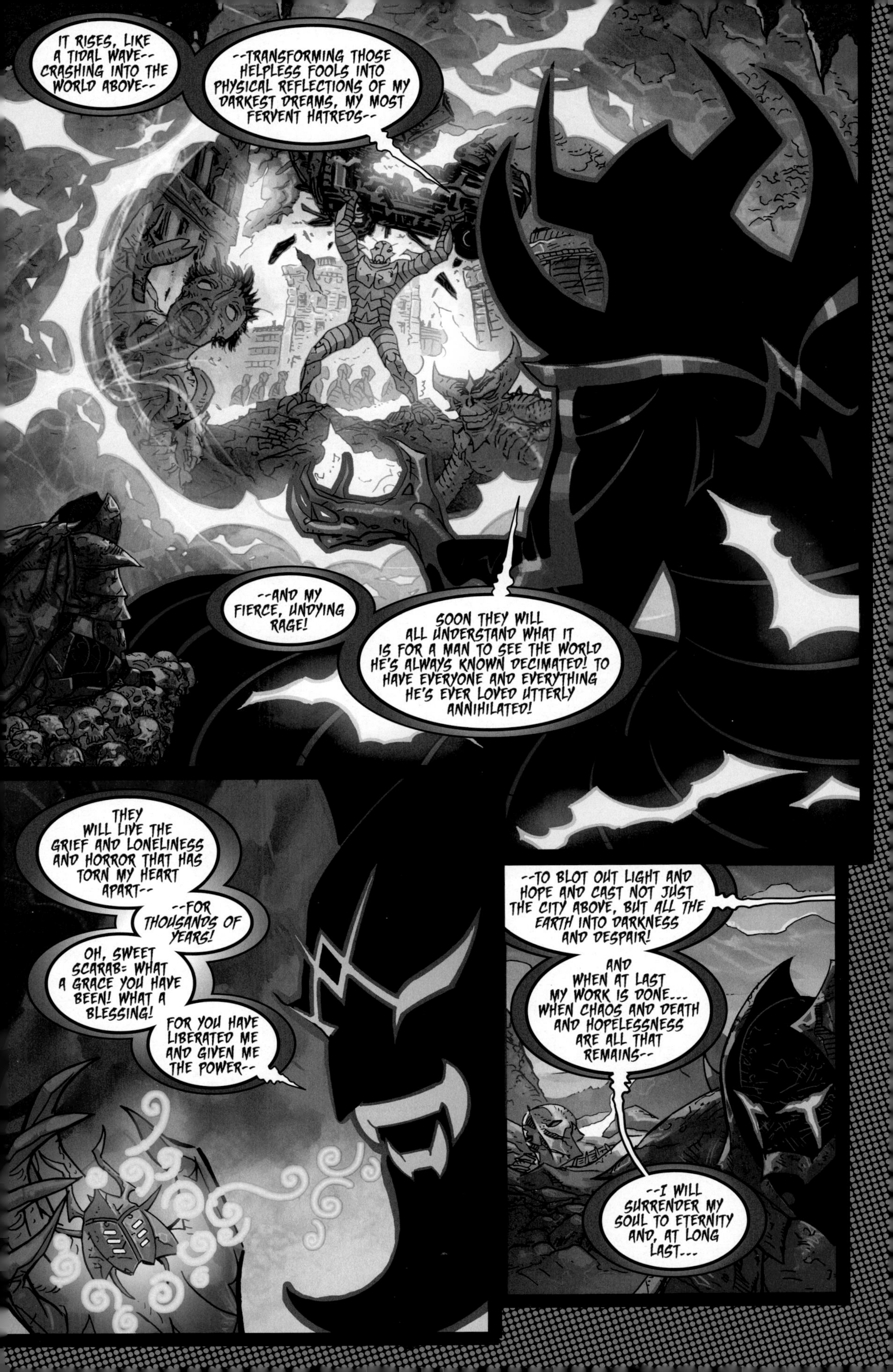
IT RISES, LIKE A TIDAL WAVE--CRASHING INTO THE WORLD ABOVE--
--TRANSFORMING THOSE HELPLESS FOOLS INTO PHYSICAL REFLECTIONS OF MY DARKEST DREAMS, MY MOST FERVENT HATREDS--
--AND MY FIERCE, UNDYING RAGE!
SOON THEY WILL ALL UNDERSTAND WHAT IT IS FOR A MAN TO SEE THE WORLD HE'S ALWAYS KNOWN DECIMATED! TO HAVE EVERYONE AND EVERYTHING HE'S EVER LOVED UTTERLY ANNIHILATED!
THEY WILL LIVE THE GRIEF AND LONELINESS AND HORROR THAT HAS TORN MY HEART APART--
--FOR THOUSANDS OF YEARS!
OH, SWEET SCARAB: WHAT A GRACE YOU HAVE BEEN! WHAT A BLESSING!
FOR YOU HAVE LIBERATED ME AND GIVEN ME THE POWER--
--TO BLOT OUT LIGHT AND HOPE AND CAST NOT JUST THE CITY ABOVE, BUT ALL THE EARTH INTO DARKNESS AND DESPAIR!
AND WHEN AT LAST MY WORK IS DONE... WHEN CHAOS AND DEATH AND HOPELESSNESS ARE ALL THAT REMAINS--
--I WILL SURRENDER MY SOUL TO ETERNITY AND, AT LONG LAST...

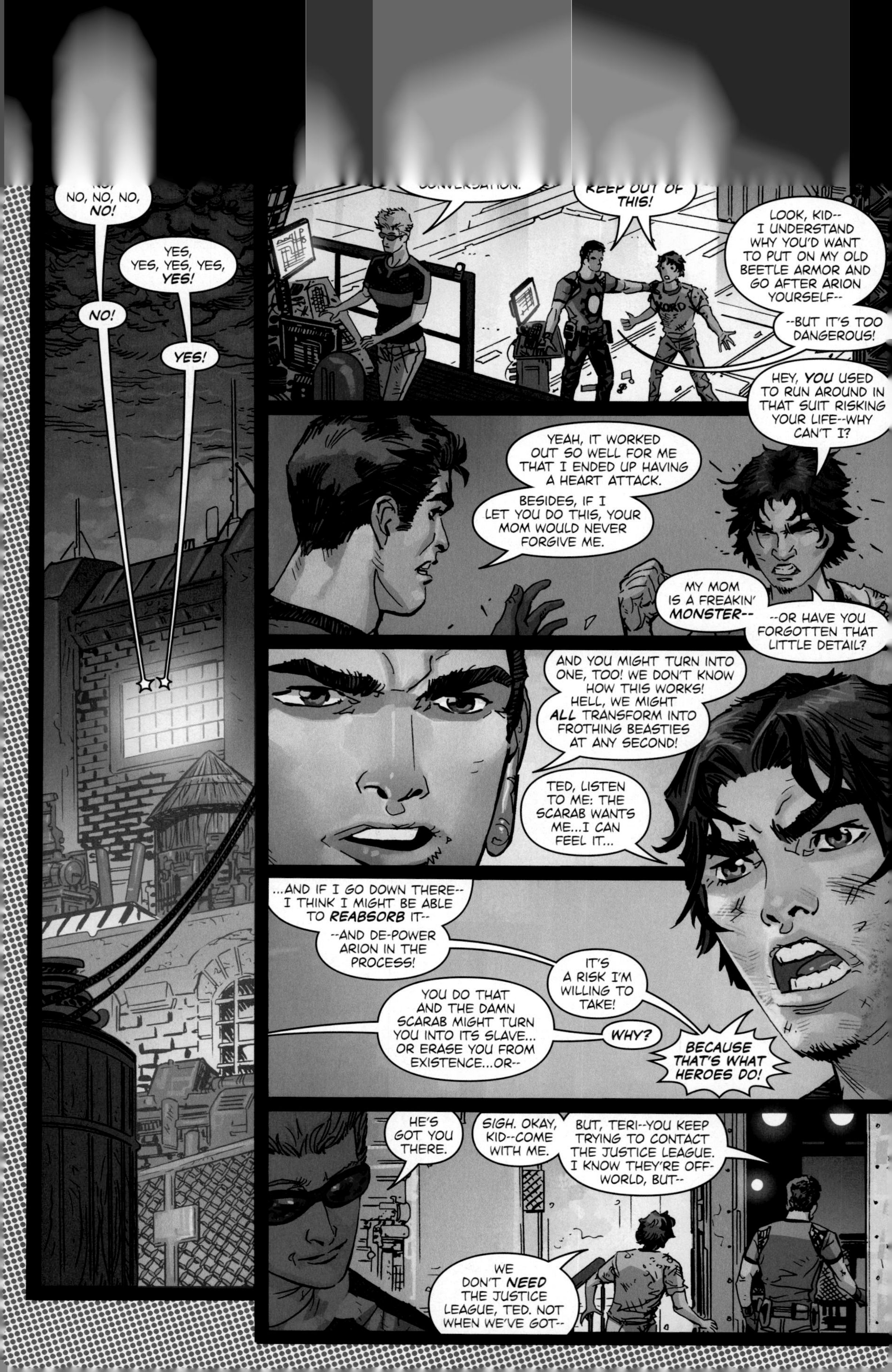
NO, NO, NO, NO!
YES, YES, YES, YES, YES!
NO!
YES!
KEEP OUT OF THIS!
LOOK, KID-- I UNDERSTAND WHY YOU'D WANT TO PUT ON MY OLD BEETLE ARMOR AND GO AFTER ARION YOURSELF--
--BUT IT'S TOO DANGEROUS!
HEY, YOU USED TO RUN AROUND IN THAT SUIT RISKING YOUR LIFE--WHY CAN'T I?
YEAH, IT WORKED OUT SO WELL FOR ME THAT I ENDED UP HAVING A HEART ATTACK.
BESIDES, IF I LET YOU DO THIS, YOUR MOM WOULD NEVER FORGIVE ME.
MY MOM IS A FREAKIN' MONSTER--
--OR HAVE YOU FORGOTTEN THAT LITTLE DETAIL?
AND YOU MIGHT TURN INTO ONE, TOO! WE DON'T KNOW HOW THIS WORKS! HELL, WE MIGHT ALL TRANSFORM INTO FROTHING BEASTIES AT ANY SECOND!
TED, LISTEN TO ME: THE SCARAB WANTS ME...I CAN FEEL IT...
...AND IF I GO DOWN THERE-- I THINK I MIGHT BE ABLE TO REABSORB IT--
--AND DE-POWER ARION IN THE PROCESS!
IT'S A RISK I'M WILLING TO TAKE!
YOU DO THAT AND THE DAMN SCARAB MIGHT TURN YOU INTO ITS SLAVE... OR ERASE YOU FROM EXISTENCE...OR--
WHY?
BECAUSE THAT'S WHAT HEROES DO!
HE'S GOT YOU THERE.
SIGH. OKAY, KID--COME WITH ME.
BUT, TERI--YOU KEEP TRYING TO CONTACT THE JUSTICE LEAGUE. I KNOW THEY'RE OFF-WORLD, BUT--
WE DON'T NEED THE JUSTICE LEAGUE, TED. NOT WHEN WE'VE GOT--

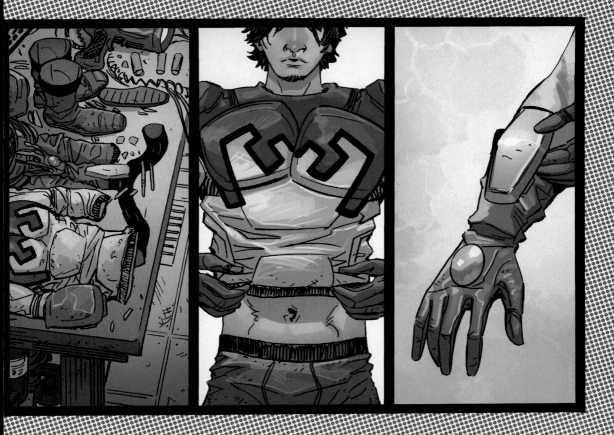

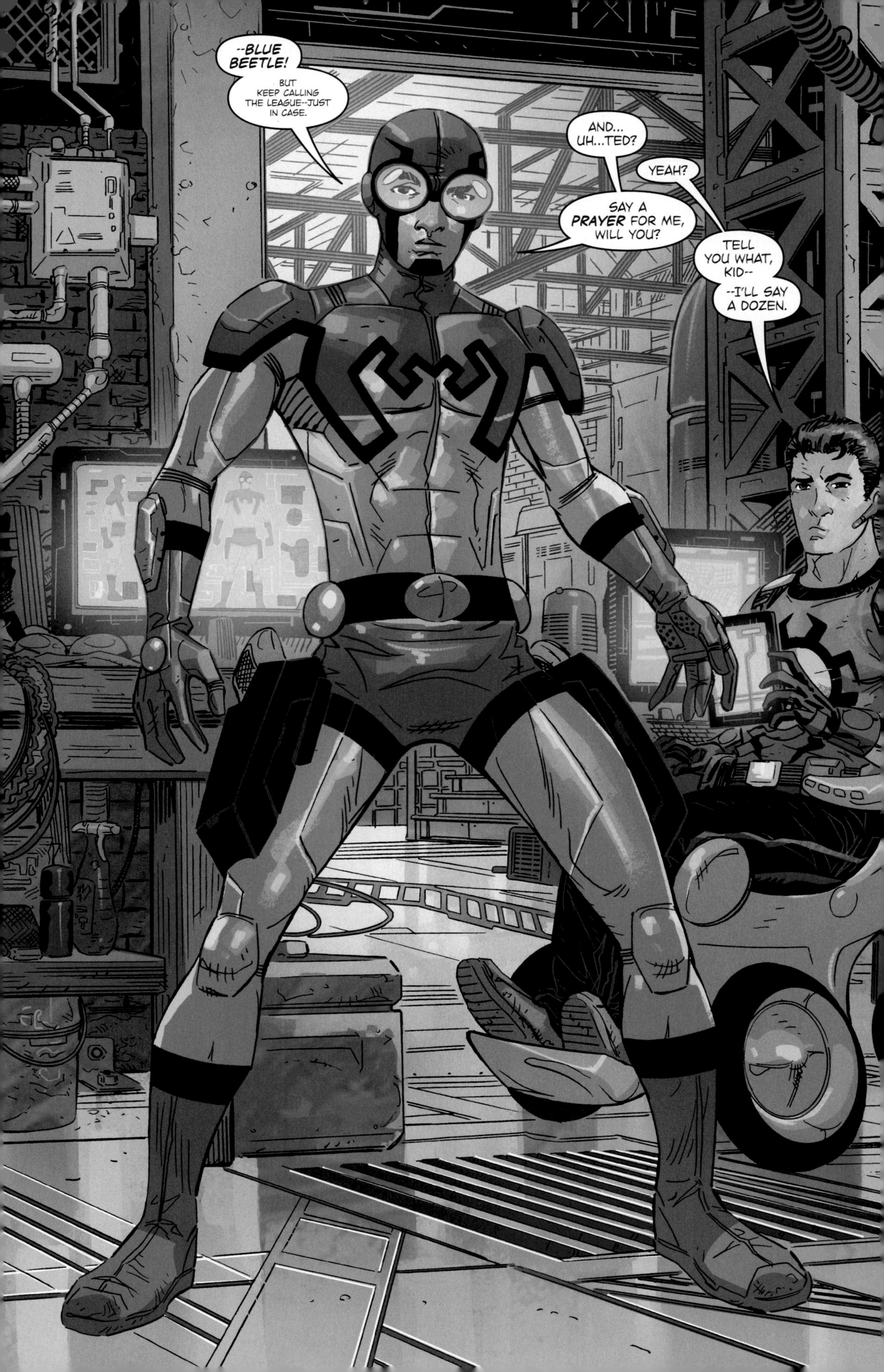
--BLUE BEETLE!
BUT KEEP CALLING THE LEAGUE--JUST IN CASE.
AND... UH...TED?
YEAH?
SAY A PRAYER FOR ME, WILL YOU?
TELL YOU WHAT, KID--
--I'LL SAY A DOZEN.

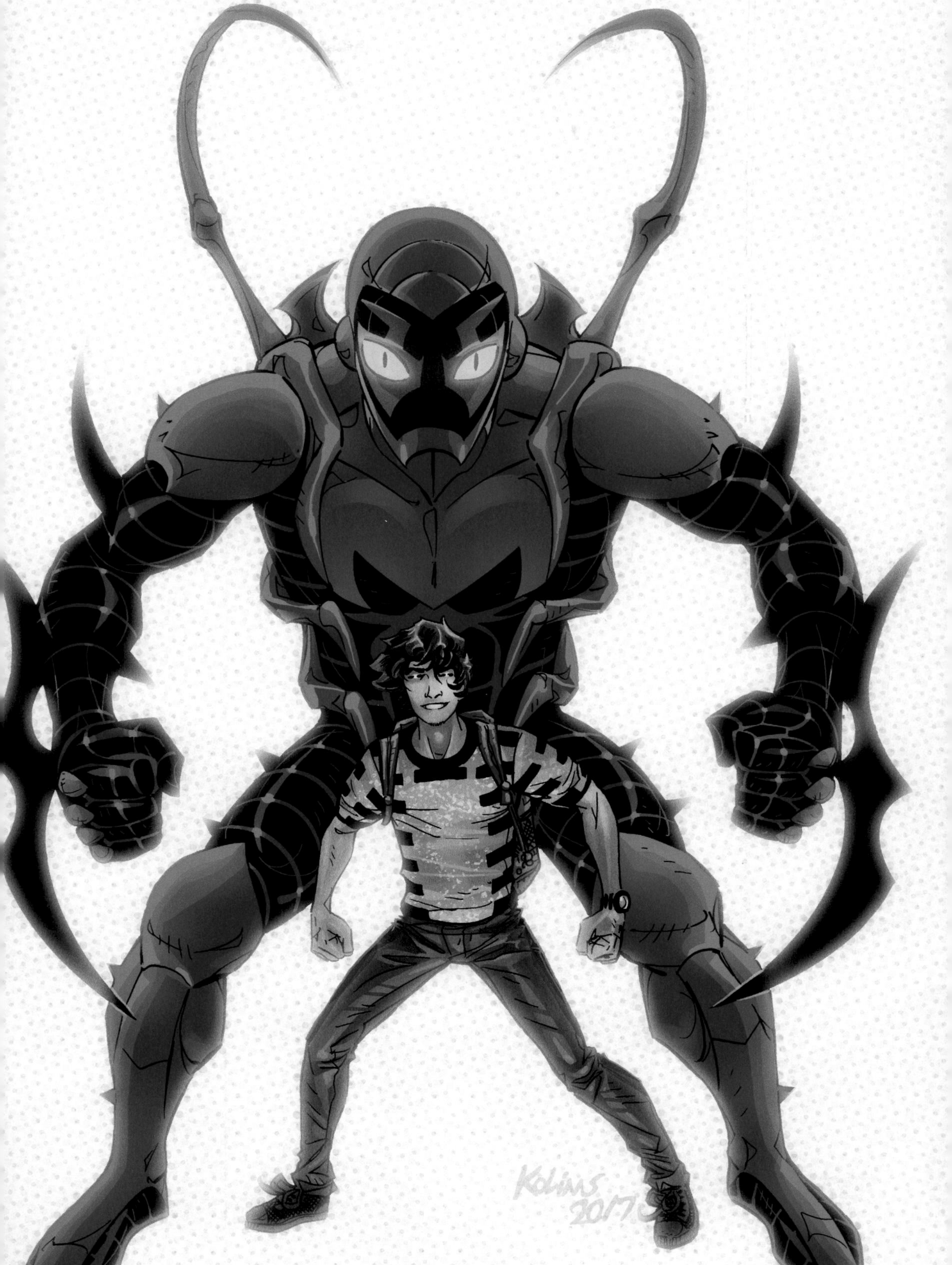
Kolins
2017

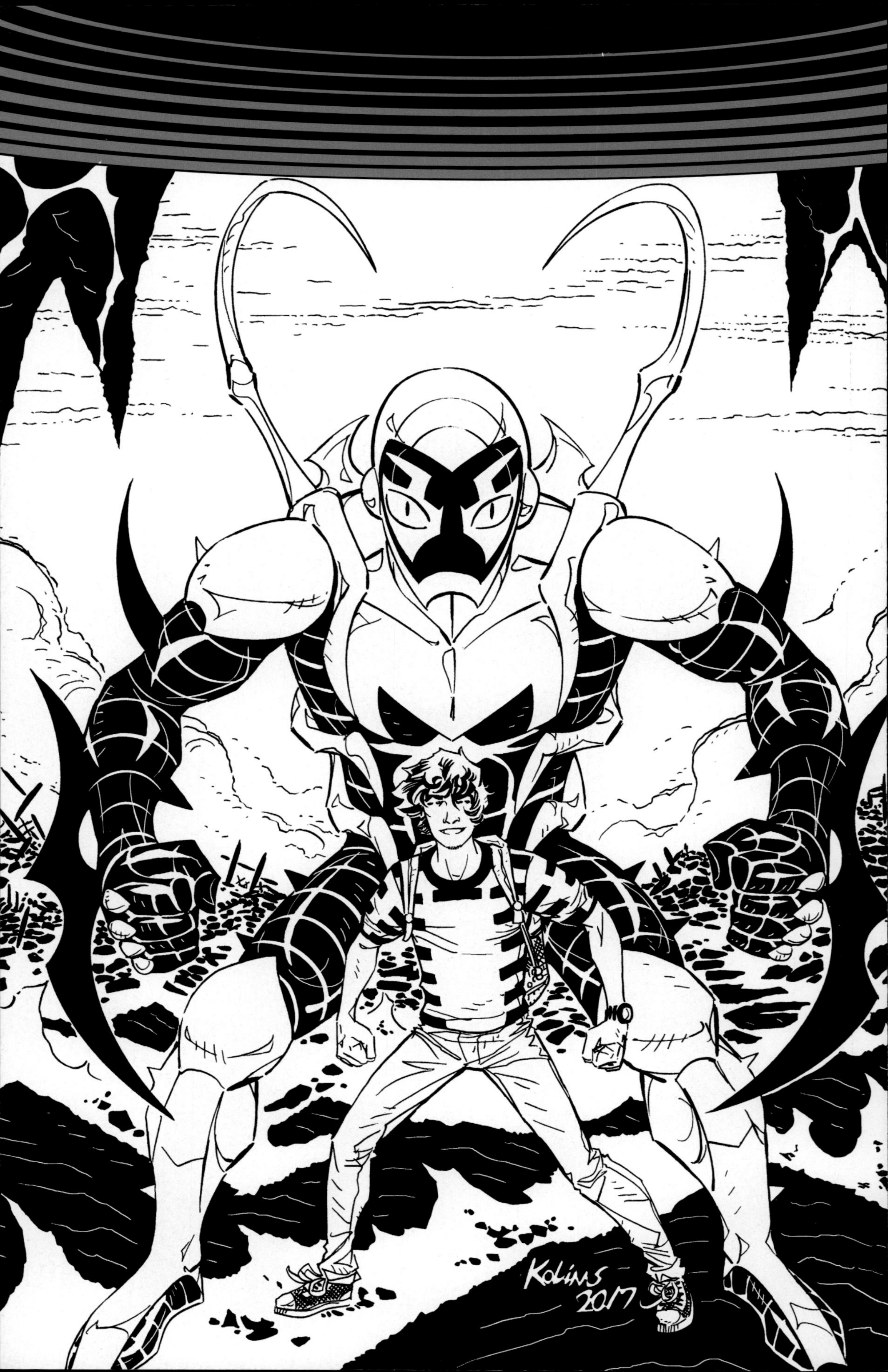
KOLINS
2017

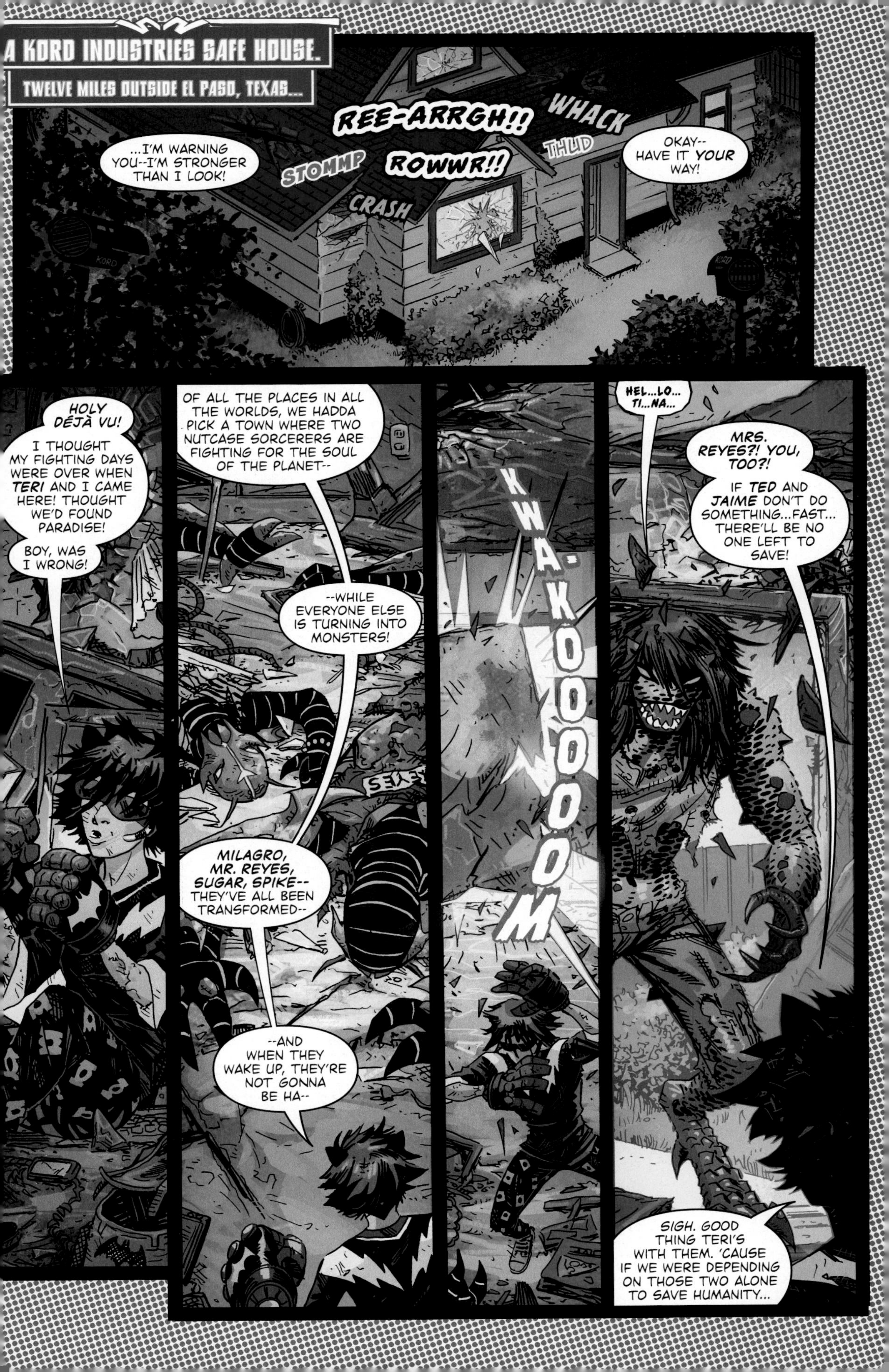
A KORD INDUSTRIES SAFE HOUSE.
TWELVE MILES OUTSIDE EL PASO, TEXAS...
...I'M WARNING YOU--I'M STRONGER THAN I LOOK!
STOMMP
REE-ARRGH!!
ROWWR!!
CRASH
WHACK
THUD
OKAY-- HAVE IT YOUR WAY!
HOLY DÉJÀ VU!
I THOUGHT MY FIGHTING DAYS WERE OVER WHEN TERI AND I CAME HERE! THOUGHT WE'D FOUND PARADISE!
BOY, WAS I WRONG!
OF ALL THE PLACES IN ALL THE WORLDS, WE HADDA PICK A TOWN WHERE TWO NUTCASE SORCERERS ARE FIGHTING FOR THE SOUL OF THE PLANET--
--WHILE EVERYONE ELSE IS TURNING INTO MONSTERS!
MILAGRO, MR. REYES, SUGAR, SPIKE-- THEY'VE ALL BEEN TRANSFORMED--
--AND WHEN THEY WAKE UP, THEY'RE NOT GONNA BE HA--
KWA-KOOOOOOM
HEL...LO... TI...NA...
MRS. REYES?! YOU, TOO?!
IF TED AND JAIME DON'T DO SOMETHING...FAST... THERE'LL BE NO ONE LEFT TO SAVE!
SIGH. GOOD THING TERI'S WITH THEM. 'CAUSE IF WE WERE DEPENDING ON THOSE TWO ALONE TO SAVE HUMANITY...

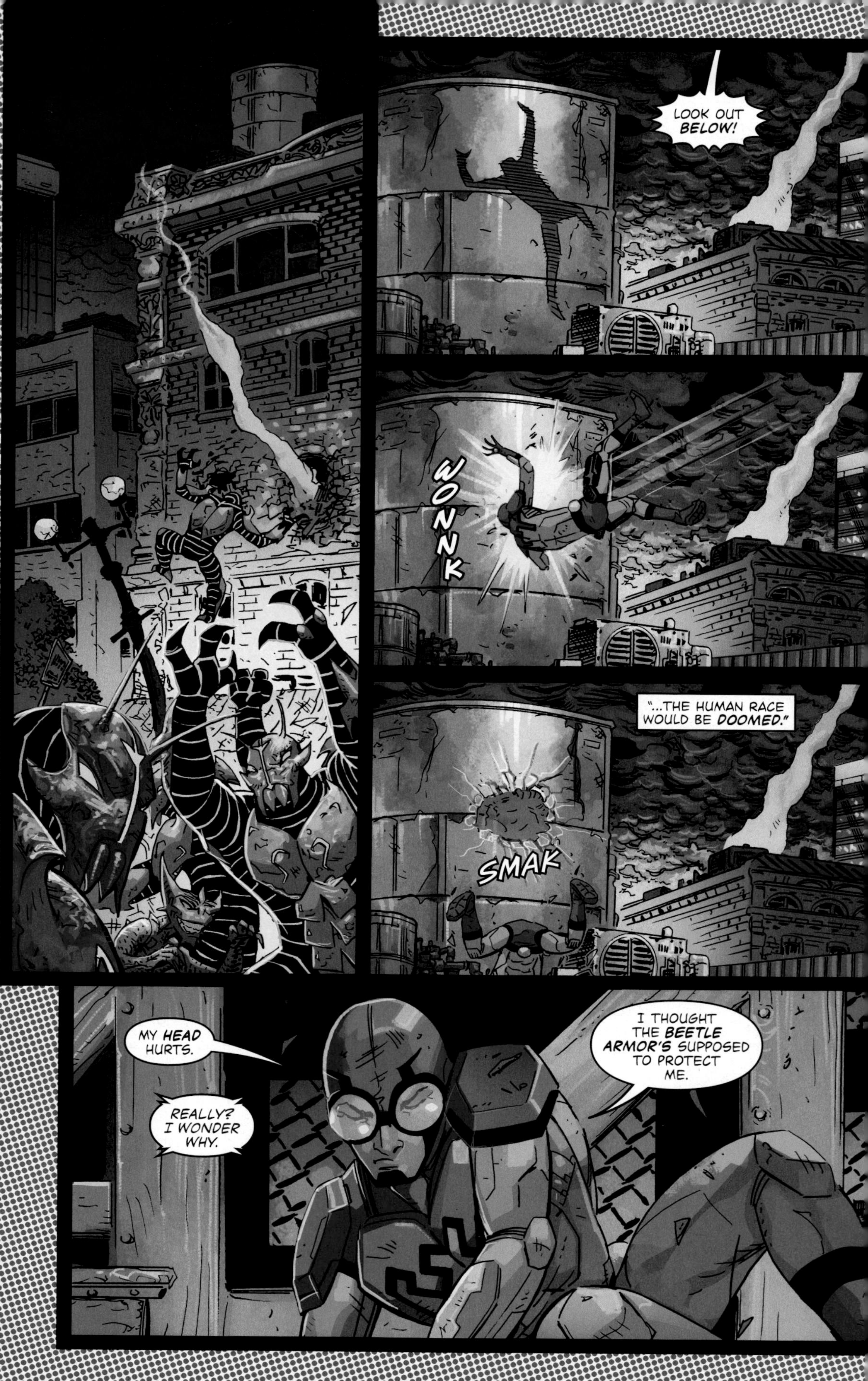
LOOK OUT BELOW!
WONNK
"...THE HUMAN RACE WOULD BE DOOMED."
SMAK
MY HEAD HURTS.
I THOUGHT THE BEETLE ARMOR'S SUPPOSED TO PROTECT ME.
REALLY? I WONDER WHY.

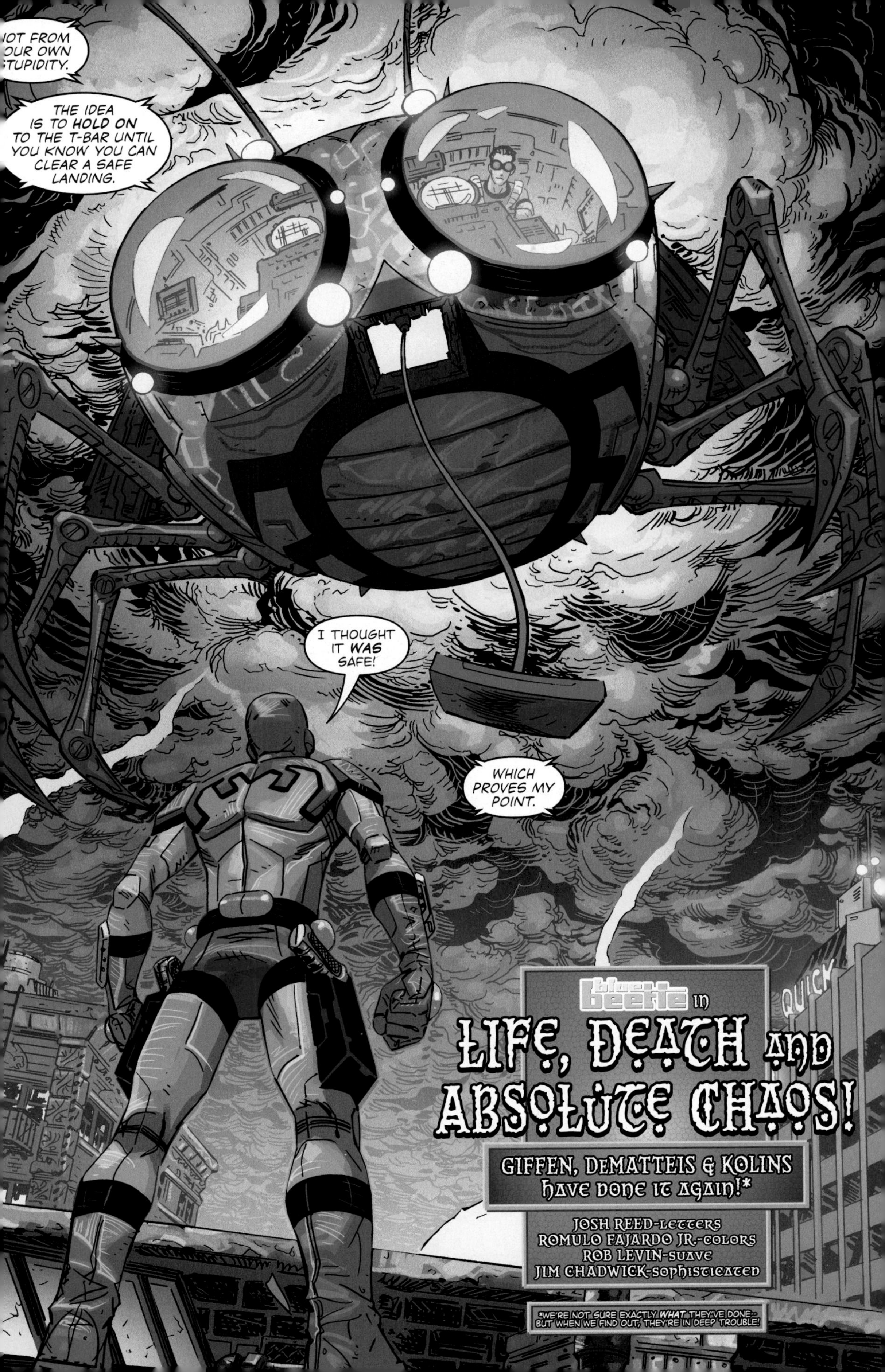

NOT FROM YOUR OWN STUPIDITY.
THE IDEA IS TO HOLD ON TO THE T-BAR UNTIL YOU KNOW YOU CAN CLEAR A SAFE LANDING.
I THOUGHT IT WAS SAFE!
WHICH PROVES MY POINT.
blue beetle in
LIFE, DEATH AND ABSOLUTE CHAOS!
GIFFEN, DEMATTEIS & KOLINS have done it again!*
JOSH REED-letters
ROMULO FAJARDO JR.-colors
ROB LEVIN-suave
JIM CHADWICK-sophisticated
*WE'RE NOT SURE EXACTLY WHAT THEY'VE DONE-- BUT WHEN WE FIND OUT, THEY'RE IN DEEP TROUBLE!
QUICK

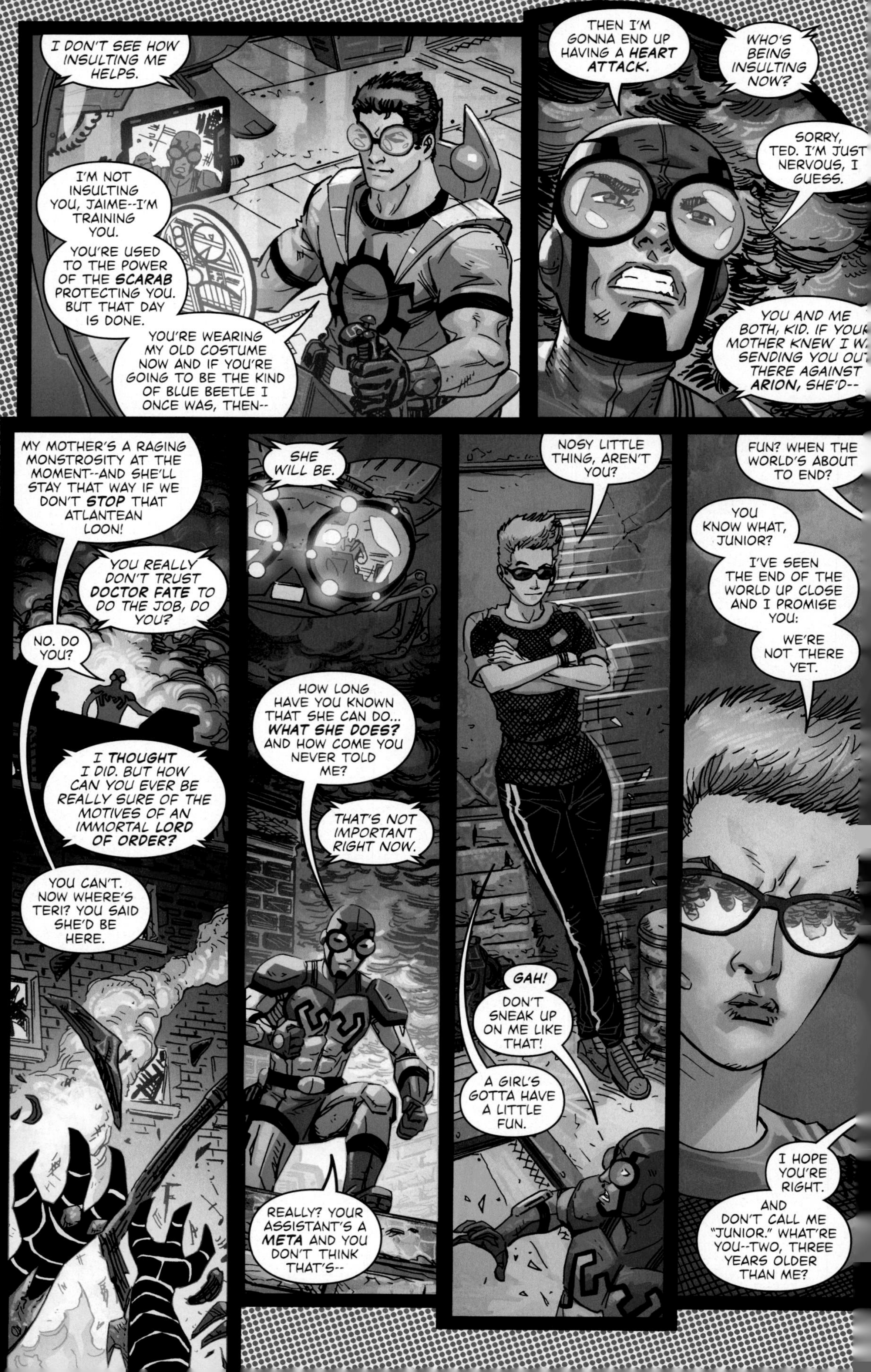
I DON'T SEE HOW INSULTING ME HELPS.
I'M NOT INSULTING YOU, JAIME--I'M TRAINING YOU.
YOU'RE USED TO THE POWER OF THE **SCARAB** PROTECTING YOU. BUT THAT DAY IS DONE.
YOU'RE WEARING MY OLD COSTUME NOW AND IF YOU'RE GOING TO BE THE KIND OF BLUE BEETLE I ONCE WAS, THEN--
THEN I'M GONNA END UP HAVING A **HEART ATTACK.**
WHO'S BEING INSULTING NOW?
SORRY, TED. I'M JUST NERVOUS, I GUESS.
MY MOTHER'S A RAGING MONSTROSITY AT THE MOMENT--AND SHE'LL STAY THAT WAY IF WE DON'T **STOP** THAT ATLANTEAN LOON!
YOU REALLY DON'T TRUST **DOCTOR FATE** TO DO THE JOB, DO YOU?
NO. DO YOU?
*I **THOUGHT** I DID. BUT HOW CAN YOU EVER BE REALLY SURE OF THE MOTIVES OF AN IMMORTAL **LORD OF ORDER?***
YOU CAN'T. NOW WHERE'S TERI? YOU SAID SHE'D BE HERE.
SHE WILL BE.
HOW LONG HAVE YOU KNOWN THAT SHE CAN DO... ***WHAT SHE DOES?*** AND HOW COME YOU NEVER TOLD ME?
THAT'S NOT IMPORTANT RIGHT NOW.
REALLY? YOUR ASSISTANT'S A **META** AND YOU DON'T THINK THAT'S--
NOSY LITTLE THING, AREN'T YOU?
GAH! DON'T SNEAK UP ON ME LIKE THAT!
A GIRL'S GOTTA HAVE A LITTLE FUN.
FUN? WHEN THE WORLD'S ABOUT TO END?
YOU KNOW WHAT, JUNIOR?
I'VE SEEN THE END OF THE WORLD UP CLOSE AND I PROMISE YOU:
WE'RE NOT THERE YET.
I HOPE YOU'RE RIGHT.
AND DON'T CALL ME "JUNIOR." WHAT'RE YOU--TWO, THREE YEARS OLDER THAN ME?

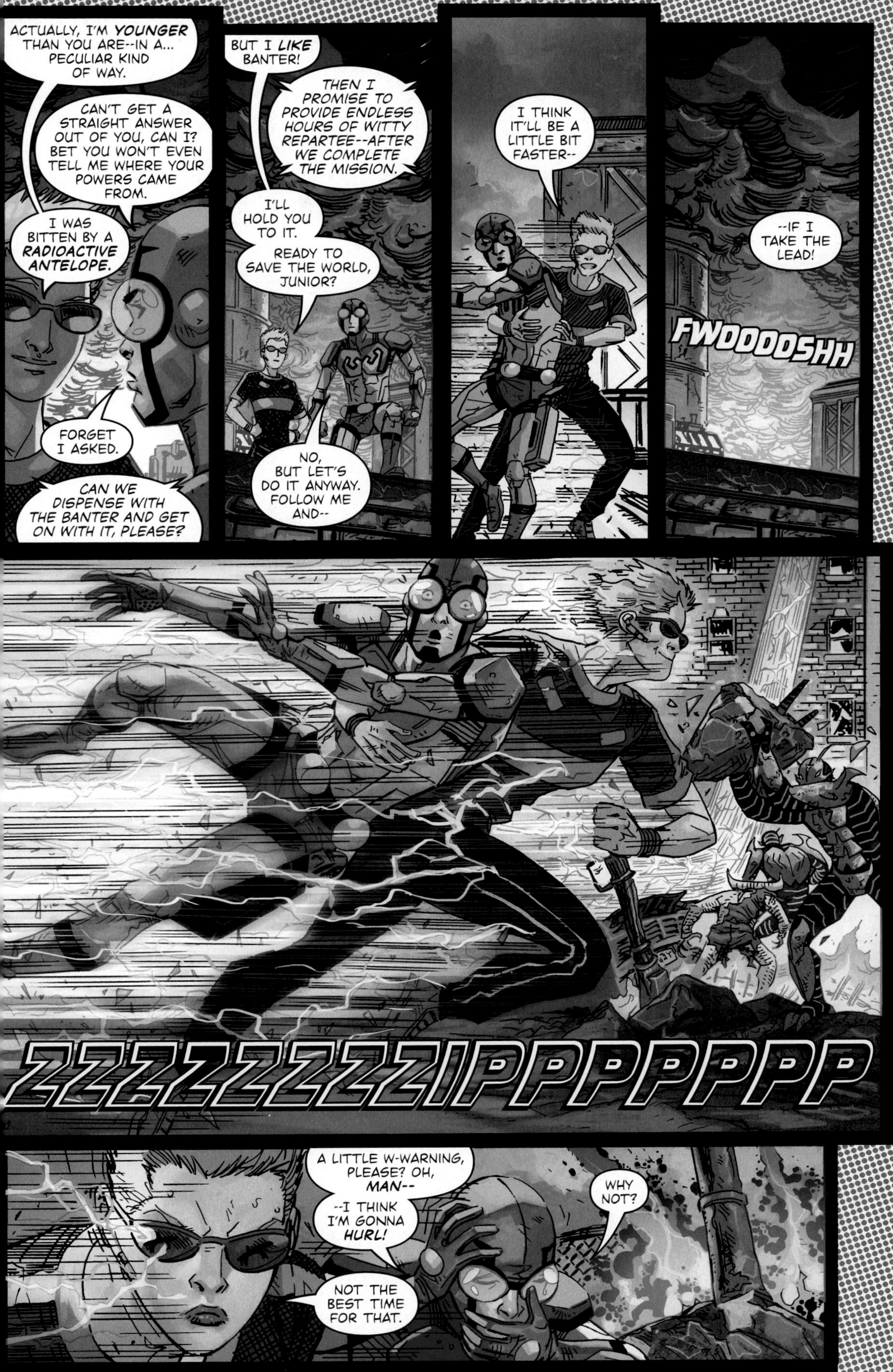

ACTUALLY, I'M YOUNGER THAN YOU ARE--IN A... PECULIAR KIND OF WAY.
CAN'T GET A STRAIGHT ANSWER OUT OF YOU, CAN I? BET YOU WON'T EVEN TELL ME WHERE YOUR POWERS CAME FROM.
I WAS BITTEN BY A RADIOACTIVE ANTELOPE.
FORGET I ASKED.
CAN WE DISPENSE WITH THE BANTER AND GET ON WITH IT, PLEASE?
BUT I LIKE BANTER!
THEN I PROMISE TO PROVIDE ENDLESS HOURS OF WITTY REPARTEE--AFTER WE COMPLETE THE MISSION.
I'LL HOLD YOU TO IT.
READY TO SAVE THE WORLD, JUNIOR?
NO, BUT LET'S DO IT ANYWAY. FOLLOW ME AND--
I THINK IT'LL BE A LITTLE BIT FASTER--
--IF I TAKE THE LEAD!
FWOOOOSHH
ZZZZZZZZZIPPPPPPPP
A LITTLE W-WARNING, PLEASE? OH, MAN--
--I THINK I'M GONNA HURL!
NOT THE BEST TIME FOR THAT.
WHY NOT?

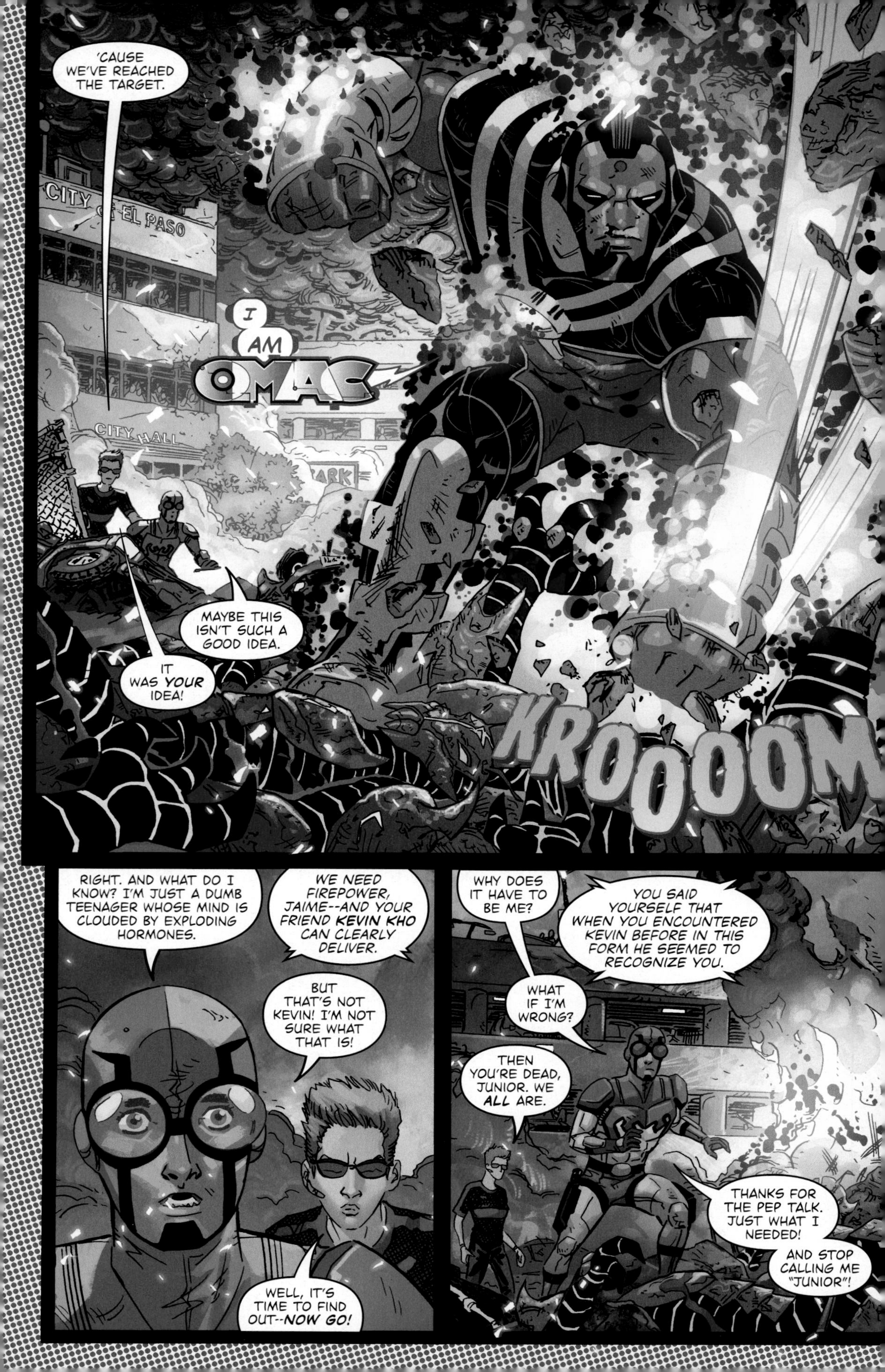
'CAUSE WE'VE REACHED THE TARGET.
CITY OF EL PASO
CITY HALL
I AM OMAC
MAYBE THIS ISN'T SUCH A GOOD IDEA.
IT WAS **YOUR** IDEA!
KROOOOOM
RIGHT. AND WHAT DO I KNOW? I'M JUST A DUMB TEENAGER WHOSE MIND IS CLOUDED BY EXPLODING HORMONES.
WE NEED FIREPOWER, JAIME--AND YOUR FRIEND **KEVIN KHO** CAN CLEARLY DELIVER.
BUT THAT'S NOT KEVIN! I'M NOT SURE WHAT THAT IS!
WELL, IT'S TIME TO FIND OUT--**NOW GO!**
WHY DOES IT HAVE TO BE ME?
YOU SAID YOURSELF THAT WHEN YOU ENCOUNTERED KEVIN BEFORE IN THIS FORM HE SEEMED TO RECOGNIZE YOU.
WHAT IF I'M WRONG?
THEN YOU'RE DEAD, JUNIOR. WE **ALL** ARE.
THANKS FOR THE PEP TALK. JUST WHAT I NEEDED!
AND STOP CALLING ME "JUNIOR"!

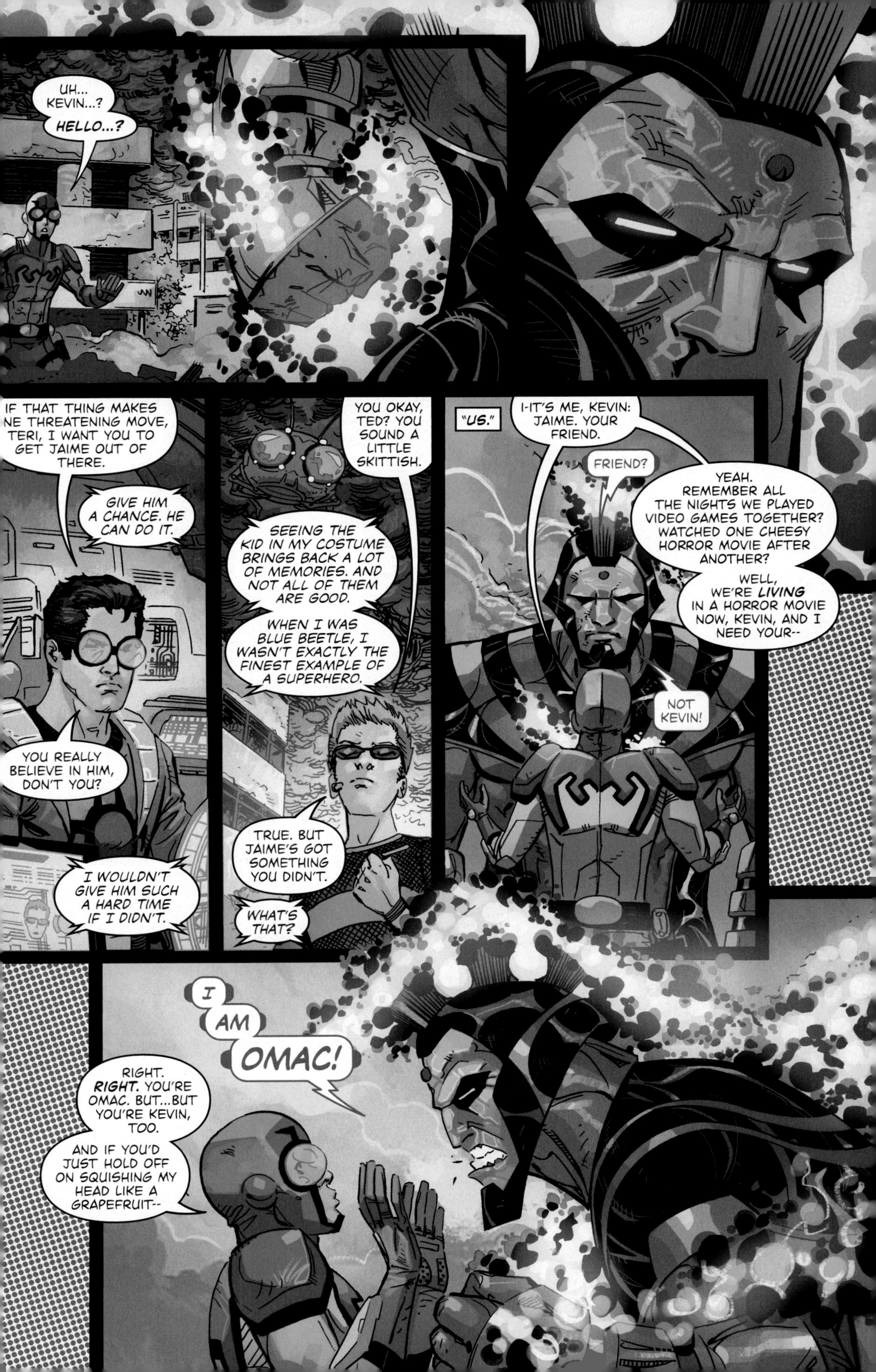

UH... KEVIN...? **HELLO...?**
IF THAT THING MAKES NE THREATENING MOVE, TERI, I WANT YOU TO GET JAIME OUT OF THERE.
GIVE HIM A CHANCE. HE CAN DO IT.
YOU REALLY BELIEVE IN HIM, DON'T YOU?
I WOULDN'T GIVE HIM SUCH A HARD TIME IF I DIDN'T.
YOU OKAY, TED? YOU SOUND A LITTLE SKITTISH.
SEEING THE KID IN MY COSTUME BRINGS BACK A LOT OF MEMORIES. AND NOT ALL OF THEM ARE GOOD.
WHEN I WAS BLUE BEETLE, I WASN'T EXACTLY THE FINEST EXAMPLE OF A SUPERHERO.
TRUE. BUT JAIME'S GOT SOMETHING YOU DIDN'T.
WHAT'S THAT?
"*US.*"
I-IT'S ME, KEVIN: JAIME. YOUR FRIEND.
FRIEND?
YEAH. REMEMBER ALL THE NIGHTS WE PLAYED VIDEO GAMES TOGETHER? WATCHED ONE CHEESY HORROR MOVIE AFTER ANOTHER?
WELL, WE'RE ***LIVING*** IN A HORROR MOVIE NOW, KEVIN, AND I NEED YOUR--
NOT KEVIN!
I AM OMAC!
RIGHT. ***RIGHT.*** YOU'RE OMAC. BUT...BUT YOU'RE KEVIN, TOO.
AND IF YOU'D JUST HOLD OFF ON SQUISHING MY HEAD LIKE A GRAPEFRUIT--

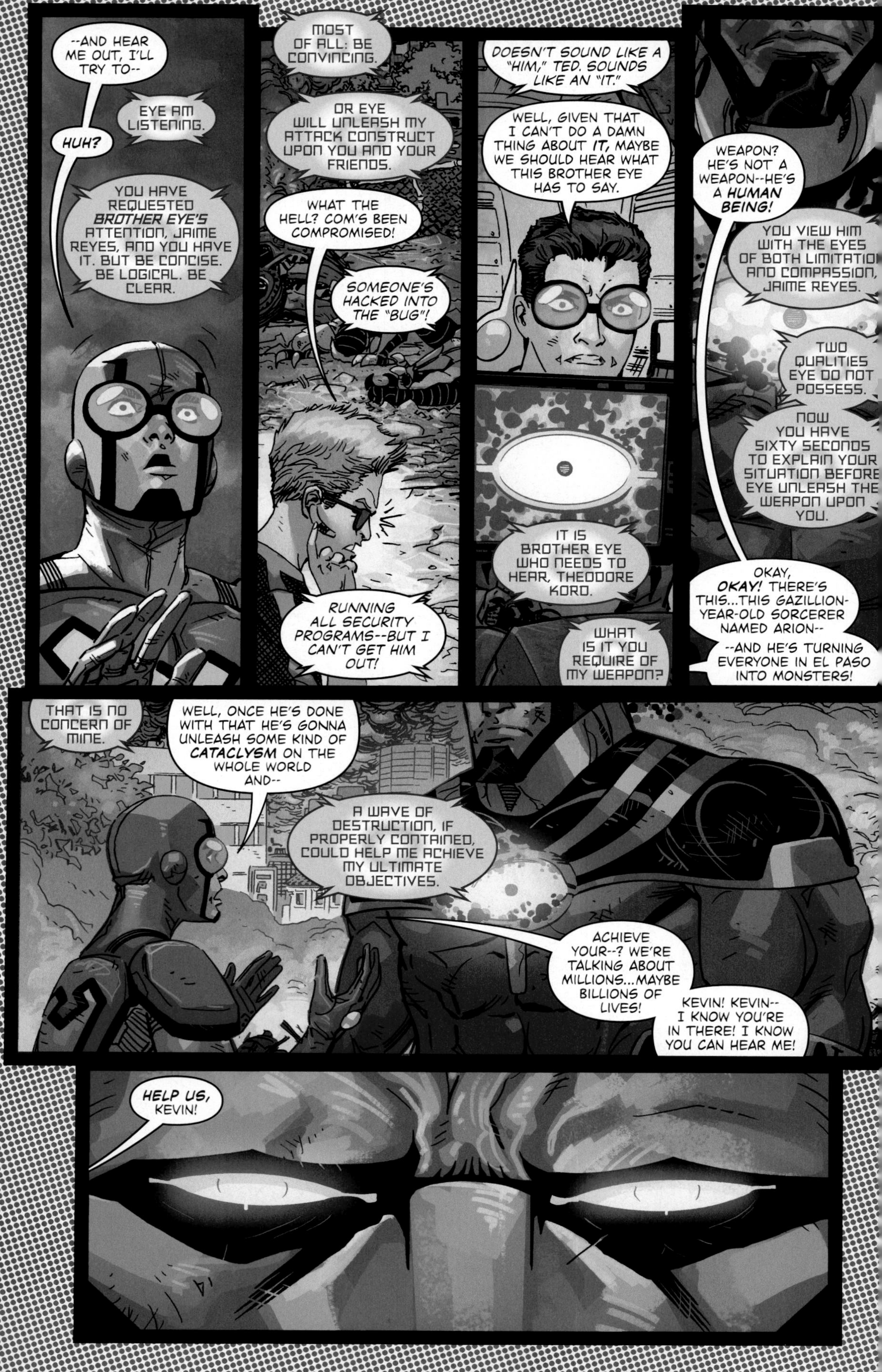

--AND HEAR ME OUT, I'LL TRY TO--
EYE AM LISTENING.
HUH?
YOU HAVE REQUESTED BROTHER EYE'S ATTENTION, JAIME REYES, AND YOU HAVE IT. BUT BE CONCISE. BE LOGICAL. BE CLEAR.
MOST OF ALL: BE CONVINCING.
OR EYE WILL UNLEASH MY ATTACK CONSTRUCT UPON YOU AND YOUR FRIENDS.
WHAT THE HELL? COM'S BEEN COMPROMISED!
SOMEONE'S HACKED INTO THE "BUG"!
RUNNING ALL SECURITY PROGRAMS--BUT I CAN'T GET HIM OUT!
DOESN'T SOUND LIKE A "HIM," TED. SOUNDS LIKE AN "IT."
WELL, GIVEN THAT I CAN'T DO A DAMN THING ABOUT IT, MAYBE WE SHOULD HEAR WHAT THIS BROTHER EYE HAS TO SAY.
IT IS BROTHER EYE WHO NEEDS TO HEAR, THEODORE KORD.
WHAT IS IT YOU REQUIRE OF MY WEAPON?
WEAPON? HE'S NOT A WEAPON--HE'S A HUMAN BEING!
YOU VIEW HIM WITH THE EYES OF BOTH LIMITATIO AND COMPASSION, JAIME REYES.
TWO QUALITIES EYE DO NOT POSSESS.
NOW YOU HAVE SIXTY SECONDS TO EXPLAIN YOUR SITUATION BEFORE EYE UNLEASH THE WEAPON UPON YOU.
OKAY, OKAY! THERE'S THIS...THIS GAZILLION-YEAR-OLD SORCERER NAMED ARION--
--AND HE'S TURNING EVERYONE IN EL PASO INTO MONSTERS!
THAT IS NO CONCERN OF MINE.
WELL, ONCE HE'S DONE WITH THAT HE'S GONNA UNLEASH SOME KIND OF CATACLYSM ON THE WHOLE WORLD AND--
A WAVE OF DESTRUCTION, IF PROPERLY CONTAINED, COULD HELP ME ACHIEVE MY ULTIMATE OBJECTIVES.
ACHIEVE YOUR--? WE'RE TALKING ABOUT MILLIONS...MAYBE BILLIONS OF LIVES!
KEVIN! KEVIN-- I KNOW YOU'RE IN THERE! I KNOW YOU CAN HEAR ME!
HELP US, KEVIN!

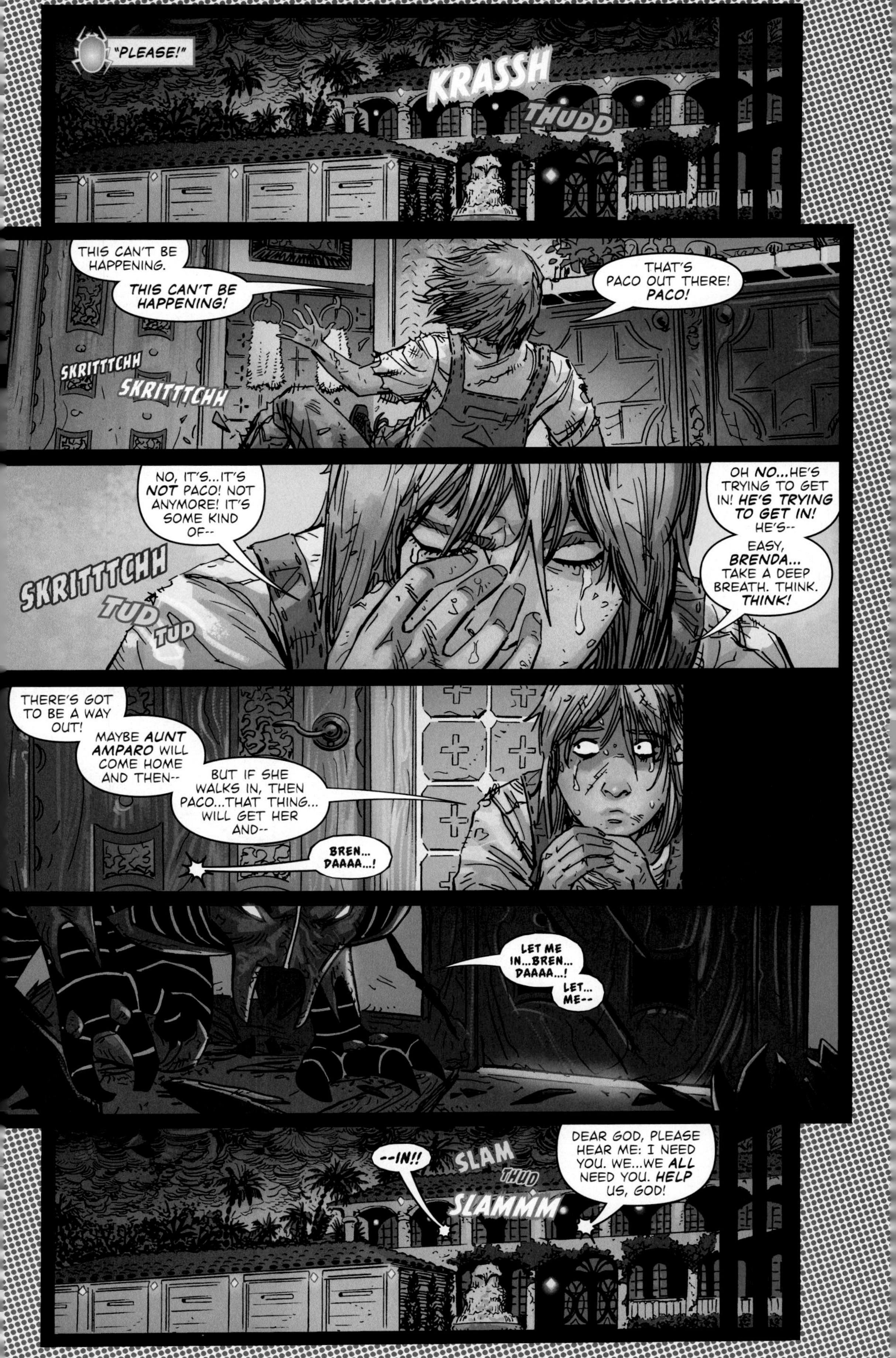
"PLEASE!"
KRASSH
THUDD
THIS CAN'T BE HAPPENING.
THIS CAN'T BE HAPPENING!
THAT'S PACO OUT THERE! PACO!
SKRITTTCHH
SKRITTTCHH
NO, IT'S...IT'S NOT PACO! NOT ANYMORE! IT'S SOME KIND OF--
SKRITTTCHH
TUD
TUD
OH NO...HE'S TRYING TO GET IN! HE'S TRYING TO GET IN! HE'S--
EASY, BRENDA... TAKE A DEEP BREATH. THINK. THINK!
THERE'S GOT TO BE A WAY OUT!
MAYBE AUNT AMPARO WILL COME HOME AND THEN--
BUT IF SHE WALKS IN, THEN PACO...THAT THING... WILL GET HER AND--
BREN... DAAAA...!
LET ME IN...BREN... DAAAA...!
LET... ME--
--IN!!
SLAM
THUD
SLAMMM
DEAR GOD, PLEASE HEAR ME: I NEED YOU. WE...WE ALL NEED YOU. HELP US, GOD!

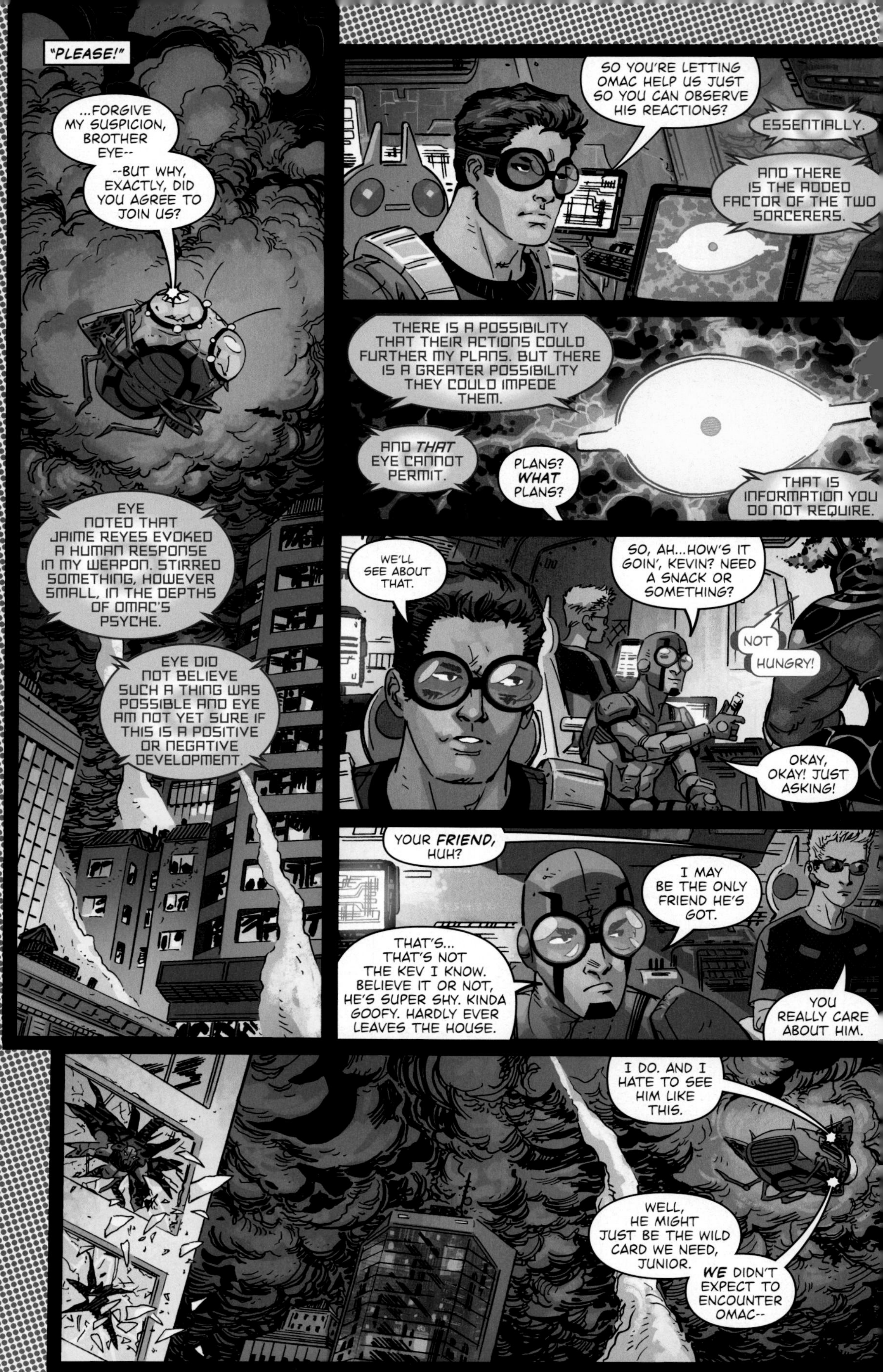
"PLEASE!"
...FORGIVE MY SUSPICION, BROTHER EYE--
--BUT WHY, EXACTLY, DID YOU AGREE TO JOIN US?
SO YOU'RE LETTING OMAC HELP US JUST SO YOU CAN OBSERVE HIS REACTIONS?
ESSENTIALLY.
AND THERE IS THE ADDED FACTOR OF THE TWO SORCERERS.
THERE IS A POSSIBILITY THAT THEIR ACTIONS COULD FURTHER MY PLANS. BUT THERE IS A GREATER POSSIBILITY THEY COULD IMPEDE THEM.
AND THAT EYE CANNOT PERMIT.
PLANS? WHAT PLANS?
THAT IS INFORMATION YOU DO NOT REQUIRE.
EYE NOTED THAT JAIME REYES EVOKED A HUMAN RESPONSE IN MY WEAPON. STIRRED SOMETHING, HOWEVER SMALL, IN THE DEPTHS OF OMAC'S PSYCHE.
EYE DID NOT BELIEVE SUCH A THING WAS POSSIBLE AND EYE AM NOT YET SURE IF THIS IS A POSITIVE OR NEGATIVE DEVELOPMENT.
WE'LL SEE ABOUT THAT.
SO, AH...HOW'S IT GOIN', KEVIN? NEED A SNACK OR SOMETHING?
NOT
HUNGRY!
OKAY, OKAY! JUST ASKING!
YOUR FRIEND, HUH?
I MAY BE THE ONLY FRIEND HE'S GOT.
THAT'S... THAT'S NOT THE KEV I KNOW. BELIEVE IT OR NOT, HE'S SUPER SHY. KINDA GOOFY. HARDLY EVER LEAVES THE HOUSE.
YOU REALLY CARE ABOUT HIM.
I DO. AND I HATE TO SEE HIM LIKE THIS.
WELL, HE MIGHT JUST BE THE WILD CARD WE NEED, JUNIOR.
WE DIDN'T EXPECT TO ENCOUNTER OMAC--

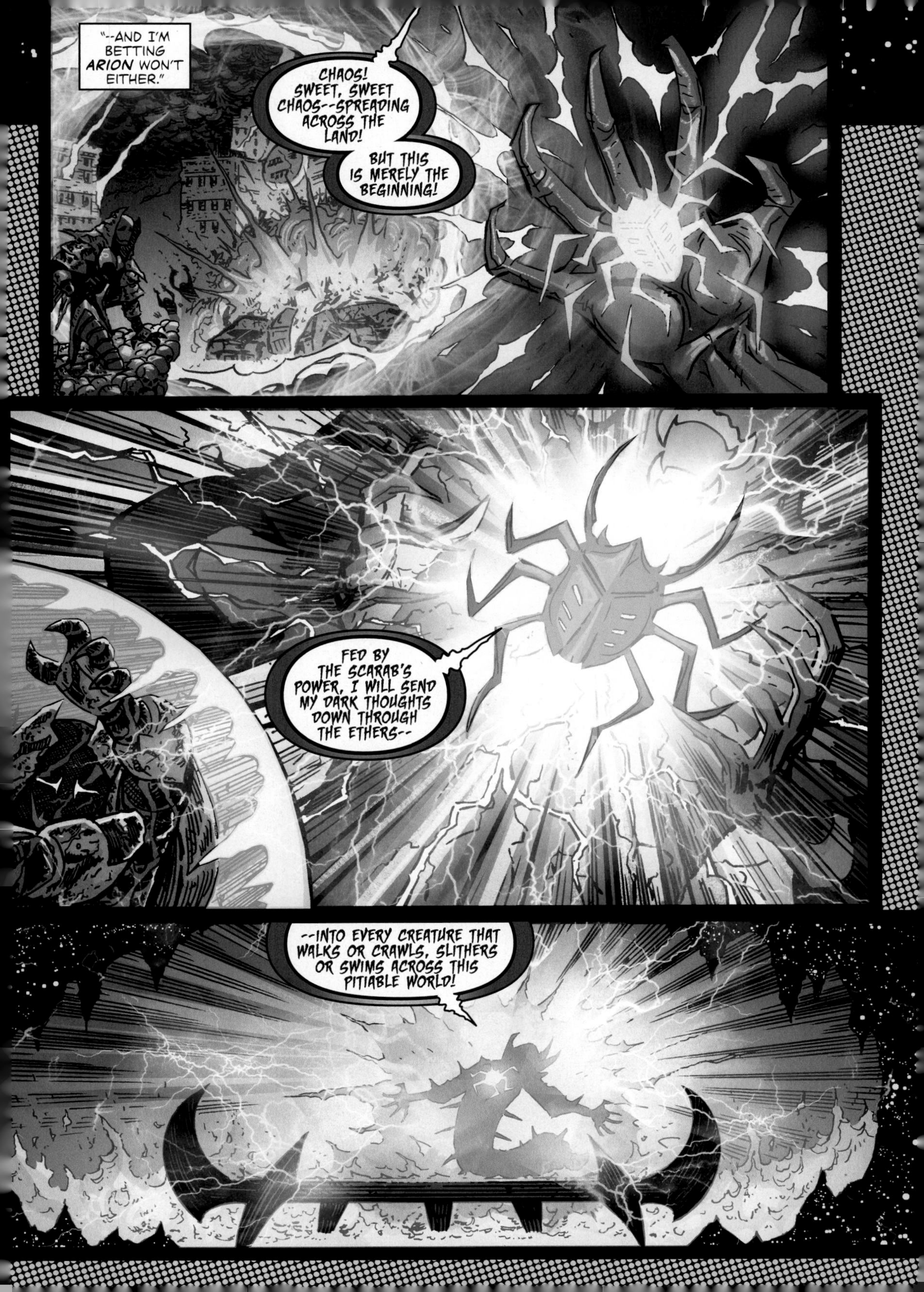
"--AND I'M BETTING ARION WON'T EITHER."
CHAOS! SWEET, SWEET CHAOS--SPREADING ACROSS THE LAND!
BUT THIS IS MERELY THE BEGINNING!
FED BY THE SCARAB'S POWER, I WILL SEND MY DARK THOUGHTS DOWN THROUGH THE ETHERS--
--INTO EVERY CREATURE THAT WALKS OR CRAWLS, SLITHERS OR SWIMS ACROSS THIS PITIABLE WORLD!

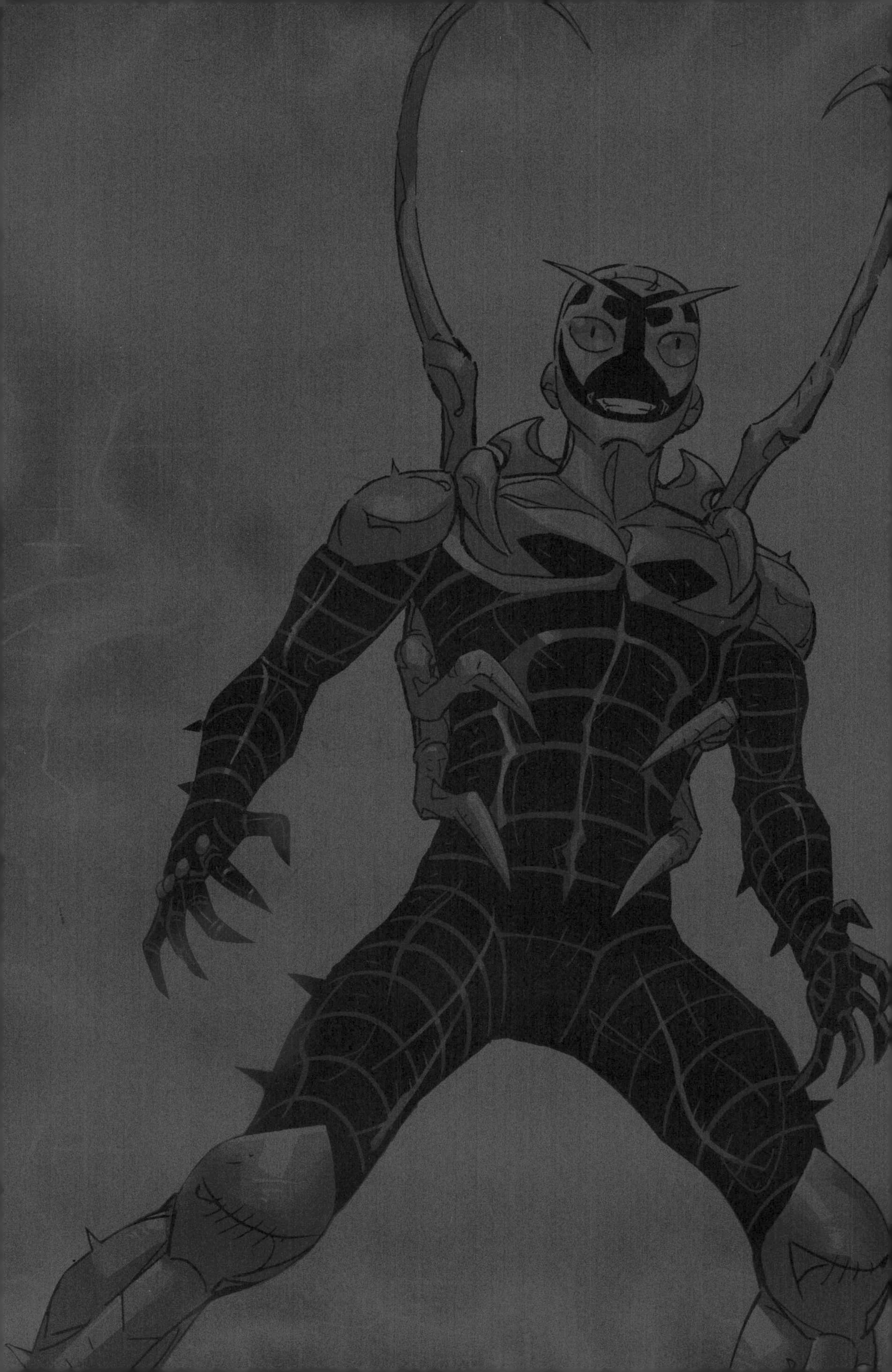

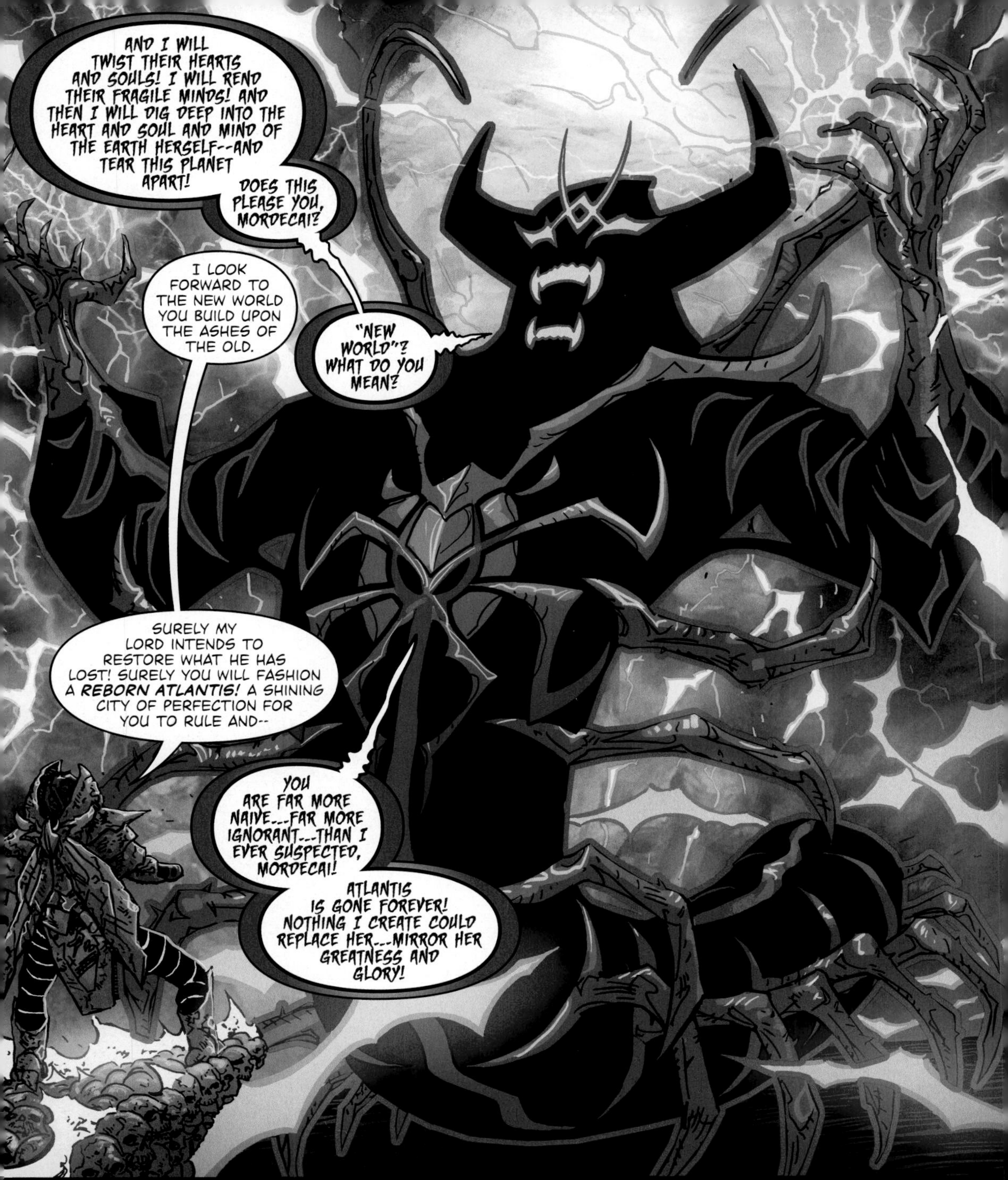
AND I WILL TWIST THEIR HEARTS AND SOULS! I WILL REND THEIR FRAGILE MINDS! AND THEN I WILL DIG DEEP INTO THE HEART AND SOUL AND MIND OF THE EARTH HERSELF--AND TEAR THIS PLANET APART!
DOES THIS PLEASE YOU, MORDECAI?
I LOOK FORWARD TO THE NEW WORLD YOU BUILD UPON THE ASHES OF THE OLD.
"NEW WORLD"? WHAT DO YOU MEAN?
SURELY MY LORD INTENDS TO RESTORE WHAT HE HAS LOST! SURELY YOU WILL FASHION A **REBORN ATLANTIS!** A SHINING CITY OF PERFECTION FOR YOU TO RULE AND--
YOU ARE FAR MORE NAIVE---FAR MORE IGNORANT---THAN I EVER SUSPECTED, MORDECAI!
ATLANTIS IS GONE FOREVER! NOTHING I CREATE COULD REPLACE HER---MIRROR HER GREATNESS AND GLORY!
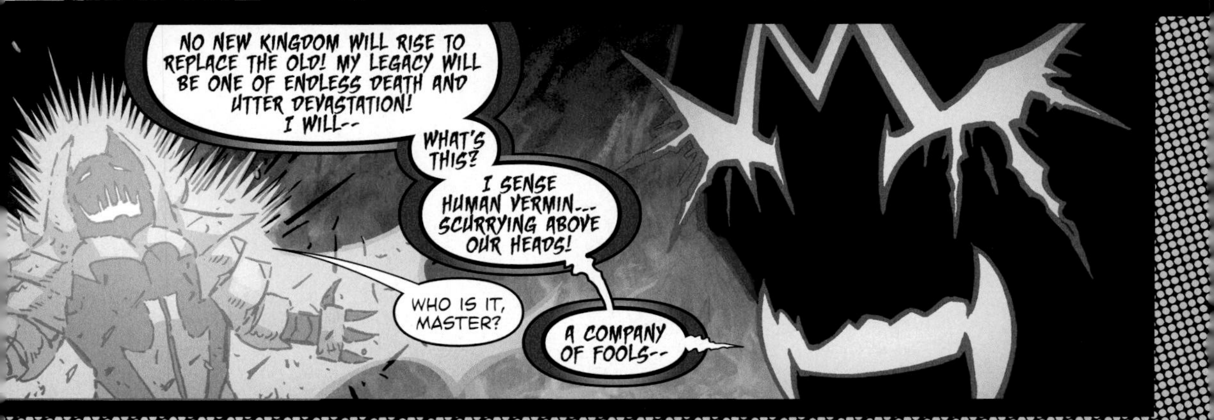
NO NEW KINGDOM WILL RISE TO REPLACE THE OLD! MY LEGACY WILL BE ONE OF ENDLESS DEATH AND UTTER DEVASTATION! I WILL--
WHAT'S THIS?
I SENSE HUMAN VERMIN--- SCURRYING ABOVE OUR HEADS!
WHO IS IT, MASTER?
A COMPANY OF FOOLS--

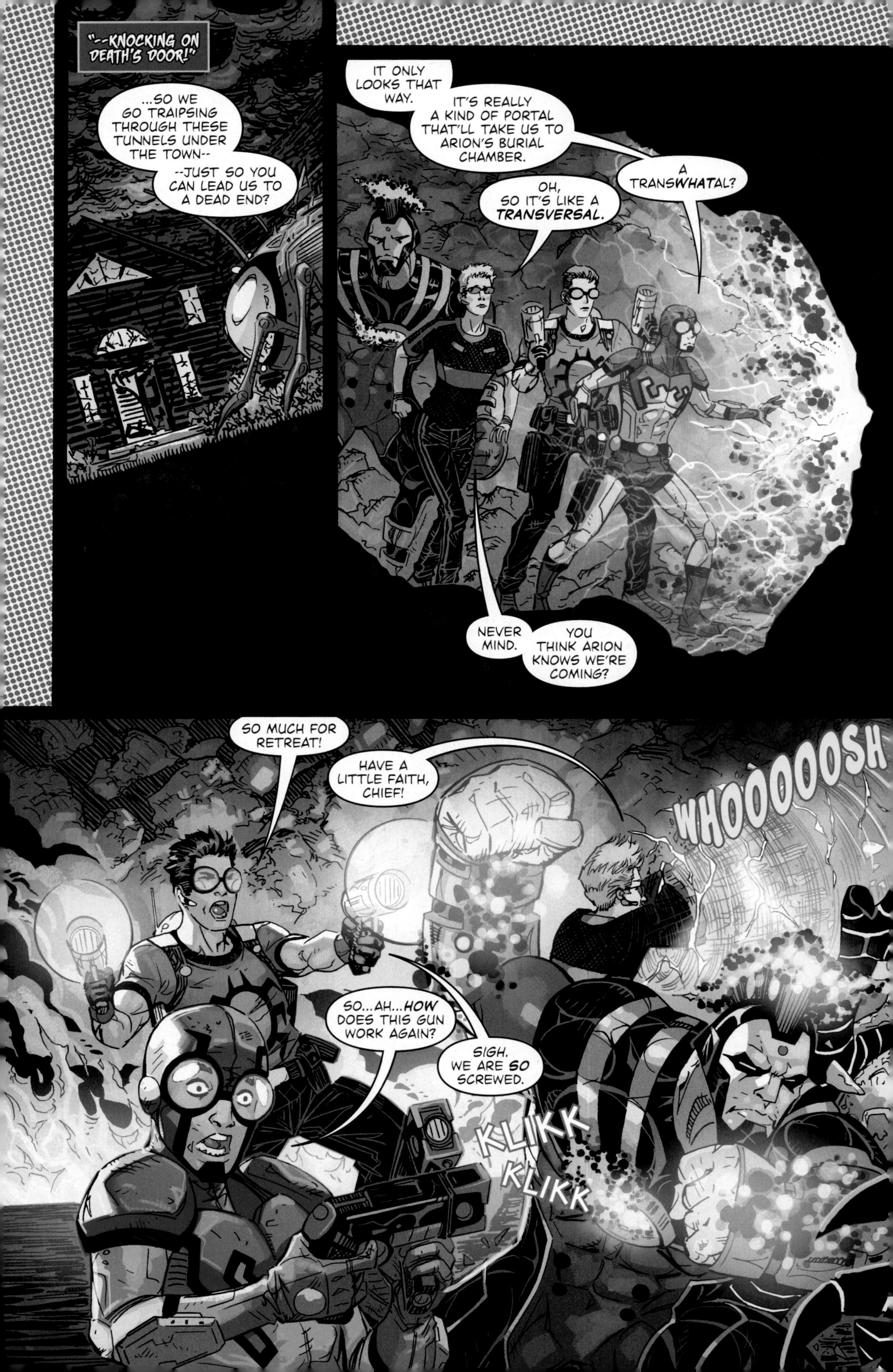
"--KNOCKING ON DEATH'S DOOR!"
...SO WE GO TRAIPSING THROUGH THESE TUNNELS UNDER THE TOWN--
--JUST SO YOU CAN LEAD US TO A DEAD END?
IT ONLY LOOKS THAT WAY.
IT'S REALLY A KIND OF PORTAL THAT'LL TAKE US TO ARION'S BURIAL CHAMBER.
OH, SO IT'S LIKE A **TRANSVERSAL.**
A TRANS**WHAT**AL?
NEVER MIND.
YOU THINK ARION KNOWS WE'RE COMING?
SO MUCH FOR RETREAT!
HAVE A LITTLE FAITH, CHIEF!
WHOOOOOSH
SO...AH...**HOW** DOES THIS GUN WORK AGAIN?
SIGH. WE ARE **SO** SCREWED.
KLIKK
KLIKK

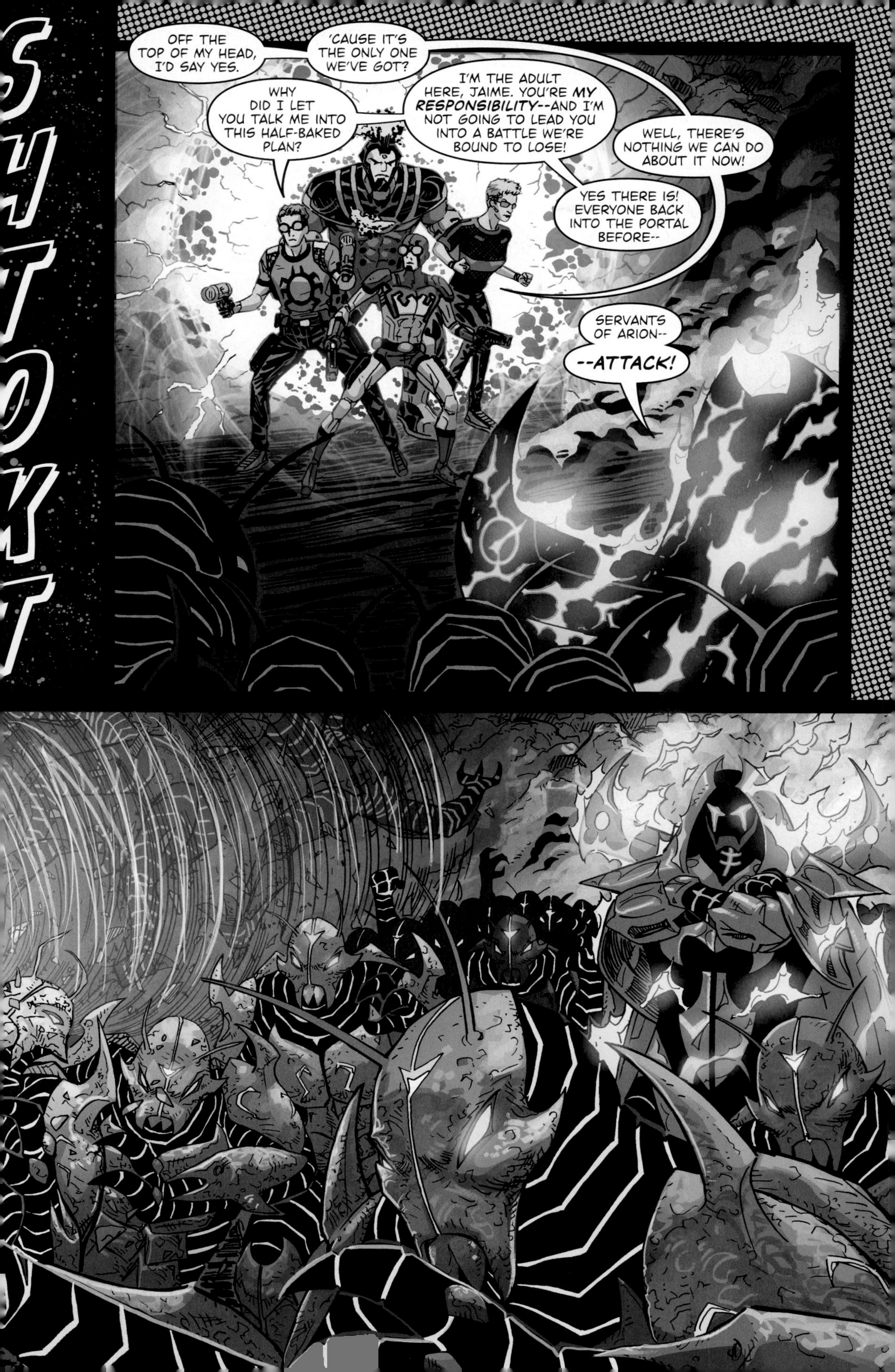
WHY DID I LET YOU TALK ME INTO THIS HALF-BAKED PLAN?
OFF THE TOP OF MY HEAD, I'D SAY YES.
'CAUSE IT'S THE ONLY ONE WE'VE GOT?
I'M THE ADULT HERE, JAIME. YOU'RE **MY *RESPONSIBILITY***--AND I'M NOT GOING TO LEAD YOU INTO A BATTLE WE'RE BOUND TO LOSE!
WELL, THERE'S NOTHING WE CAN DO ABOUT IT NOW!
YES THERE IS! EVERYONE BACK INTO THE PORTAL BEFORE--
SERVANTS OF ARION--
--ATTACK!

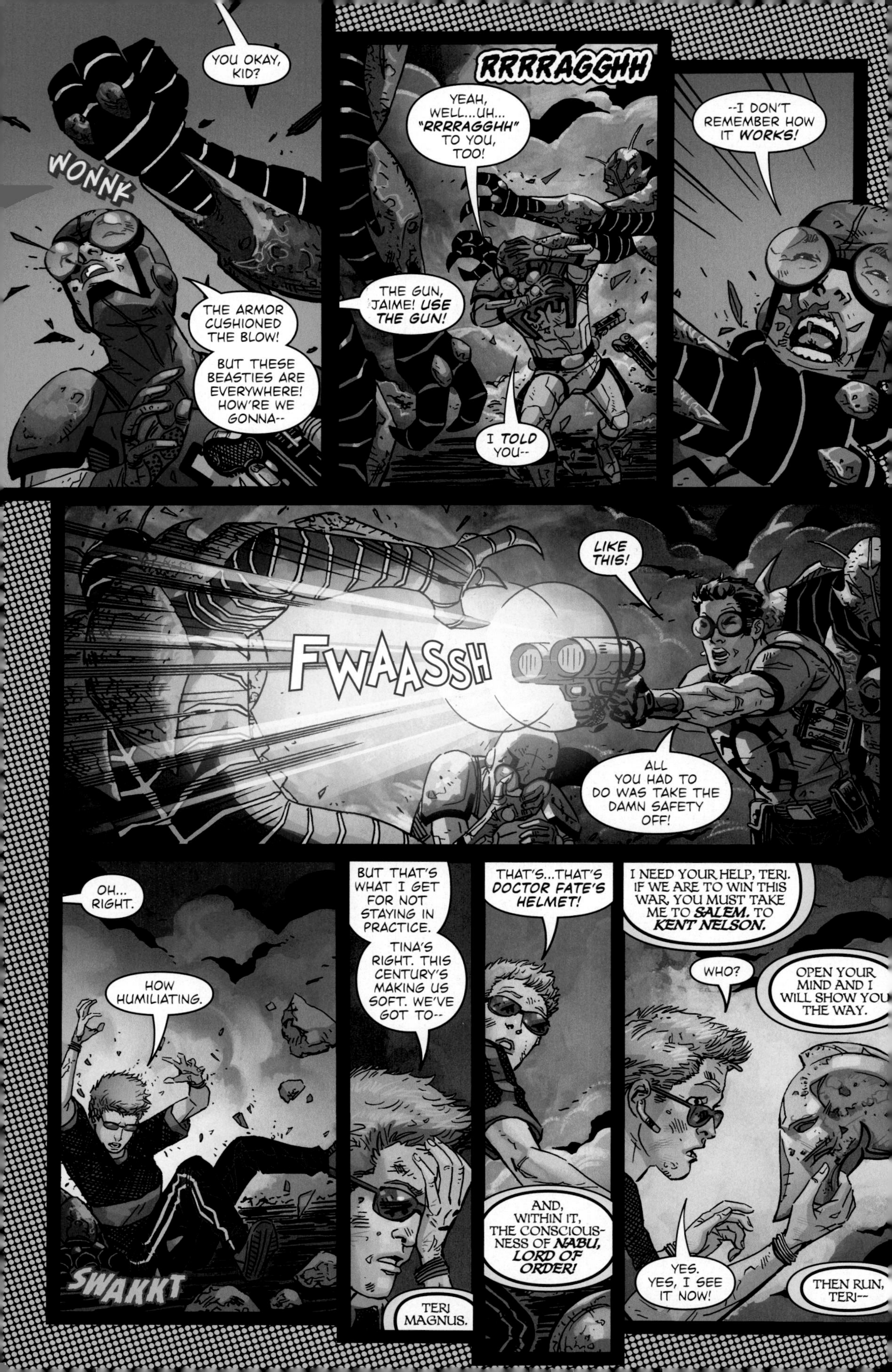

YOU OKAY, KID?
WONNK
THE ARMOR CUSHIONED THE BLOW!
BUT THESE BEASTIES ARE EVERYWHERE! HOW'RE WE GONNA--
RRRRAGGHH
YEAH, WELL...UH... "RRRRAGGHH" TO YOU, TOO!
THE GUN, JAIME! USE THE GUN!
I TOLD YOU--
--I DON'T REMEMBER HOW IT WORKS!
LIKE THIS!
FWAASSH
ALL YOU HAD TO DO WAS TAKE THE DAMN SAFETY OFF!
OH... RIGHT.
HOW HUMILIATING.
SWAKKT
BUT THAT'S WHAT I GET FOR NOT STAYING IN PRACTICE.
TINA'S RIGHT. THIS CENTURY'S MAKING US SOFT. WE'VE GOT TO--
TERI MAGNUS.
THAT'S...THAT'S DOCTOR FATE'S HELMET!
AND, WITHIN IT, THE CONSCIOUS-NESS OF NABU, LORD OF ORDER!
I NEED YOUR HELP, TERI. IF WE ARE TO WIN THIS WAR, YOU MUST TAKE ME TO SALEM. TO KENT NELSON.
WHO?
OPEN YOUR MIND AND I WILL SHOW YOU THE WAY.
YES. YES, I SEE IT NOW!
THEN RUN, TERI--

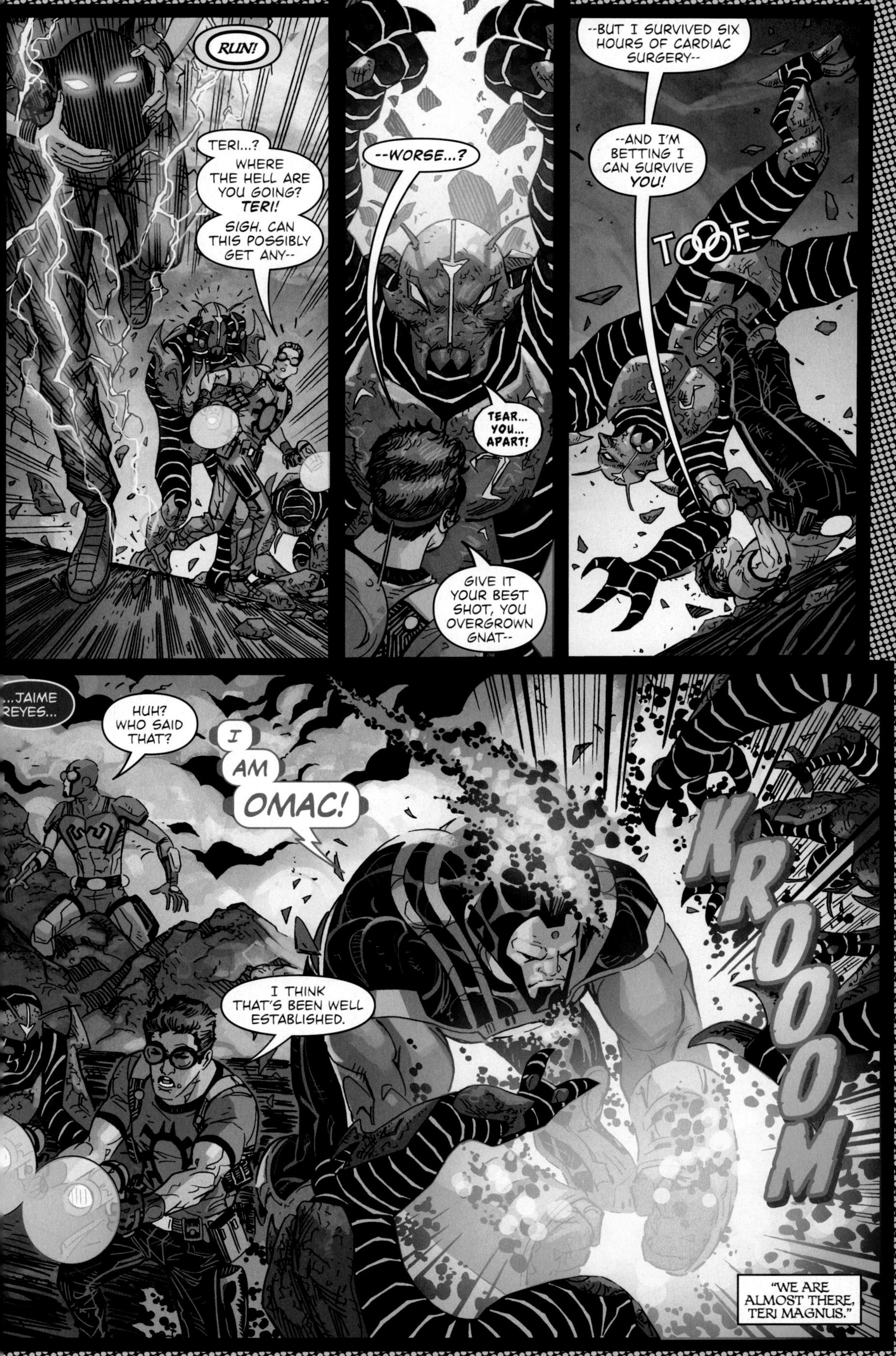
RUN!
TERI...? WHERE THE HELL ARE YOU GOING? TERI!
SIGH. CAN THIS POSSIBLY GET ANY--
--WORSE...?
TEAR... YOU... APART!
GIVE IT YOUR BEST SHOT, YOU OVERGROWN GNAT--
--BUT I SURVIVED SIX HOURS OF CARDIAC SURGERY--
--AND I'M BETTING I CAN SURVIVE YOU!
TOOF
...JAIME REYES...
HUH? WHO SAID THAT?
I AM OMAC!
I THINK THAT'S BEEN WELL ESTABLISHED.
KROOOOM
"WE ARE ALMOST THERE, TERI MAGNUS."

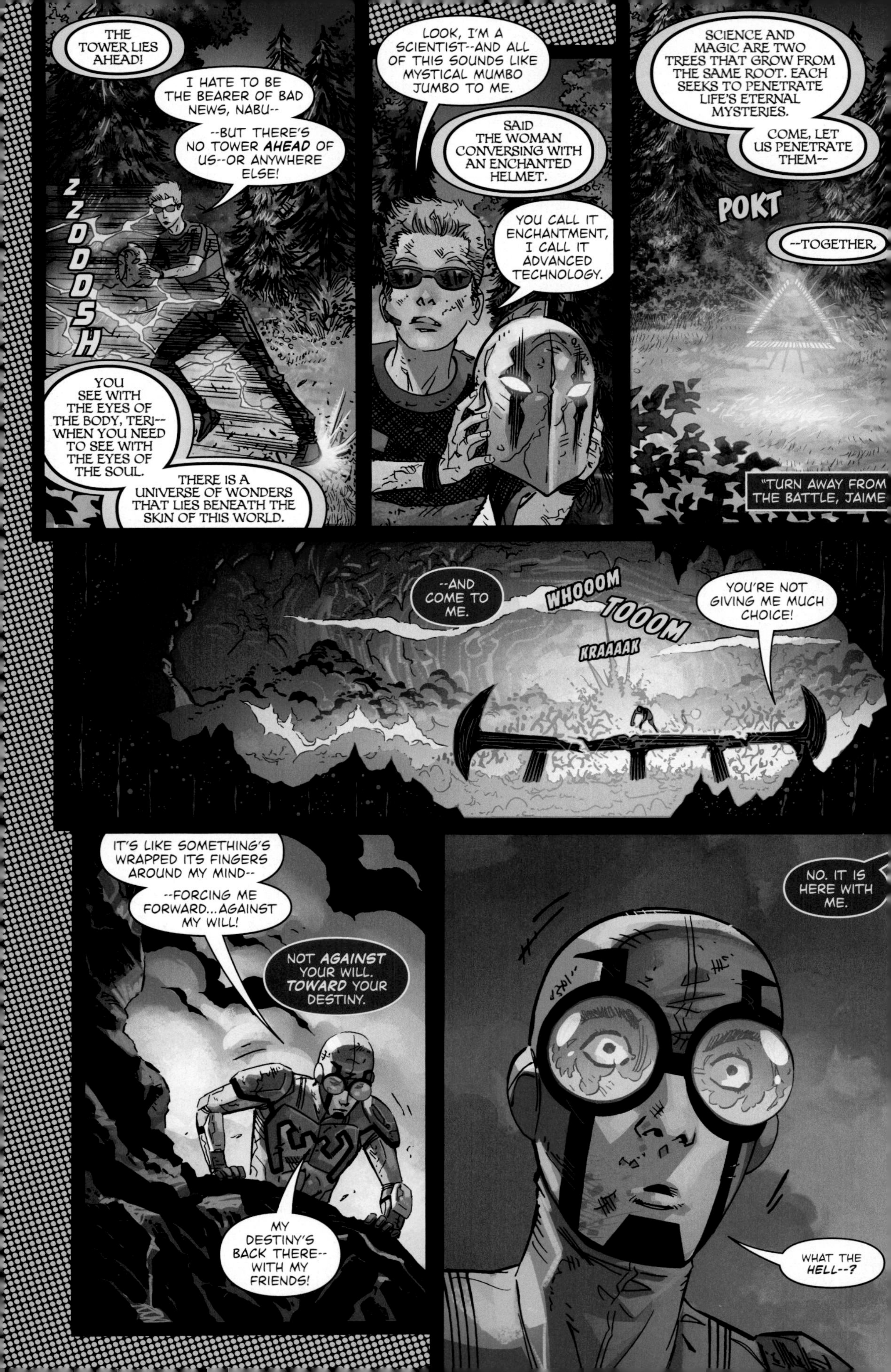
THE TOWER LIES AHEAD!
I HATE TO BE THE BEARER OF BAD NEWS, NABU--
--BUT THERE'S NO TOWER AHEAD OF US--OR ANYWHERE ELSE!
ZZDDDSH
YOU SEE WITH THE EYES OF THE BODY, TERI--WHEN YOU NEED TO SEE WITH THE EYES OF THE SOUL.
THERE IS A UNIVERSE OF WONDERS THAT LIES BENEATH THE SKIN OF THIS WORLD.
LOOK, I'M A SCIENTIST--AND ALL OF THIS SOUNDS LIKE MYSTICAL MUMBO JUMBO TO ME.
SAID THE WOMAN CONVERSING WITH AN ENCHANTED HELMET.
YOU CALL IT ENCHANTMENT, I CALL IT ADVANCED TECHNOLOGY.
SCIENCE AND MAGIC ARE TWO TREES THAT GROW FROM THE SAME ROOT. EACH SEEKS TO PENETRATE LIFE'S ETERNAL MYSTERIES.
COME, LET US PENETRATE THEM--
POKT
--TOGETHER.
"TURN AWAY FROM THE BATTLE, JAIME
--AND COME TO ME.
WHOOOM
TOOOM
KRAAAAK
YOU'RE NOT GIVING ME MUCH CHOICE!
IT'S LIKE SOMETHING'S WRAPPED ITS FINGERS AROUND MY MIND--
--FORCING ME FORWARD...AGAINST MY WILL!
NOT AGAINST YOUR WILL. TOWARD YOUR DESTINY.
MY DESTINY'S BACK THERE--WITH MY FRIENDS!
NO. IT IS HERE WITH ME.
WHAT THE HELL--?

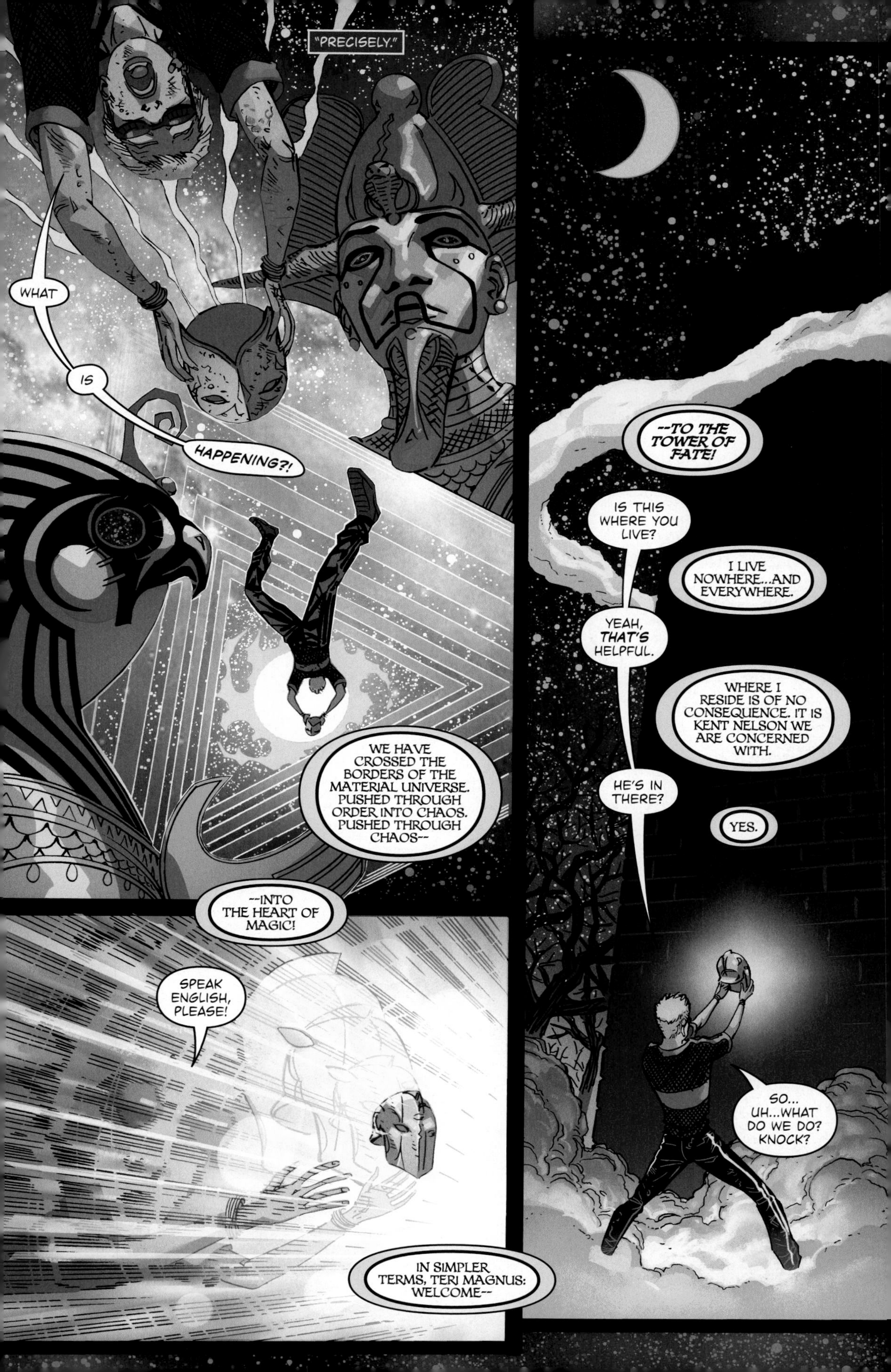
"PRECISELY."
WHAT IS HAPPENING?!
WE HAVE CROSSED THE BORDERS OF THE MATERIAL UNIVERSE. PUSHED THROUGH ORDER INTO CHAOS. PUSHED THROUGH CHAOS--
--INTO THE HEART OF MAGIC!
SPEAK ENGLISH, PLEASE!
IN SIMPLER TERMS, TERI MAGNUS: WELCOME--
--TO THE TOWER OF FATE!
IS THIS WHERE YOU LIVE?
I LIVE NOWHERE...AND EVERYWHERE.
YEAH, THAT'S HELPFUL.
WHERE I RESIDE IS OF NO CONSEQUENCE. IT IS KENT NELSON WE ARE CONCERNED WITH.
HE'S IN THERE?
YES.
SO... UH...WHAT DO WE DO? KNOCK?

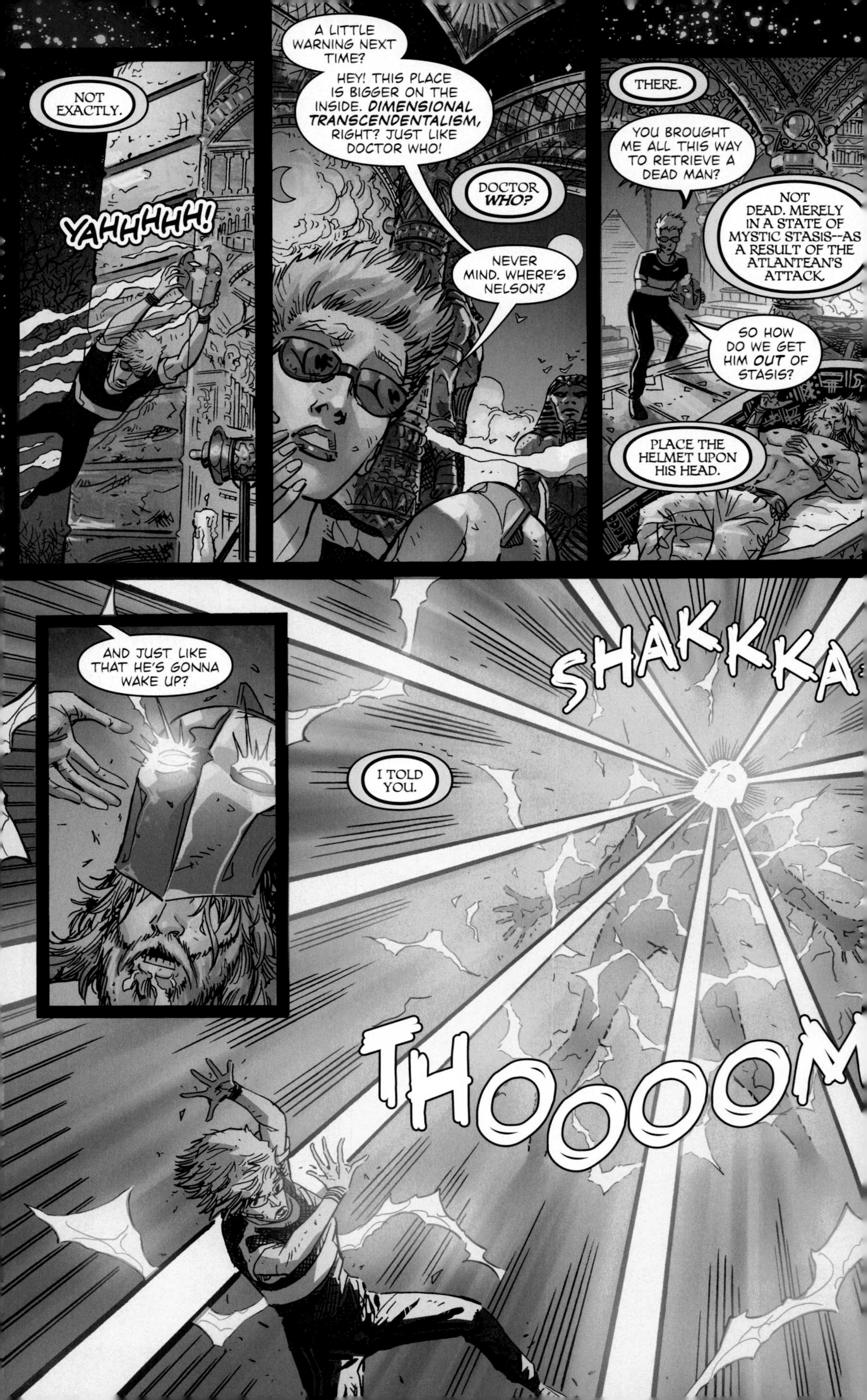
NOT EXACTLY.
YAHHHHH!
A LITTLE WARNING NEXT TIME?
HEY! THIS PLACE IS BIGGER ON THE INSIDE. DIMENSIONAL TRANSCENDENTALISM, RIGHT? JUST LIKE DOCTOR WHO!
DOCTOR WHO?
NEVER MIND. WHERE'S NELSON?
THERE.
YOU BROUGHT ME ALL THIS WAY TO RETRIEVE A DEAD MAN?
NOT DEAD. MERELY IN A STATE OF MYSTIC STASIS--AS A RESULT OF THE ATLANTEAN'S ATTACK.
SO HOW DO WE GET HIM OUT OF STASIS?
PLACE THE HELMET UPON HIS HEAD.
AND JUST LIKE THAT HE'S GONNA WAKE UP?
I TOLD YOU.
SHAKKKA-
THOOOOM

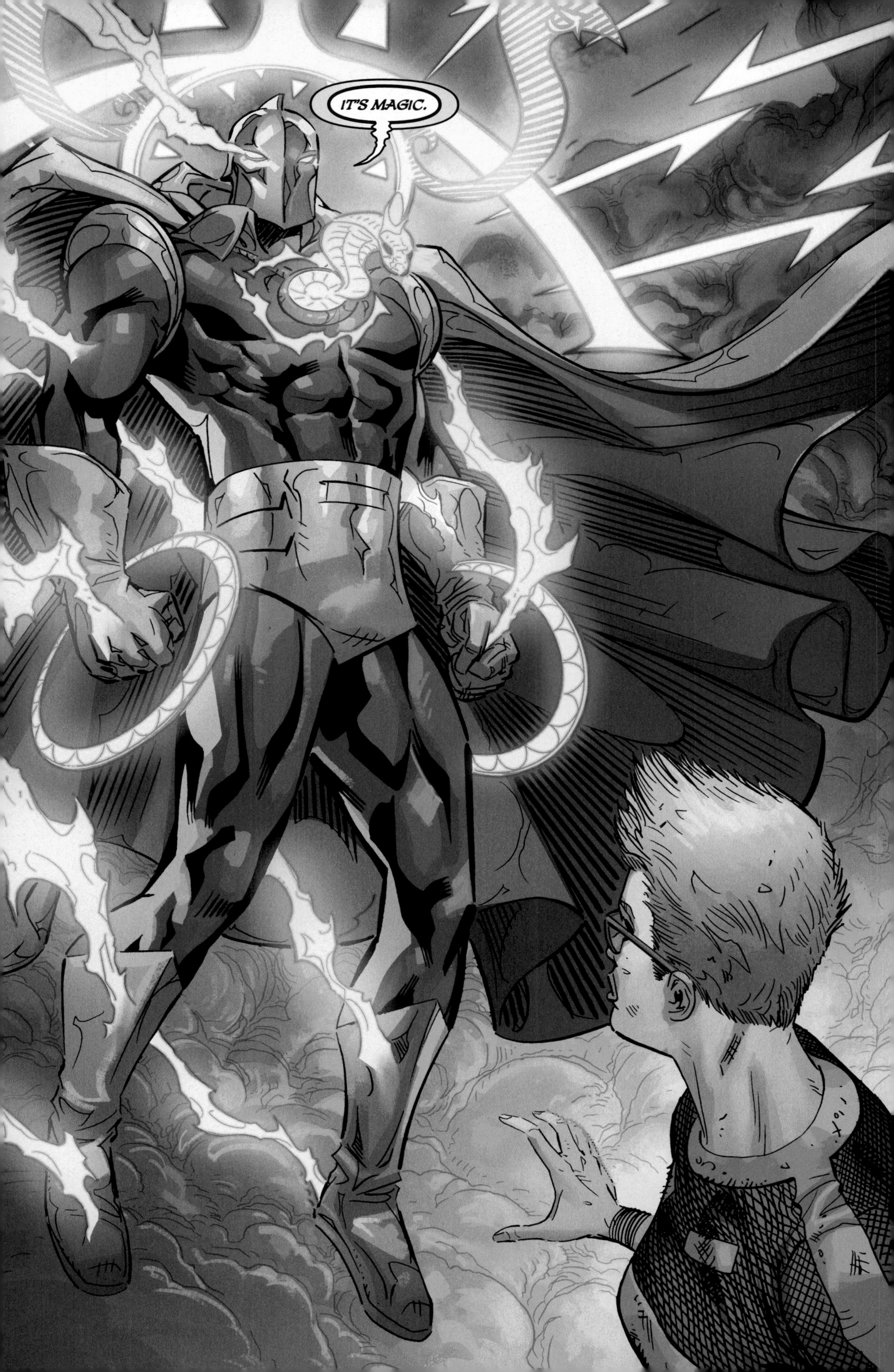
IT'S MAGIC.

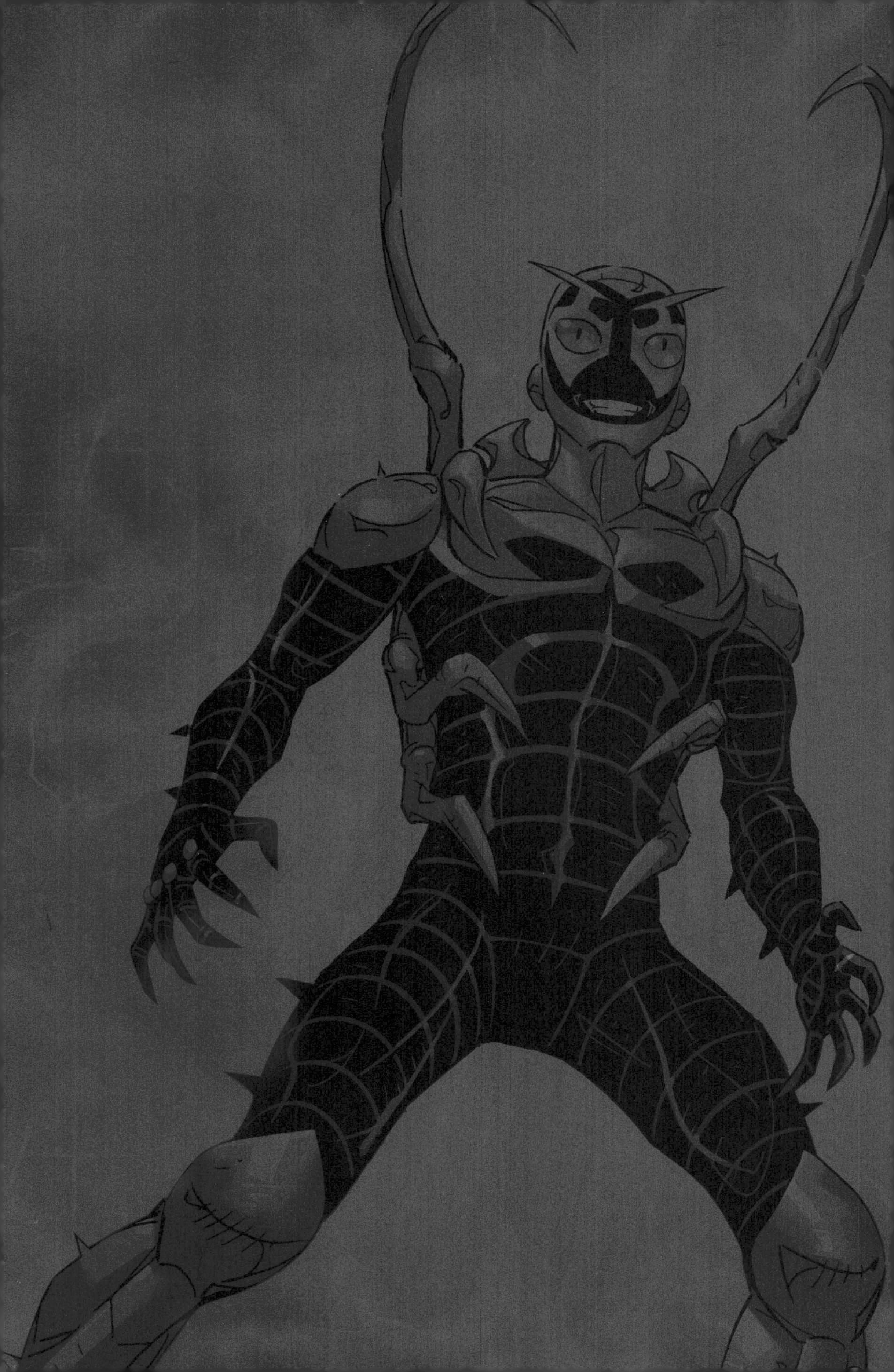

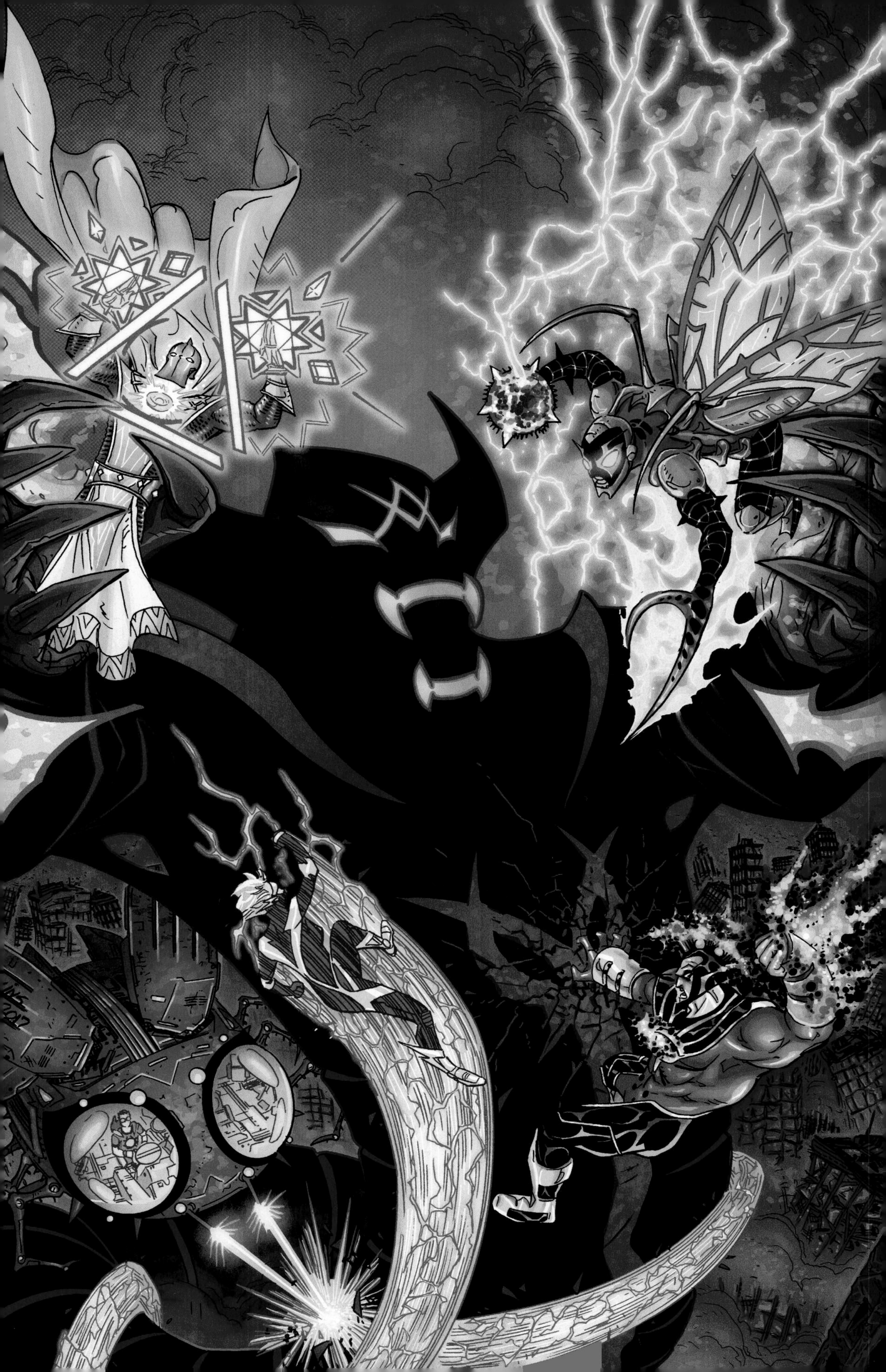

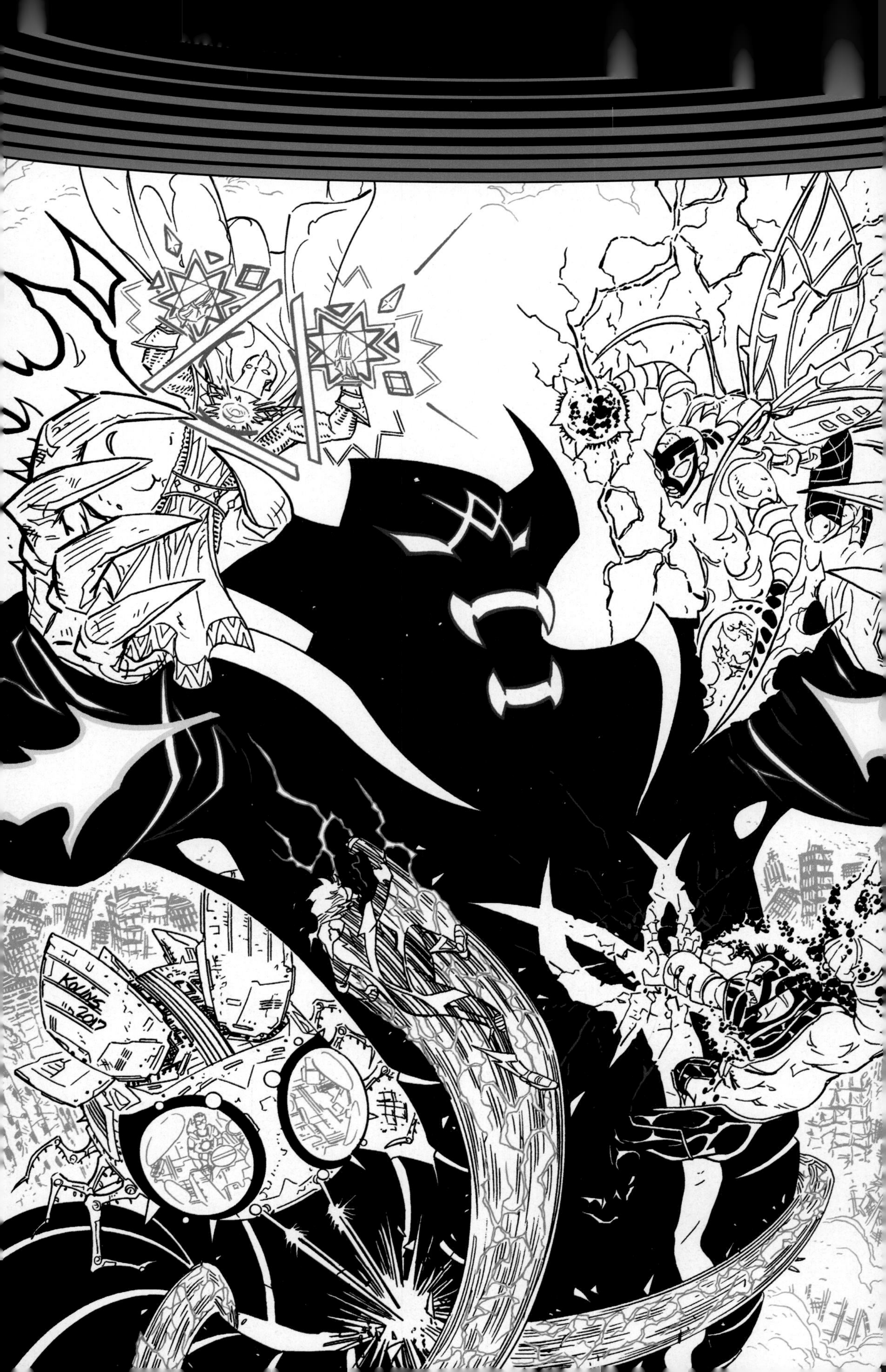
KOLINS
2017

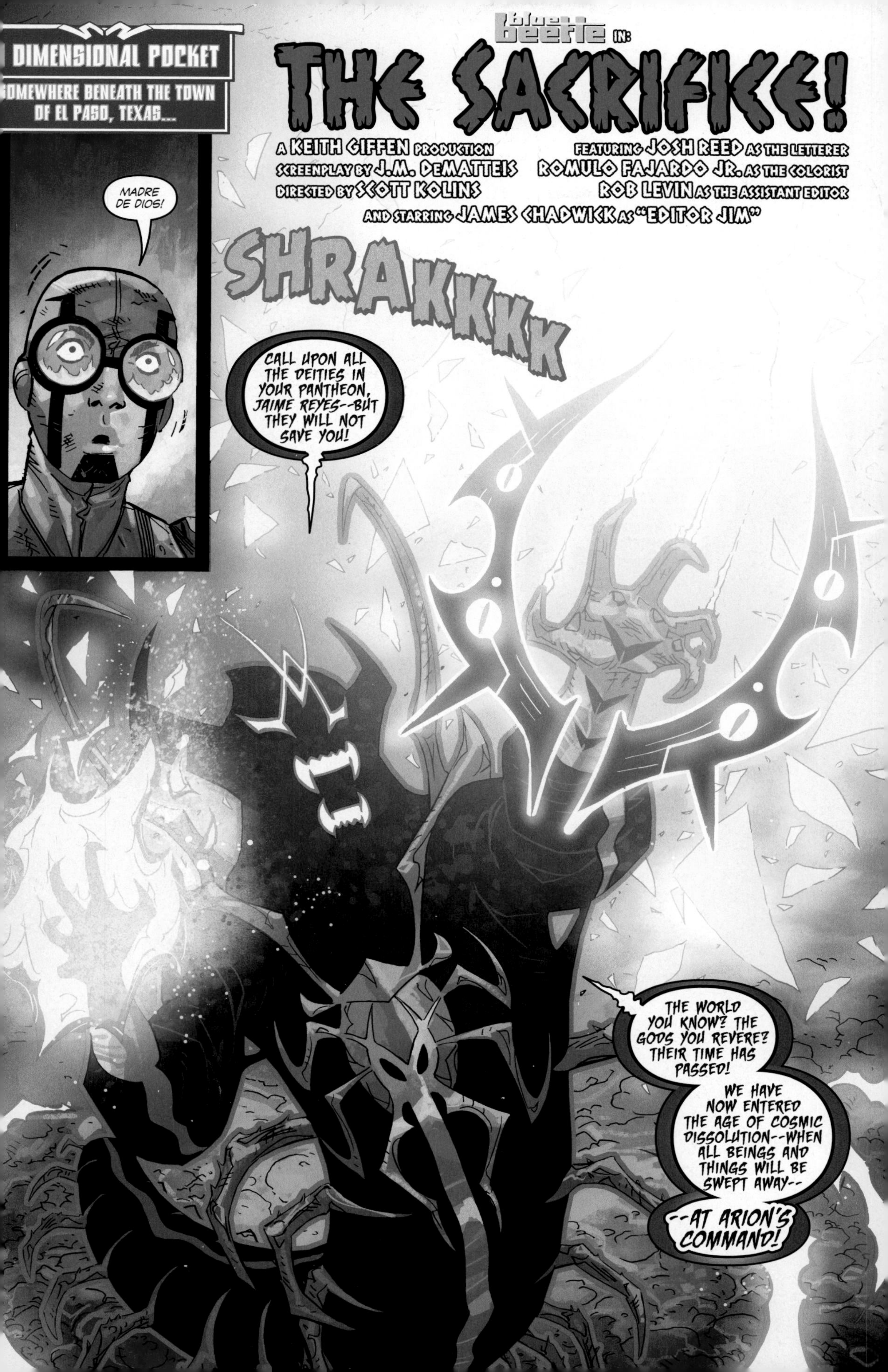
Blue Beetle in:
THE SACRIFICE!
A KEITH GIFFEN PRODUCTION
SCREENPLAY BY J.M. DEMATTEIS
DIRECTED BY SCOTT KOLINS
FEATURING JOSH REED AS THE LETTERER
ROMULO FAJARDO JR. AS THE COLORIST
ROB LEVIN AS THE ASSISTANT EDITOR
AND STARRING JAMES CHADWICK AS "EDITOR JIM"
DIMENSIONAL POCKET
SOMEWHERE BENEATH THE TOWN OF EL PASO, TEXAS...
MADRE DE DIOS!
SHRAKKKKK
CALL UPON ALL THE DEITIES IN YOUR PANTHEON, JAIME REYES--BUT THEY WILL NOT SAVE YOU!
THE WORLD YOU KNOW? THE GODS YOU REVERE? THEIR TIME HAS PASSED!
WE HAVE NOW ENTERED THE AGE OF COSMIC DISSOLUTION--WHEN ALL BEINGS AND THINGS WILL BE SWEPT AWAY--
--AT ARION'S COMMAND!

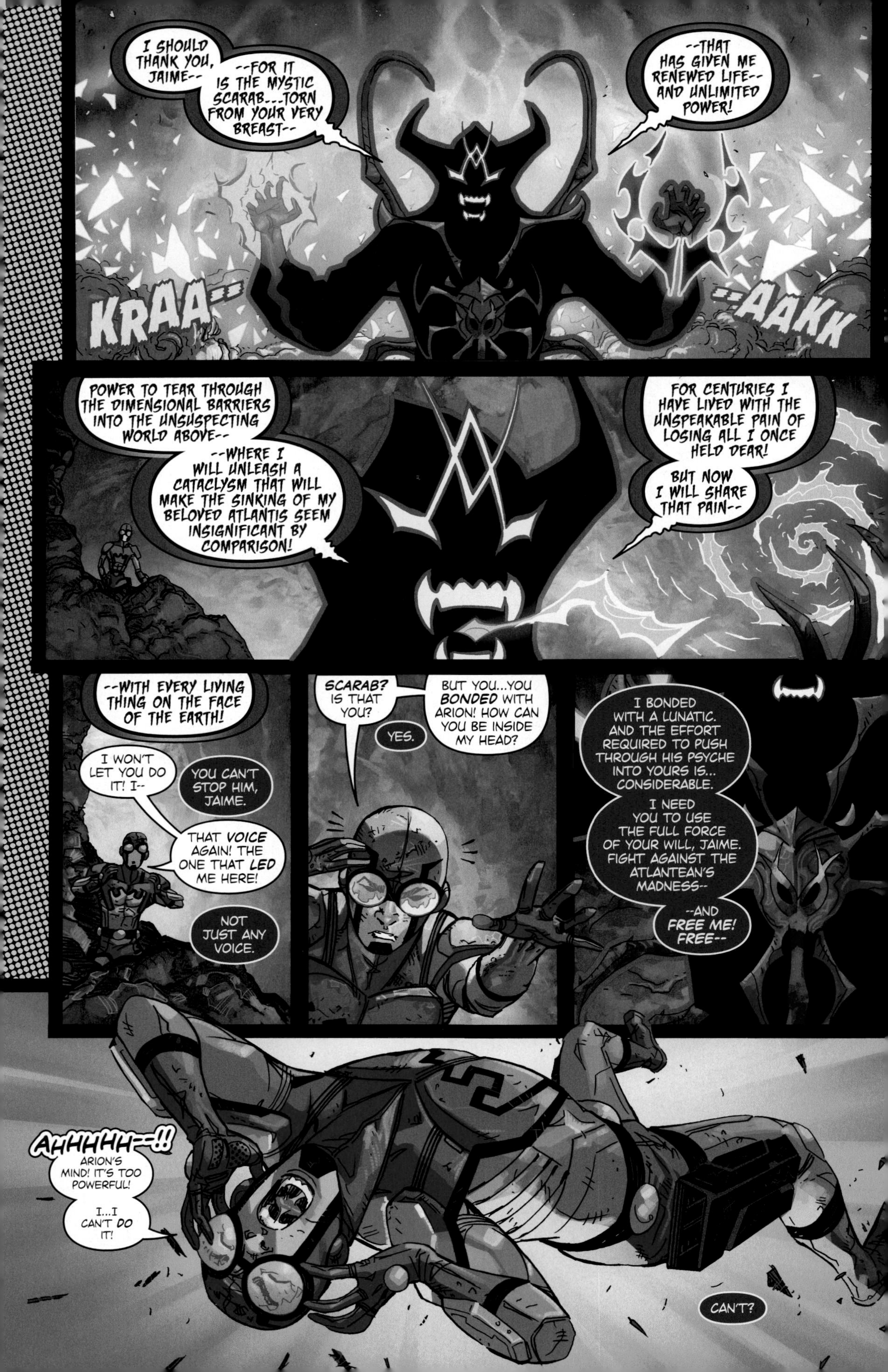
I SHOULD THANK YOU, JAIME--
--FOR IT IS THE MYSTIC SCARAB---TORN FROM YOUR VERY BREAST--
--THAT HAS GIVEN ME RENEWED LIFE--AND UNLIMITED POWER!
KRAA--
--AAKK
POWER TO TEAR THROUGH THE DIMENSIONAL BARRIERS INTO THE UNSUSPECTING WORLD ABOVE--
--WHERE I WILL UNLEASH A CATACLYSM THAT WILL MAKE THE SINKING OF MY BELOVED ATLANTIS SEEM INSIGNIFICANT BY COMPARISON!
FOR CENTURIES I HAVE LIVED WITH THE UNSPEAKABLE PAIN OF LOSING ALL I ONCE HELD DEAR!
BUT NOW I WILL SHARE THAT PAIN--
--WITH EVERY LIVING THING ON THE FACE OF THE EARTH!
I WON'T LET YOU DO IT! I--
YOU CAN'T STOP HIM, JAIME.
THAT VOICE AGAIN! THE ONE THAT LED ME HERE!
NOT JUST ANY VOICE.
SCARAB? IS THAT YOU?
YES.
BUT YOU...YOU BONDED WITH ARION! HOW CAN YOU BE INSIDE MY HEAD?
I BONDED WITH A LUNATIC. AND THE EFFORT REQUIRED TO PUSH THROUGH HIS PSYCHE INTO YOURS IS... CONSIDERABLE.
I NEED YOU TO USE THE FULL FORCE OF YOUR WILL, JAIME. FIGHT AGAINST THE ATLANTEAN'S MADNESS--
--AND FREE ME! FREE--
AHHHHH--!!
ARION'S MIND! IT'S TOO POWERFUL!
I...I CAN'T DO IT!
CAN'T?

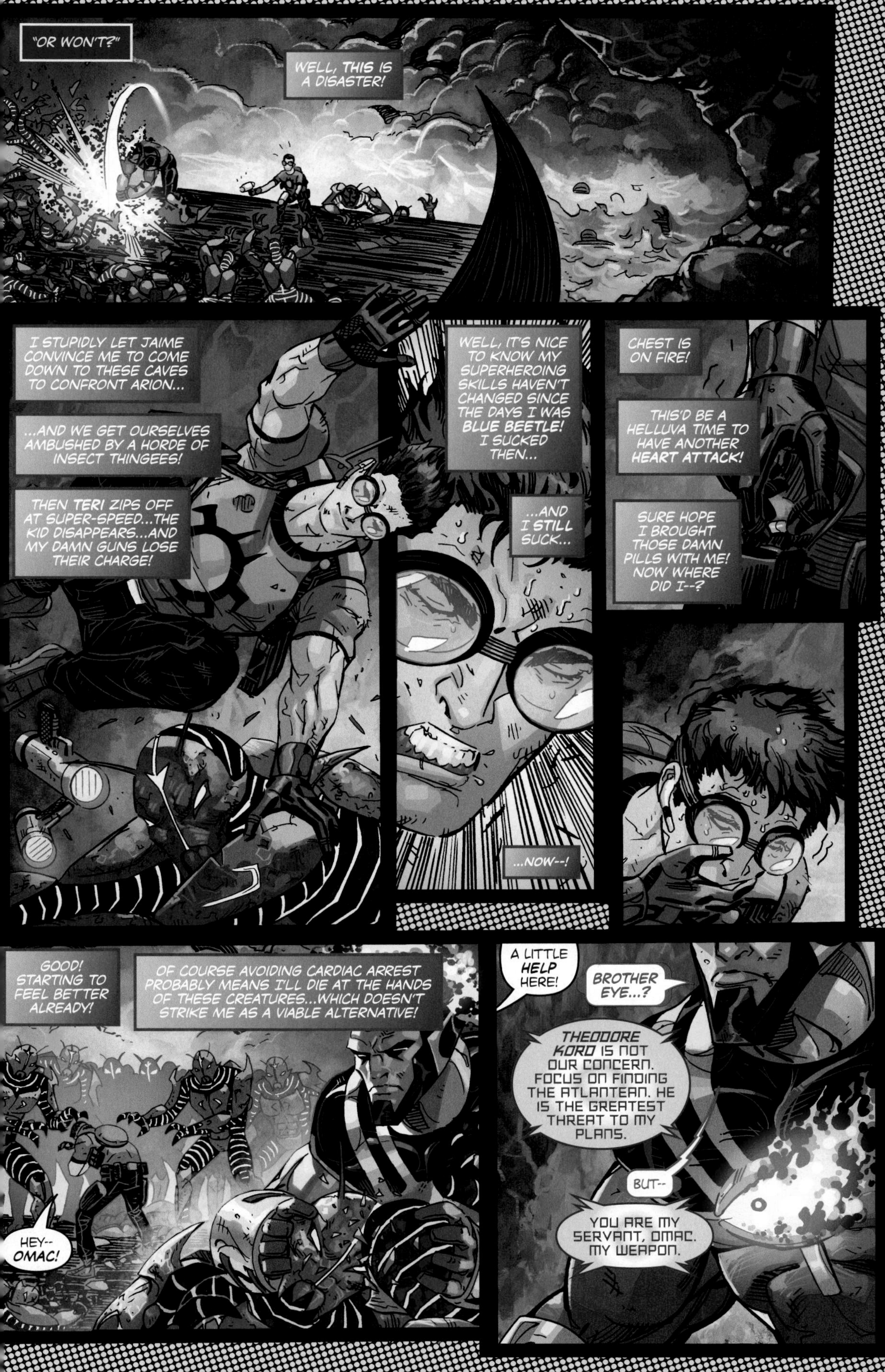
"OR WON'T?"
WELL, THIS IS A DISASTER!
I STUPIDLY LET JAIME CONVINCE ME TO COME DOWN TO THESE CAVES TO CONFRONT ARION...
...AND WE GET OURSELVES AMBUSHED BY A HORDE OF INSECT THINGEES!
THEN TERI ZIPS OFF AT SUPER-SPEED...THE KID DISAPPEARS...AND MY DAMN GUNS LOSE THEIR CHARGE!
WELL, IT'S NICE TO KNOW MY SUPERHEROING SKILLS HAVEN'T CHANGED SINCE THE DAYS I WAS BLUE BEETLE! I SUCKED THEN...
...AND I STILL SUCK...
...NOW--!
CHEST IS ON FIRE!
THIS'D BE A HELLUVA TIME TO HAVE ANOTHER HEART ATTACK!
SURE HOPE I BROUGHT THOSE DAMN PILLS WITH ME! NOW WHERE DID I--?
GOOD! STARTING TO FEEL BETTER ALREADY!
OF COURSE AVOIDING CARDIAC ARREST PROBABLY MEANS I'LL DIE AT THE HANDS OF THESE CREATURES...WHICH DOESN'T STRIKE ME AS A VIABLE ALTERNATIVE!
HEY-- OMAC!
A LITTLE HELP HERE!
BROTHER EYE...?
THEODORE KORD IS NOT OUR CONCERN. FOCUS ON FINDING THE ATLANTEAN. HE IS THE GREATEST THREAT TO MY PLANS.
BUT--
YOU ARE MY SERVANT, OMAC. MY WEAPON.

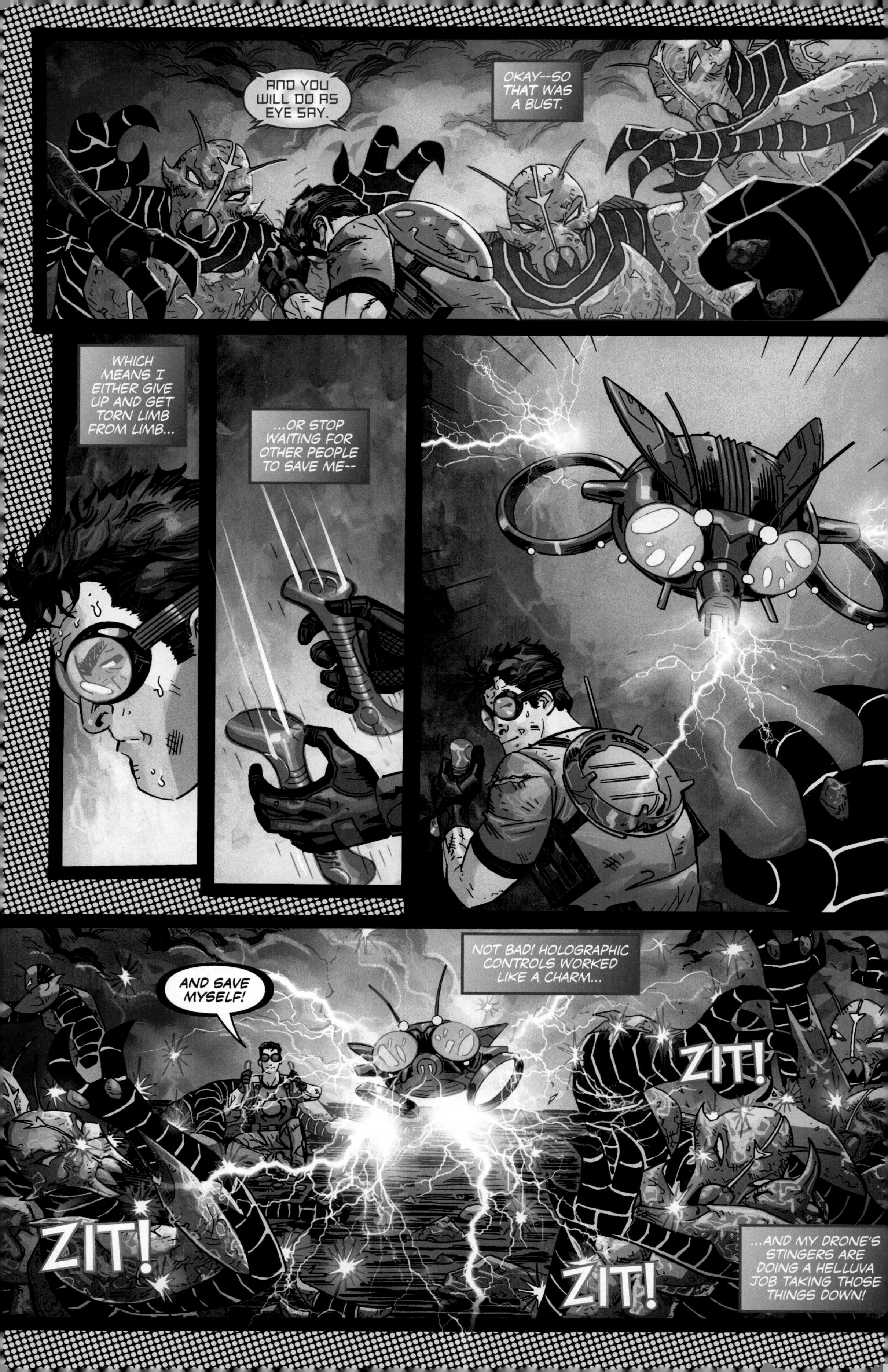
AND YOU WILL DO AS EYE SAY.
OKAY--SO THAT WAS A BUST.
WHICH MEANS I EITHER GIVE UP AND GET TORN LIMB FROM LIMB...
...OR STOP WAITING FOR OTHER PEOPLE TO SAVE ME--
AND SAVE MYSELF!
NOT BAD! HOLOGRAPHIC CONTROLS WORKED LIKE A CHARM...
ZIT!
ZIT!
ZIT!
...AND MY DRONE'S STINGERS ARE DOING A HELLUVA JOB TAKING THOSE THINGS DOWN!

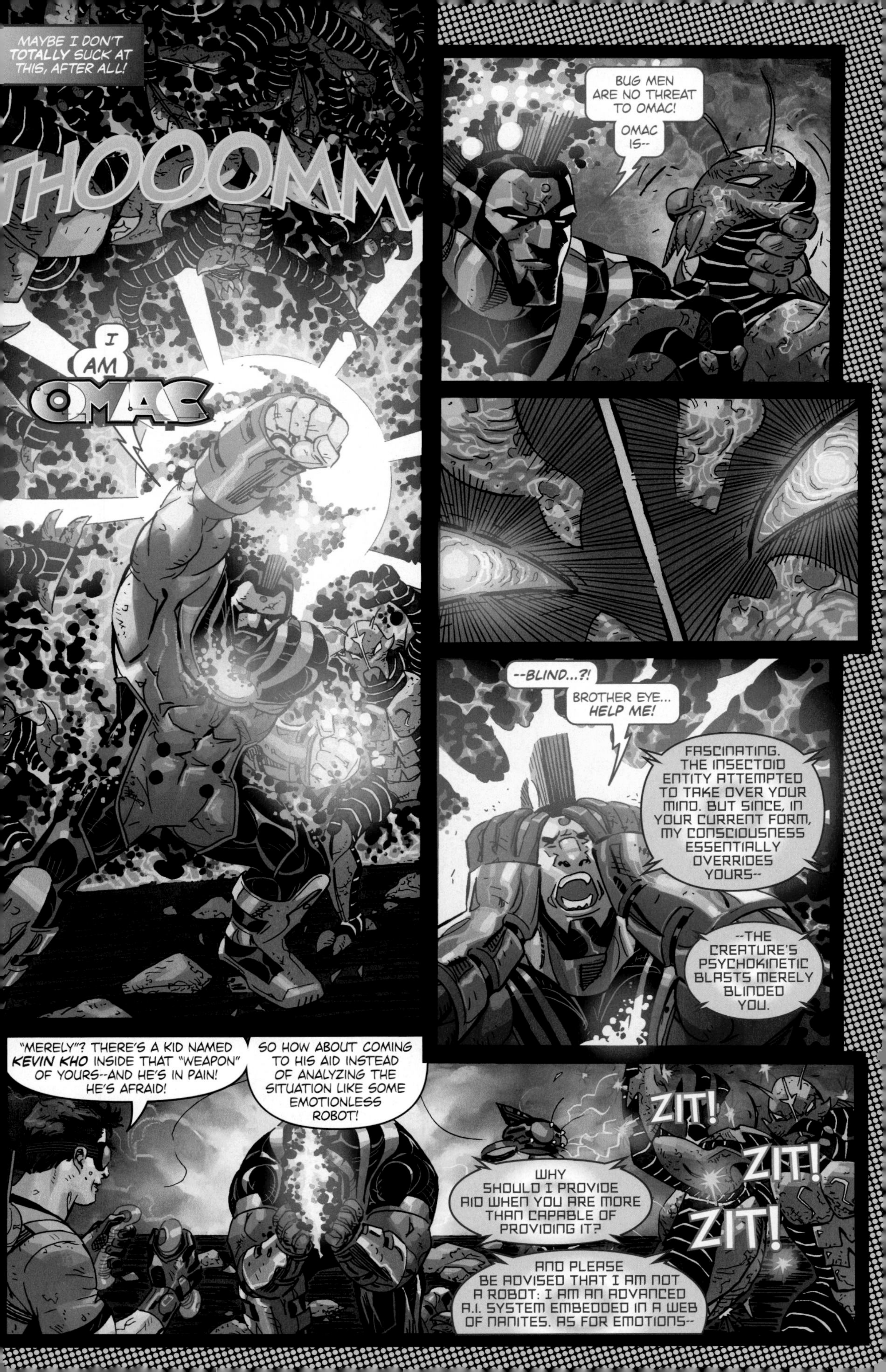
MAYBE I DON'T TOTALLY SUCK AT THIS, AFTER ALL!
THOOOMM
I AM O.M.A.C.
BUG MEN ARE NO THREAT TO OMAC!
OMAC IS--
--BLIND...?!
BROTHER EYE... HELP ME!
FASCINATING. THE INSECTOID ENTITY ATTEMPTED TO TAKE OVER YOUR MIND. BUT SINCE, IN YOUR CURRENT FORM, MY CONSCIOUSNESS ESSENTIALLY OVERRIDES YOURS--
--THE CREATURE'S PSYCHOKINETIC BLASTS MERELY BLINDED YOU.
"MERELY"? THERE'S A KID NAMED KEVIN KHO INSIDE THAT "WEAPON" OF YOURS--AND HE'S IN PAIN! HE'S AFRAID!
SO HOW ABOUT COMING TO HIS AID INSTEAD OF ANALYZING THE SITUATION LIKE SOME EMOTIONLESS ROBOT!
ZIT!
ZIT!
ZIT!
WHY SHOULD I PROVIDE AID WHEN YOU ARE MORE THAN CAPABLE OF PROVIDING IT?
AND PLEASE BE ADVISED THAT I AM NOT A ROBOT: I AM AN ADVANCED A.I. SYSTEM EMBEDDED IN A WEB OF NANITES. AS FOR EMOTIONS--

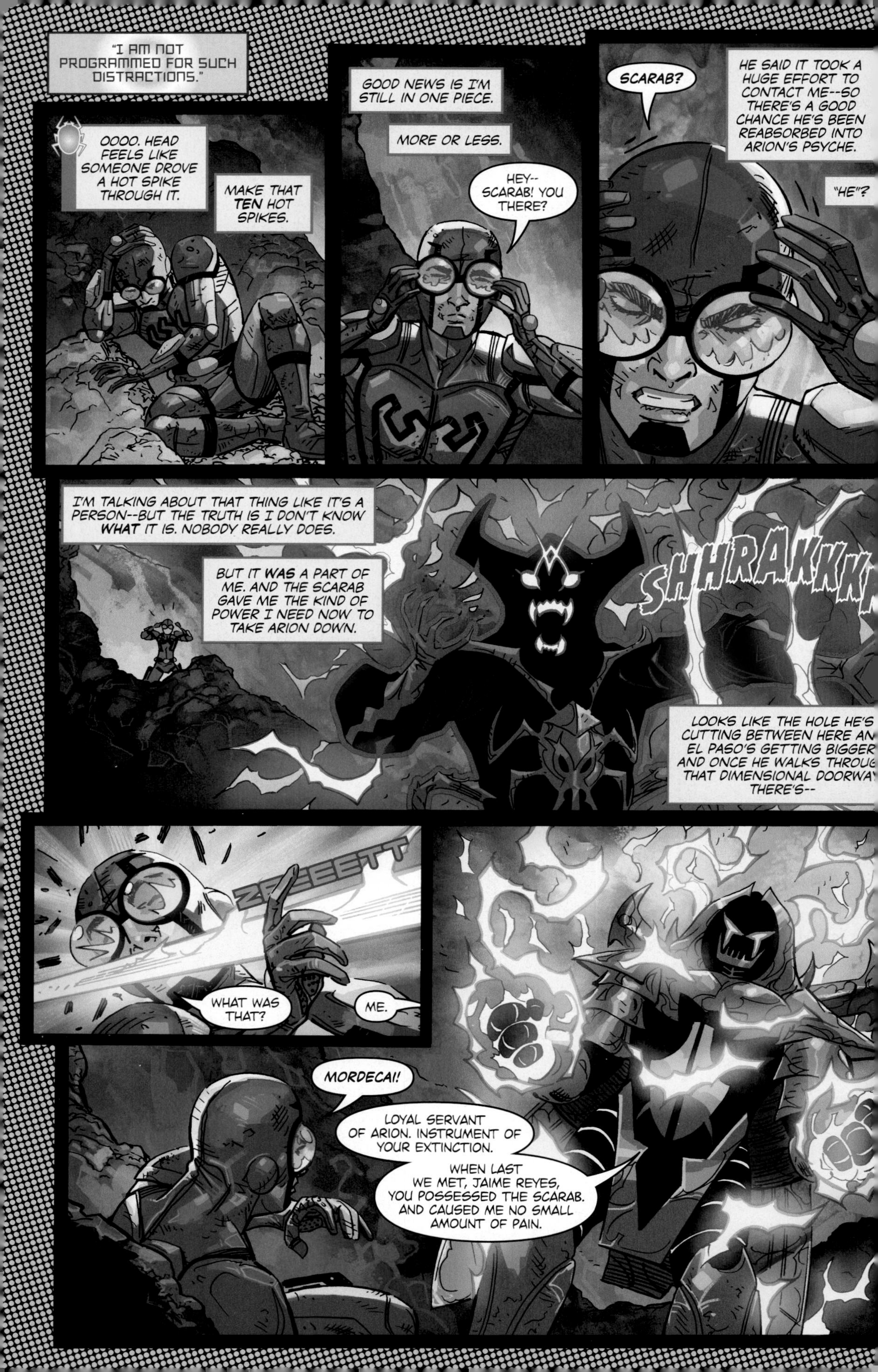
"I AM NOT PROGRAMMED FOR SUCH DISTRACTIONS."
OOOO. HEAD FEELS LIKE SOMEONE DROVE A HOT SPIKE THROUGH IT.
MAKE THAT TEN HOT SPIKES.
GOOD NEWS IS I'M STILL IN ONE PIECE.
MORE OR LESS.
HEY-- SCARAB! YOU THERE?
SCARAB?
HE SAID IT TOOK A HUGE EFFORT TO CONTACT ME--SO THERE'S A GOOD CHANCE HE'S BEEN REABSORBED INTO ARION'S PSYCHE.
"HE"?
I'M TALKING ABOUT THAT THING LIKE IT'S A PERSON--BUT THE TRUTH IS I DON'T KNOW WHAT IT IS. NOBODY REALLY DOES.
BUT IT WAS A PART OF ME. AND THE SCARAB GAVE ME THE KIND OF POWER I NEED NOW TO TAKE ARION DOWN.
SHHRAKKK
LOOKS LIKE THE HOLE HE'S CUTTING BETWEEN HERE AN EL PASO'S GETTING BIGGER AND ONCE HE WALKS THROUG THAT DIMENSIONAL DOORWAY THERE'S--
ZREEETT
WHAT WAS THAT?
ME.
MORDECAI!
LOYAL SERVANT OF ARION. INSTRUMENT OF YOUR EXTINCTION.
WHEN LAST WE MET, JAIME REYES, YOU POSSESSED THE SCARAB. AND CAUSED ME NO SMALL AMOUNT OF PAIN.

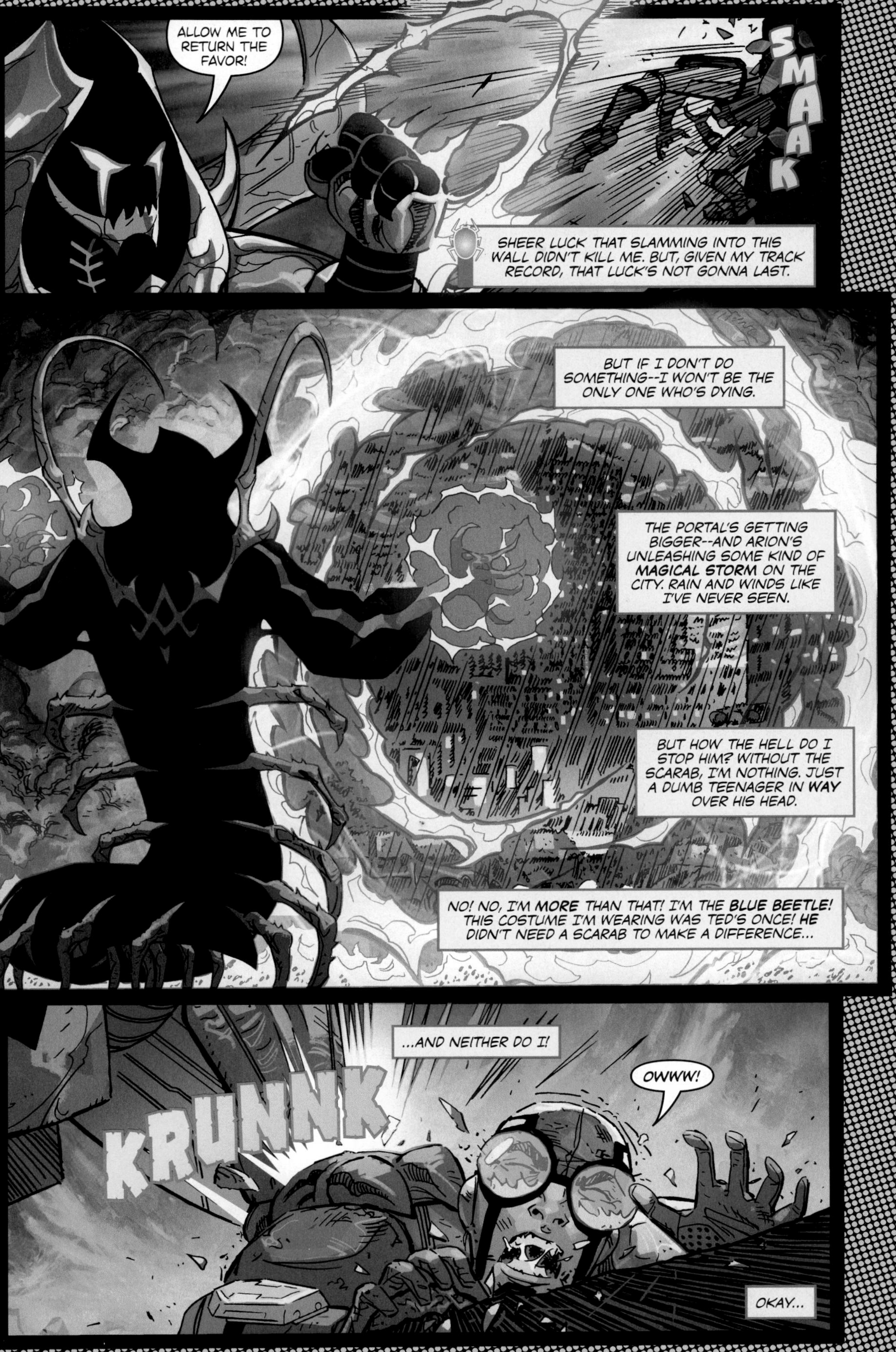
ALLOW ME TO RETURN THE FAVOR!
SMAAK
SHEER LUCK THAT SLAMMING INTO THIS WALL DIDN'T KILL ME. BUT, GIVEN MY TRACK RECORD, THAT LUCK'S NOT GONNA LAST.
BUT IF I DON'T DO SOMETHING--I WON'T BE THE ONLY ONE WHO'S DYING.
THE PORTAL'S GETTING BIGGER--AND ARION'S UNLEASHING SOME KIND OF MAGICAL STORM ON THE CITY. RAIN AND WINDS LIKE I'VE NEVER SEEN.
BUT HOW THE HELL DO I STOP HIM? WITHOUT THE SCARAB, I'M NOTHING. JUST A DUMB TEENAGER IN WAY OVER HIS HEAD.
NO! NO, I'M MORE THAN THAT! I'M THE BLUE BEETLE! THIS COSTUME I'M WEARING WAS TED'S ONCE! HE DIDN'T NEED A SCARAB TO MAKE A DIFFERENCE...
...AND NEITHER DO I!
OWWW!
KRUNNK
OKAY...

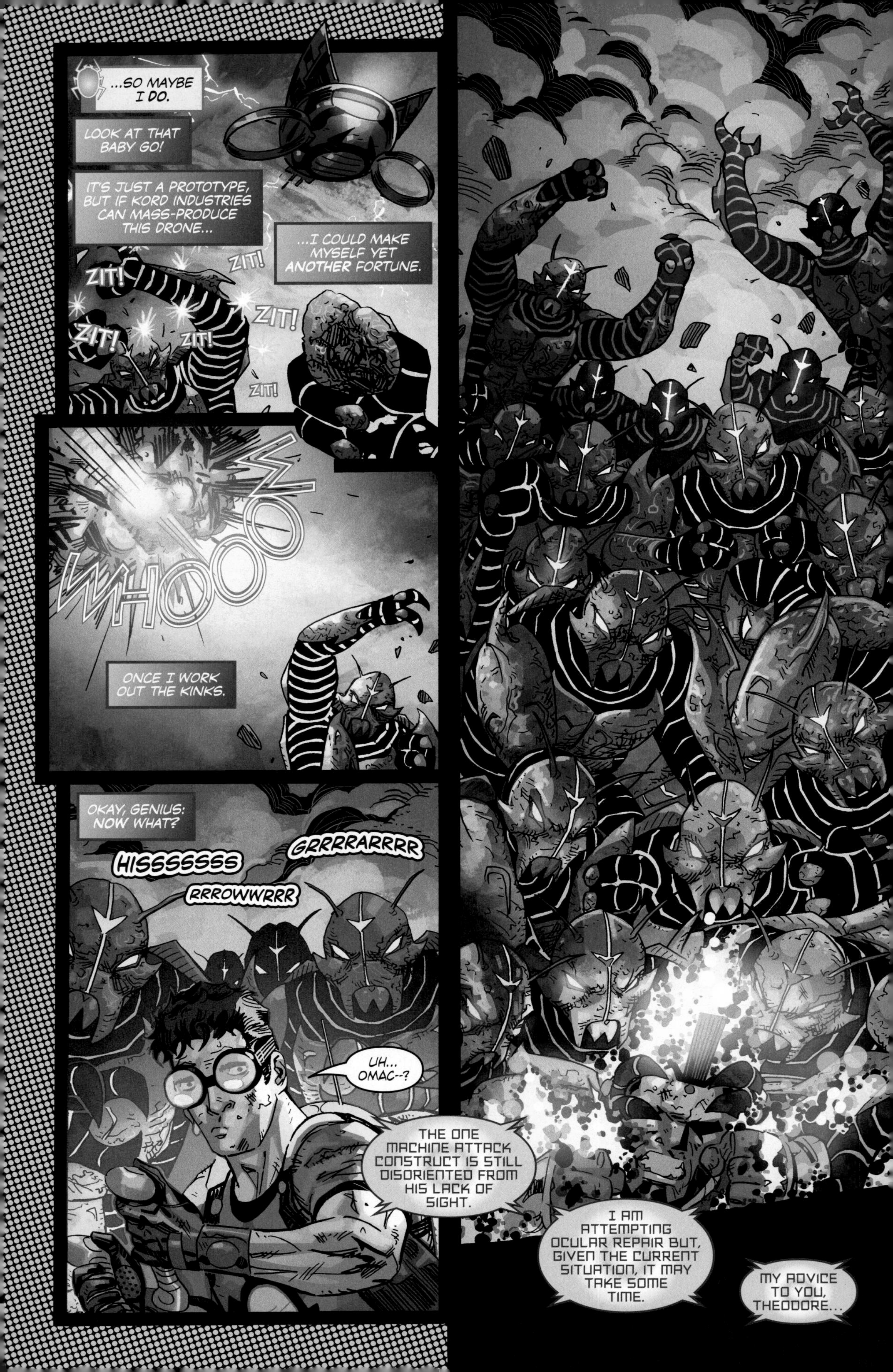

...SO MAYBE I DO.
LOOK AT THAT BABY GO!
IT'S JUST A PROTOTYPE, BUT IF KORD INDUSTRIES CAN MASS-PRODUCE THIS DRONE...
...I COULD MAKE MYSELF YET ANOTHER FORTUNE.
ZIT!
ZIT!
ZIT!
ZIT!
ZIT!
ZIT!
WHOOOOOOSH
ONCE I WORK OUT THE KINKS.
OKAY, GENIUS: NOW WHAT?
HISSSSSSS
GRRRRARRRR
RRROWWRRR
UH... OMAC--?
THE ONE MACHINE ATTACK CONSTRUCT IS STILL DISORIENTED FROM HIS LACK OF SIGHT.
I AM ATTEMPTING OCULAR REPAIR BUT, GIVEN THE CURRENT SITUATION, IT MAY TAKE SOME TIME.
MY ADVICE TO YOU, THEODORE...

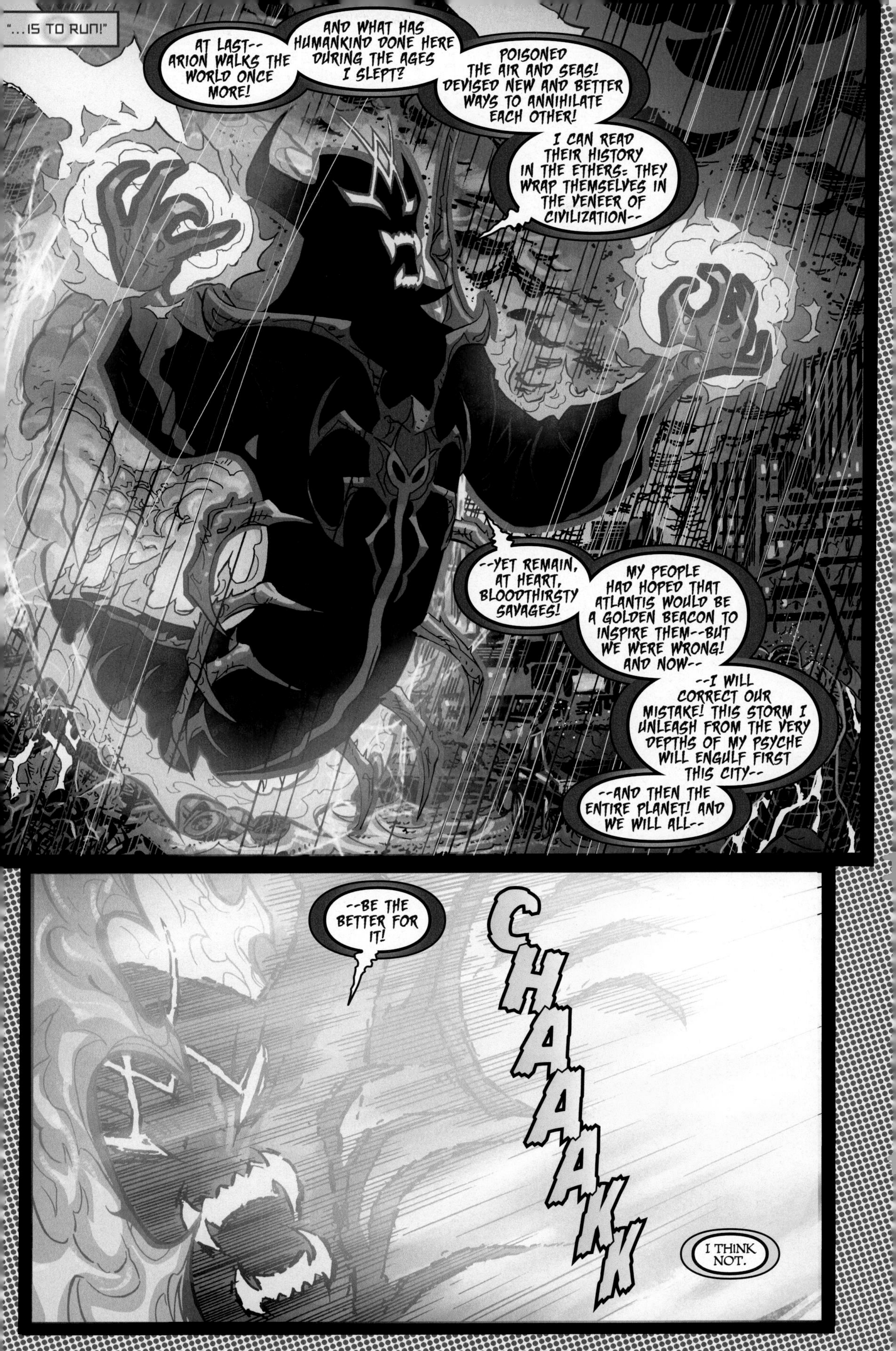
"...IS TO RUN!"
AT LAST--ARION WALKS THE WORLD ONCE MORE!
AND WHAT HAS HUMANKIND DONE HERE DURING THE AGES I SLEPT?
POISONED THE AIR AND SEAS! DEVISED NEW AND BETTER WAYS TO ANNIHILATE EACH OTHER!
I CAN READ THEIR HISTORY IN THE ETHERS: THEY WRAP THEMSELVES IN THE VENEER OF CIVILIZATION--
--YET REMAIN, AT HEART, BLOODTHIRSTY SAVAGES!
MY PEOPLE HAD HOPED THAT ATLANTIS WOULD BE A GOLDEN BEACON TO INSPIRE THEM--BUT WE WERE WRONG! AND NOW--
--I WILL CORRECT OUR MISTAKE! THIS STORM I UNLEASH FROM THE VERY DEPTHS OF MY PSYCHE WILL ENGULF FIRST THIS CITY--
--AND THEN THE ENTIRE PLANET! AND WE WILL ALL--
--BE THE BETTER FOR IT!
CHAAAKK
I THINK NOT.

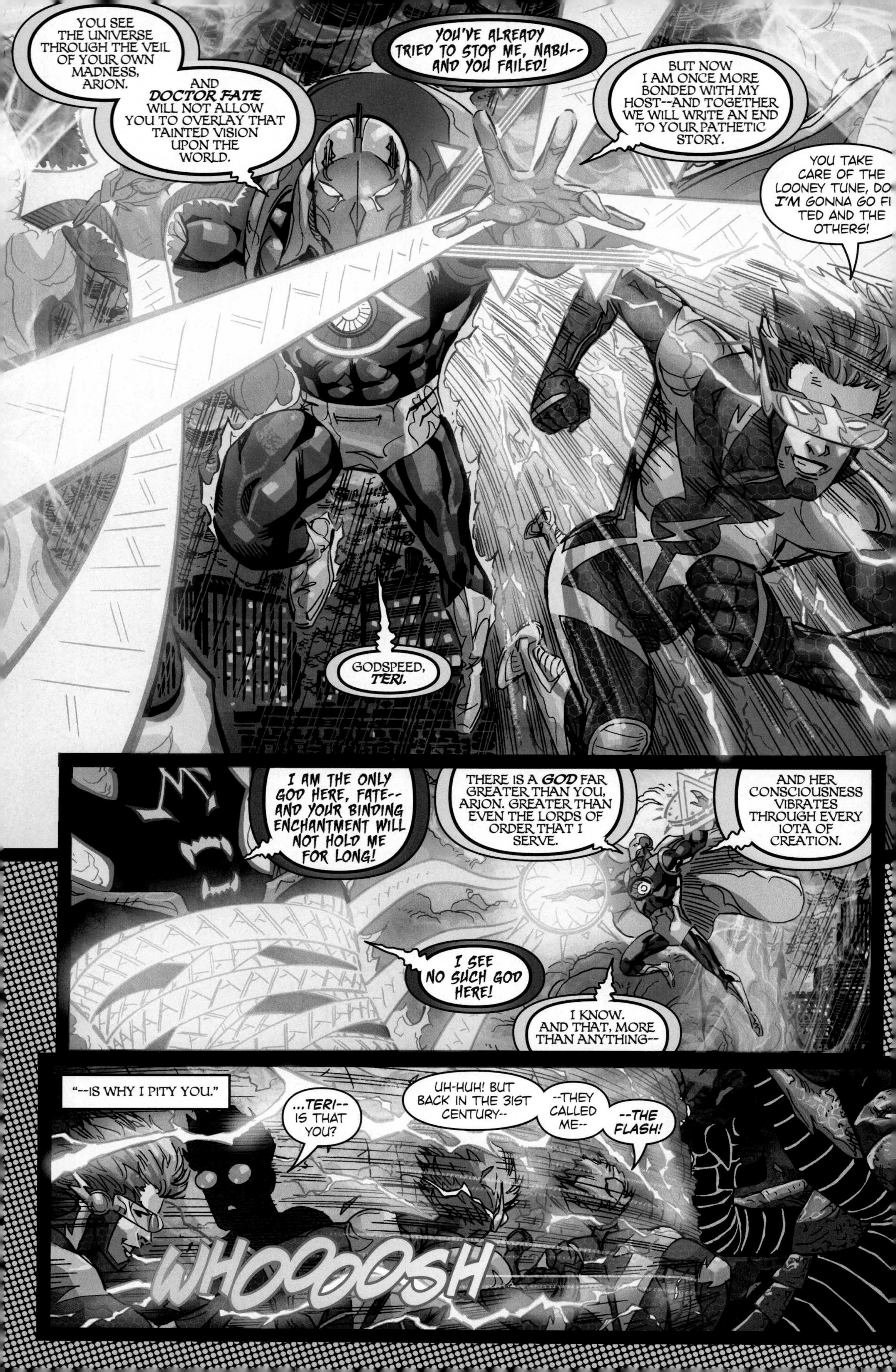
YOU SEE THE UNIVERSE THROUGH THE VEIL OF YOUR OWN MADNESS, ARION.
AND DOCTOR FATE WILL NOT ALLOW YOU TO OVERLAY THAT TAINTED VISION UPON THE WORLD.
YOU'VE ALREADY TRIED TO STOP ME, NABU-- AND YOU FAILED!
BUT NOW I AM ONCE MORE BONDED WITH MY HOST--AND TOGETHER WE WILL WRITE AN END TO YOUR PATHETIC STORY.
YOU TAKE CARE OF THE LOONEY TUNE, DO I'M GONNA GO FI TED AND THE OTHERS!
GODSPEED, TERI.
I AM THE ONLY GOD HERE, FATE-- AND YOUR BINDING ENCHANTMENT WILL NOT HOLD ME FOR LONG!
THERE IS A GOD FAR GREATER THAN YOU, ARION. GREATER THAN EVEN THE LORDS OF ORDER THAT I SERVE.
AND HER CONSCIOUSNESS VIBRATES THROUGH EVERY IOTA OF CREATION.
I SEE NO SUCH GOD HERE!
I KNOW. AND THAT, MORE THAN ANYTHING--
"--IS WHY I PITY YOU."
...TERI-- IS THAT YOU?
UH-HUH! BUT BACK IN THE 31ST CENTURY--
--THEY CALLED ME--
--THE FLASH!
WHOOOOOSH

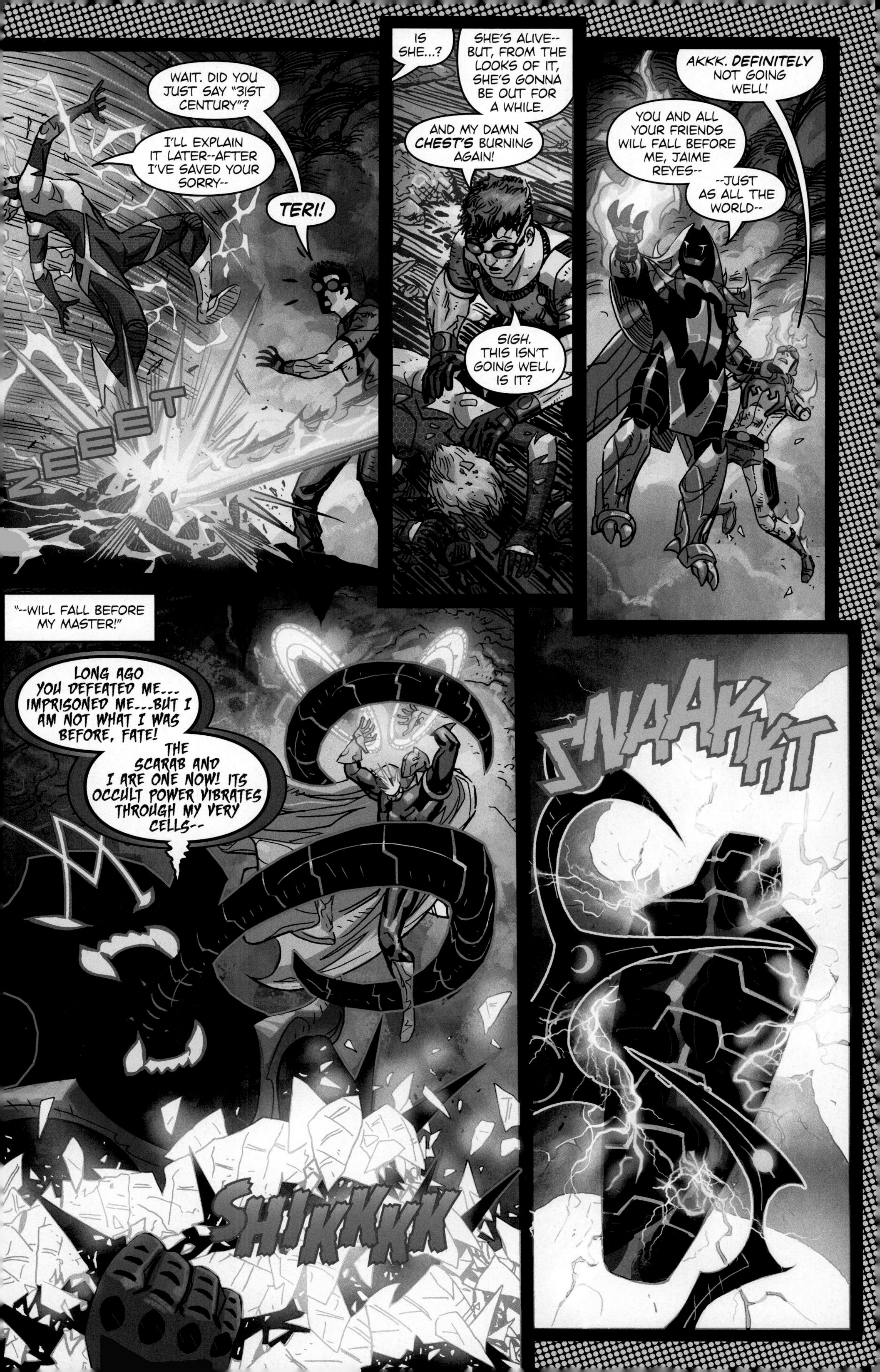
WAIT. DID YOU JUST SAY "31ST CENTURY"?
I'LL EXPLAIN IT LATER--AFTER I'VE SAVED YOUR SORRY--
TERI!
ZEEEET
IS SHE...?
SHE'S ALIVE--BUT, FROM THE LOOKS OF IT, SHE'S GONNA BE OUT FOR A WHILE.
AND MY DAMN CHEST'S BURNING AGAIN!
SIGH. THIS ISN'T GOING WELL, IS IT?
AKKK. DEFINITELY NOT GOING WELL!
YOU AND ALL YOUR FRIENDS WILL FALL BEFORE ME, JAIME REYES--
--JUST AS ALL THE WORLD--
"--WILL FALL BEFORE MY MASTER!"
LONG AGO YOU DEFEATED ME... IMPRISONED ME...BUT I AM NOT WHAT I WAS BEFORE, FATE!
THE SCARAB AND I ARE ONE NOW! ITS OCCULT POWER VIBRATES THROUGH MY VERY CELLS--
SHIKKKK
SNAAKKT

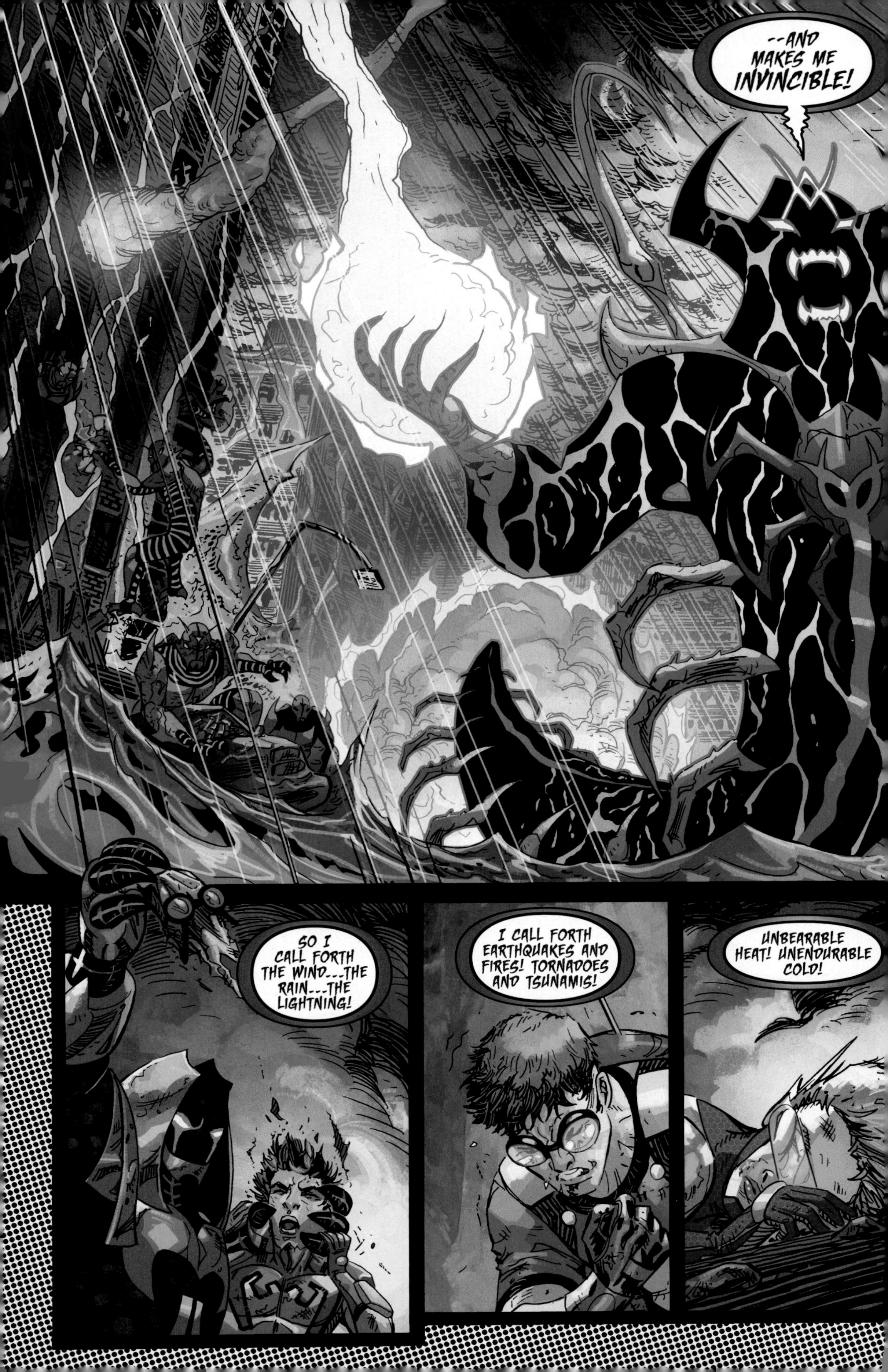
--AND MAKES ME INVINCIBLE!
SO I CALL FORTH THE WIND--THE RAIN--THE LIGHTNING!
I CALL FORTH EARTHQUAKES AND FIRES! TORNADOES AND TSUNAMIS!
UNBEARABLE HEAT! UNENDURABLE COLD!

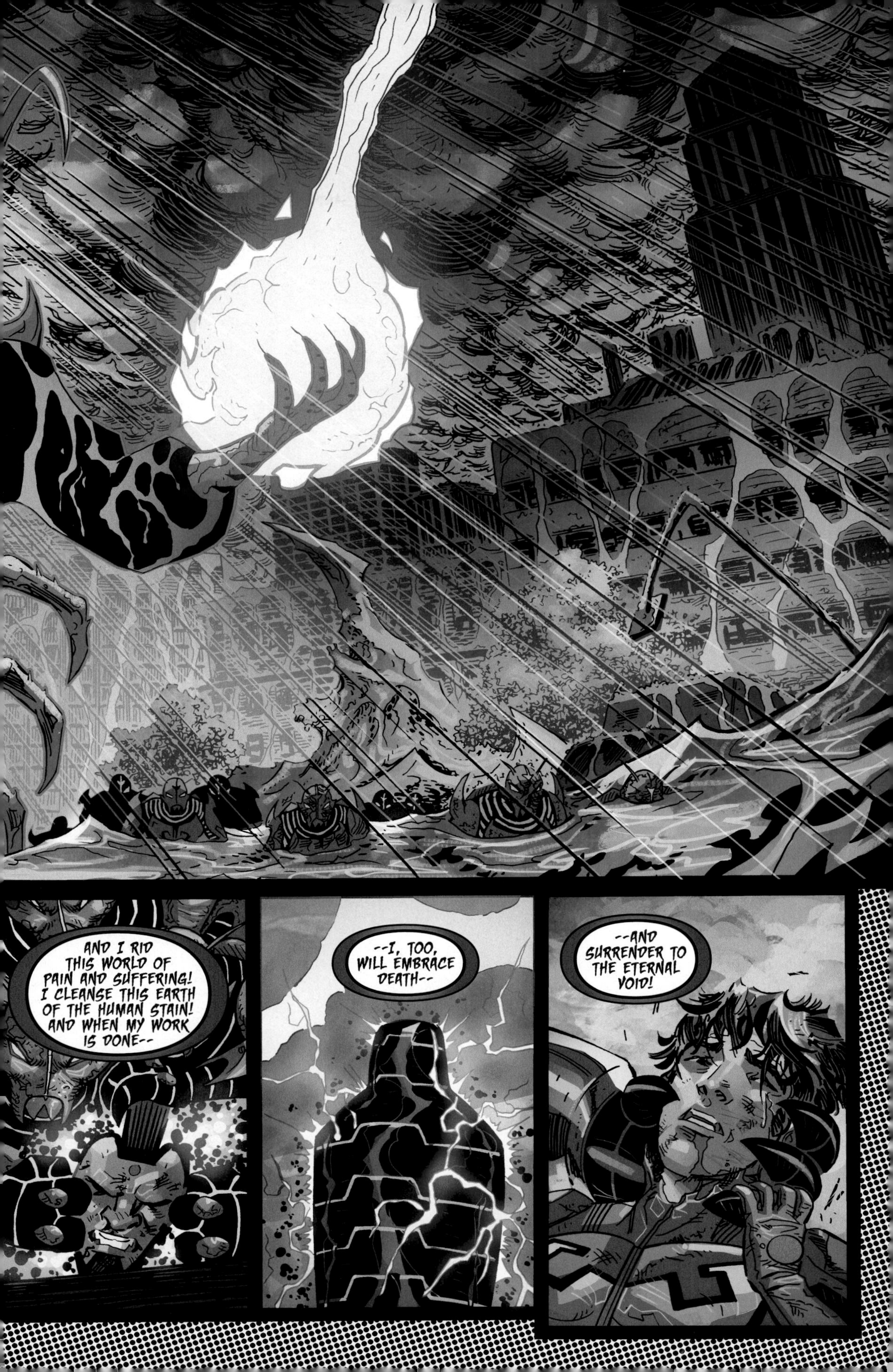
AND I RID THIS WORLD OF PAIN AND SUFFERING! I CLEANSE THIS EARTH OF THE HUMAN STAIN! AND WHEN MY WORK IS DONE--
--I, TOO, WILL EMBRACE DEATH--
--AND SURRENDER TO THE ETERNAL VOID!

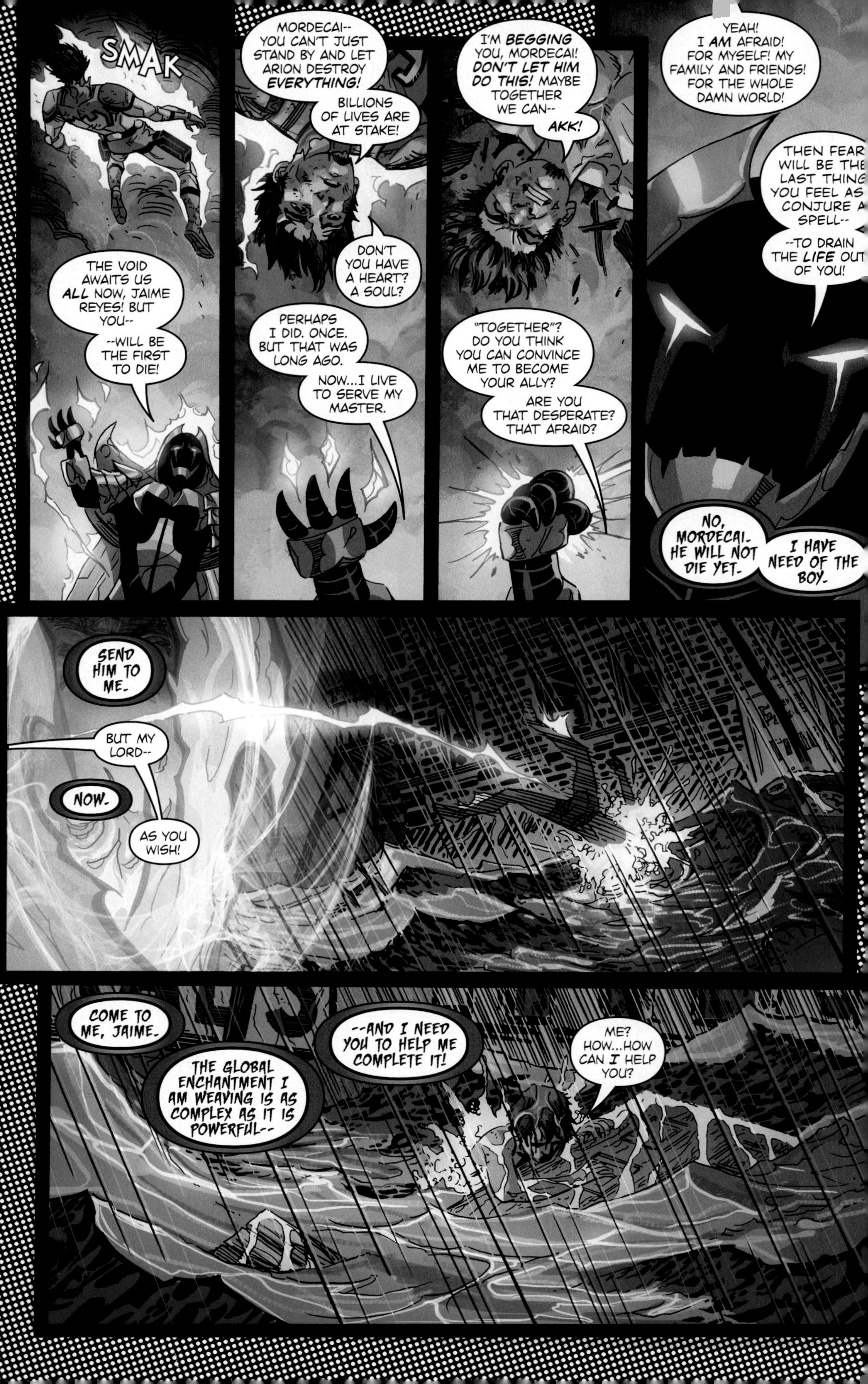
SMAK
THE VOID AWAITS US ALL NOW, JAIME REYES! BUT YOU--
--WILL BE THE FIRST TO DIE!
MORDECAI-- YOU CAN'T JUST STAND BY AND LET ARION DESTROY EVERYTHING!
BILLIONS OF LIVES ARE AT STAKE!
DON'T YOU HAVE A HEART? A SOUL?
PERHAPS I DID. ONCE. BUT THAT WAS LONG AGO.
NOW...I LIVE TO SERVE MY MASTER.
I'M BEGGING YOU, MORDECAI! DON'T LET HIM DO THIS! MAYBE TOGETHER WE CAN--
AKK!
"TOGETHER"? DO YOU THINK YOU CAN CONVINCE ME TO BECOME YOUR ALLY?
ARE YOU THAT DESPERATE? THAT AFRAID?
YEAH! I AM AFRAID! FOR MYSELF! MY FAMILY AND FRIENDS! FOR THE WHOLE DAMN WORLD!
THEN FEAR WILL BE THE LAST THING YOU FEEL AS CONJURE A SPELL--
--TO DRAIN THE LIFE OUT OF YOU!
NO, MORDECAI. HE WILL NOT DIE YET.
I HAVE NEED OF THE BOY.
SEND HIM TO ME.
BUT MY LORD--
NOW.
AS YOU WISH!
COME TO ME, JAIME.
THE GLOBAL ENCHANTMENT I AM WEAVING IS AS COMPLEX AS IT IS POWERFUL--
--AND I NEED YOU TO HELP ME COMPLETE IT!
ME? HOW...HOW CAN I HELP YOU?

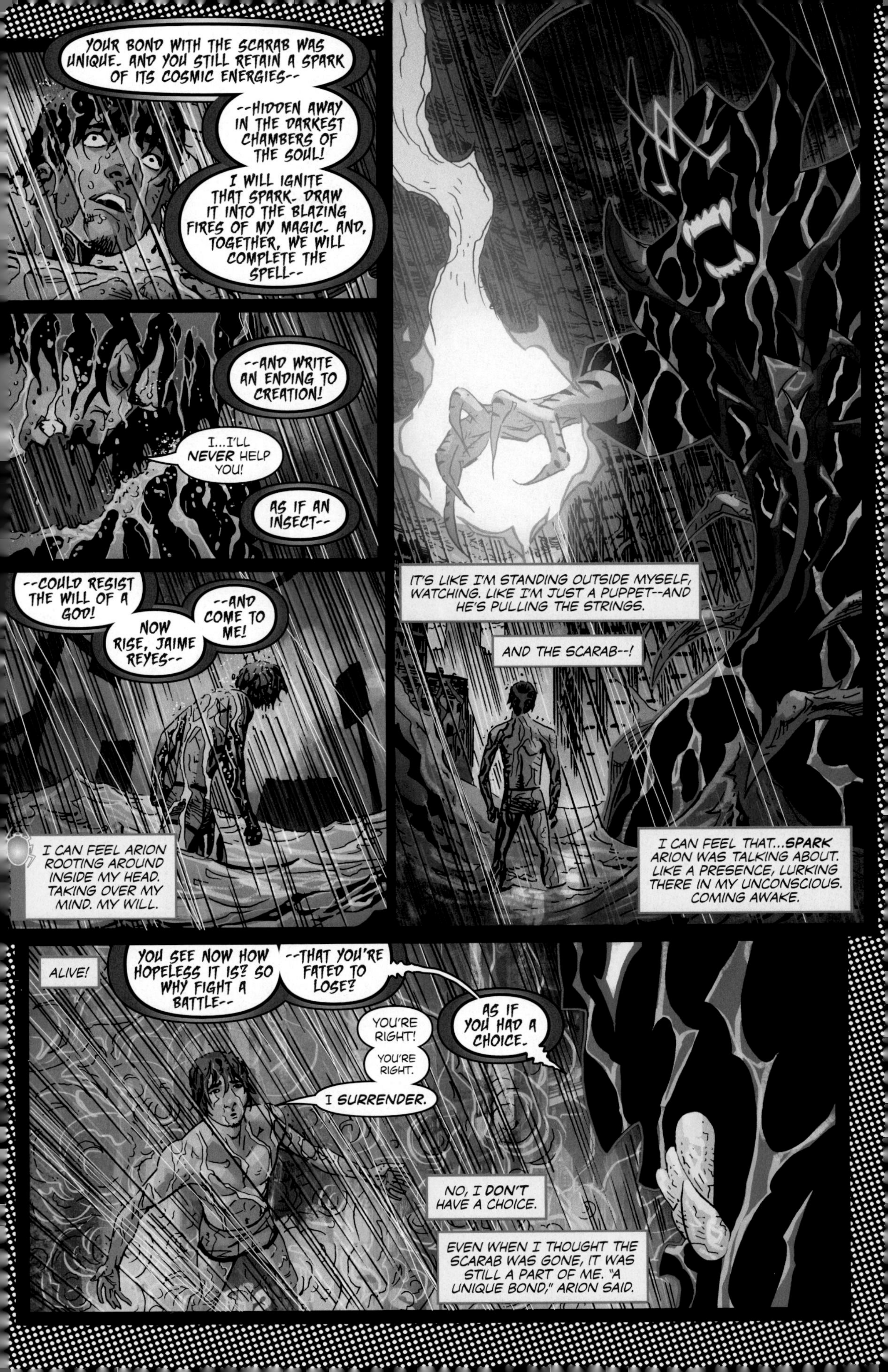
YOUR BOND WITH THE SCARAB WAS UNIQUE. AND YOU STILL RETAIN A SPARK OF ITS COSMIC ENERGIES--
--HIDDEN AWAY IN THE DARKEST CHAMBERS OF THE SOUL!
I WILL IGNITE THAT SPARK. DRAW IT INTO THE BLAZING FIRES OF MY MAGIC. AND, TOGETHER, WE WILL COMPLETE THE SPELL--
--AND WRITE AN ENDING TO CREATION!
I...I'LL NEVER HELP YOU!
AS IF AN INSECT--
--COULD RESIST THE WILL OF A GOD!
NOW RISE, JAIME REYES--
--AND COME TO ME!
I CAN FEEL ARION ROOTING AROUND INSIDE MY HEAD. TAKING OVER MY MIND. MY WILL.
IT'S LIKE I'M STANDING OUTSIDE MYSELF, WATCHING. LIKE I'M JUST A PUPPET--AND HE'S PULLING THE STRINGS.
AND THE SCARAB--!
I CAN FEEL THAT...SPARK ARION WAS TALKING ABOUT. LIKE A PRESENCE, LURKING THERE IN MY UNCONSCIOUS. COMING AWAKE.
ALIVE!
YOU SEE NOW HOW HOPELESS IT IS? SO WHY FIGHT A BATTLE--
--THAT YOU'RE FATED TO LOSE?
AS IF YOU HAD A CHOICE.
YOU'RE RIGHT!
YOU'RE RIGHT.
I SURRENDER.
NO, I DON'T HAVE A CHOICE.
EVEN WHEN I THOUGHT THE SCARAB WAS GONE, IT WAS STILL A PART OF ME. "A UNIQUE BOND," ARION SAID.

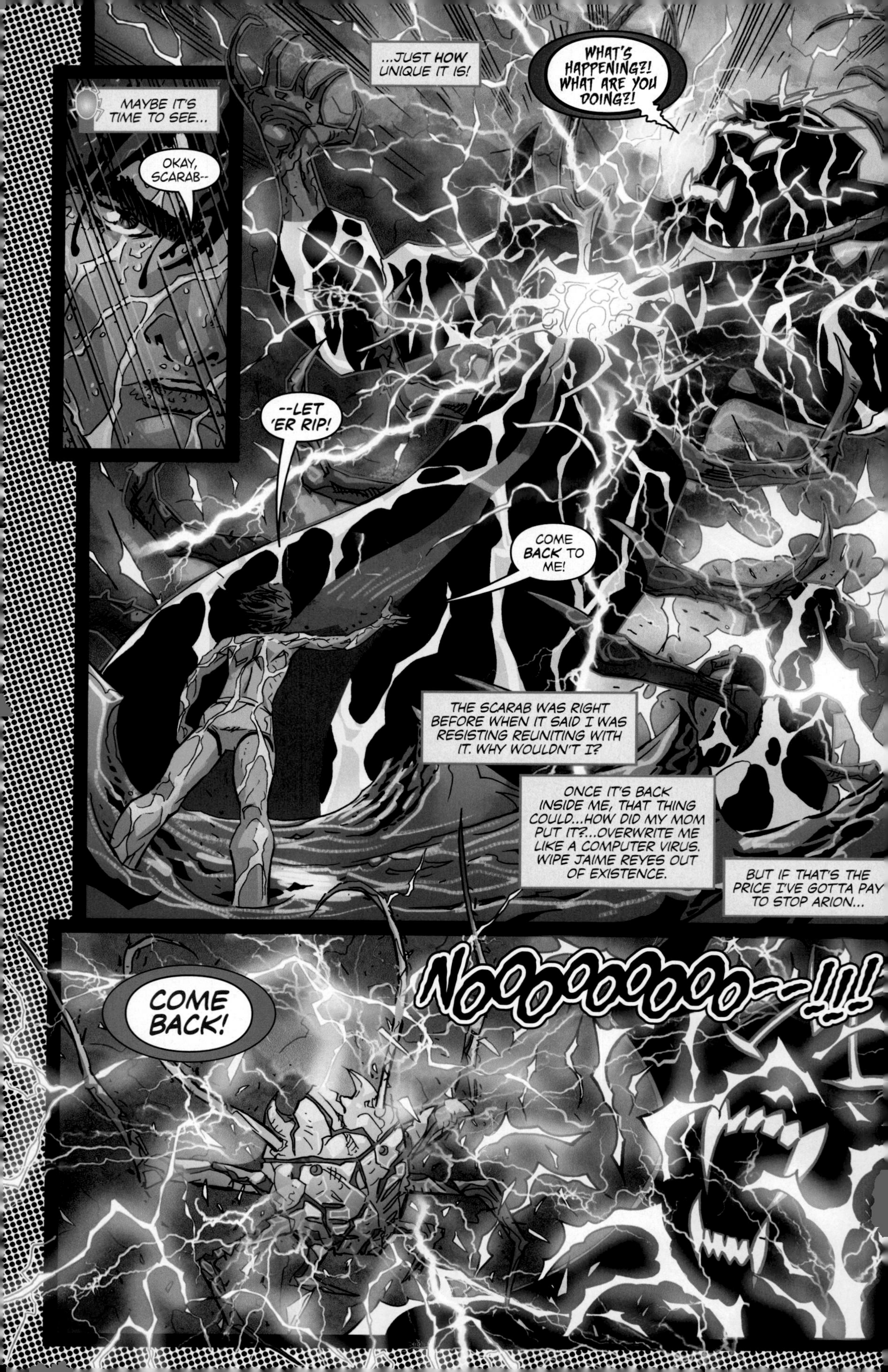
MAYBE IT'S TIME TO SEE...
OKAY, SCARAB--
...JUST HOW UNIQUE IT IS!
WHAT'S HAPPENING?! WHAT ARE YOU DOING?!
--LET 'ER RIP!
COME BACK TO ME!
THE SCARAB WAS RIGHT BEFORE WHEN IT SAID I WAS RESISTING REUNITING WITH IT. WHY WOULDN'T I?
ONCE IT'S BACK INSIDE ME, THAT THING COULD...HOW DID MY MOM PUT IT?...OVERWRITE ME LIKE A COMPUTER VIRUS. WIPE JAIME REYES OUT OF EXISTENCE.
BUT IF THAT'S THE PRICE I'VE GOTTA PAY TO STOP ARION...
COME BACK!
NOOOOOOOOOO--!!!

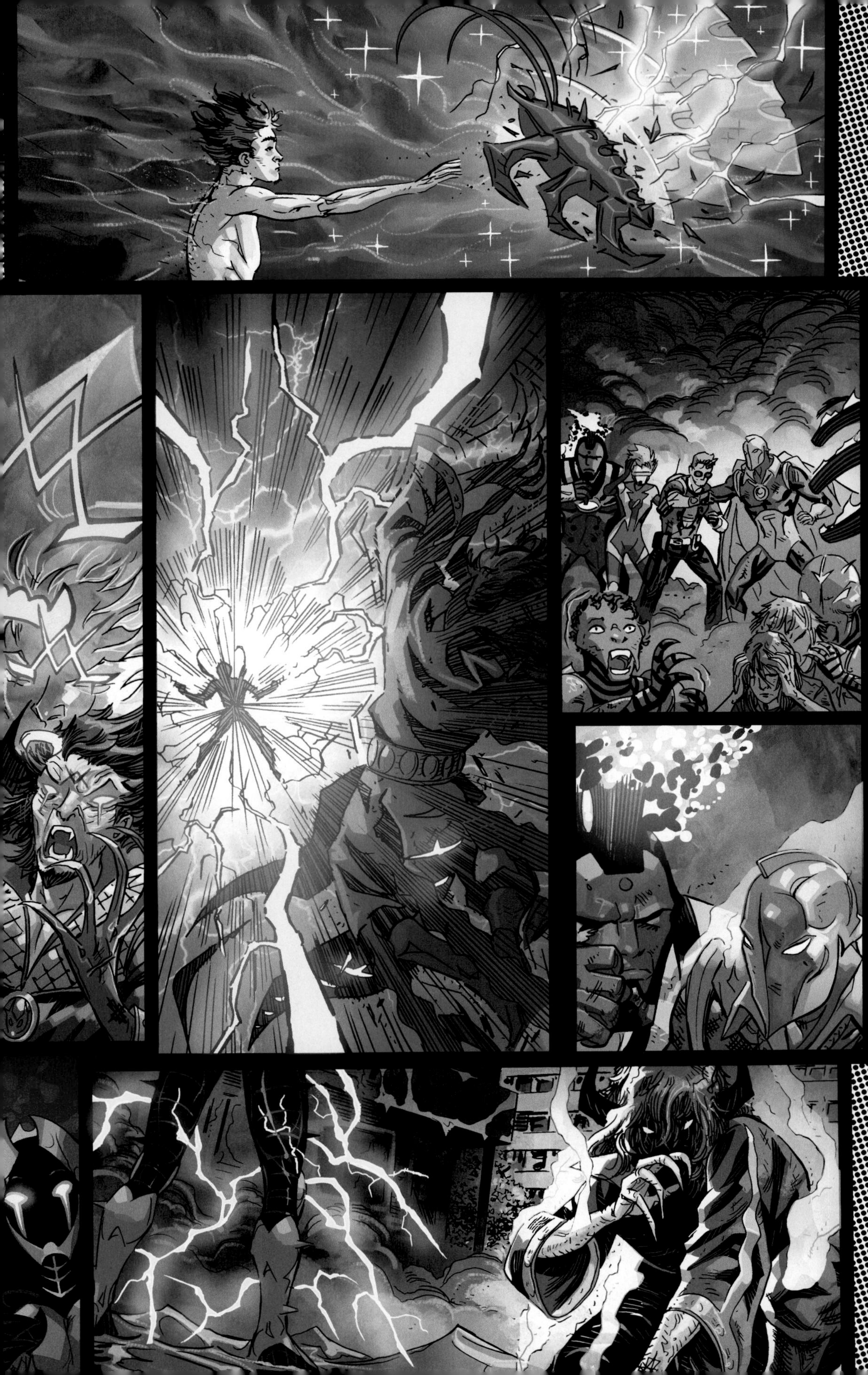

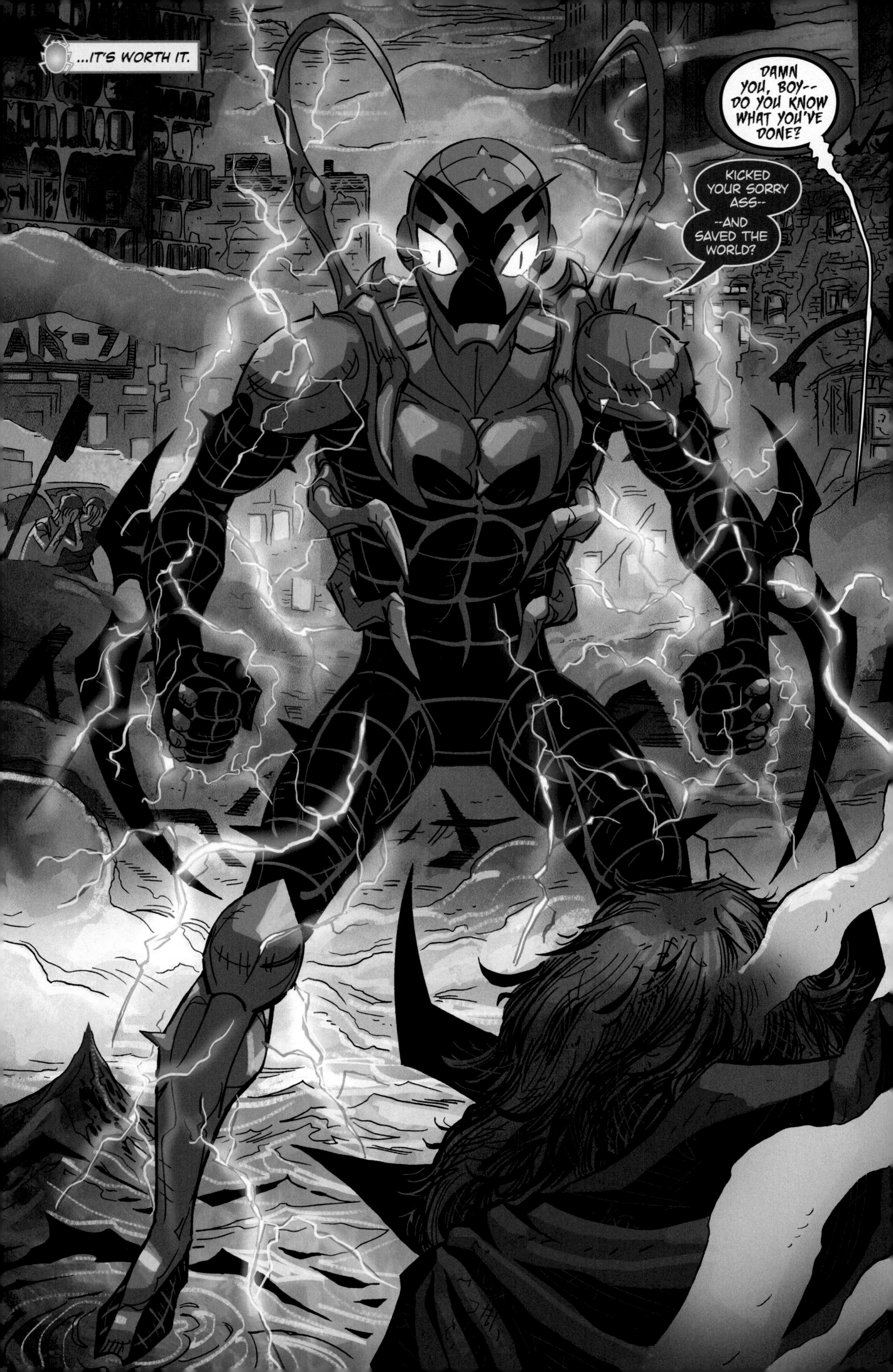
...IT'S WORTH IT.
DAMN YOU, BOY-- DO YOU KNOW WHAT YOU'VE DONE?
KICKED YOUR SORRY ASS--
--AND SAVED THE WORLD?

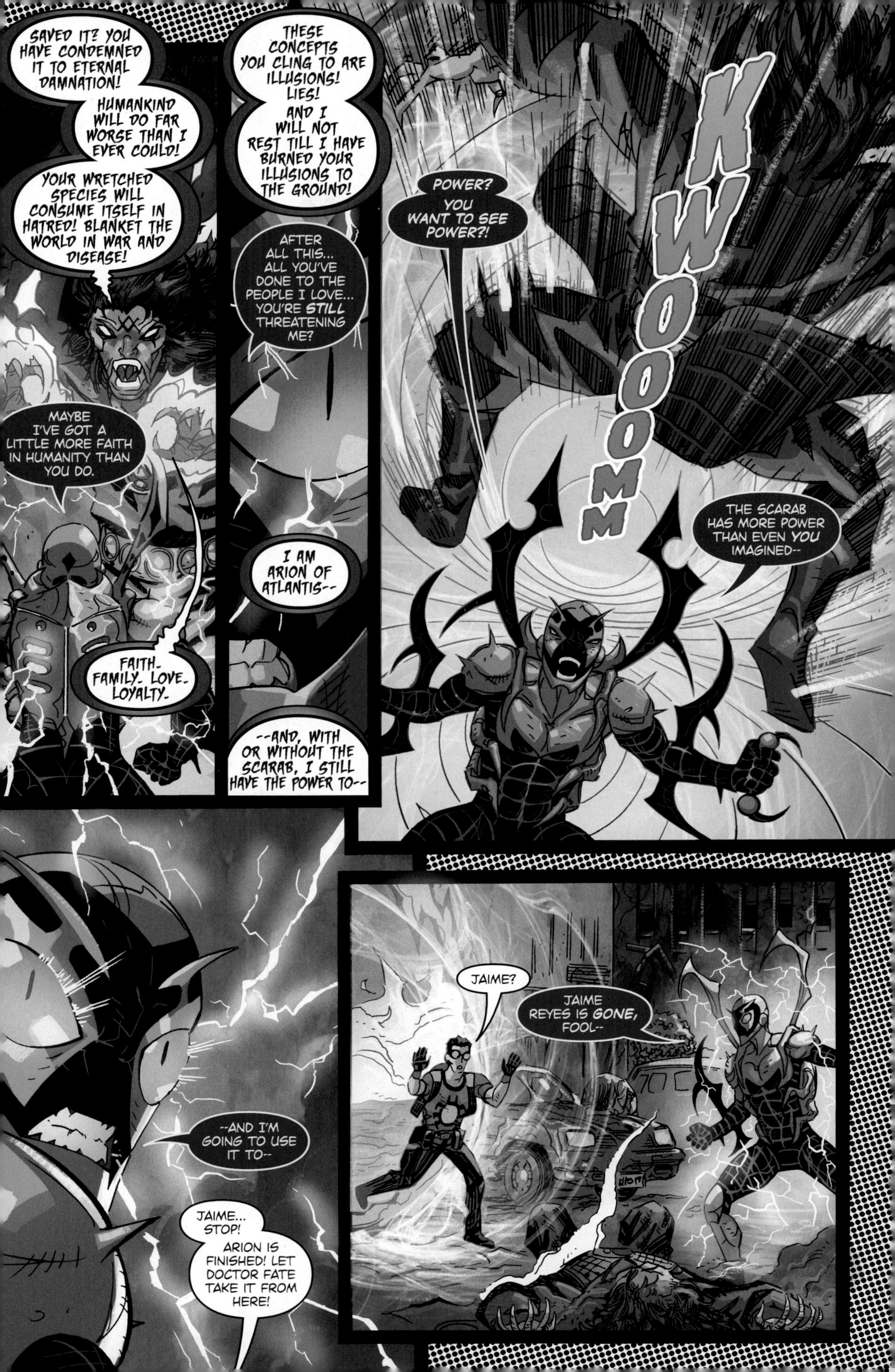
SAVED IT? YOU HAVE CONDEMNED IT TO ETERNAL DAMNATION!
HUMANKIND WILL DO FAR WORSE THAN I EVER COULD!
YOUR WRETCHED SPECIES WILL CONSUME ITSELF IN HATRED! BLANKET THE WORLD IN WAR AND DISEASE!
MAYBE I'VE GOT A LITTLE MORE FAITH IN HUMANITY THAN YOU DO.
FAITH. FAMILY. LOVE. LOYALTY.
THESE CONCEPTS YOU CLING TO ARE ILLUSIONS! LIES!
AND I WILL NOT REST TILL I HAVE BURNED YOUR ILLUSIONS TO THE GROUND!
AFTER ALL THIS... ALL YOU'VE DONE TO THE PEOPLE I LOVE... YOU'RE STILL THREATENING ME?
I AM ARION OF ATLANTIS--
--AND, WITH OR WITHOUT THE SCARAB, I STILL HAVE THE POWER TO--
POWER? YOU WANT TO SEE POWER?!
KKWOOOOOMM
THE SCARAB HAS MORE POWER THAN EVEN YOU IMAGINED--
--AND I'M GOING TO USE IT TO--
JAIME... STOP!
ARION IS FINISHED! LET DOCTOR FATE TAKE IT FROM HERE!
JAIME?
JAIME REYES IS GONE, FOOL--

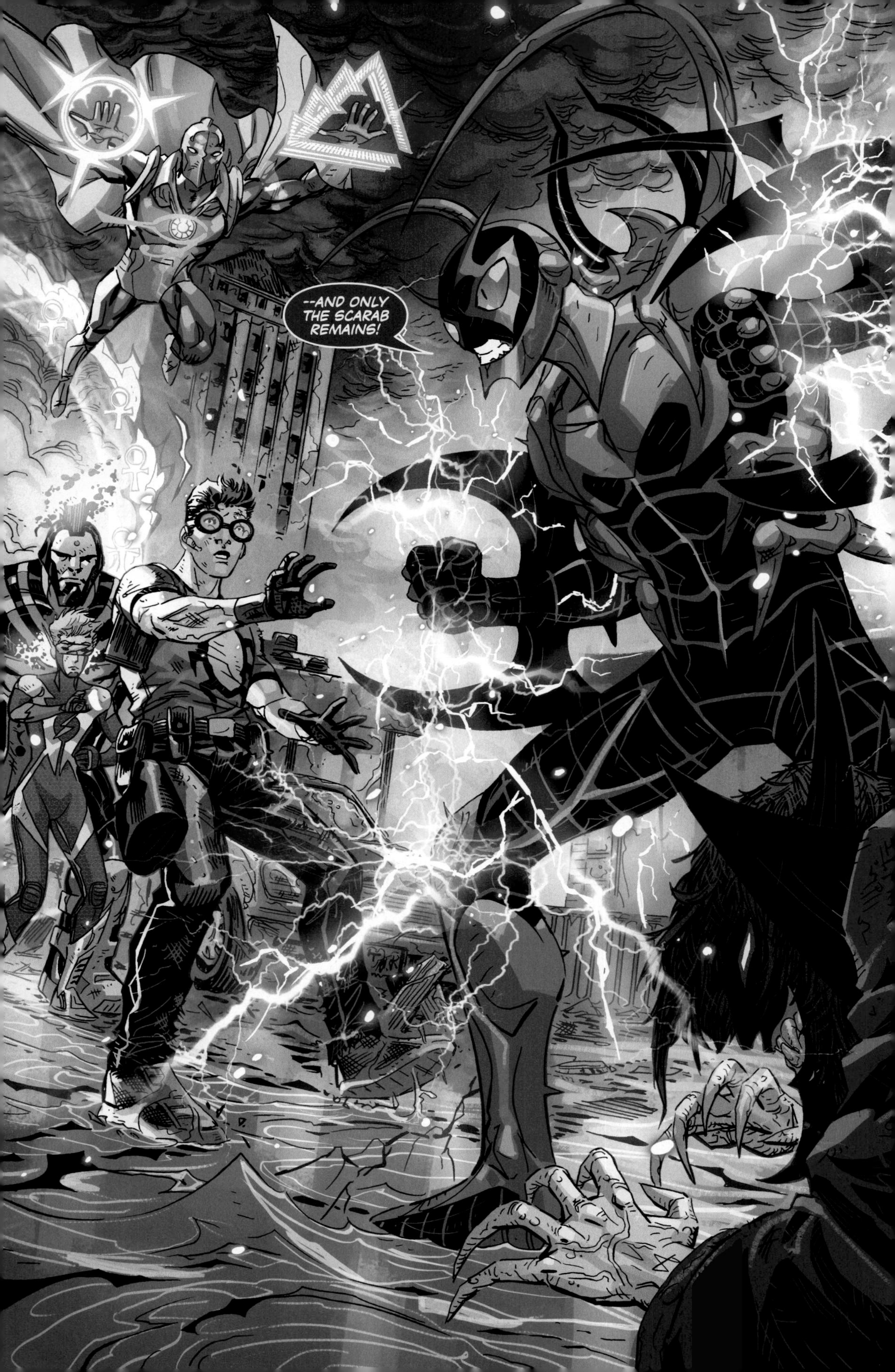
--AND ONLY THE SCARAB REMAINS!

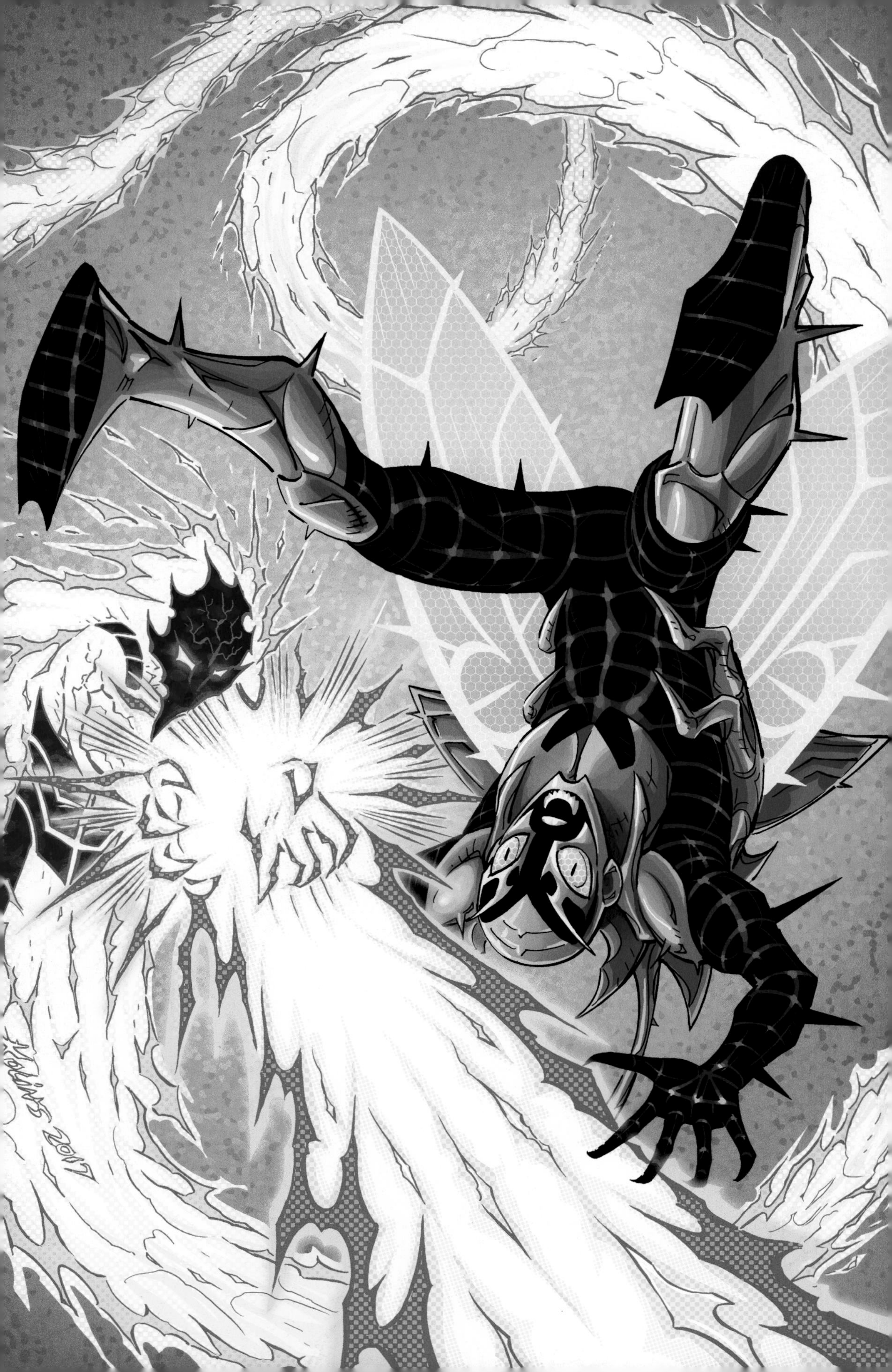

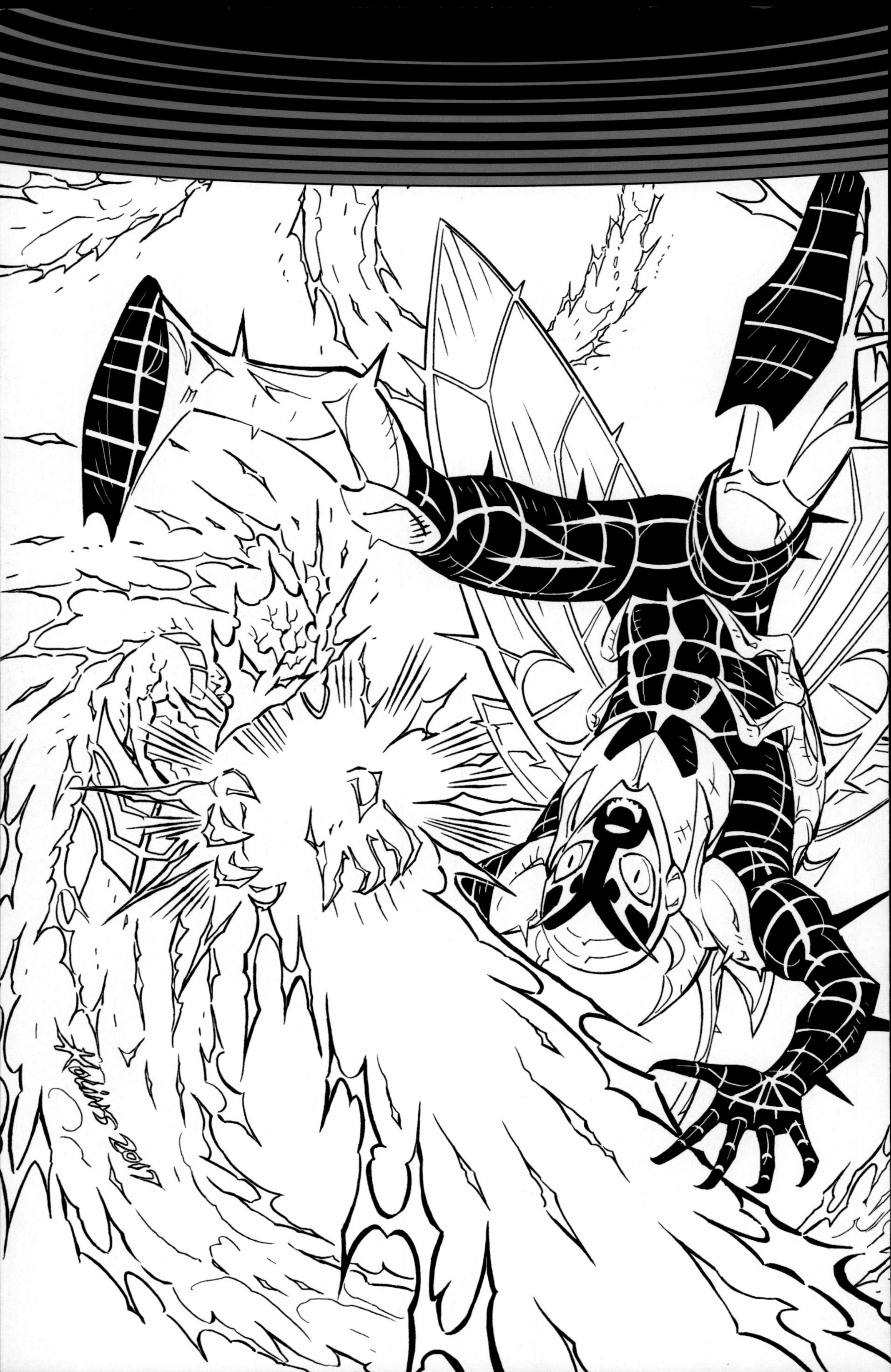

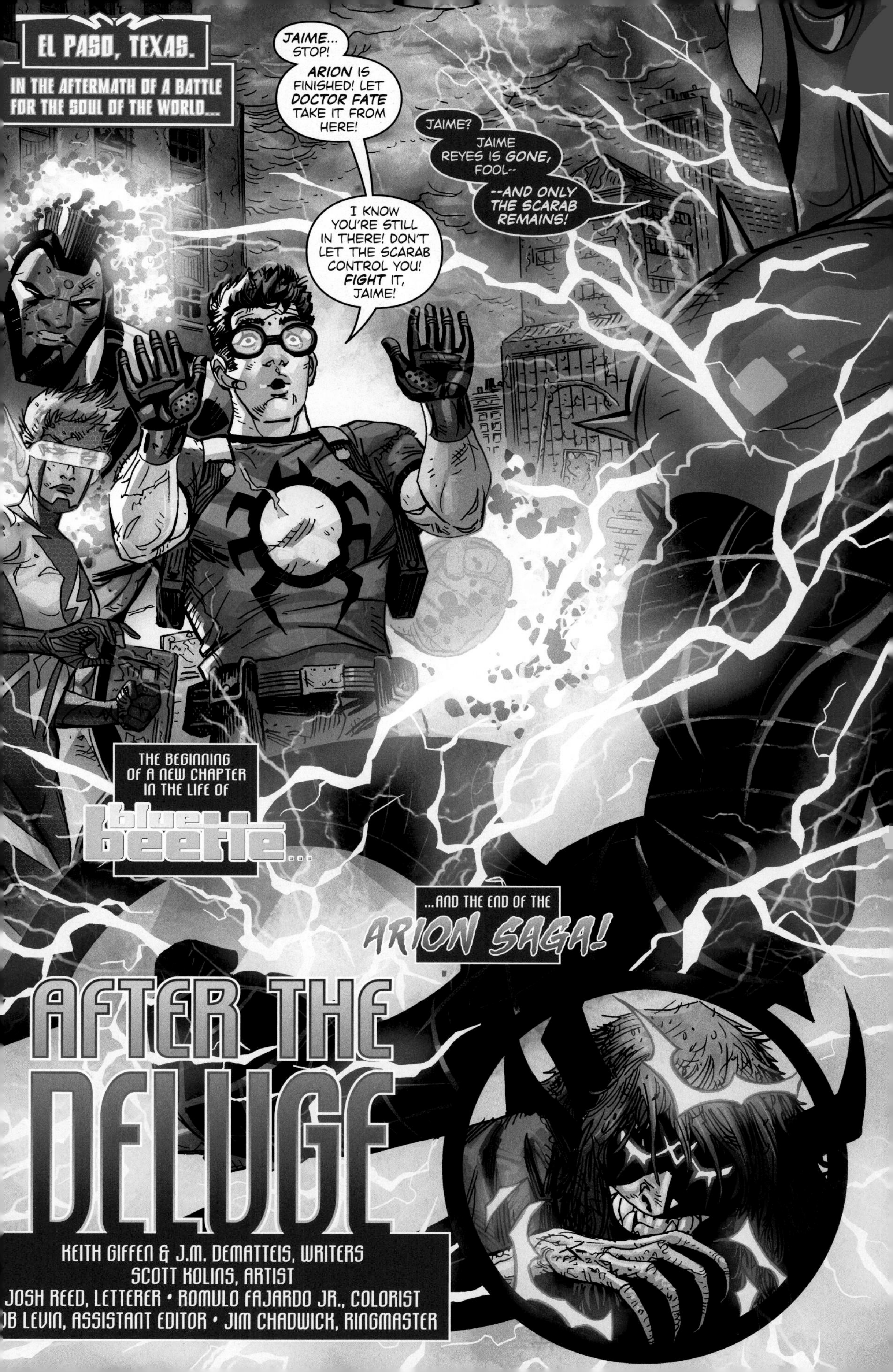
EL PASO, TEXAS.
IN THE AFTERMATH OF A BATTLE FOR THE SOUL OF THE WORLD...
JAIME... STOP!
ARION IS FINISHED! LET DOCTOR FATE TAKE IT FROM HERE!
I KNOW YOU'RE STILL IN THERE! DON'T LET THE SCARAB CONTROL YOU! FIGHT IT, JAIME!
JAIME?
JAIME REYES IS GONE, FOOL--
--AND ONLY THE SCARAB REMAINS!
THE BEGINNING OF A NEW CHAPTER IN THE LIFE OF
blue beetle...
...AND THE END OF THE
ARION SAGA!
AFTER THE DELUGE
KEITH GIFFEN & J.M. DEMATTEIS, WRITERS
SCOTT KOLINS, ARTIST
JOSH REED, LETTERER • ROMULO FAJARDO JR., COLORIST
JB LEVIN, ASSISTANT EDITOR • JIM CHADWICK, RINGMASTER

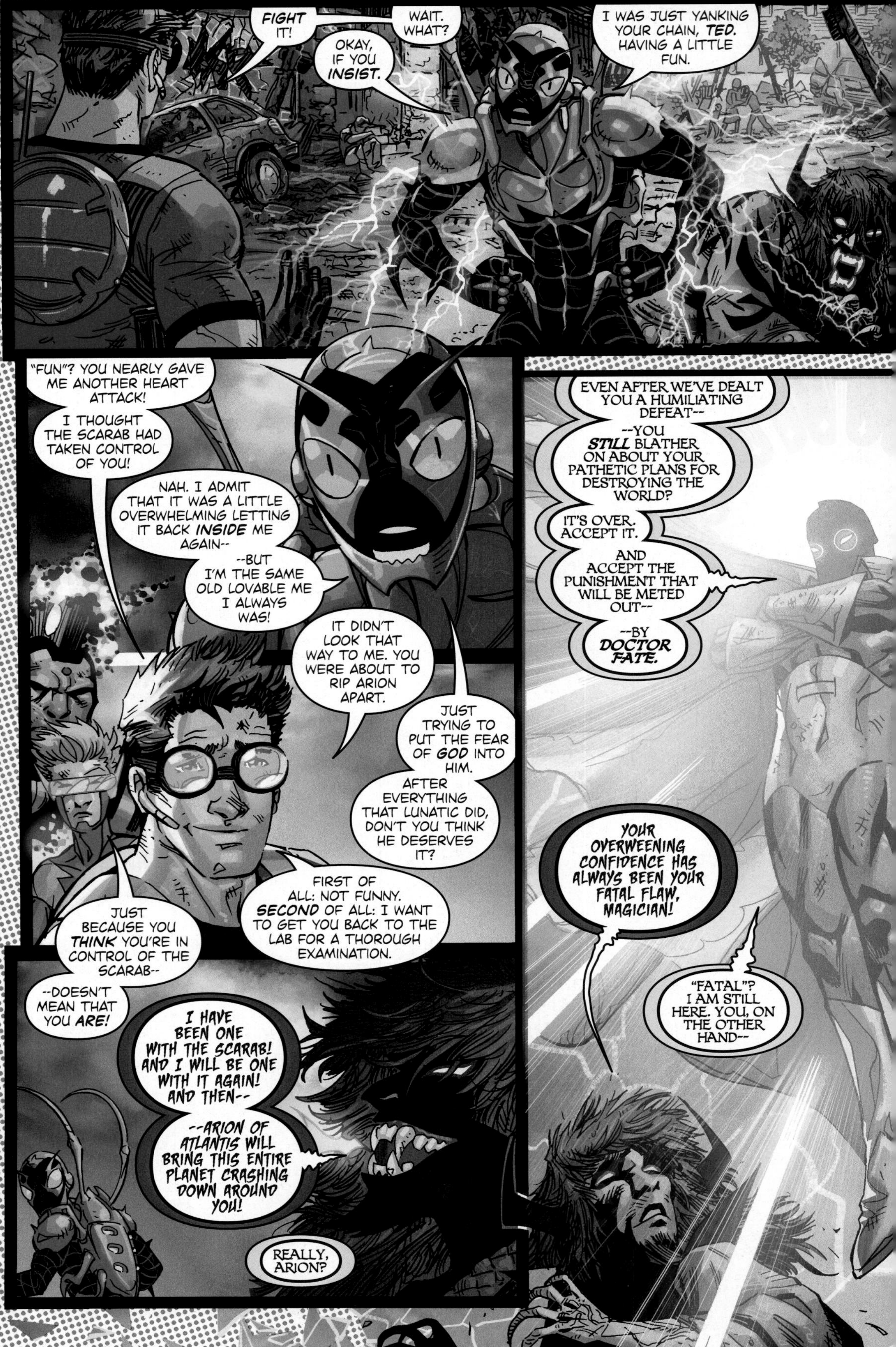
FIGHT IT!
WAIT. WHAT?
OKAY, IF YOU INSIST.
I WAS JUST YANKING YOUR CHAIN, TED. HAVING A LITTLE FUN.
"FUN"? YOU NEARLY GAVE ME ANOTHER HEART ATTACK!
I THOUGHT THE SCARAB HAD TAKEN CONTROL OF YOU!
NAH. I ADMIT THAT IT WAS A LITTLE OVERWHELMING LETTING IT BACK INSIDE ME AGAIN--
--BUT I'M THE SAME OLD LOVABLE ME I ALWAYS WAS!
IT DIDN'T LOOK THAT WAY TO ME. YOU WERE ABOUT TO RIP ARION APART.
JUST TRYING TO PUT THE FEAR OF GOD INTO HIM.
AFTER EVERYTHING THAT LUNATIC DID, DON'T YOU THINK HE DESERVES IT?
FIRST OF ALL: NOT FUNNY. SECOND OF ALL: I WANT TO GET YOU BACK TO THE LAB FOR A THOROUGH EXAMINATION.
JUST BECAUSE YOU THINK YOU'RE IN CONTROL OF THE SCARAB--
--DOESN'T MEAN THAT YOU ARE!
I HAVE BEEN ONE WITH THE SCARAB! AND I WILL BE ONE WITH IT AGAIN! AND THEN--
--ARION OF ATLANTIS WILL BRING THIS ENTIRE PLANET CRASHING DOWN AROUND YOU!
REALLY, ARION?
EVEN AFTER WE'VE DEALT YOU A HUMILIATING DEFEAT--
--YOU STILL BLATHER ON ABOUT YOUR PATHETIC PLANS FOR DESTROYING THE WORLD?
IT'S OVER. ACCEPT IT.
AND ACCEPT THE PUNISHMENT THAT WILL BE METED OUT--
--BY DOCTOR FATE.
YOUR OVERWEENING CONFIDENCE HAS ALWAYS BEEN YOUR FATAL FLAW, MAGICIAN!
"FATAL"? I AM STILL HERE. YOU, ON THE OTHER HAND--

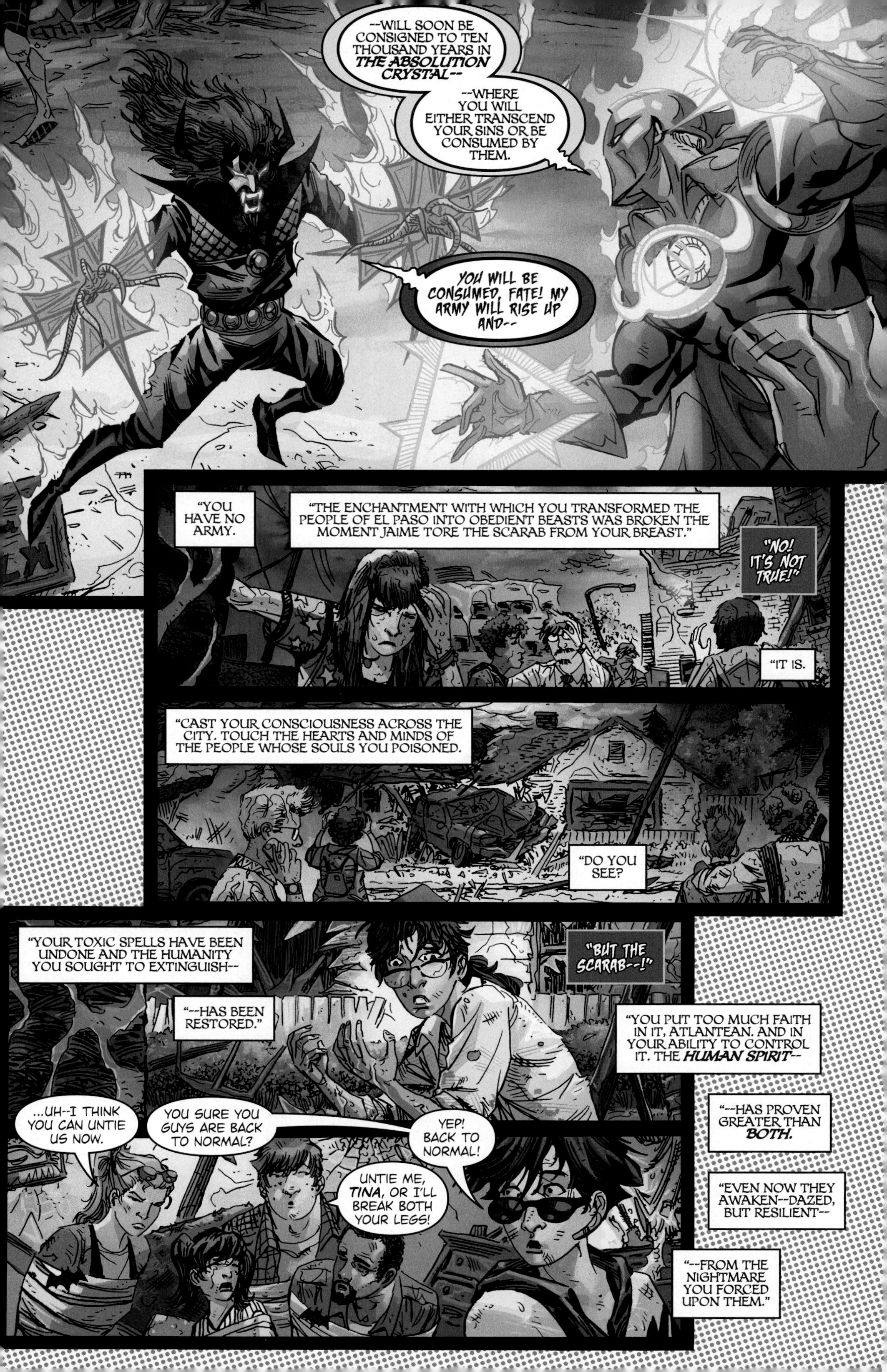
--WILL SOON BE CONSIGNED TO TEN THOUSAND YEARS IN THE ABSOLUTION CRYSTAL--
--WHERE YOU WILL EITHER TRANSCEND YOUR SINS OR BE CONSUMED BY THEM.
YOU WILL BE CONSUMED, FATE! MY ARMY WILL RISE UP AND--
"YOU HAVE NO ARMY.
"THE ENCHANTMENT WITH WHICH YOU TRANSFORMED THE PEOPLE OF EL PASO INTO OBEDIENT BEASTS WAS BROKEN THE MOMENT JAIME TORE THE SCARAB FROM YOUR BREAST."
"NO! IT'S NOT TRUE!"
"IT IS.
"CAST YOUR CONSCIOUSNESS ACROSS THE CITY. TOUCH THE HEARTS AND MINDS OF THE PEOPLE WHOSE SOULS YOU POISONED.
"DO YOU SEE?
"YOUR TOXIC SPELLS HAVE BEEN UNDONE AND THE HUMANITY YOU SOUGHT TO EXTINGUISH--
"BUT THE SCARAB--!"
"--HAS BEEN RESTORED."
"YOU PUT TOO MUCH FAITH IN IT, ATLANTEAN. AND IN YOUR ABILITY TO CONTROL IT. THE HUMAN SPIRIT--
...UH--I THINK YOU CAN UNTIE US NOW.
YOU SURE YOU GUYS ARE BACK TO NORMAL?
YEP! BACK TO NORMAL!
UNTIE ME, TINA, OR I'LL BREAK BOTH YOUR LEGS!
"--HAS PROVEN GREATER THAN BOTH.
"EVEN NOW THEY AWAKEN--DAZED, BUT RESILIENT--
"--FROM THE NIGHTMARE YOU FORCED UPON THEM."

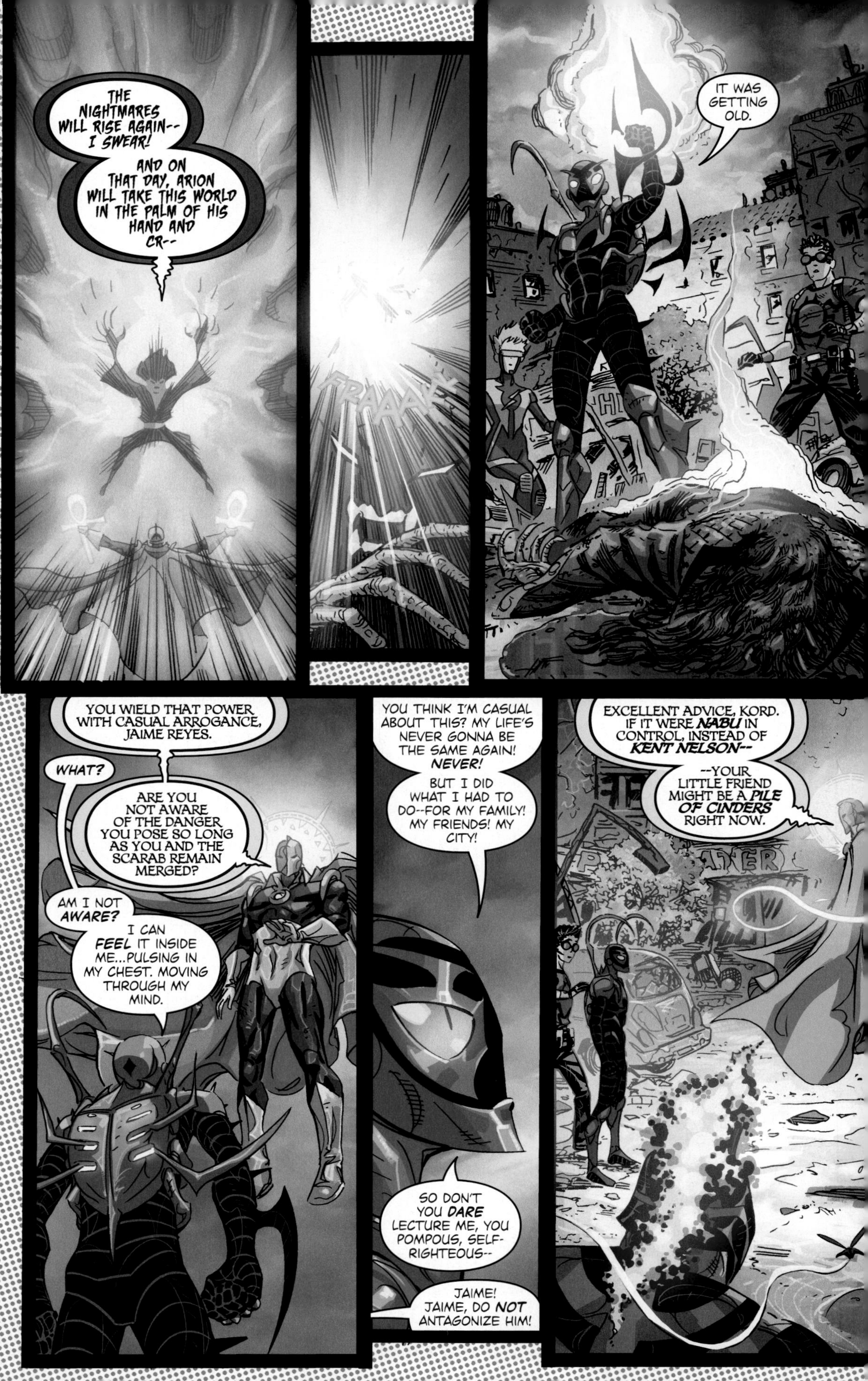
THE NIGHTMARES WILL RISE AGAIN-- I SWEAR!
AND ON THAT DAY, ARION WILL TAKE THIS WORLD IN THE PALM OF HIS HAND AND CR--
FRAAAK
IT WAS GETTING OLD.
YOU WIELD THAT POWER WITH CASUAL ARROGANCE, JAIME REYES.
WHAT?
ARE YOU NOT AWARE OF THE DANGER YOU POSE SO LONG AS YOU AND THE SCARAB REMAIN MERGED?
AM I NOT AWARE?
I CAN FEEL IT INSIDE ME...PULSING IN MY CHEST. MOVING THROUGH MY MIND.
YOU THINK I'M CASUAL ABOUT THIS? MY LIFE'S NEVER GONNA BE THE SAME AGAIN! NEVER!
BUT I DID WHAT I HAD TO DO--FOR MY FAMILY! MY FRIENDS! MY CITY!
SO DON'T YOU DARE LECTURE ME, YOU POMPOUS, SELF-RIGHTEOUS--
JAIME! JAIME, DO NOT ANTAGONIZE HIM!
EXCELLENT ADVICE, KORD. IF IT WERE NABU IN CONTROL, INSTEAD OF KENT NELSON--
--YOUR LITTLE FRIEND MIGHT BE A PILE OF CINDERS RIGHT NOW.

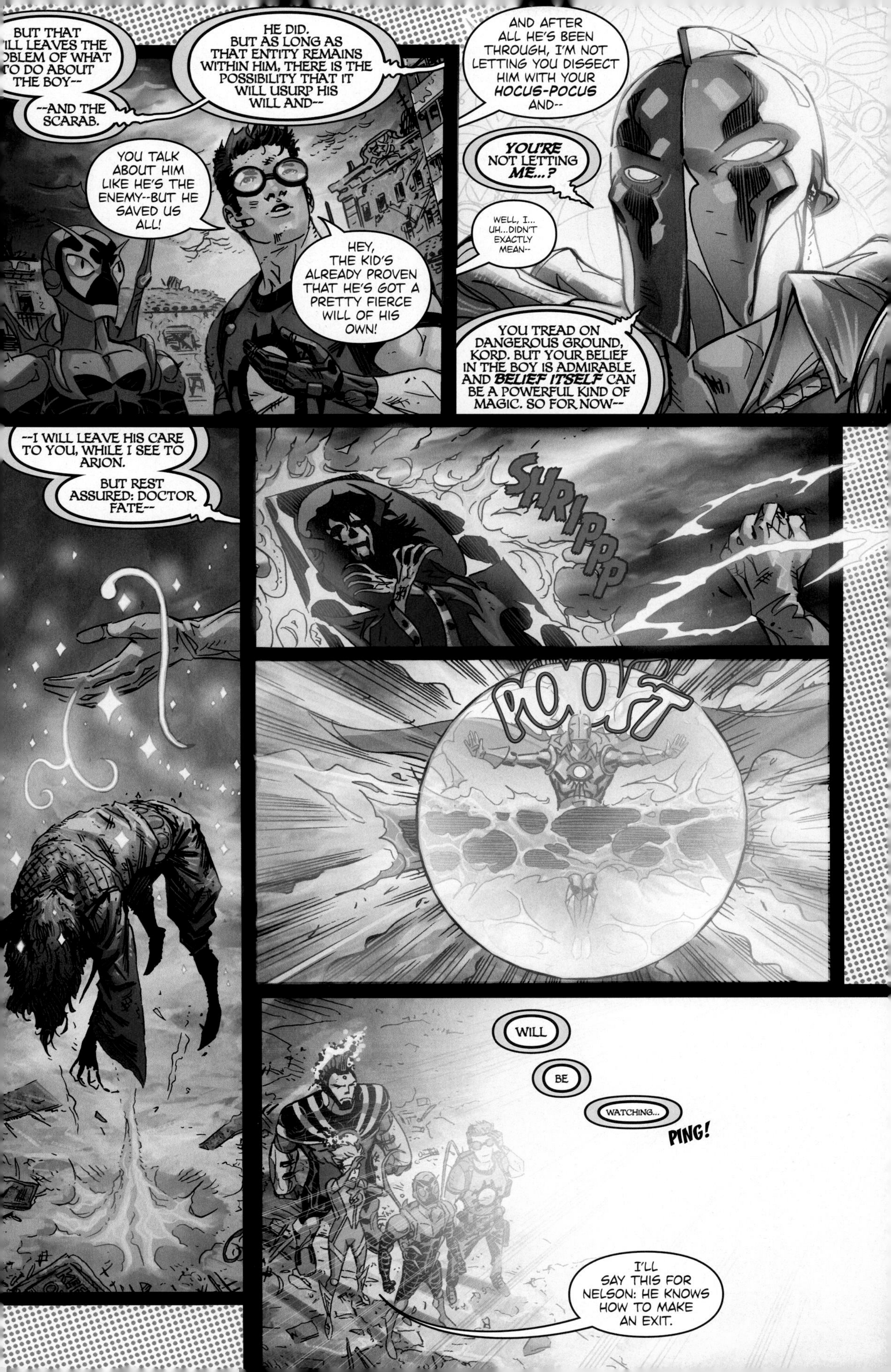
BUT THAT STILL LEAVES THE PROBLEM OF WHAT TO DO ABOUT THE BOY--
--AND THE SCARAB.
HE DID. BUT AS LONG AS THAT ENTITY REMAINS WITHIN HIM, THERE IS THE POSSIBILITY THAT IT WILL USURP HIS WILL AND--
YOU TALK ABOUT HIM LIKE HE'S THE ENEMY--BUT HE SAVED US ALL!
HEY, THE KID'S ALREADY PROVEN THAT HE'S GOT A PRETTY FIERCE WILL OF HIS OWN!
AND AFTER ALL HE'S BEEN THROUGH, I'M NOT LETTING YOU DISSECT HIM WITH YOUR HOCUS-POCUS AND--
YOU'RE NOT LETTING ME...?
WELL, I... UH...DIDN'T EXACTLY MEAN--
YOU TREAD ON DANGEROUS GROUND, KORD. BUT YOUR BELIEF IN THE BOY IS ADMIRABLE. AND BELIEF ITSELF CAN BE A POWERFUL KIND OF MAGIC. SO FOR NOW--
--I WILL LEAVE HIS CARE TO YOU, WHILE I SEE TO ARION.
BUT REST ASSURED: DOCTOR FATE--
SHRIPPP
WILL
BE
WATCHING...
PING!
I'LL SAY THIS FOR NELSON: HE KNOWS HOW TO MAKE AN EXIT.

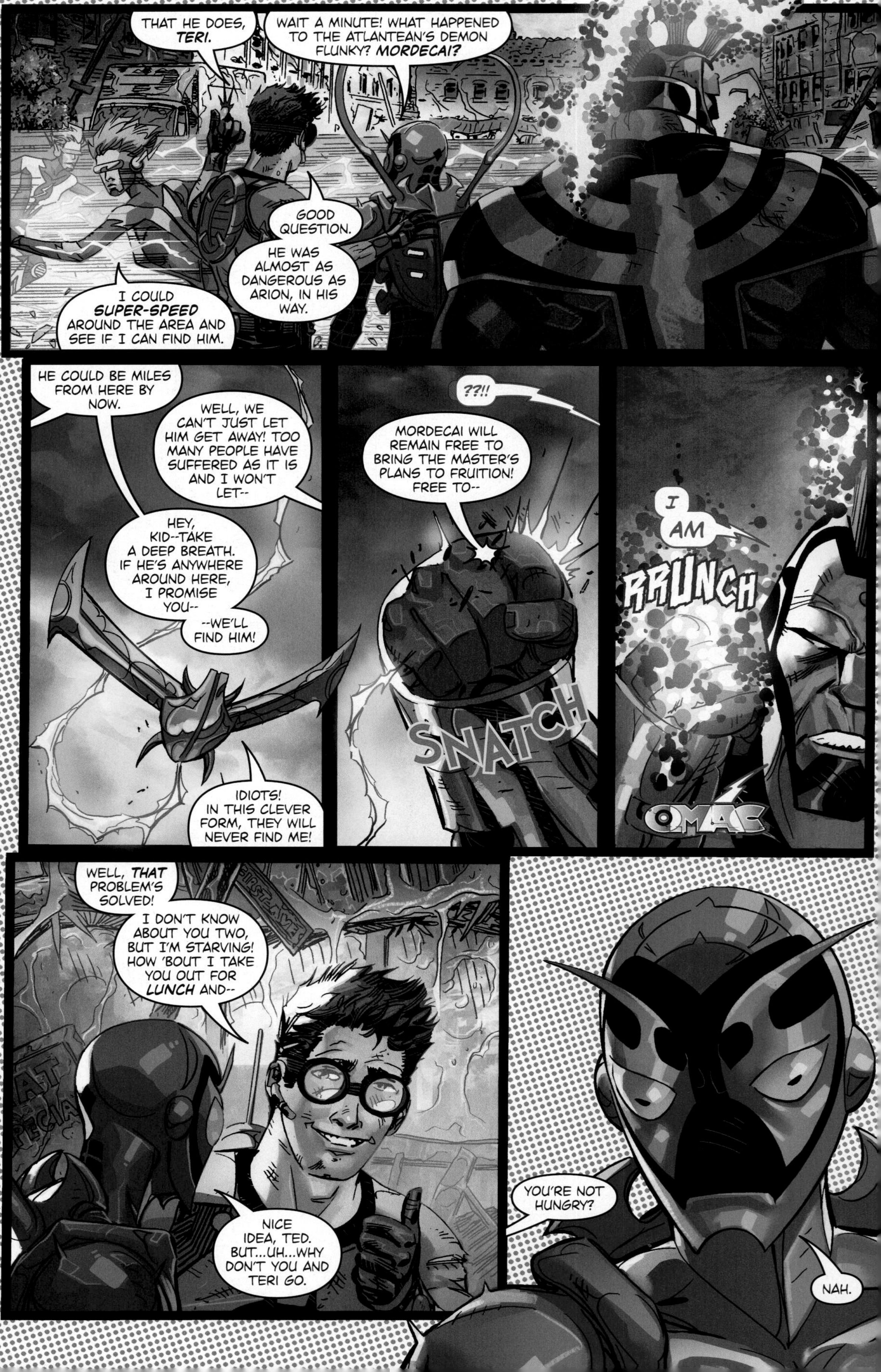
THAT HE DOES, TERI.
WAIT A MINUTE! WHAT HAPPENED TO THE ATLANTEAN'S DEMON FLUNKY? MORDECAI?
GOOD QUESTION.
HE WAS ALMOST AS DANGEROUS AS ARION, IN HIS WAY.
I COULD SUPER-SPEED AROUND THE AREA AND SEE IF I CAN FIND HIM.
HE COULD BE MILES FROM HERE BY NOW.
WELL, WE CAN'T JUST LET HIM GET AWAY! TOO MANY PEOPLE HAVE SUFFERED AS IT IS AND I WON'T LET--
HEY, KID--TAKE A DEEP BREATH. IF HE'S ANYWHERE AROUND HERE, I PROMISE YOU--
--WE'LL FIND HIM!
IDIOTS! IN THIS CLEVER FORM, THEY WILL NEVER FIND ME!
??!!
MORDECAI WILL REMAIN FREE TO BRING THE MASTER'S PLANS TO FRUITION! FREE TO--
SNATCH
I AM
RRUNCH
OMAC
WELL, THAT PROBLEM'S SOLVED!
I DON'T KNOW ABOUT YOU TWO, BUT I'M STARVING! HOW 'BOUT I TAKE YOU OUT FOR LUNCH AND--
NICE IDEA, TED. BUT...UH...WHY DON'T YOU AND TERI GO.
YOU'RE NOT HUNGRY?
NAH.

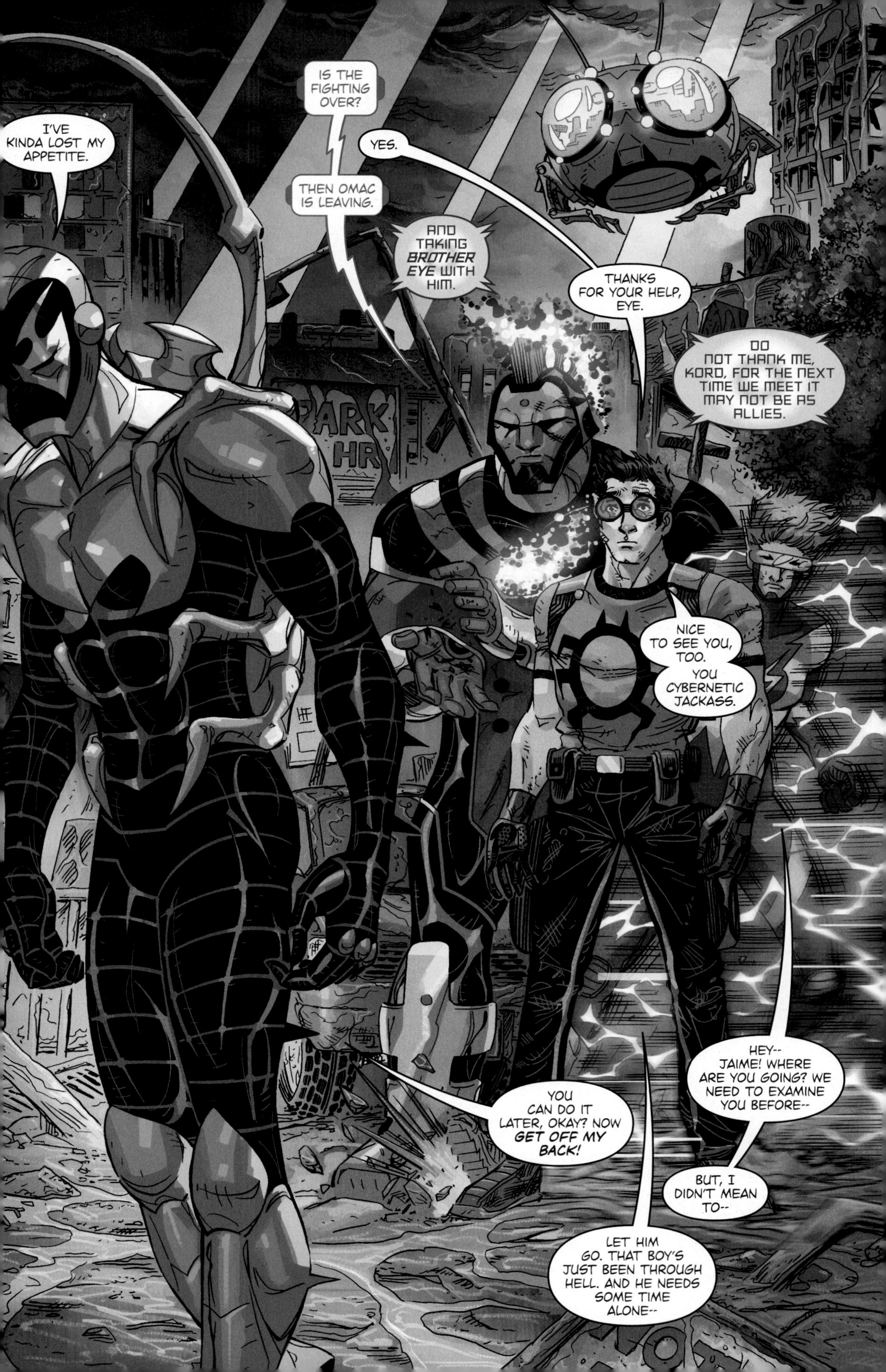

I'VE KINDA LOST MY APPETITE.
IS THE FIGHTING OVER?
YES.
THEN OMAC IS LEAVING.
AND TAKING BROTHER EYE WITH HIM.
THANKS FOR YOUR HELP, EYE.
DO NOT THANK ME, KORD, FOR THE NEXT TIME WE MEET IT MAY NOT BE AS ALLIES.
NICE TO SEE YOU, TOO.
YOU CYBERNETIC JACKASS.
HEY-- JAIME! WHERE ARE YOU GOING? WE NEED TO EXAMINE YOU BEFORE--
YOU CAN DO IT LATER, OKAY? NOW GET OFF MY BACK!
BUT, I DIDN'T MEAN TO--
LET HIM GO. THAT BOY'S JUST BEEN THROUGH HELL. AND HE NEEDS SOME TIME ALONE--

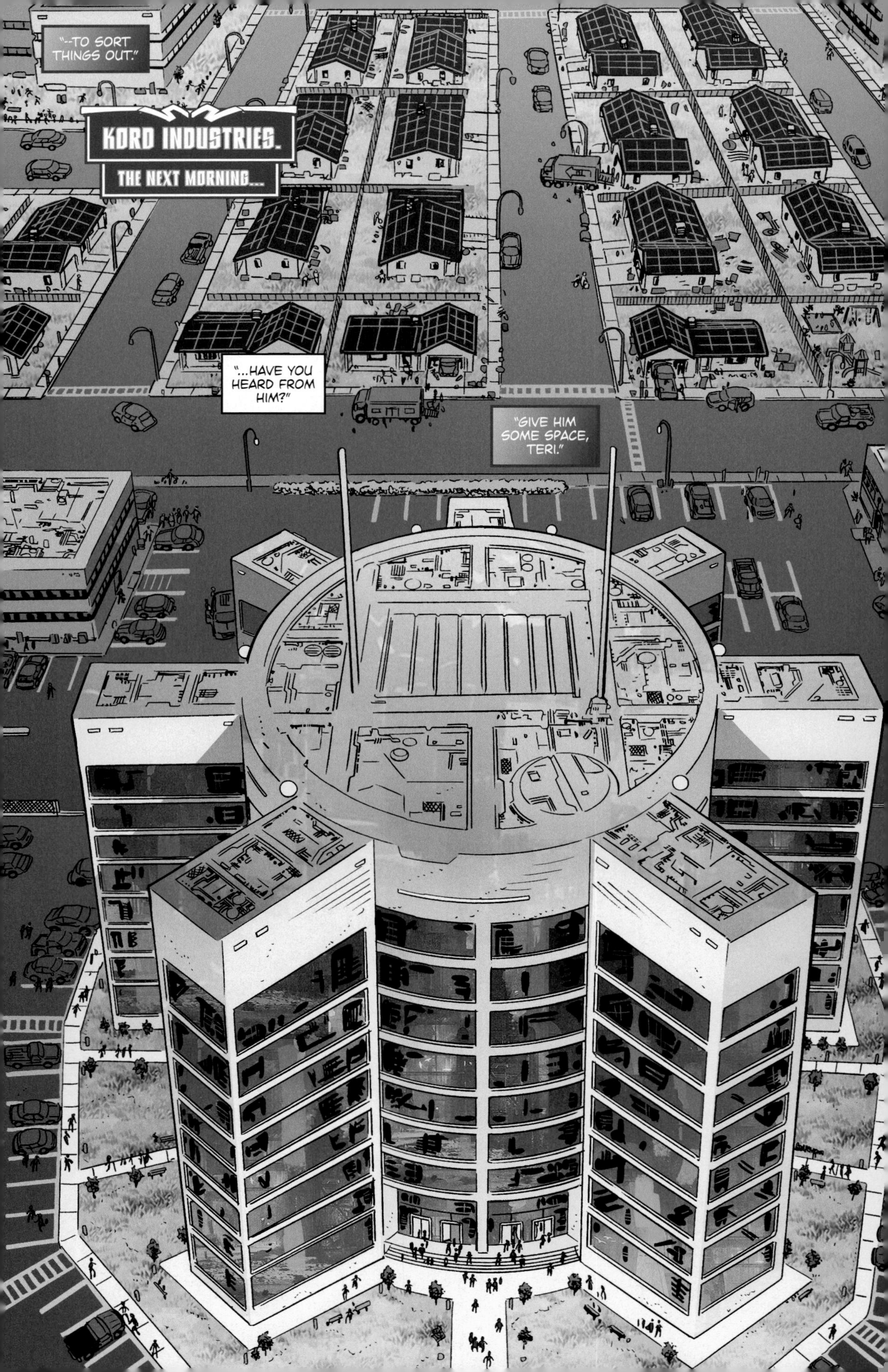

"--TO SORT THINGS OUT."
KORD INDUSTRIES.
THE NEXT MORNING...
"...HAVE YOU HEARD FROM HIM?"
"GIVE HIM SOME SPACE, TERI."

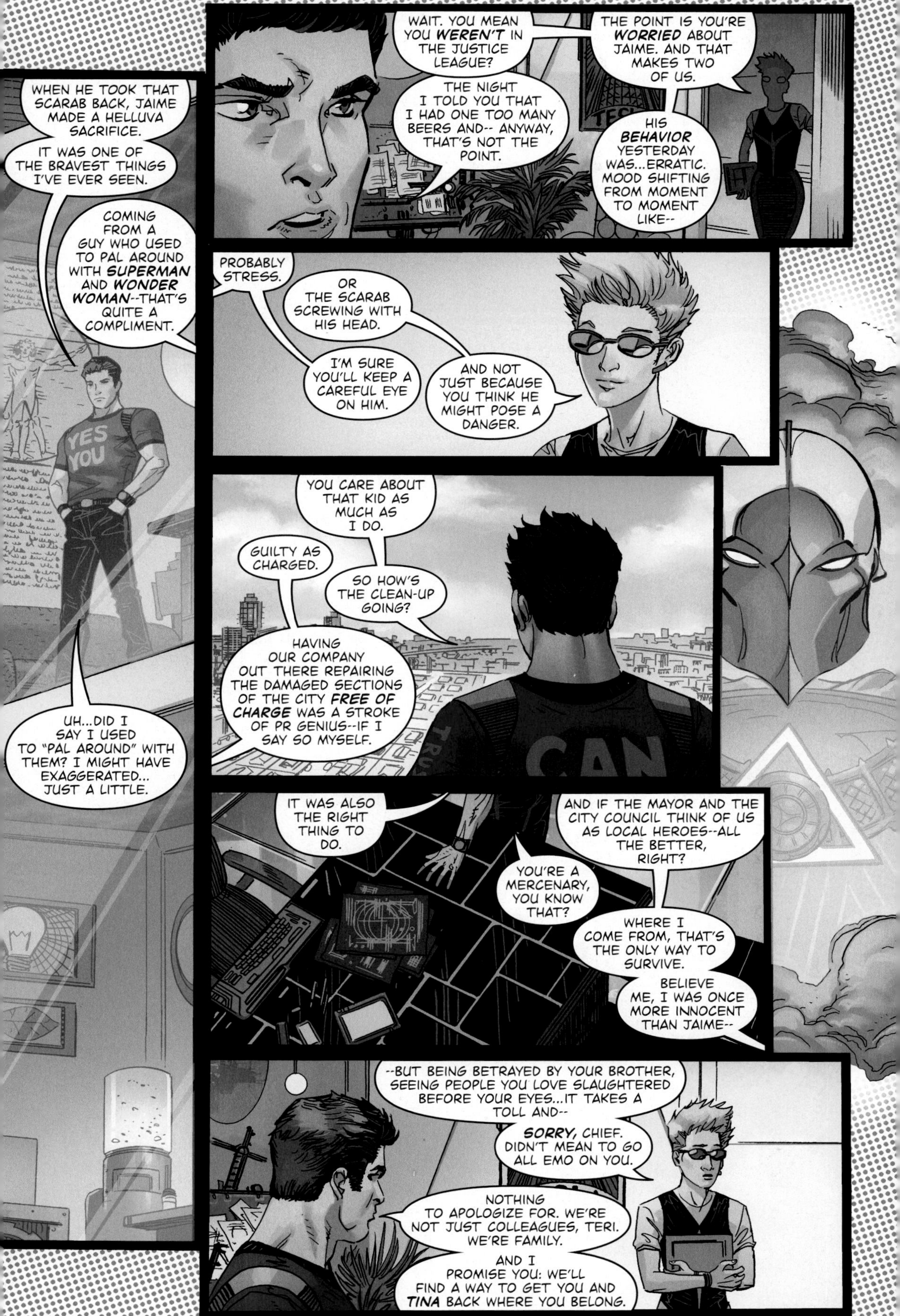

WHEN HE TOOK THAT SCARAB BACK, JAIME MADE A HELLUVA SACRIFICE.
IT WAS ONE OF THE BRAVEST THINGS I'VE EVER SEEN.
COMING FROM A GUY WHO USED TO PAL AROUND WITH **SUPERMAN** AND **WONDER WOMAN**--THAT'S QUITE A COMPLIMENT.
UH...DID I SAY I USED TO "PAL AROUND" WITH THEM? I MIGHT HAVE EXAGGERATED... JUST A LITTLE.
WAIT. YOU MEAN YOU **WEREN'T** IN THE JUSTICE LEAGUE?
THE NIGHT I TOLD YOU THAT I HAD ONE TOO MANY BEERS AND-- ANYWAY, THAT'S NOT THE POINT.
THE POINT IS YOU'RE **WORRIED** ABOUT JAIME. AND THAT MAKES TWO OF US.
HIS **BEHAVIOR** YESTERDAY WAS...ERRATIC. MOOD SHIFTING FROM MOMENT TO MOMENT LIKE--
PROBABLY STRESS.
OR THE SCARAB SCREWING WITH HIS HEAD.
I'M SURE YOU'LL KEEP A CAREFUL EYE ON HIM.
AND NOT JUST BECAUSE YOU THINK HE MIGHT POSE A DANGER.
YOU CARE ABOUT THAT KID AS MUCH AS I DO.
GUILTY AS CHARGED.
SO HOW'S THE CLEAN-UP GOING?
HAVING OUR COMPANY OUT THERE REPAIRING THE DAMAGED SECTIONS OF THE CITY **FREE OF CHARGE** WAS A STROKE OF PR GENIUS--IF I SAY SO MYSELF.
IT WAS ALSO THE RIGHT THING TO DO.
AND IF THE MAYOR AND THE CITY COUNCIL THINK OF US AS LOCAL HEROES--ALL THE BETTER, RIGHT?
YOU'RE A MERCENARY, YOU KNOW THAT?
WHERE I COME FROM, THAT'S THE ONLY WAY TO SURVIVE.
BELIEVE ME, I WAS ONCE MORE INNOCENT THAN JAIME--
--BUT BEING BETRAYED BY YOUR BROTHER, SEEING PEOPLE YOU LOVE SLAUGHTERED BEFORE YOUR EYES...IT TAKES A TOLL AND--
SORRY, CHIEF. DIDN'T MEAN TO GO ALL EMO ON YOU.
NOTHING TO APOLOGIZE FOR. WE'RE NOT JUST COLLEAGUES, TERI. WE'RE FAMILY.
AND I PROMISE YOU: WE'LL FIND A WAY TO GET YOU AND **TINA** BACK WHERE YOU BELONG.

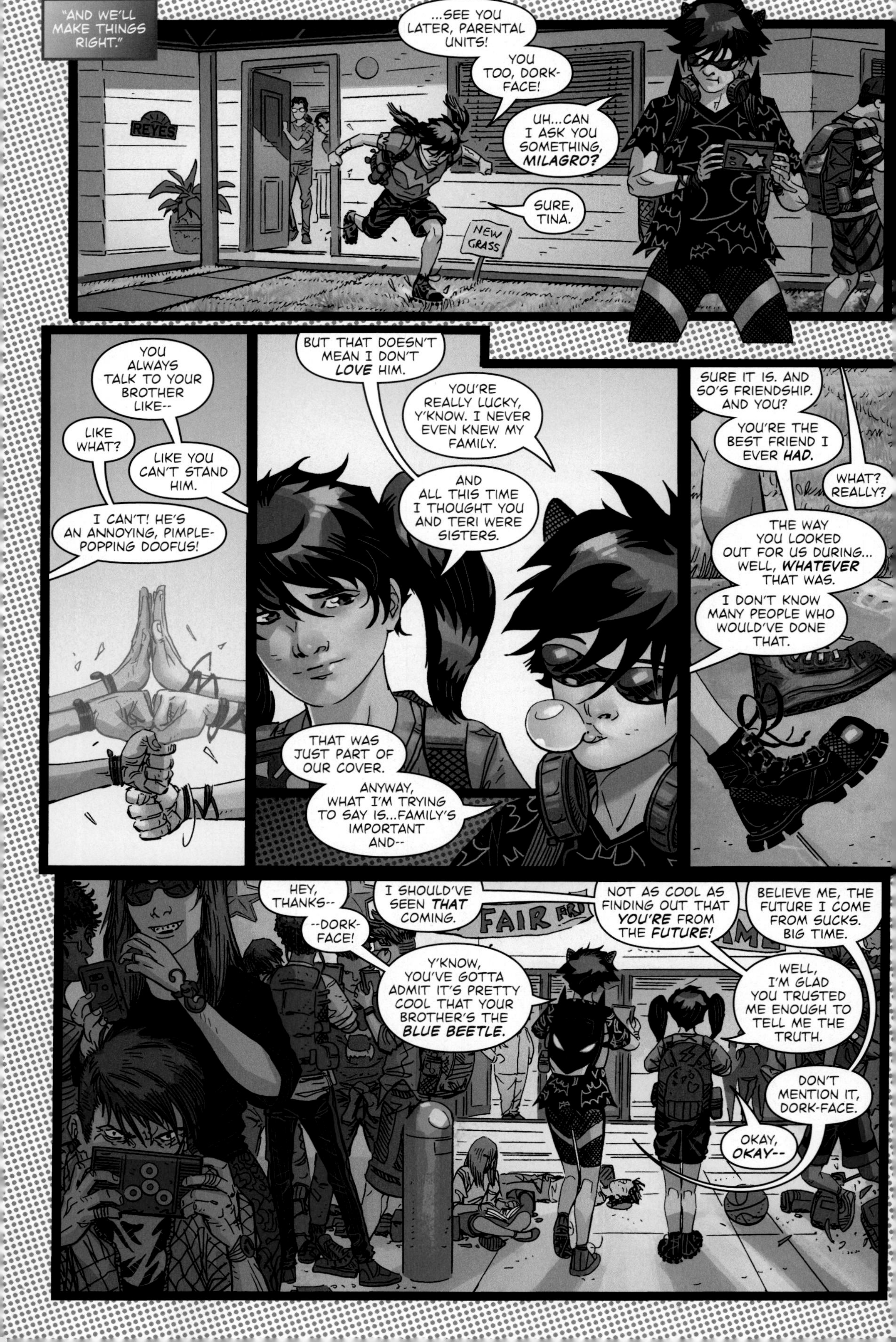
"AND WE'LL MAKE THINGS RIGHT."
...SEE YOU LATER, PARENTAL UNITS!
YOU TOO, DORK-FACE!
UH...CAN I ASK YOU SOMETHING, MILAGRO?
SURE, TINA.
REYES
NEW GRASS
YOU ALWAYS TALK TO YOUR BROTHER LIKE--
LIKE WHAT?
LIKE YOU CAN'T STAND HIM.
I CAN'T! HE'S AN ANNOYING, PIMPLE-POPPING DOOFUS!
BUT THAT DOESN'T MEAN I DON'T LOVE HIM.
YOU'RE REALLY LUCKY, Y'KNOW. I NEVER EVEN KNEW MY FAMILY.
AND ALL THIS TIME I THOUGHT YOU AND TERI WERE SISTERS.
THAT WAS JUST PART OF OUR COVER.
ANYWAY, WHAT I'M TRYING TO SAY IS...FAMILY'S IMPORTANT AND--
SURE IT IS. AND SO'S FRIENDSHIP. AND YOU?
YOU'RE THE BEST FRIEND I EVER HAD.
WHAT? REALLY?
THE WAY YOU LOOKED OUT FOR US DURING... WELL, WHATEVER THAT WAS.
I DON'T KNOW MANY PEOPLE WHO WOULD'VE DONE THAT.
HEY, THANKS--
--DORK-FACE!
I SHOULD'VE SEEN THAT COMING.
Y'KNOW, YOU'VE GOTTA ADMIT IT'S PRETTY COOL THAT YOUR BROTHER'S THE BLUE BEETLE.
NOT AS COOL AS FINDING OUT THAT YOU'RE FROM THE FUTURE!
BELIEVE ME, THE FUTURE I COME FROM SUCKS. BIG TIME.
WELL, I'M GLAD YOU TRUSTED ME ENOUGH TO TELL ME THE TRUTH.
DON'T MENTION IT, DORK-FACE.
OKAY, OKAY--
FAIR

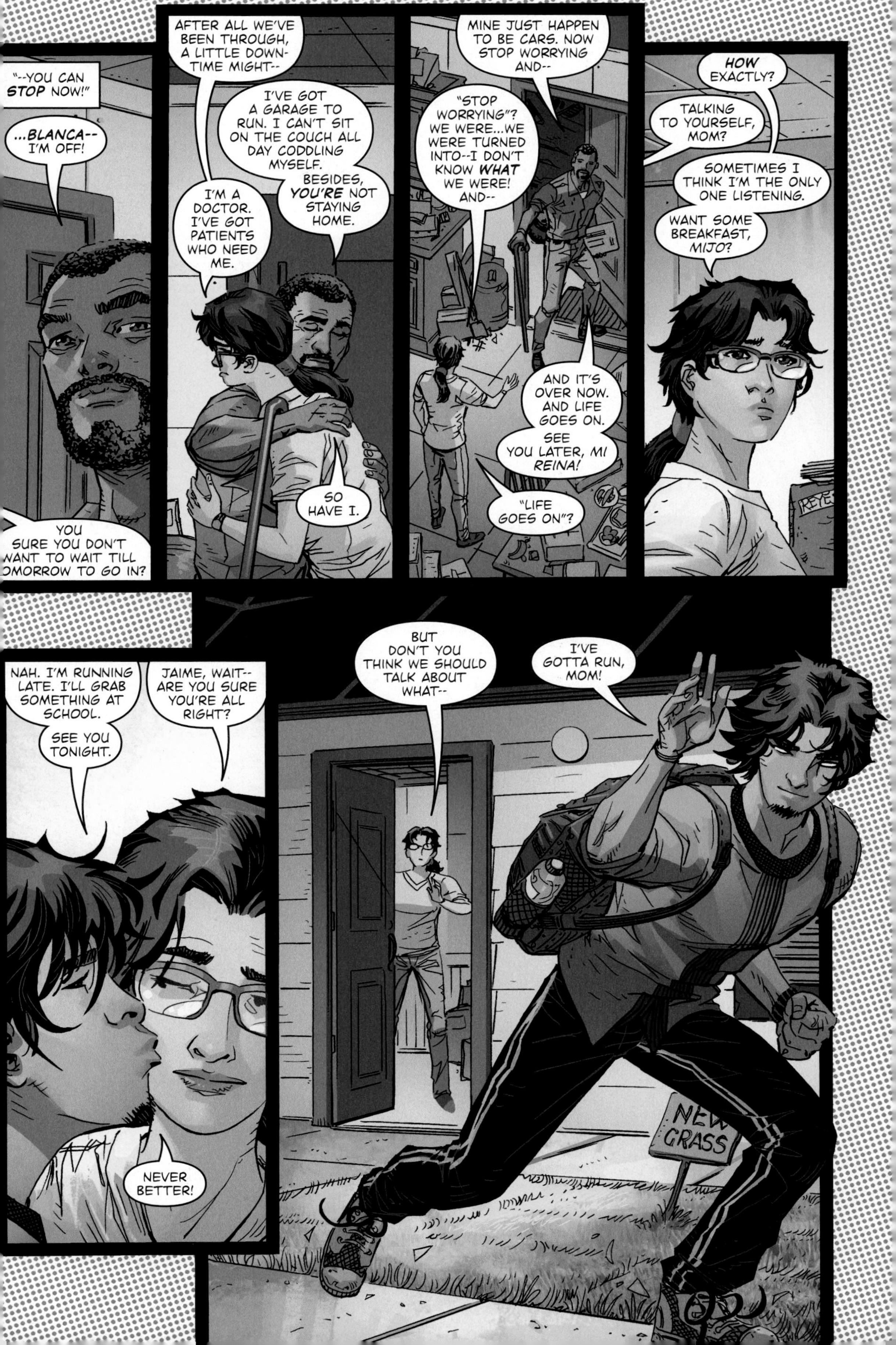
"--YOU CAN STOP NOW!"
...BLANCA-- I'M OFF!
YOU SURE YOU DON'T WANT TO WAIT TILL TOMORROW TO GO IN?
AFTER ALL WE'VE BEEN THROUGH, A LITTLE DOWN-TIME MIGHT--
I'M A DOCTOR. I'VE GOT PATIENTS WHO NEED ME.
I'VE GOT A GARAGE TO RUN. I CAN'T SIT ON THE COUCH ALL DAY CODDLING MYSELF.
BESIDES, YOU'RE NOT STAYING HOME.
SO HAVE I.
MINE JUST HAPPEN TO BE CARS. NOW STOP WORRYING AND--
"STOP WORRYING"? WE WERE...WE WERE TURNED INTO--I DON'T KNOW WHAT WE WERE! AND--
AND IT'S OVER NOW. AND LIFE GOES ON.
SEE YOU LATER, MI REINA!
"LIFE GOES ON"?
HOW EXACTLY?
TALKING TO YOURSELF, MOM?
SOMETIMES I THINK I'M THE ONLY ONE LISTENING.
WANT SOME BREAKFAST, MIJO?
REYES
NAH. I'M RUNNING LATE. I'LL GRAB SOMETHING AT SCHOOL.
SEE YOU TONIGHT.
JAIME, WAIT-- ARE YOU SURE YOU'RE ALL RIGHT?
NEVER BETTER!
BUT DON'T YOU THINK WE SHOULD TALK ABOUT WHAT--
I'VE GOTTA RUN, MOM!
NEW GRASS

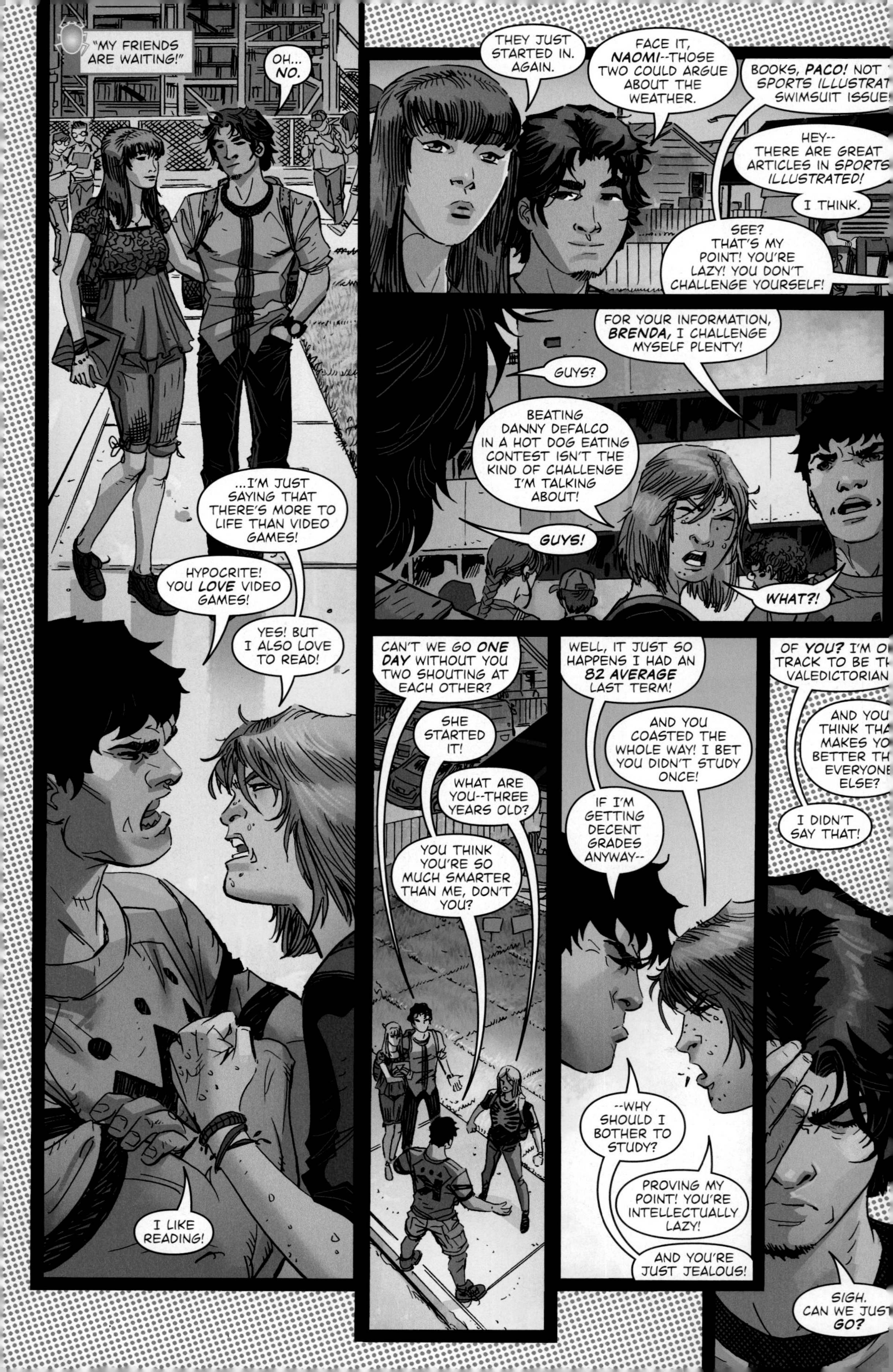

"MY FRIENDS ARE WAITING!"
OH... NO.
THEY JUST STARTED IN. AGAIN.
FACE IT, NAOMI--THOSE TWO COULD ARGUE ABOUT THE WEATHER.
BOOKS, PACO! NOT SPORTS ILLUSTRAT SWIMSUIT ISSUE
HEY-- THERE ARE GREAT ARTICLES IN SPORTS ILLUSTRATED!
I THINK.
SEE? THAT'S MY POINT! YOU'RE LAZY! YOU DON'T CHALLENGE YOURSELF!
FOR YOUR INFORMATION, BRENDA, I CHALLENGE MYSELF PLENTY!
GUYS?
BEATING DANNY DeFALCO IN A HOT DOG EATING CONTEST ISN'T THE KIND OF CHALLENGE I'M TALKING ABOUT!
GUYS!
WHAT?!
...I'M JUST SAYING THAT THERE'S MORE TO LIFE THAN VIDEO GAMES!
HYPOCRITE! YOU LOVE VIDEO GAMES!
YES! BUT I ALSO LOVE TO READ!
I LIKE READING!
CAN'T WE GO ONE DAY WITHOUT YOU TWO SHOUTING AT EACH OTHER?
SHE STARTED IT!
WHAT ARE YOU--THREE YEARS OLD?
YOU THINK YOU'RE SO MUCH SMARTER THAN ME, DON'T YOU?
WELL, IT JUST SO HAPPENS I HAD AN 82 AVERAGE LAST TERM!
AND YOU COASTED THE WHOLE WAY! I BET YOU DIDN'T STUDY ONCE!
IF I'M GETTING DECENT GRADES ANYWAY--
--WHY SHOULD I BOTHER TO STUDY?
PROVING MY POINT! YOU'RE INTELLECTUALLY LAZY!
AND YOU'RE JUST JEALOUS!
OF YOU? I'M O TRACK TO BE TH VALEDICTORIAN
AND YOU THINK THA MAKES YO BETTER TH EVERYONE ELSE?
I DIDN'T SAY THAT!
SIGH. CAN WE JUS GO?

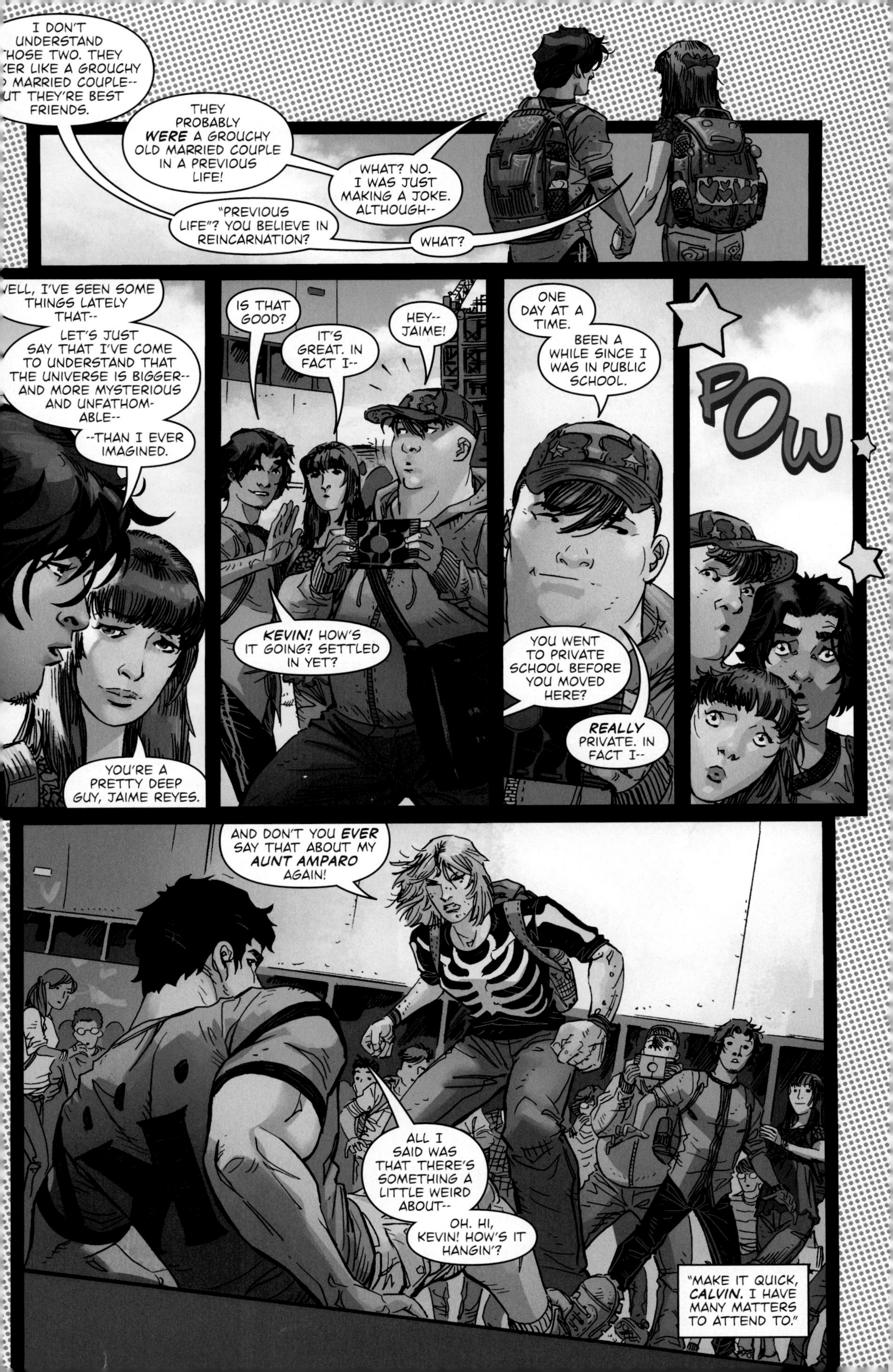
I DON'T UNDERSTAND THOSE TWO. THEY ...KE LIKE A GROUCHY ...D MARRIED COUPLE-- ...UT THEY'RE BEST FRIENDS.
THEY PROBABLY WERE A GROUCHY OLD MARRIED COUPLE IN A PREVIOUS LIFE!
WHAT? NO. I WAS JUST MAKING A JOKE. ALTHOUGH--
"PREVIOUS LIFE"? YOU BELIEVE IN REINCARNATION?
WHAT?
...ELL, I'VE SEEN SOME THINGS LATELY THAT--
LET'S JUST SAY THAT I'VE COME TO UNDERSTAND THAT THE UNIVERSE IS BIGGER--
AND MORE MYSTERIOUS AND UNFATHOM-ABLE--
--THAN I EVER IMAGINED.
YOU'RE A PRETTY DEEP GUY, JAIME REYES.
IS THAT GOOD?
IT'S GREAT. IN FACT I--
HEY-- JAIME!
KEVIN! HOW'S IT GOING? SETTLED IN YET?
ONE DAY AT A TIME.
BEEN A WHILE SINCE I WAS IN PUBLIC SCHOOL.
YOU WENT TO PRIVATE SCHOOL BEFORE YOU MOVED HERE?
REALLY PRIVATE. IN FACT I--
POW
AND DON'T YOU EVER SAY THAT ABOUT MY AUNT AMPARO AGAIN!
ALL I SAID WAS THAT THERE'S SOMETHING A LITTLE WEIRD ABOUT--
OH. HI, KEVIN! HOW'S IT HANGIN'?
"MAKE IT QUICK, CALVIN. I HAVE MANY MATTERS TO ATTEND TO."

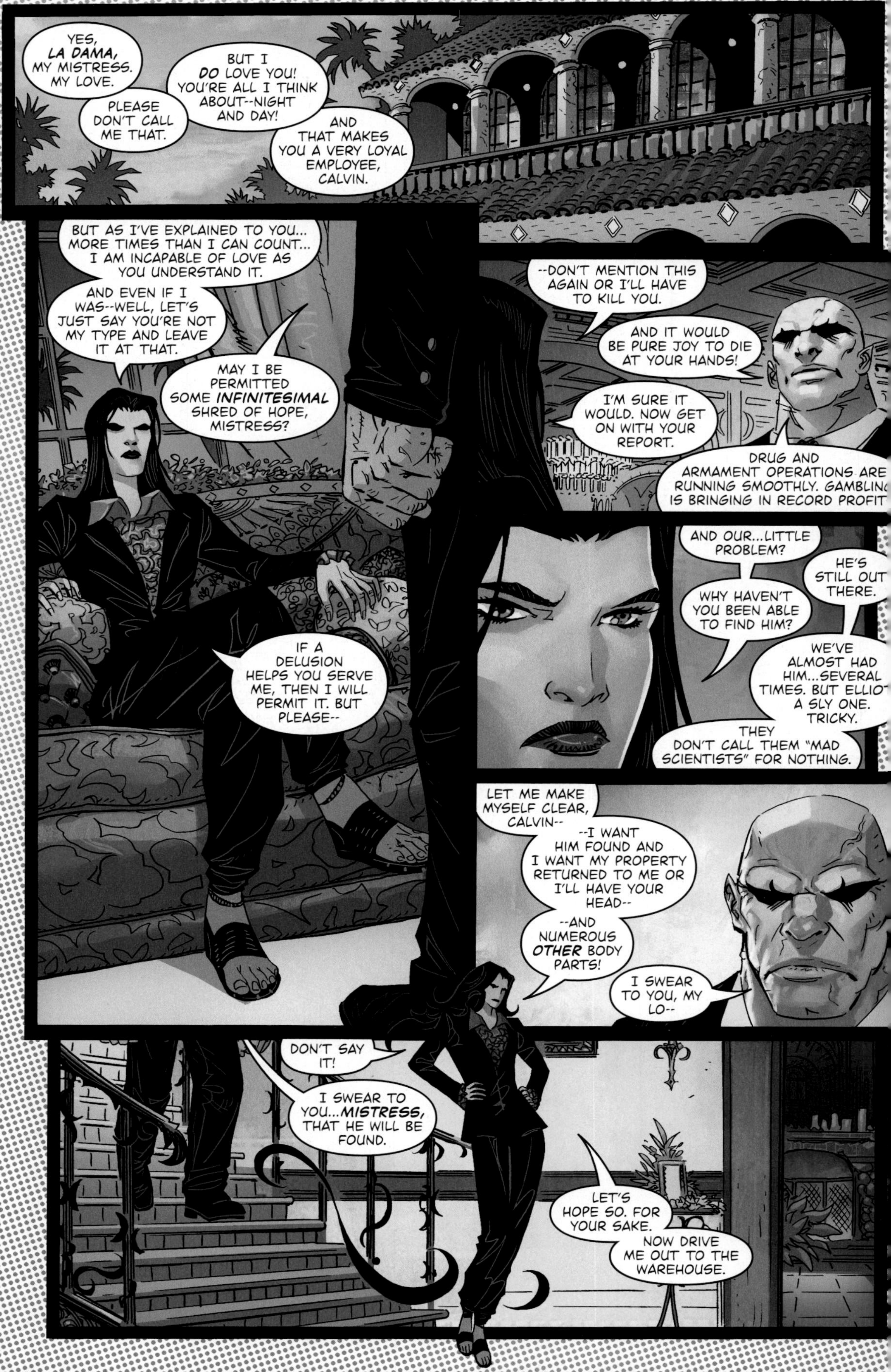
YES, LA DAMA, MY MISTRESS. MY LOVE.
PLEASE DON'T CALL ME THAT.
BUT I DO LOVE YOU! YOU'RE ALL I THINK ABOUT--NIGHT AND DAY!
AND THAT MAKES YOU A VERY LOYAL EMPLOYEE, CALVIN.
BUT AS I'VE EXPLAINED TO YOU... MORE TIMES THAN I CAN COUNT... I AM INCAPABLE OF LOVE AS YOU UNDERSTAND IT.
AND EVEN IF I WAS--WELL, LET'S JUST SAY YOU'RE NOT MY TYPE AND LEAVE IT AT THAT.
MAY I BE PERMITTED SOME INFINITESIMAL SHRED OF HOPE, MISTRESS?
IF A DELUSION HELPS YOU SERVE ME, THEN I WILL PERMIT IT. BUT PLEASE--
--DON'T MENTION THIS AGAIN OR I'LL HAVE TO KILL YOU.
AND IT WOULD BE PURE JOY TO DIE AT YOUR HANDS!
I'M SURE IT WOULD. NOW GET ON WITH YOUR REPORT.
DRUG AND ARMAMENT OPERATIONS ARE RUNNING SMOOTHLY. GAMBLING IS BRINGING IN RECORD PROFIT
AND OUR...LITTLE PROBLEM?
WHY HAVEN'T YOU BEEN ABLE TO FIND HIM?
HE'S STILL OUT THERE.
WE'VE ALMOST HAD HIM...SEVERAL TIMES. BUT ELLIOT A SLY ONE. TRICKY.
THEY DON'T CALL THEM "MAD SCIENTISTS" FOR NOTHING.
LET ME MAKE MYSELF CLEAR, CALVIN--
--I WANT HIM FOUND AND I WANT MY PROPERTY RETURNED TO ME OR I'LL HAVE YOUR HEAD--
--AND NUMEROUS OTHER BODY PARTS!
I SWEAR TO YOU, MY LO--
DON'T SAY IT!
I SWEAR TO YOU...MISTRESS, THAT HE WILL BE FOUND.
LET'S HOPE SO. FOR YOUR SAKE.
NOW DRIVE ME OUT TO THE WAREHOUSE.

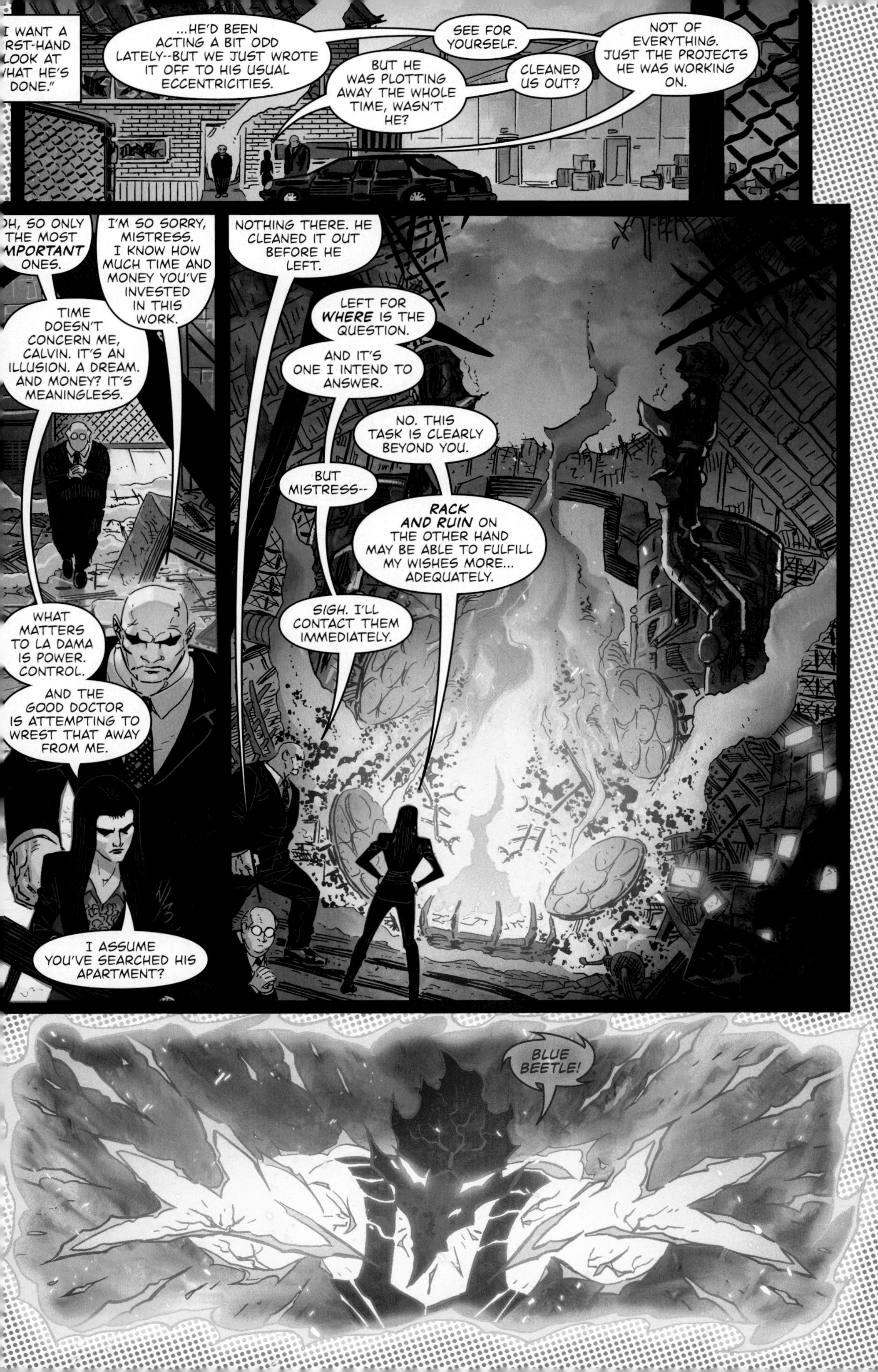

I WANT A RST-HAND LOOK AT WHAT HE'S DONE."
...HE'D BEEN ACTING A BIT ODD LATELY--BUT WE JUST WROTE IT OFF TO HIS USUAL ECCENTRICITIES.
BUT HE WAS PLOTTING AWAY THE WHOLE TIME, WASN'T HE?
SEE FOR YOURSELF.
CLEANED US OUT?
NOT OF EVERYTHING. JUST THE PROJECTS HE WAS WORKING ON.
OH, SO ONLY THE MOST *IMPORTANT* ONES.
I'M SO SORRY, MISTRESS. I KNOW HOW MUCH TIME AND MONEY YOU'VE INVESTED IN THIS WORK.
TIME DOESN'T CONCERN ME, CALVIN. IT'S AN ILLUSION. A DREAM. AND MONEY? IT'S MEANINGLESS.
WHAT MATTERS TO LA DAMA IS POWER. CONTROL.
AND THE GOOD DOCTOR IS ATTEMPTING TO WREST THAT AWAY FROM ME.
I ASSUME YOU'VE SEARCHED HIS APARTMENT?
NOTHING THERE. HE CLEANED IT OUT BEFORE HE LEFT.
LEFT FOR *WHERE* IS THE QUESTION.
AND IT'S ONE I INTEND TO ANSWER.
NO. THIS TASK IS CLEARLY BEYOND YOU.
BUT MISTRESS--
RACK AND RUIN ON THE OTHER HAND MAY BE ABLE TO FULFILL MY WISHES MORE... ADEQUATELY.
SIGH. I'LL CONTACT THEM IMMEDIATELY.
BLUE BEETLE!

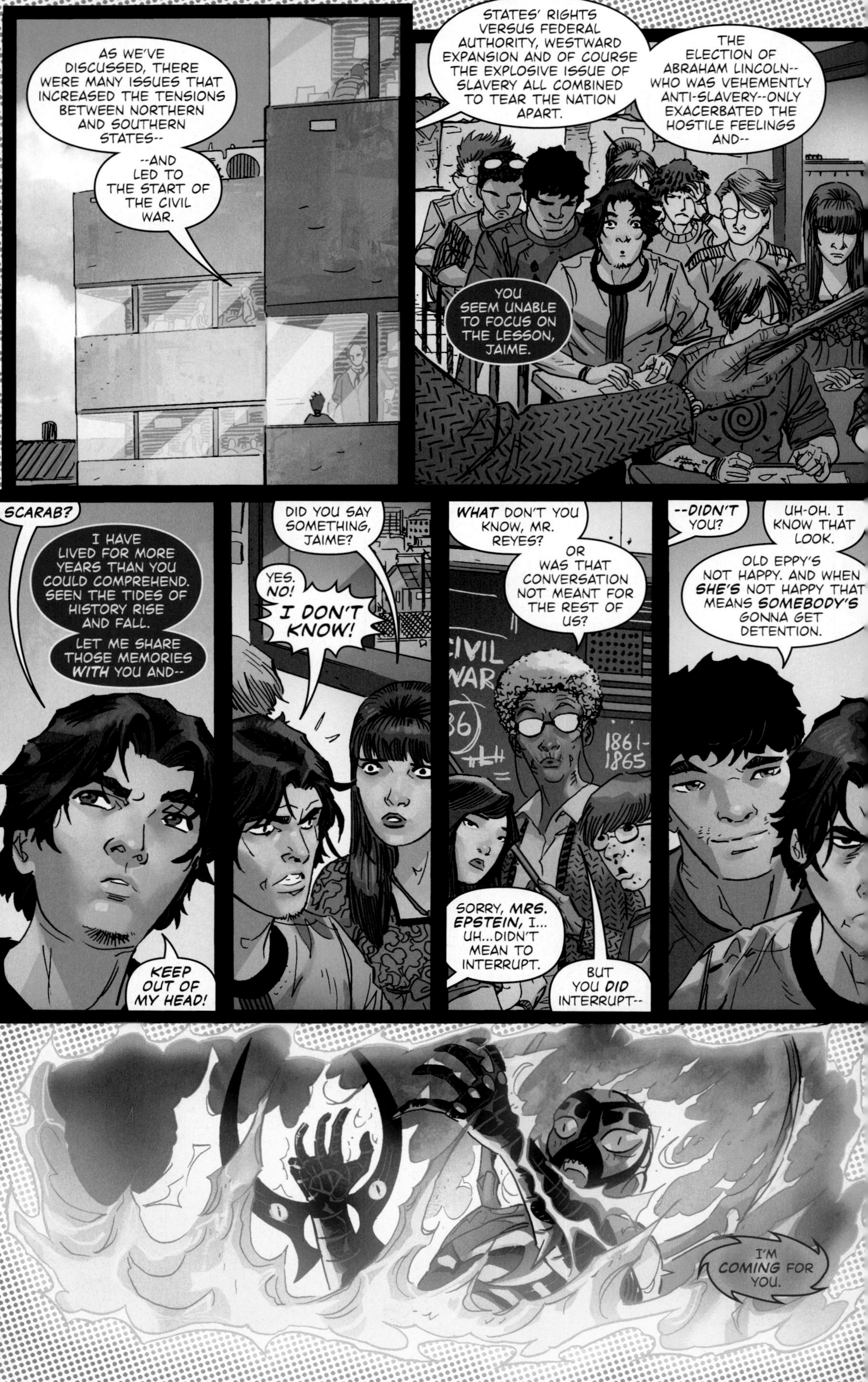
AS WE'VE DISCUSSED, THERE WERE MANY ISSUES THAT INCREASED THE TENSIONS BETWEEN NORTHERN AND SOUTHERN STATES--
--AND LED TO THE START OF THE CIVIL WAR.
STATES' RIGHTS VERSUS FEDERAL AUTHORITY, WESTWARD EXPANSION AND OF COURSE THE EXPLOSIVE ISSUE OF SLAVERY ALL COMBINED TO TEAR THE NATION APART.
THE ELECTION OF ABRAHAM LINCOLN--WHO WAS VEHEMENTLY ANTI-SLAVERY--ONLY EXACERBATED THE HOSTILE FEELINGS AND--
YOU SEEM UNABLE TO FOCUS ON THE LESSON, JAIME.
SCARAB?
I HAVE LIVED FOR MORE YEARS THAN YOU COULD COMPREHEND. SEEN THE TIDES OF HISTORY RISE AND FALL.
LET ME SHARE THOSE MEMORIES WITH YOU AND--
KEEP OUT OF MY HEAD!
DID YOU SAY SOMETHING, JAIME?
YES. NO!
I DON'T KNOW!
WHAT DON'T YOU KNOW, MR. REYES?
OR WAS THAT CONVERSATION NOT MEANT FOR THE REST OF US?
CIVIL WAR
1861-1865
SORRY, MRS. EPSTEIN, I... UH...DIDN'T MEAN TO INTERRUPT.
BUT YOU DID INTERRUPT--
--DIDN'T YOU?
UH-OH. I KNOW THAT LOOK.
OLD EPPY'S NOT HAPPY. AND WHEN SHE'S NOT HAPPY THAT MEANS SOMEBODY'S GONNA GET DETENTION.
I'M COMING FOR YOU.

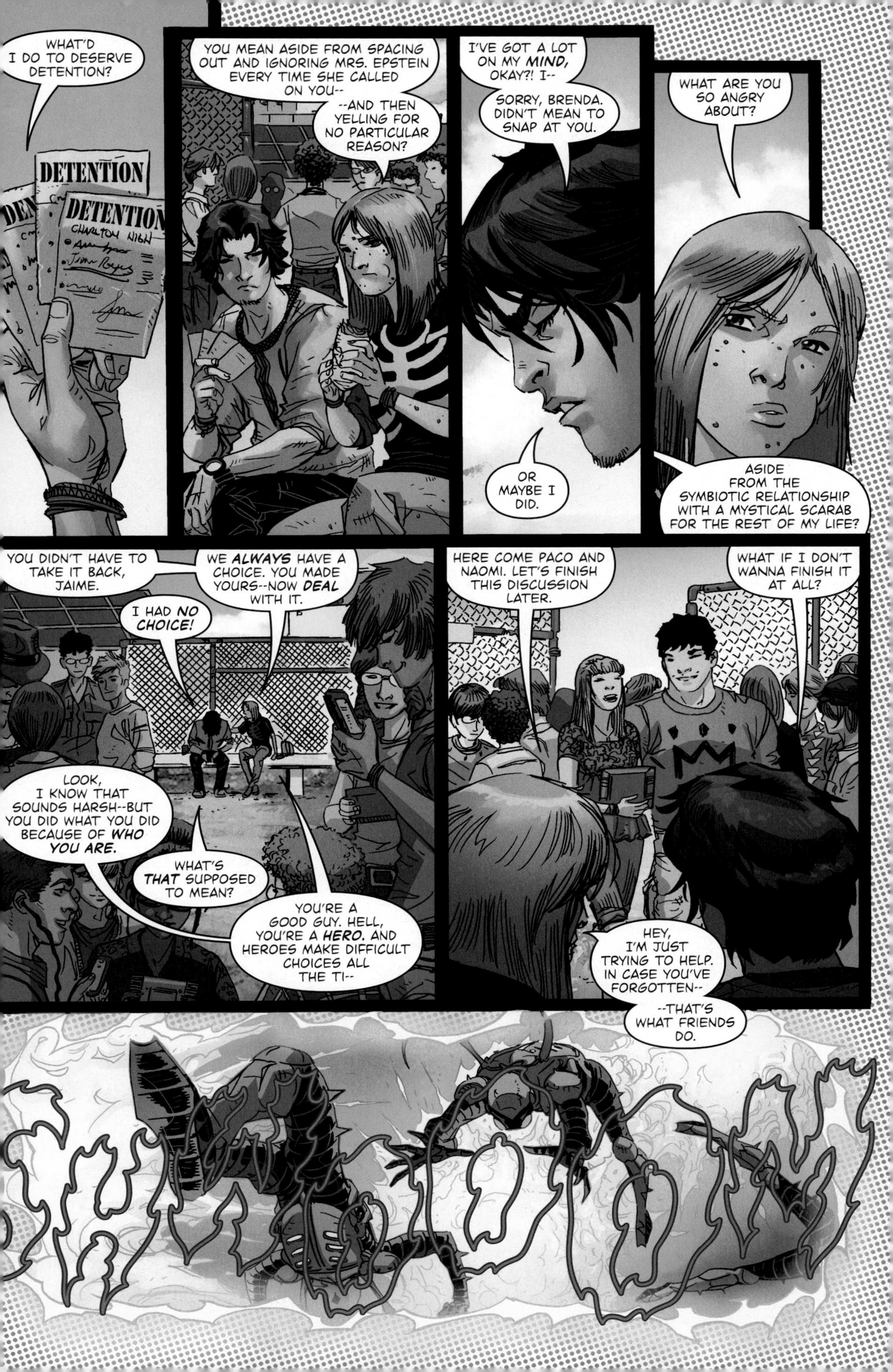

WHAT'D I DO TO DESERVE DETENTION?
DETENTION
DETENTION
CHARLTON HIGH
YOU MEAN ASIDE FROM SPACING OUT AND IGNORING MRS. EPSTEIN EVERY TIME SHE CALLED ON YOU--
--AND THEN YELLING FOR NO PARTICULAR REASON?
I'VE GOT A LOT ON MY *MIND*, OKAY?! I--
SORRY, BRENDA. DIDN'T MEAN TO SNAP AT YOU.
OR MAYBE I DID.
WHAT ARE YOU SO ANGRY ABOUT?
ASIDE FROM THE SYMBIOTIC RELATIONSHIP WITH A MYSTICAL SCARAB FOR THE REST OF MY LIFE?
YOU DIDN'T HAVE TO TAKE IT BACK, JAIME.
I HAD *NO CHOICE!*
WE *ALWAYS* HAVE A CHOICE. YOU MADE YOURS--NOW *DEAL* WITH IT.
LOOK, I KNOW THAT SOUNDS HARSH--BUT YOU DID WHAT YOU DID BECAUSE OF *WHO YOU ARE.*
WHAT'S *THAT* SUPPOSED TO MEAN?
YOU'RE A GOOD GUY. HELL, YOU'RE A *HERO.* AND HEROES MAKE DIFFICULT CHOICES ALL THE TI--
HERE COME PACO AND NAOMI. LET'S FINISH THIS DISCUSSION LATER.
WHAT IF I DON'T WANNA FINISH IT AT ALL?
HEY, I'M JUST TRYING TO HELP. IN CASE YOU'VE FORGOTTEN--
--THAT'S WHAT FRIENDS DO.

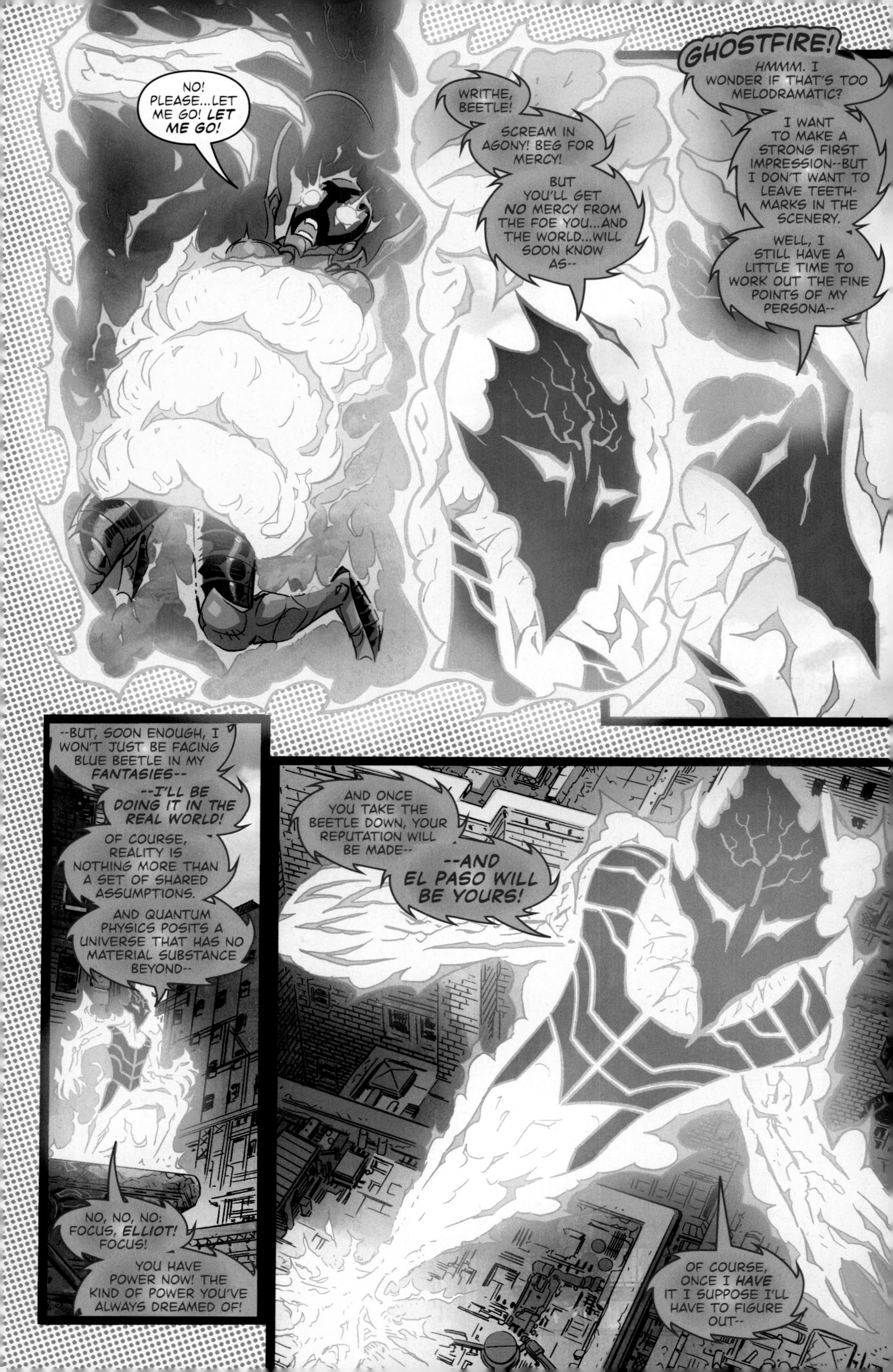
NO! PLEASE...LET ME GO! LET ME GO!
WRITHE, BEETLE!
SCREAM IN AGONY! BEG FOR MERCY!
BUT YOU'LL GET NO MERCY FROM THE FOE YOU...AND THE WORLD...WILL SOON KNOW AS--
GHOSTFIRE!
HMMM. I WONDER IF THAT'S TOO MELODRAMATIC?
I WANT TO MAKE A STRONG FIRST IMPRESSION--BUT I DON'T WANT TO LEAVE TEETH-MARKS IN THE SCENERY.
WELL, I STILL HAVE A LITTLE TIME TO WORK OUT THE FINE POINTS OF MY PERSONA--
--BUT, SOON ENOUGH, I WON'T JUST BE FACING BLUE BEETLE IN MY FANTASIES--
--I'LL BE DOING IT IN THE REAL WORLD!
OF COURSE, REALITY IS NOTHING MORE THAN A SET OF SHARED ASSUMPTIONS.
AND QUANTUM PHYSICS POSITS A UNIVERSE THAT HAS NO MATERIAL SUBSTANCE BEYOND--
NO, NO, NO: FOCUS, ELLIOT! FOCUS!
YOU HAVE POWER NOW! THE KIND OF POWER YOU'VE ALWAYS DREAMED OF!
AND ONCE YOU TAKE THE BEETLE DOWN, YOUR REPUTATION WILL BE MADE--
--AND EL PASO WILL BE YOURS!
OF COURSE, ONCE I HAVE IT I SUPPOSE I'LL HAVE TO FIGURE OUT--

"--WHAT I'M GOING TO DO WITH IT!"

YOU ARE RESTLESS, JAIME. THIS...DETENTION SEEMS TO HAVE AGITATED YOU.

SINCE WHEN DO YOU CARE? AND SINCE WHEN ARE YOU SO CHATTY?

NEVER BEFORE HAVE I BEEN RE-BONDED WITH A HOST. I AM ATTEMPTING TO ESTABLISH A MORE FELICITOUS RELATIONSHIP.

OR YOU'RE TRYING TO MANIPULATE ME.

WHY WOULD I DO THAT?

BECAUSE ALL THE TESTS TED AND MY MOM DID BEFORE INDICATED THAT YOU WERE ON THE VERGE OF...WHAT'D THEY SAY?... OVERWRITING MY PERSONALITY?

IT WAS NEVER MY INTENTION TO DO THAT.

BASICALLY ERASING ME FROM EXISTENCE.

SOMETIMES THE INITIAL BONDING EXPERIENCE SETS OFF CERTAIN PROTOCOLS THAT NEED TO BE ADJUSTED. MODIFIED.

IT IS NOT EASY FINDING THE CORRECT INTERNAL BALANCE WITH MY HOST.

NOW WHY DON'T I TRUST YOU?

YOU HAVE NO CHOICE BUT TO TRUST ME, JAIME. AND I HAVE NO CHOICE--

--BUT TO TRUST YOU IN RETURN.

YEAH? WELL SOMEONE TOLD ME TODAY THAT WE ALWAYS HAVE A CHOICE. NOW SHUT UP, WILL YOU?

AND LEAVE ME ALONE!

MR. REYES...? ARE YOU ALL RIGHT?

SIGH. FINE, MRS. EPSTEIN.

YOU DON'T SEEM FINE. YOU USED TO BE ONE OF MY BEST STUDENTS, JAIME, BUT LATELY--

ARE YOU HAVING TROUBLE AT HOME?

NO TROUBLE, MRS. EPSTEIN. REALLY.

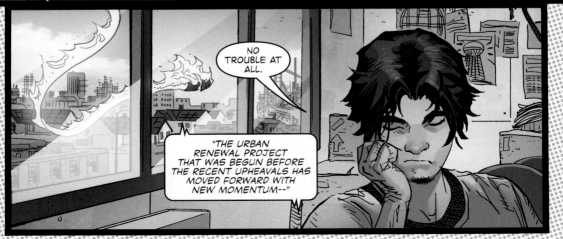

NO TROUBLE AT ALL.

"THE URBAN RENEWAL PROJECT THAT WAS BEGUN BEFORE THE RECENT UPHEAVALS HAS MOVED FORWARD WITH NEW MOMENTUM--"

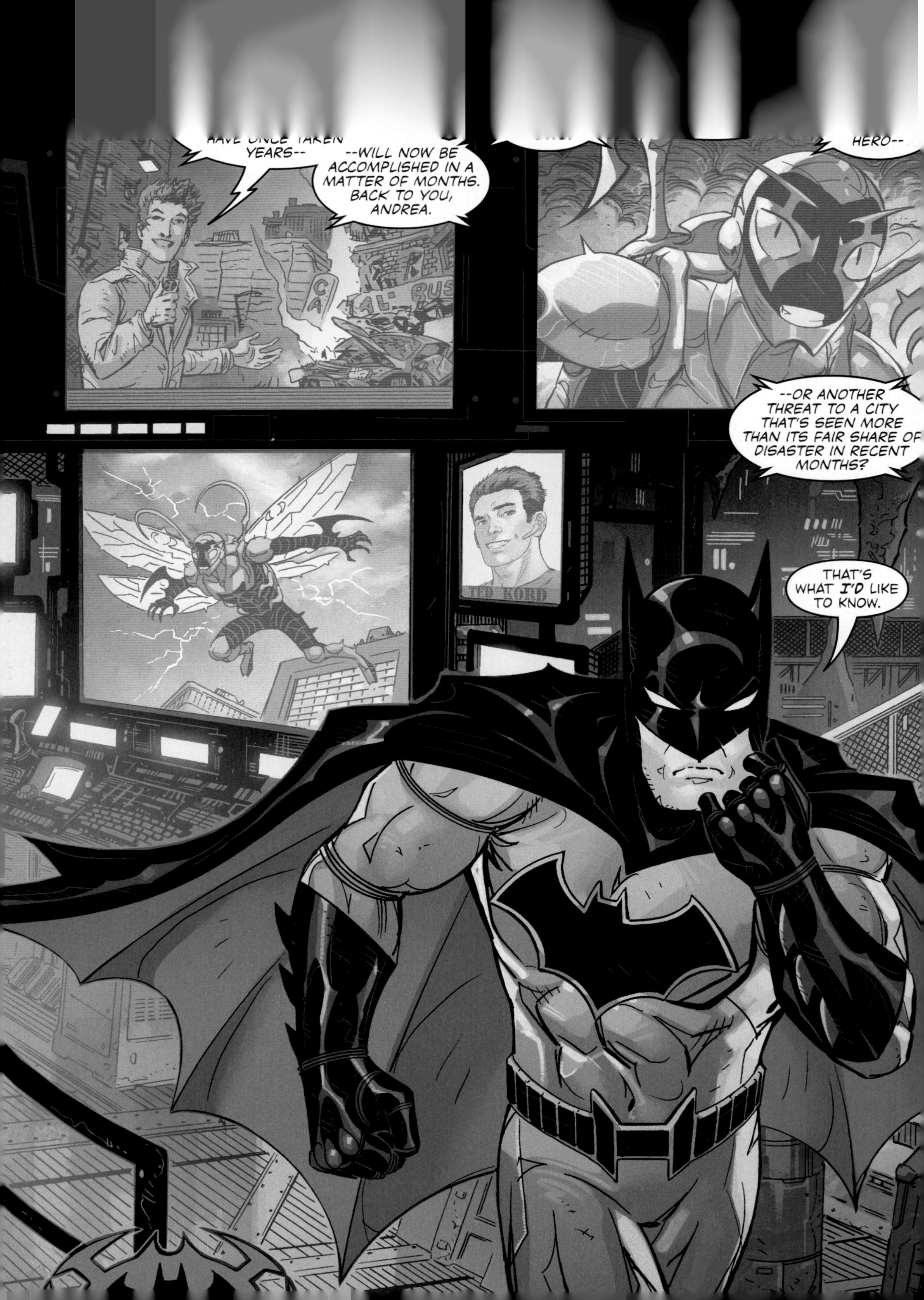
YEARS--
--WILL NOW BE ACCOMPLISHED IN A MATTER OF MONTHS. BACK TO YOU, ANDREA.
HERO--
--OR ANOTHER THREAT TO A CITY THAT'S SEEN MORE THAN ITS FAIR SHARE OF DISASTER IN RECENT MONTHS?
TED KORD
THAT'S WHAT I'D LIKE TO KNOW.

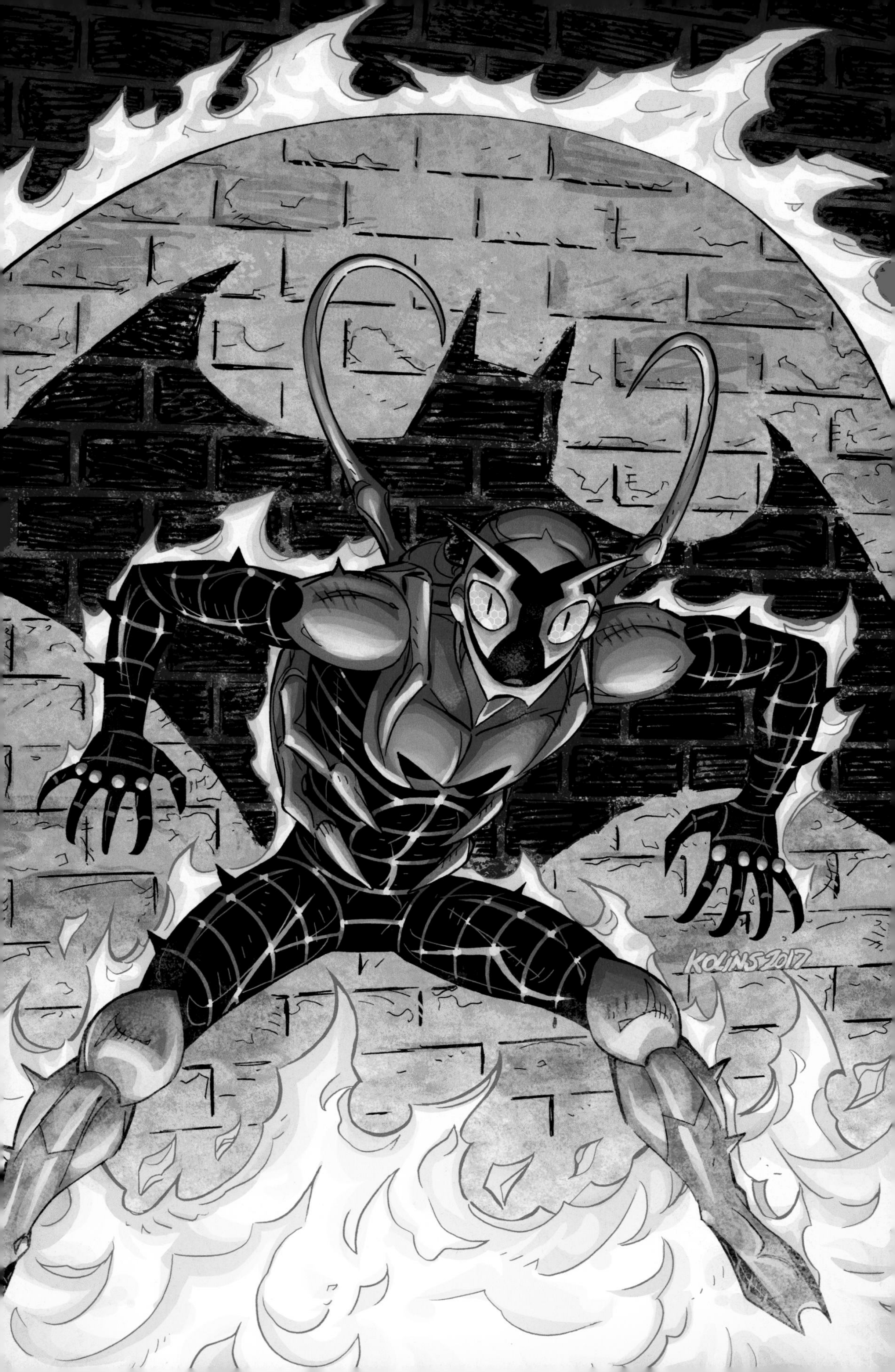
KOLINS2017

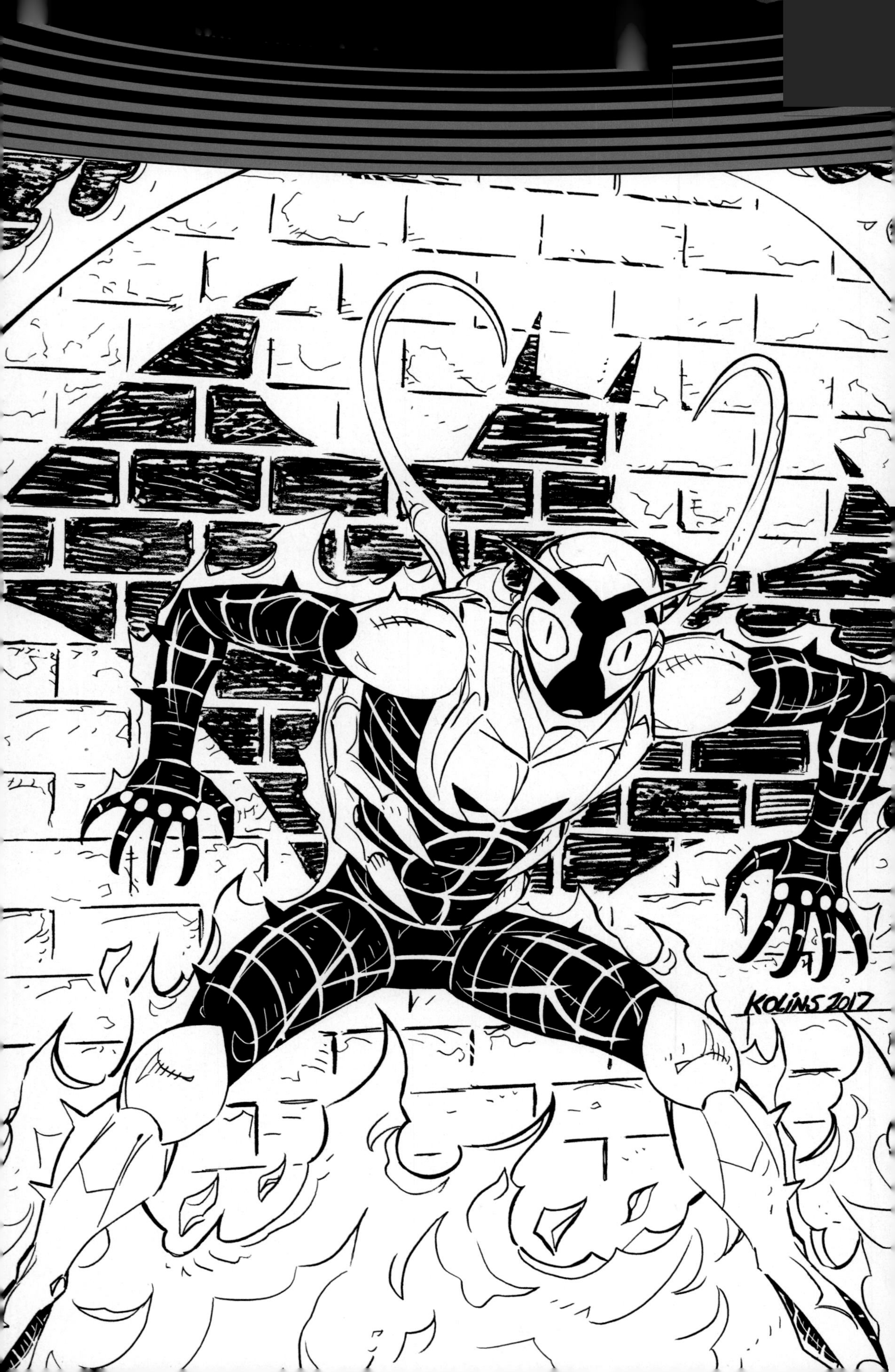
KOLINS 2017

blue beetle
EL PASO, TEXAS.
THE HEADQUARTERS OF KORD INDUSTRIES...
I'VE BEEN STANDING HERE FOR ALMOST FIVE MINUTES, KORD.
YIKES!
ISN'T IT ABOUT TIME YOU NOTICED?
WHY
KORD
TWO BEETLES-- AND A BAT!
JUST ONE MORE ISSUE TO GO FOR THE TEAM OF
KEITH GIFFEN, J.M. DEMATTEIS & SCOTT KOLINS
AND NO ONE'S HAPPIER THAN
JOSH REED, LETTERER • ROMULO FAJARDO JR., COLORIST
ROB LEVIN, ASSISTANT EDITOR • JIM CHADWICK, HECTORED AND HARRIED
BATMAN CREATED BY BOB KANE WITH BILL FINGER

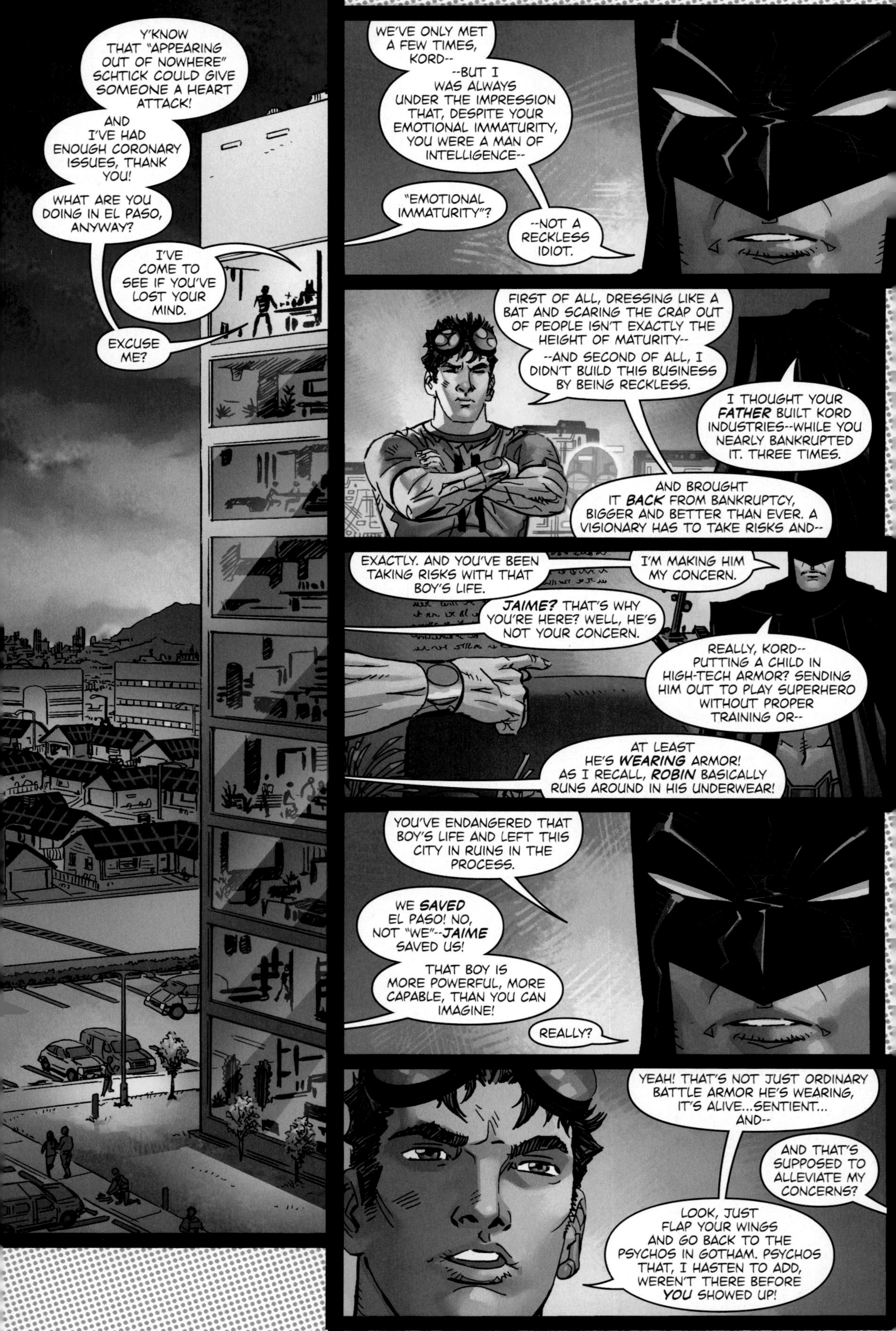
Y'KNOW THAT "APPEARING OUT OF NOWHERE" SCHTICK COULD GIVE SOMEONE A HEART ATTACK!
AND I'VE HAD ENOUGH CORONARY ISSUES, THANK YOU!
WHAT ARE YOU DOING IN EL PASO, ANYWAY?
I'VE COME TO SEE IF YOU'VE LOST YOUR MIND.
EXCUSE ME?
WE'VE ONLY MET A FEW TIMES, KORD--
--BUT I WAS ALWAYS UNDER THE IMPRESSION THAT, DESPITE YOUR EMOTIONAL IMMATURITY, YOU WERE A MAN OF INTELLIGENCE--
"EMOTIONAL IMMATURITY"?
--NOT A RECKLESS IDIOT.
FIRST OF ALL, DRESSING LIKE A BAT AND SCARING THE CRAP OUT OF PEOPLE ISN'T EXACTLY THE HEIGHT OF MATURITY--
--AND SECOND OF ALL, I DIDN'T BUILD THIS BUSINESS BY BEING RECKLESS.
I THOUGHT YOUR FATHER BUILT KORD INDUSTRIES--WHILE YOU NEARLY BANKRUPTED IT. THREE TIMES.
AND BROUGHT IT BACK FROM BANKRUPTCY, BIGGER AND BETTER THAN EVER. A VISIONARY HAS TO TAKE RISKS AND--
EXACTLY. AND YOU'VE BEEN TAKING RISKS WITH THAT BOY'S LIFE.
JAIME? THAT'S WHY YOU'RE HERE? WELL, HE'S NOT YOUR CONCERN.
I'M MAKING HIM MY CONCERN.
REALLY, KORD-- PUTTING A CHILD IN HIGH-TECH ARMOR? SENDING HIM OUT TO PLAY SUPERHERO WITHOUT PROPER TRAINING OR--
AT LEAST HE'S WEARING ARMOR! AS I RECALL, ROBIN BASICALLY RUNS AROUND IN HIS UNDERWEAR!
YOU'VE ENDANGERED THAT BOY'S LIFE AND LEFT THIS CITY IN RUINS IN THE PROCESS.
WE SAVED EL PASO! NO, NOT "WE"--JAIME SAVED US!
THAT BOY IS MORE POWERFUL, MORE CAPABLE, THAN YOU CAN IMAGINE!
REALLY?
YEAH! THAT'S NOT JUST ORDINARY BATTLE ARMOR HE'S WEARING, IT'S ALIVE...SENTIENT... AND--
AND THAT'S SUPPOSED TO ALLEVIATE MY CONCERNS?
LOOK, JUST FLAP YOUR WINGS AND GO BACK TO THE PSYCHOS IN GOTHAM. PSYCHOS THAT, I HASTEN TO ADD, WEREN'T THERE BEFORE YOU SHOWED UP!

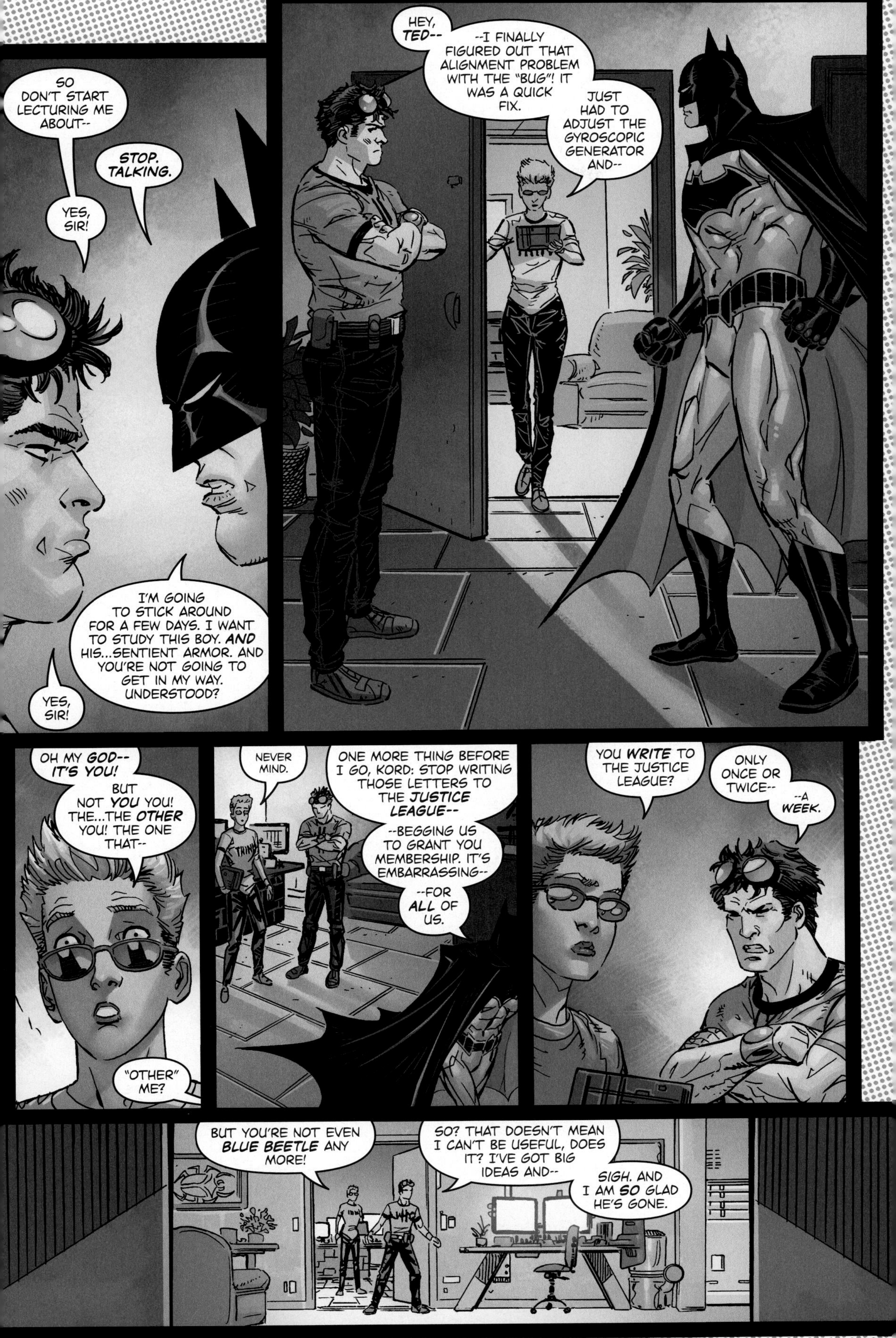
SO DON'T START LECTURING ME ABOUT--
STOP. TALKING.
YES, SIR!
I'M GOING TO STICK AROUND FOR A FEW DAYS. I WANT TO STUDY THIS BOY. AND HIS...SENTIENT ARMOR. AND YOU'RE NOT GOING TO GET IN MY WAY. UNDERSTOOD?
YES, SIR!
HEY, TED--
--I FINALLY FIGURED OUT THAT ALIGNMENT PROBLEM WITH THE "BUG"! IT WAS A QUICK FIX.
JUST HAD TO ADJUST THE GYROSCOPIC GENERATOR AND--
OH MY GOD-- IT'S YOU!
BUT NOT YOU YOU! THE...THE OTHER YOU! THE ONE THAT--
"OTHER" ME?
NEVER MIND.
ONE MORE THING BEFORE I GO, KORD: STOP WRITING THOSE LETTERS TO THE JUSTICE LEAGUE--
--BEGGING US TO GRANT YOU MEMBERSHIP. IT'S EMBARRASSING--
--FOR ALL OF US.
YOU WRITE TO THE JUSTICE LEAGUE?
ONLY ONCE OR TWICE--
--A WEEK.
BUT YOU'RE NOT EVEN BLUE BEETLE ANY MORE!
SO? THAT DOESN'T MEAN I CAN'T BE USEFUL, DOES IT? I'VE GOT BIG IDEAS AND--
SIGH. AND I AM SO GLAD HE'S GONE.

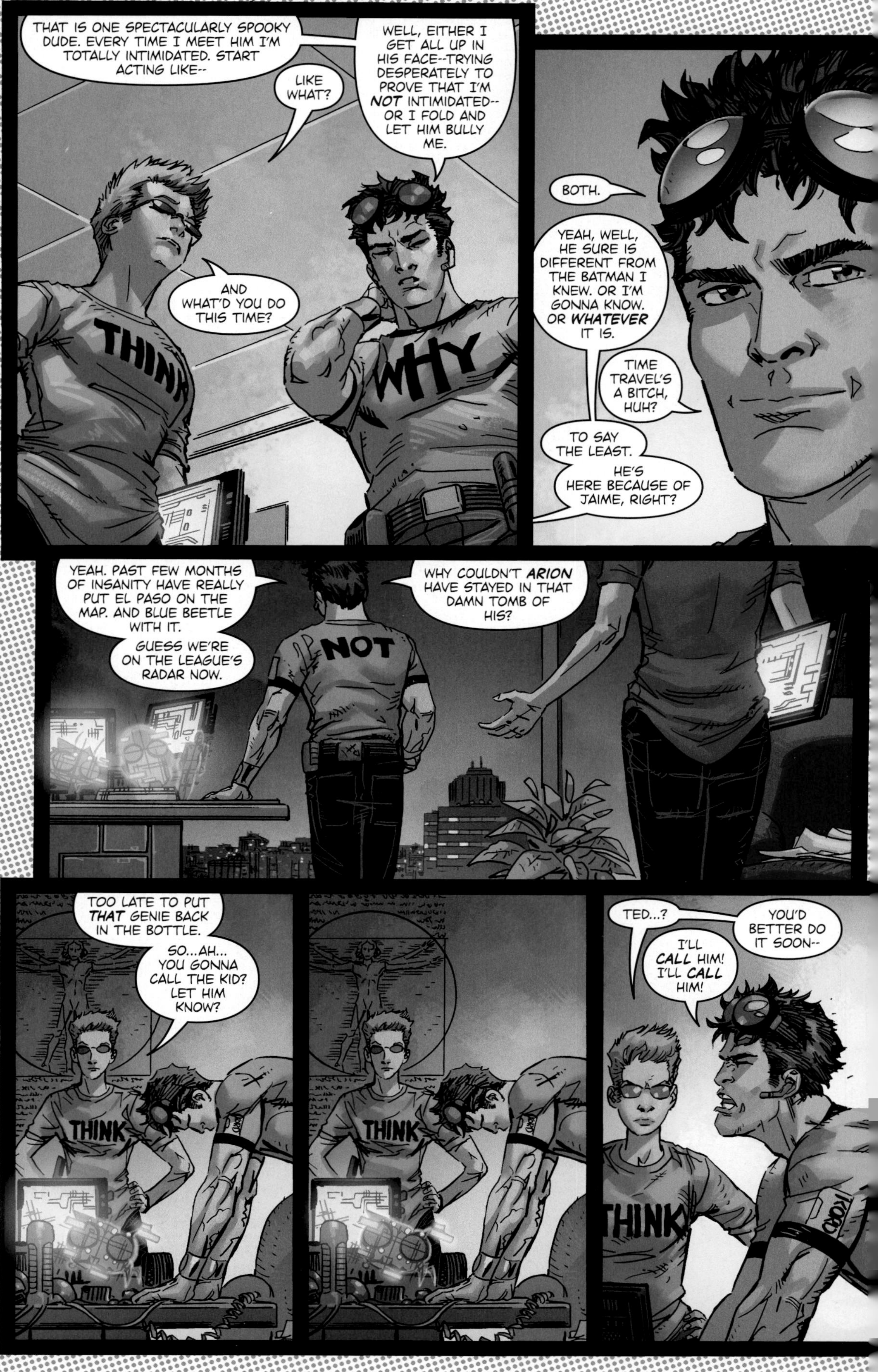
THAT IS ONE SPECTACULARLY SPOOKY DUDE. EVERY TIME I MEET HIM I'M TOTALLY INTIMIDATED. START ACTING LIKE--
LIKE WHAT?
WELL, EITHER I GET ALL UP IN HIS FACE--TRYING DESPERATELY TO PROVE THAT I'M NOT INTIMIDATED--OR I FOLD AND LET HIM BULLY ME.
AND WHAT'D YOU DO THIS TIME?
THINK
WHY
BOTH.
YEAH, WELL, HE SURE IS DIFFERENT FROM THE BATMAN I KNEW. OR I'M GONNA KNOW. OR WHATEVER IT IS.
TIME TRAVEL'S A BITCH, HUH?
TO SAY THE LEAST.
HE'S HERE BECAUSE OF JAIME, RIGHT?
YEAH. PAST FEW MONTHS OF INSANITY HAVE REALLY PUT EL PASO ON THE MAP. AND BLUE BEETLE WITH IT.
GUESS WE'RE ON THE LEAGUE'S RADAR NOW.
WHY COULDN'T ARION HAVE STAYED IN THAT DAMN TOMB OF HIS?
NOT
TOO LATE TO PUT THAT GENIE BACK IN THE BOTTLE.
SO...AH... YOU GONNA CALL THE KID? LET HIM KNOW?
THINK
THINK
TED...?
YOU'D BETTER DO IT SOON--
I'LL CALL HIM! I'LL CALL HIM!
THINK
KORD

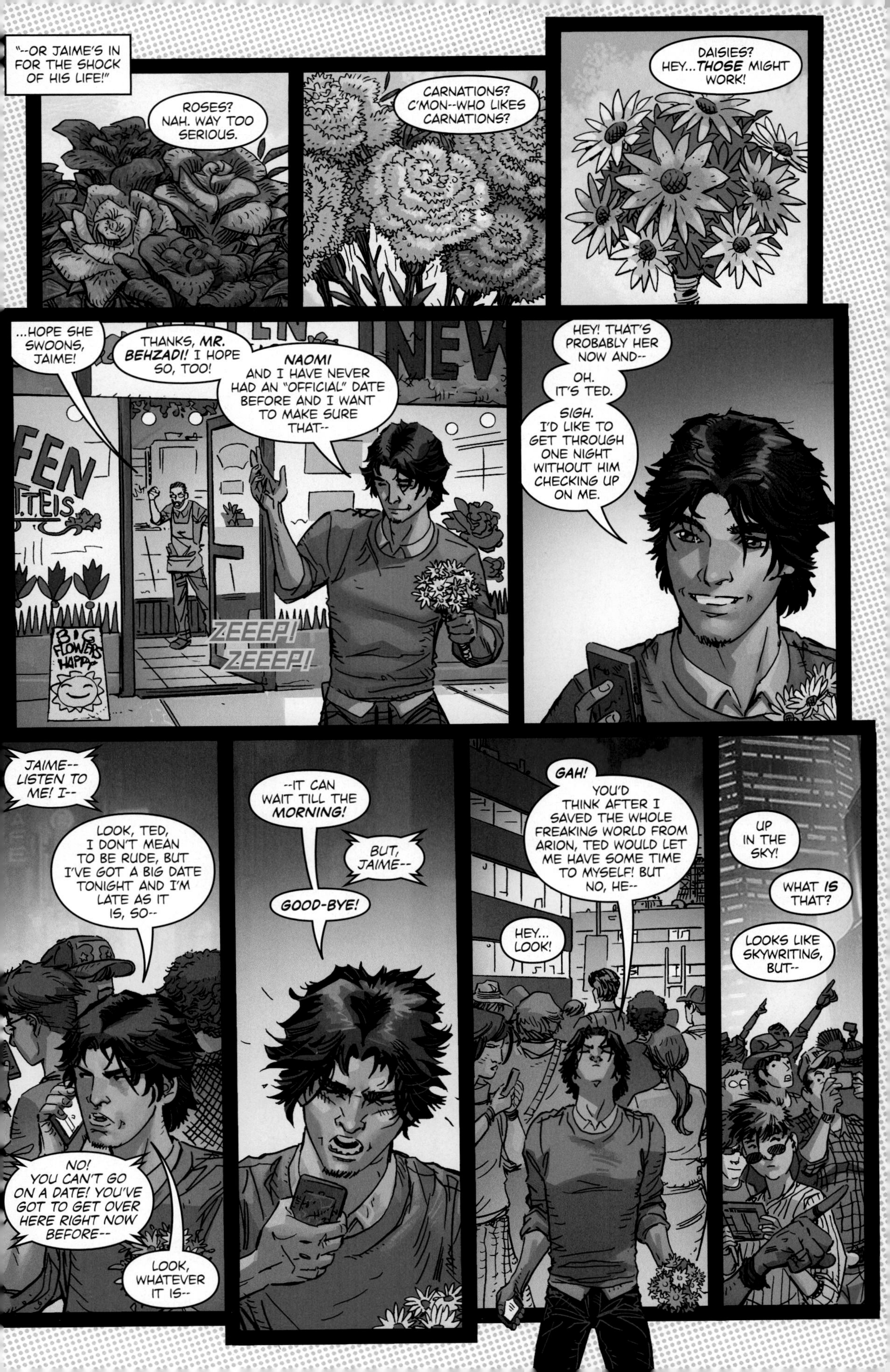
"--OR JAIME'S IN FOR THE SHOCK OF HIS LIFE!"
ROSES? NAH. WAY TOO SERIOUS.
CARNATIONS? C'MON--WHO LIKES CARNATIONS?
DAISIES? HEY...THOSE MIGHT WORK!
...HOPE SHE SWOONS, JAIME!
THANKS, MR. BEHZADI! I HOPE SO, TOO!
NAOMI AND I HAVE NEVER HAD AN "OFFICIAL" DATE BEFORE AND I WANT TO MAKE SURE THAT--
BIG FLOWERS HAPPY
ZEEEP! ZEEEP!
HEY! THAT'S PROBABLY HER NOW AND--
OH. IT'S TED.
SIGH. I'D LIKE TO GET THROUGH ONE NIGHT WITHOUT HIM CHECKING UP ON ME.
JAIME-- LISTEN TO ME! I--
LOOK, TED, I DON'T MEAN TO BE RUDE, BUT I'VE GOT A BIG DATE TONIGHT AND I'M LATE AS IT IS, SO--
NO! YOU CAN'T GO ON A DATE! YOU'VE GOT TO GET OVER HERE RIGHT NOW BEFORE--
LOOK, WHATEVER IT IS--
--IT CAN WAIT TILL THE MORNING!
BUT, JAIME--
GOOD-BYE!
GAH!
YOU'D THINK AFTER I SAVED THE WHOLE FREAKING WORLD FROM ARION, TED WOULD LET ME HAVE SOME TIME TO MYSELF! BUT NO, HE--
HEY... LOOK!
UP IN THE SKY!
WHAT IS THAT?
LOOKS LIKE SKYWRITING, BUT--

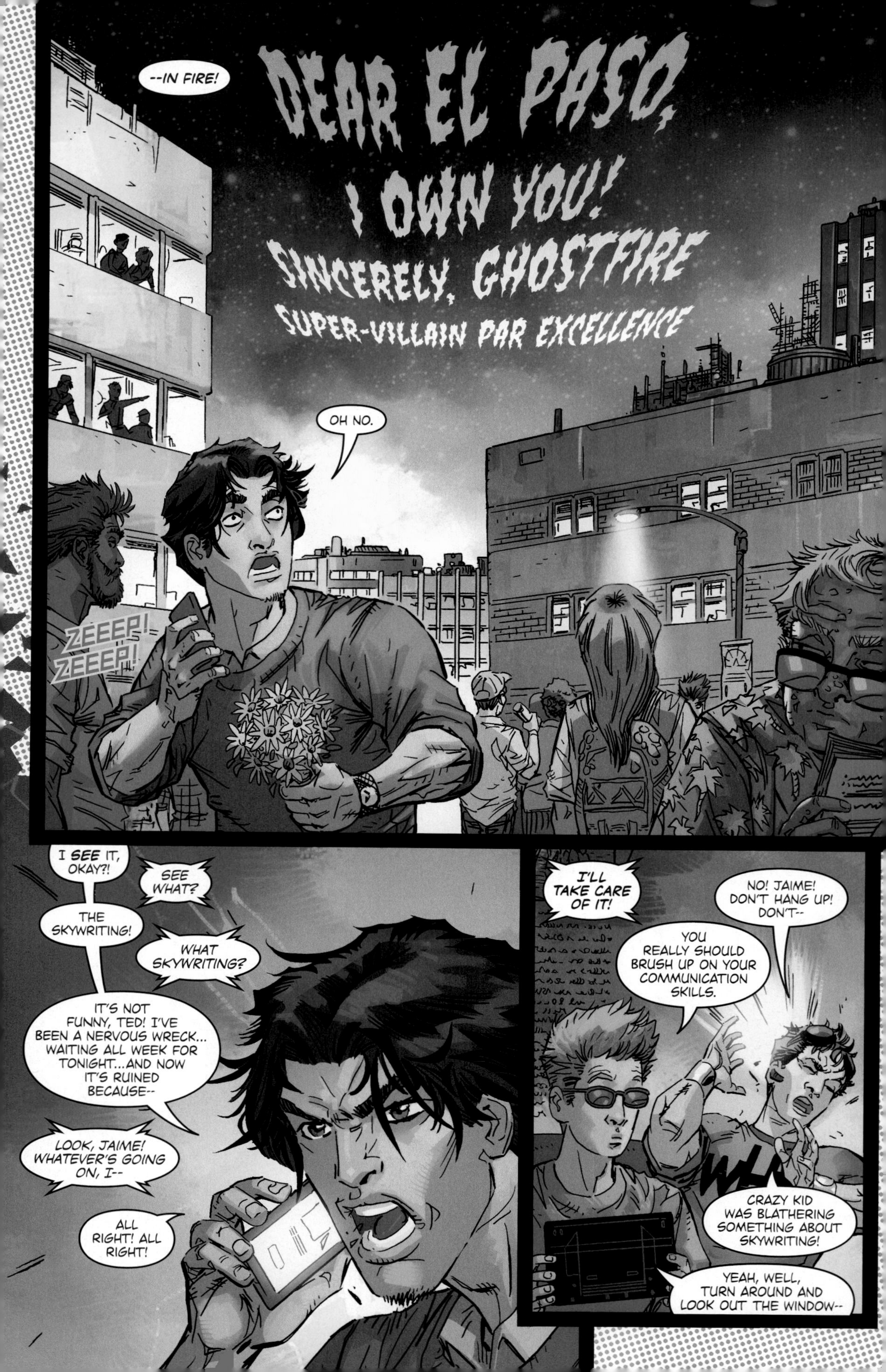
--IN FIRE!
DEAR EL PASO, I OWN YOU! SINCERELY, GHOSTFIRE SUPER-VILLAIN PAR EXCELLENCE
OH NO.
ZEEEP! ZEEEP!
I SEE IT, OKAY?!
SEE WHAT?
THE SKYWRITING!
WHAT SKYWRITING?
IT'S NOT FUNNY, TED! I'VE BEEN A NERVOUS WRECK... WAITING ALL WEEK FOR TONIGHT...AND NOW IT'S RUINED BECAUSE--
LOOK, JAIME! WHATEVER'S GOING ON, I--
ALL RIGHT! ALL RIGHT!
I'LL TAKE CARE OF IT!
NO! JAIME! DON'T HANG UP! DON'T--
YOU REALLY SHOULD BRUSH UP ON YOUR COMMUNICATION SKILLS.
CRAZY KID WAS BLATHERING SOMETHING ABOUT SKYWRITING!
YEAH, WELL, TURN AROUND AND LOOK OUT THE WINDOW--

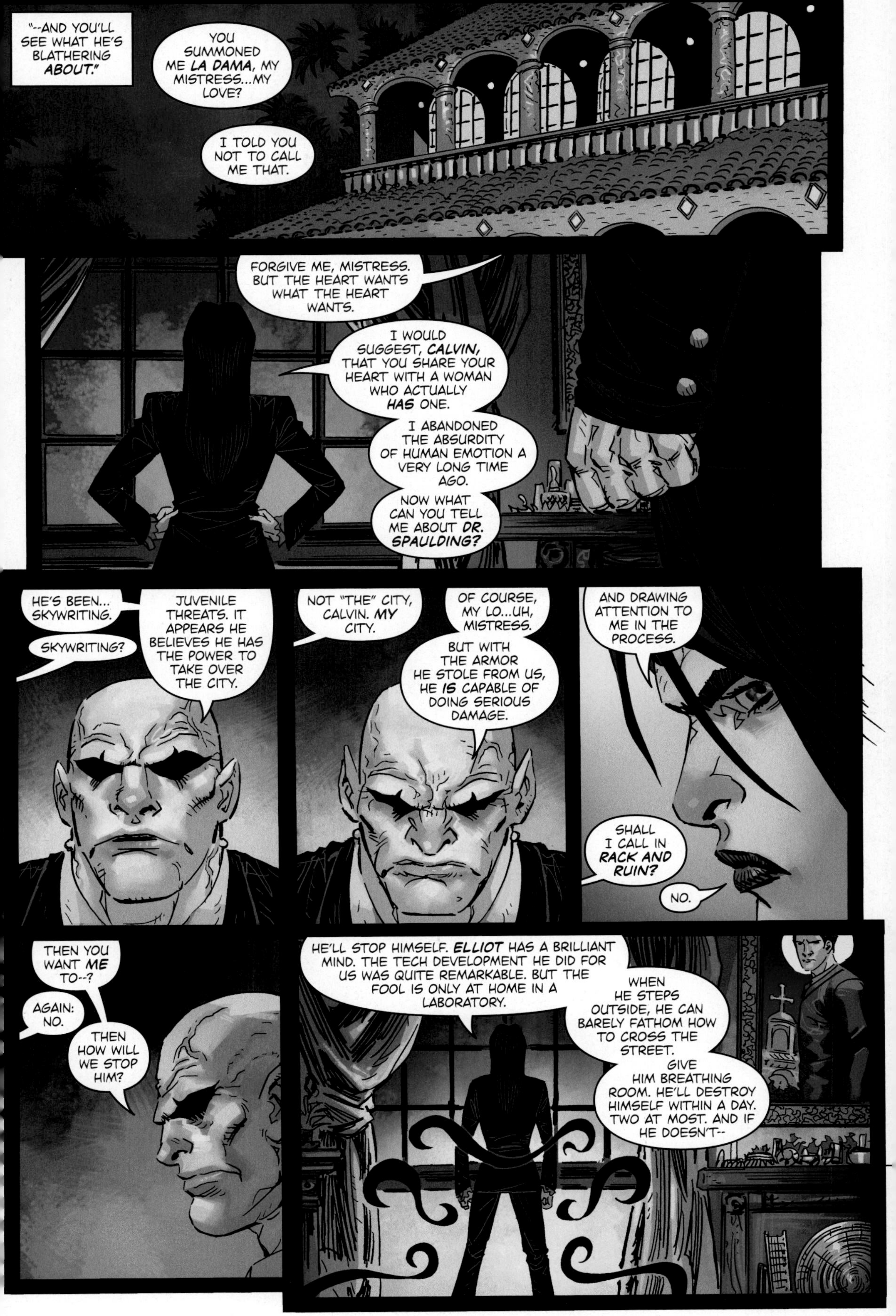
"--AND YOU'LL SEE WHAT HE'S BLATHERING ABOUT."
YOU SUMMONED ME LA DAMA, MY MISTRESS...MY LOVE?
I TOLD YOU NOT TO CALL ME THAT.
FORGIVE ME, MISTRESS. BUT THE HEART WANTS WHAT THE HEART WANTS.
I WOULD SUGGEST, CALVIN, THAT YOU SHARE YOUR HEART WITH A WOMAN WHO ACTUALLY HAS ONE.
I ABANDONED THE ABSURDITY OF HUMAN EMOTION A VERY LONG TIME AGO.
NOW WHAT CAN YOU TELL ME ABOUT DR. SPAULDING?
HE'S BEEN... SKYWRITING.
SKYWRITING?
JUVENILE THREATS. IT APPEARS HE BELIEVES HE HAS THE POWER TO TAKE OVER THE CITY.
NOT "THE" CITY, CALVIN. MY CITY.
OF COURSE, MY LO...UH, MISTRESS.
BUT WITH THE ARMOR HE STOLE FROM US, HE IS CAPABLE OF DOING SERIOUS DAMAGE.
AND DRAWING ATTENTION TO ME IN THE PROCESS.
SHALL I CALL IN RACK AND RUIN?
NO.
THEN YOU WANT ME TO--?
AGAIN: NO.
THEN HOW WILL WE STOP HIM?
HE'LL STOP HIMSELF. ELLIOT HAS A BRILLIANT MIND. THE TECH DEVELOPMENT HE DID FOR US WAS QUITE REMARKABLE. BUT THE FOOL IS ONLY AT HOME IN A LABORATORY.
WHEN HE STEPS OUTSIDE, HE CAN BARELY FATHOM HOW TO CROSS THE STREET.
GIVE HIM BREATHING ROOM. HE'LL DESTROY HIMSELF WITHIN A DAY. TWO AT MOST. AND IF HE DOESN'T--

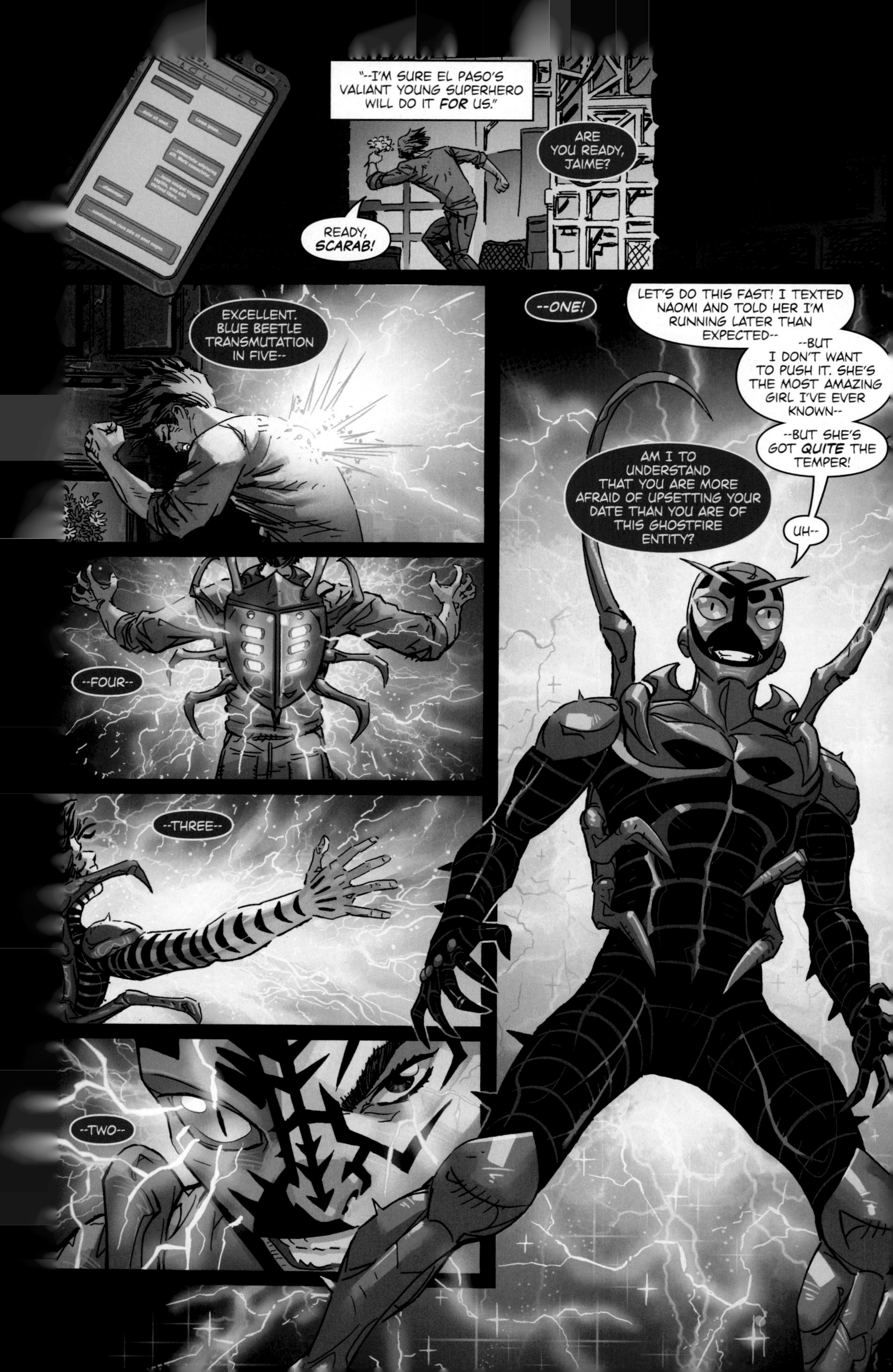
"--I'M SURE EL PASO'S VALIANT YOUNG SUPERHERO WILL DO IT FOR US."
ARE YOU READY, JAIME?
READY, SCARAB!
EXCELLENT. BLUE BEETLE TRANSMUTATION IN FIVE--
--FOUR--
--THREE--
--TWO--
--ONE!
LET'S DO THIS FAST! I TEXTED NAOMI AND TOLD HER I'M RUNNING LATER THAN EXPECTED--
--BUT I DON'T WANT TO PUSH IT. SHE'S THE MOST AMAZING GIRL I'VE EVER KNOWN--
--BUT SHE'S GOT QUITE THE TEMPER!
AM I TO UNDERSTAND THAT YOU ARE MORE AFRAID OF UPSETTING YOUR DATE THAN YOU ARE OF THIS GHOSTFIRE ENTITY?
UH--

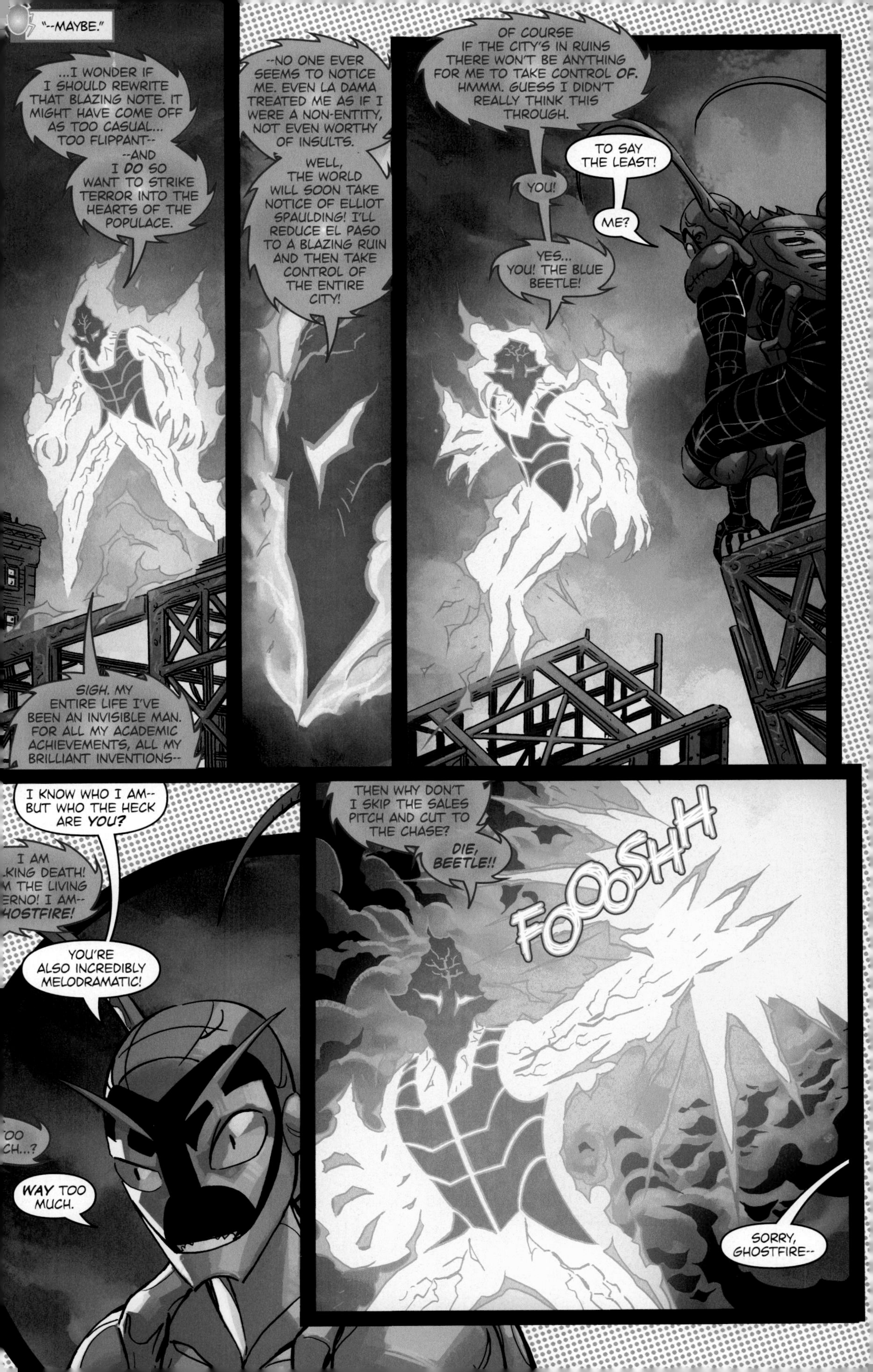

"--MAYBE."
...I WONDER IF I SHOULD REWRITE THAT BLAZING NOTE. IT MIGHT HAVE COME OFF AS TOO CASUAL... TOO FLIPPANT--
--AND I DO SO WANT TO STRIKE TERROR INTO THE HEARTS OF THE POPULACE.
SIGH. MY ENTIRE LIFE I'VE BEEN AN INVISIBLE MAN. FOR ALL MY ACADEMIC ACHIEVEMENTS, ALL MY BRILLIANT INVENTIONS--
--NO ONE EVER SEEMS TO NOTICE ME. EVEN LA DAMA TREATED ME AS IF I WERE A NON-ENTITY, NOT EVEN WORTHY OF INSULTS.
WELL, THE WORLD WILL SOON TAKE NOTICE OF ELLIOT SPAULDING! I'LL REDUCE EL PASO TO A BLAZING RUIN AND THEN TAKE CONTROL OF THE ENTIRE CITY!
OF COURSE IF THE CITY'S IN RUINS THERE WON'T BE ANYTHING FOR ME TO TAKE CONTROL OF. HMMM. GUESS I DIDN'T REALLY THINK THIS THROUGH.
TO SAY THE LEAST!
YOU!
ME?
YES... YOU! THE BLUE BEETLE!
I KNOW WHO I AM-- BUT WHO THE HECK ARE YOU?
YOU'RE ALSO INCREDIBLY MELODRAMATIC!
WAY TOO MUCH.
THEN WHY DON'T I SKIP THE SALES PITCH AND CUT TO THE CHASE?
DIE, BEETLE!!
FOOOSHH
SORRY, GHOSTFIRE--

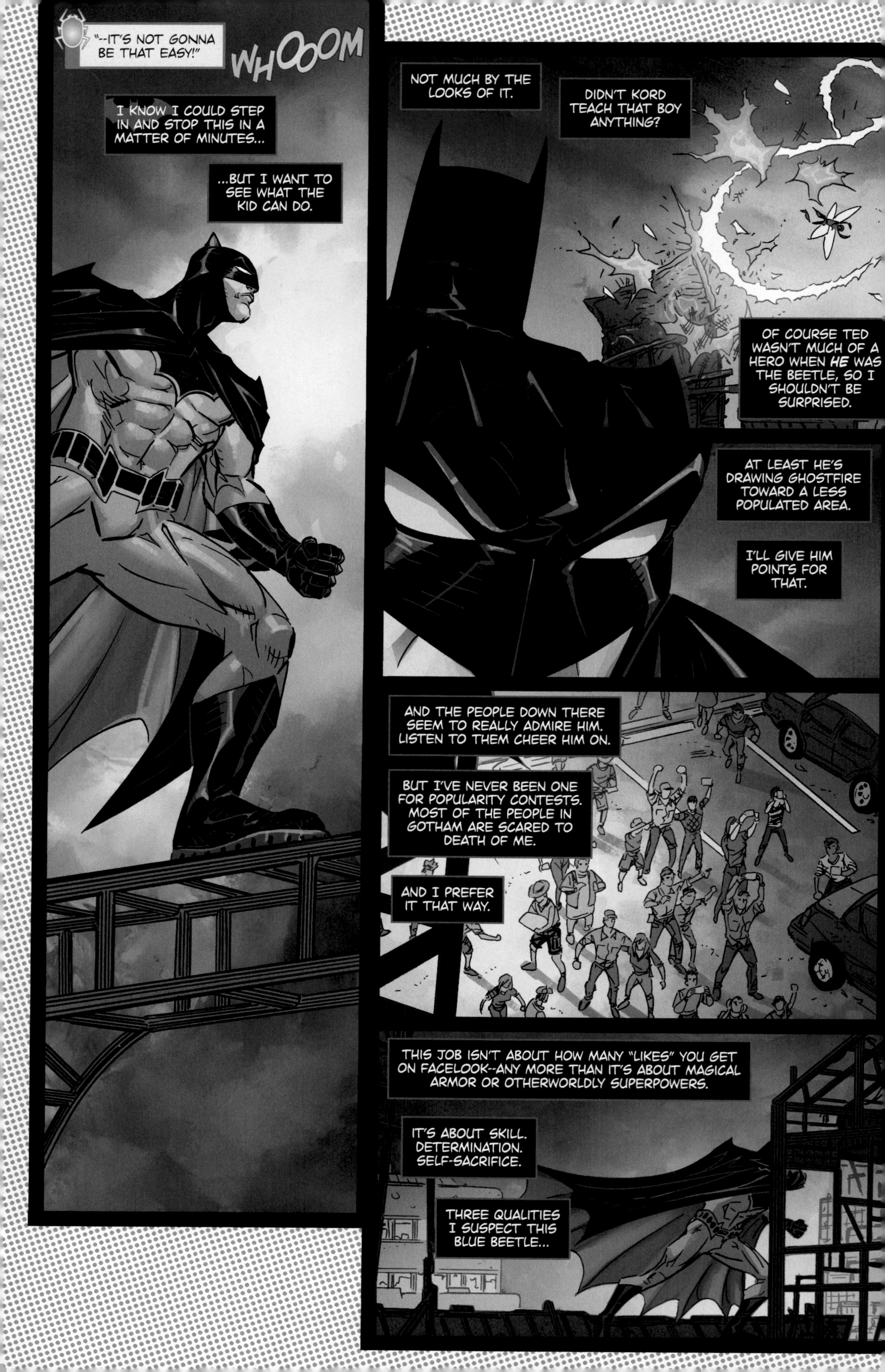
"--IT'S NOT GONNA BE THAT EASY!"
WHOOOOM
I KNOW I COULD STEP IN AND STOP THIS IN A MATTER OF MINUTES...
...BUT I WANT TO SEE WHAT THE KID CAN DO.
NOT MUCH BY THE LOOKS OF IT.
DIDN'T KORD TEACH THAT BOY ANYTHING?
OF COURSE TED WASN'T MUCH OF A HERO WHEN *HE* WAS THE BEETLE, SO I SHOULDN'T BE SURPRISED.
AT LEAST HE'S DRAWING GHOSTFIRE TOWARD A LESS POPULATED AREA.
I'LL GIVE HIM POINTS FOR THAT.
AND THE PEOPLE DOWN THERE SEEM TO REALLY ADMIRE HIM. LISTEN TO THEM CHEER HIM ON.
BUT I'VE NEVER BEEN ONE FOR POPULARITY CONTESTS. MOST OF THE PEOPLE IN GOTHAM ARE SCARED TO DEATH OF ME.
AND I PREFER IT THAT WAY.
THIS JOB ISN'T ABOUT HOW MANY "LIKES" YOU GET ON FACELOOK--ANY MORE THAN IT'S ABOUT MAGICAL ARMOR OR OTHERWORLDLY SUPERPOWERS.
IT'S ABOUT SKILL. DETERMINATION. SELF-SACRIFICE.
THREE QUALITIES I SUSPECT THIS BLUE BEETLE...

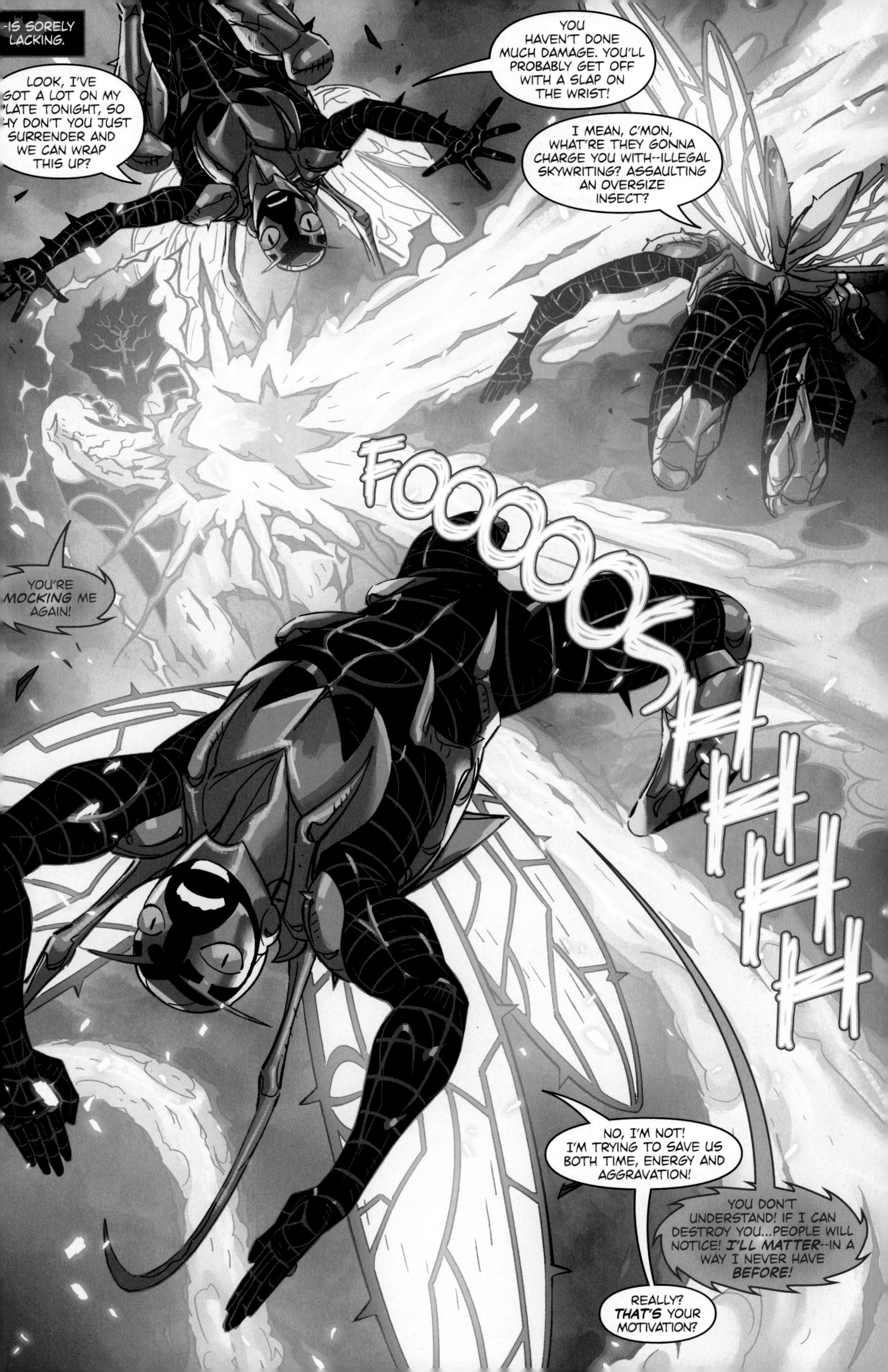

-IS SORELY LACKING.
LOOK, I'VE GOT A LOT ON MY PLATE TONIGHT, SO WHY DON'T YOU JUST SURRENDER AND WE CAN WRAP THIS UP?
YOU HAVEN'T DONE MUCH DAMAGE. YOU'LL PROBABLY GET OFF WITH A SLAP ON THE WRIST!
I MEAN, C'MON, WHAT'RE THEY GONNA CHARGE YOU WITH--ILLEGAL SKYWRITING? ASSAULTING AN OVERSIZE INSECT?
FOOOOOOSHHHHH
YOU'RE *MOCKING* ME AGAIN!
NO, I'M NOT! I'M TRYING TO SAVE US BOTH TIME, ENERGY AND AGGRAVATION!
YOU DON'T UNDERSTAND! IF I CAN DESTROY YOU...PEOPLE WILL NOTICE! ***I'LL MATTER***--IN A WAY I NEVER HAVE ***BEFORE!***
REALLY? ***THAT'S*** YOUR MOTIVATION?

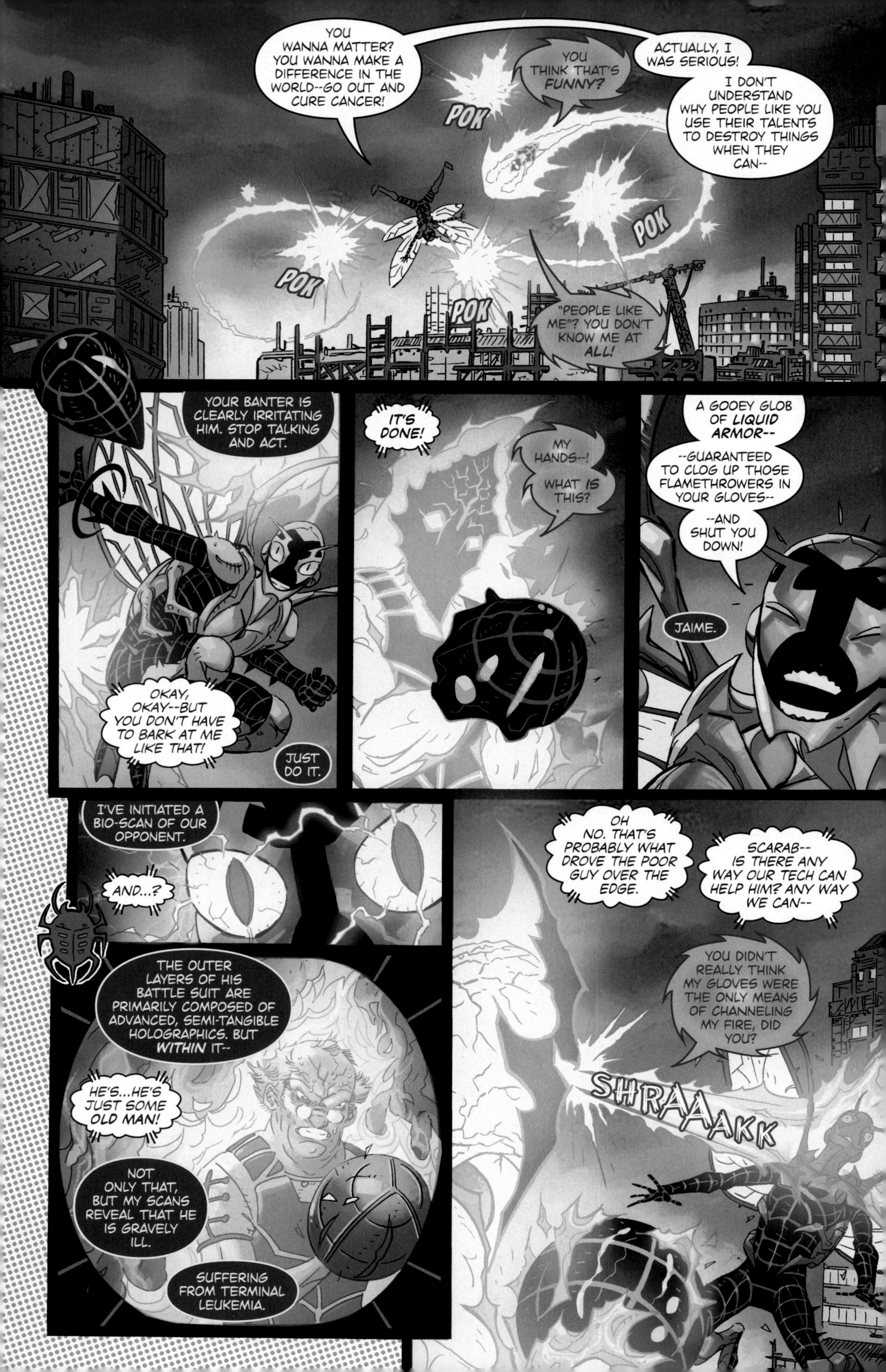
YOU WANNA MATTER? YOU WANNA MAKE A DIFFERENCE IN THE WORLD--GO OUT AND CURE CANCER!
YOU THINK THAT'S FUNNY?
ACTUALLY, I WAS SERIOUS!
I DON'T UNDERSTAND WHY PEOPLE LIKE YOU USE THEIR TALENTS TO DESTROY THINGS WHEN THEY CAN--
POK
POK
POK
POK
"PEOPLE LIKE ME"? YOU DON'T KNOW ME AT ALL!
YOUR BANTER IS CLEARLY IRRITATING HIM. STOP TALKING AND ACT.
OKAY, OKAY--BUT YOU DON'T HAVE TO BARK AT ME LIKE THAT!
JUST DO IT.
IT'S DONE!
MY HANDS--!
WHAT IS THIS?
A GOOEY GLOB OF LIQUID ARMOR--
--GUARANTEED TO CLOG UP THOSE FLAMETHROWERS IN YOUR GLOVES--
--AND SHUT YOU DOWN!
JAIME.
I'VE INITIATED A BIO-SCAN OF OUR OPPONENT.
AND...?
THE OUTER LAYERS OF HIS BATTLE SUIT ARE PRIMARILY COMPOSED OF ADVANCED, SEMI-TANGIBLE HOLOGRAPHICS. BUT WITHIN IT--
HE'S...HE'S JUST SOME OLD MAN!
NOT ONLY THAT, BUT MY SCANS REVEAL THAT HE IS GRAVELY ILL.
SUFFERING FROM TERMINAL LEUKEMIA.
OH NO. THAT'S PROBABLY WHAT DROVE THE POOR GUY OVER THE EDGE.
SCARAB-- IS THERE ANY WAY OUR TECH CAN HELP HIM? ANY WAY WE CAN--
YOU DIDN'T REALLY THINK MY GLOVES WERE THE ONLY MEANS OF CHANNELING MY FIRE, DID YOU?
SHRAAAAKK

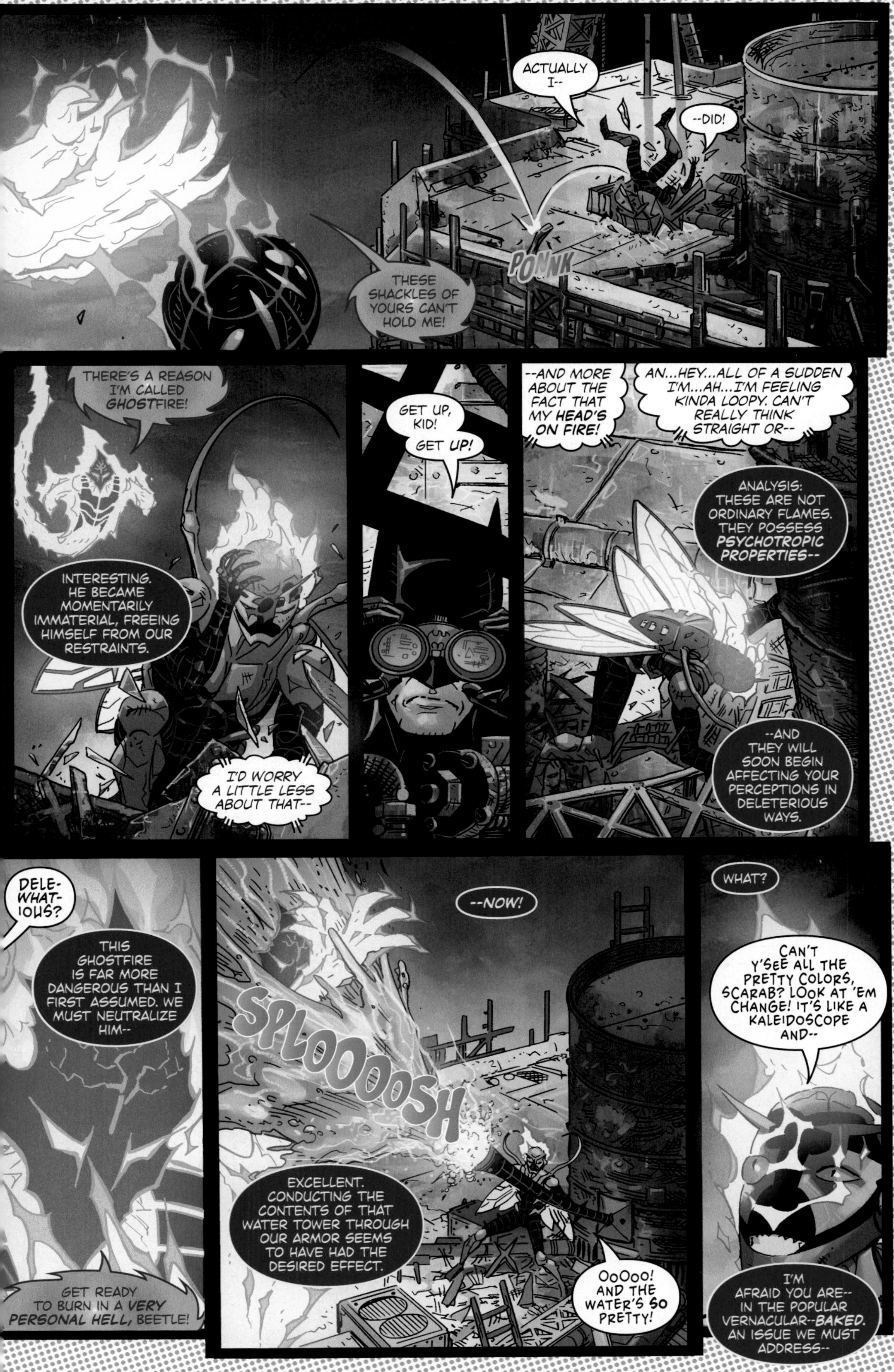
ACTUALLY I--
--DID!
PONNK
THESE SHACKLES OF YOURS CAN'T HOLD ME!
THERE'S A REASON I'M CALLED GHOSTFIRE!
INTERESTING. HE BECAME MOMENTARILY IMMATERIAL, FREEING HIMSELF FROM OUR RESTRAINTS.
I'D WORRY A LITTLE LESS ABOUT THAT--
GET UP, KID!
GET UP!
--AND MORE ABOUT THE FACT THAT MY HEAD'S ON FIRE!
AN...HEY...ALL OF A SUDDEN I'M...AH...I'M FEELING KINDA LOOPY. CAN'T REALLY THINK STRAIGHT OR--
ANALYSIS: THESE ARE NOT ORDINARY FLAMES. THEY POSSESS PSYCHOTROPIC PROPERTIES--
--AND THEY WILL SOON BEGIN AFFECTING YOUR PERCEPTIONS IN DELETERIOUS WAYS.
DELE-WHAT-IOUS?
THIS GHOSTFIRE IS FAR MORE DANGEROUS THAN I FIRST ASSUMED. WE MUST NEUTRALIZE HIM--
GET READY TO BURN IN A VERY PERSONAL HELL, BEETLE!
--NOW!
SPLOOOOOSH
EXCELLENT. CONDUCTING THE CONTENTS OF THAT WATER TOWER THROUGH OUR ARMOR SEEMS TO HAVE HAD THE DESIRED EFFECT.
OOOOO! AND THE WATER'S SO PRETTY!
WHAT?
CAN'T Y'SEE ALL THE PRETTY COLORS, SCARAB? LOOK AT 'EM CHANGE! IT'S LIKE A KALEIDOSCOPE AND--
I'M AFRAID YOU ARE--IN THE POPULAR VERNACULAR--BAKED. AN ISSUE WE MUST ADDRESS--

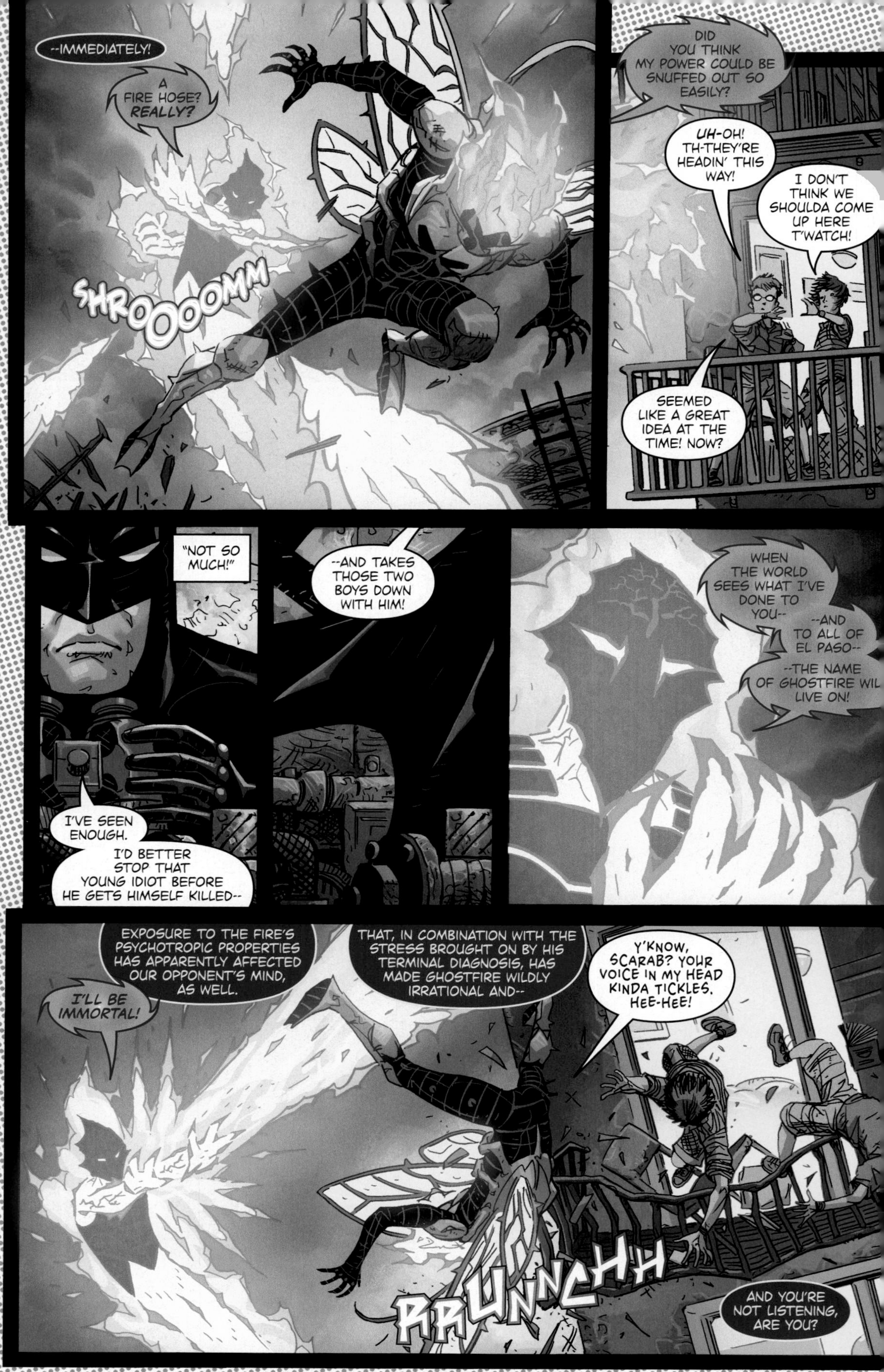
--IMMEDIATELY!
A FIRE HOSE? REALLY?
SHROOOOOMM
DID YOU THINK MY POWER COULD BE SNUFFED OUT SO EASILY?
UH-OH! TH-THEY'RE HEADIN' THIS WAY!
I DON'T THINK WE SHOULDA COME UP HERE T'WATCH!
SEEMED LIKE A GREAT IDEA AT THE TIME! NOW?
"NOT SO MUCH!"
I'VE SEEN ENOUGH.
I'D BETTER STOP THAT YOUNG IDIOT BEFORE HE GETS HIMSELF KILLED--
--AND TAKES THOSE TWO BOYS DOWN WITH HIM!
WHEN THE WORLD SEES WHAT I'VE DONE TO YOU--
--AND TO ALL OF EL PASO--
--THE NAME OF GHOSTFIRE WIL LIVE ON!
EXPOSURE TO THE FIRE'S PSYCHOTROPIC PROPERTIES HAS APPARENTLY AFFECTED OUR OPPONENT'S MIND, AS WELL.
I'LL BE IMMORTAL!
THAT, IN COMBINATION WITH THE STRESS BROUGHT ON BY HIS TERMINAL DIAGNOSIS, HAS MADE GHOSTFIRE WILDLY IRRATIONAL AND--
Y'KNOW, SCARAB? YOUR VOICE IN MY HEAD KINDA TICKLES. HEE-HEE!
RRUNNCHH
AND YOU'RE NOT LISTENING, ARE YOU?

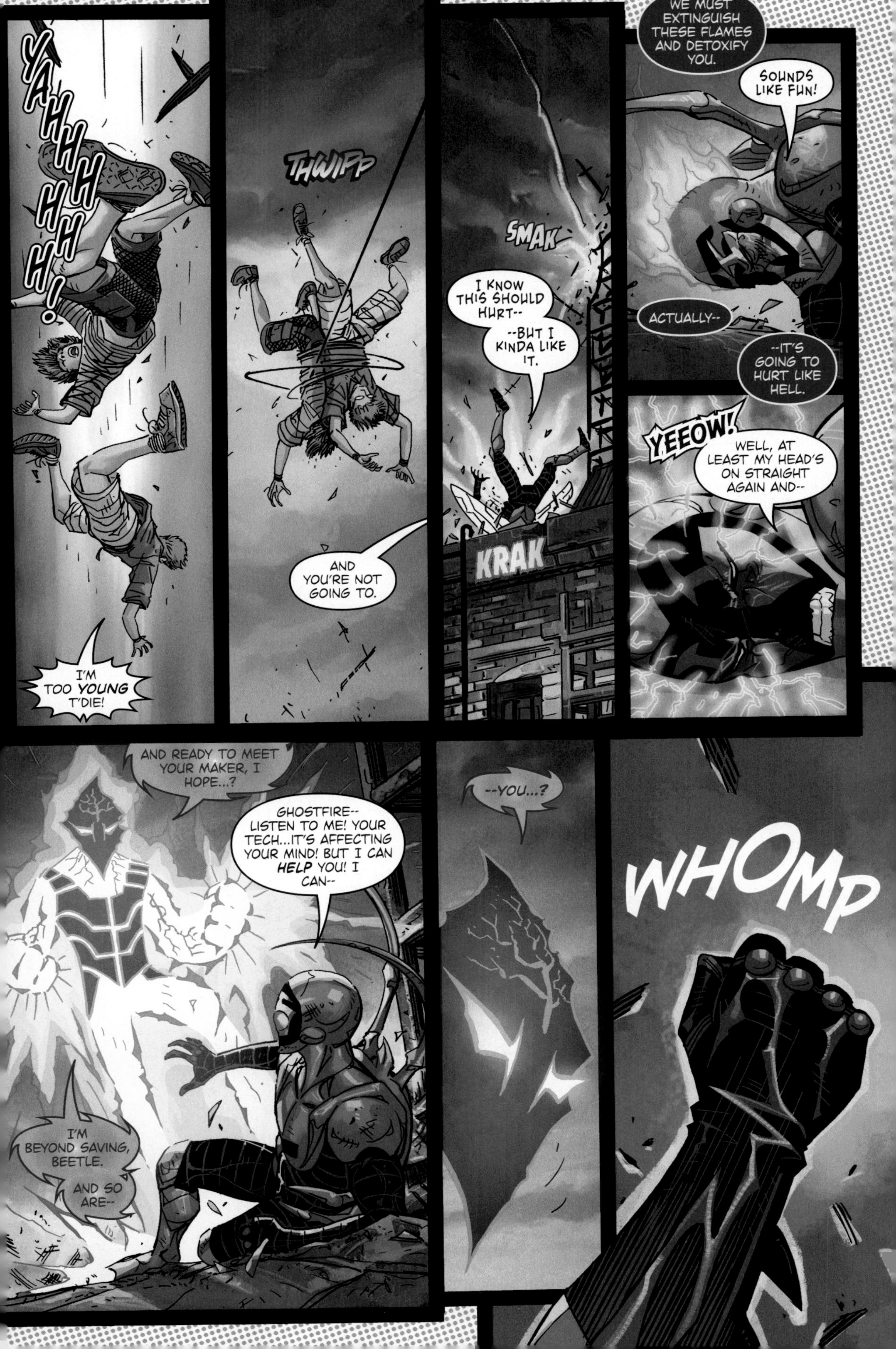
YAHHHHHHH!
I'M TOO YOUNG T'DIE!
THWIPP
AND YOU'RE NOT GOING TO.
SMAK
I KNOW THIS SHOULD HURT--
--BUT I KINDA LIKE IT.
KRAK
WE MUST EXTINGUISH THESE FLAMES AND DETOXIFY YOU.
SOUNDS LIKE FUN!
ACTUALLY--
--IT'S GOING TO HURT LIKE HELL.
YEEOW!
WELL, AT LEAST MY HEAD'S ON STRAIGHT AGAIN AND--
AND READY TO MEET YOUR MAKER, I HOPE...?
GHOSTFIRE-- LISTEN TO ME! YOUR TECH...IT'S AFFECTING YOUR MIND! BUT I CAN HELP YOU! I CAN--
I'M BEYOND SAVING, BEETLE.
AND SO ARE--
--YOU...?
WHOMP

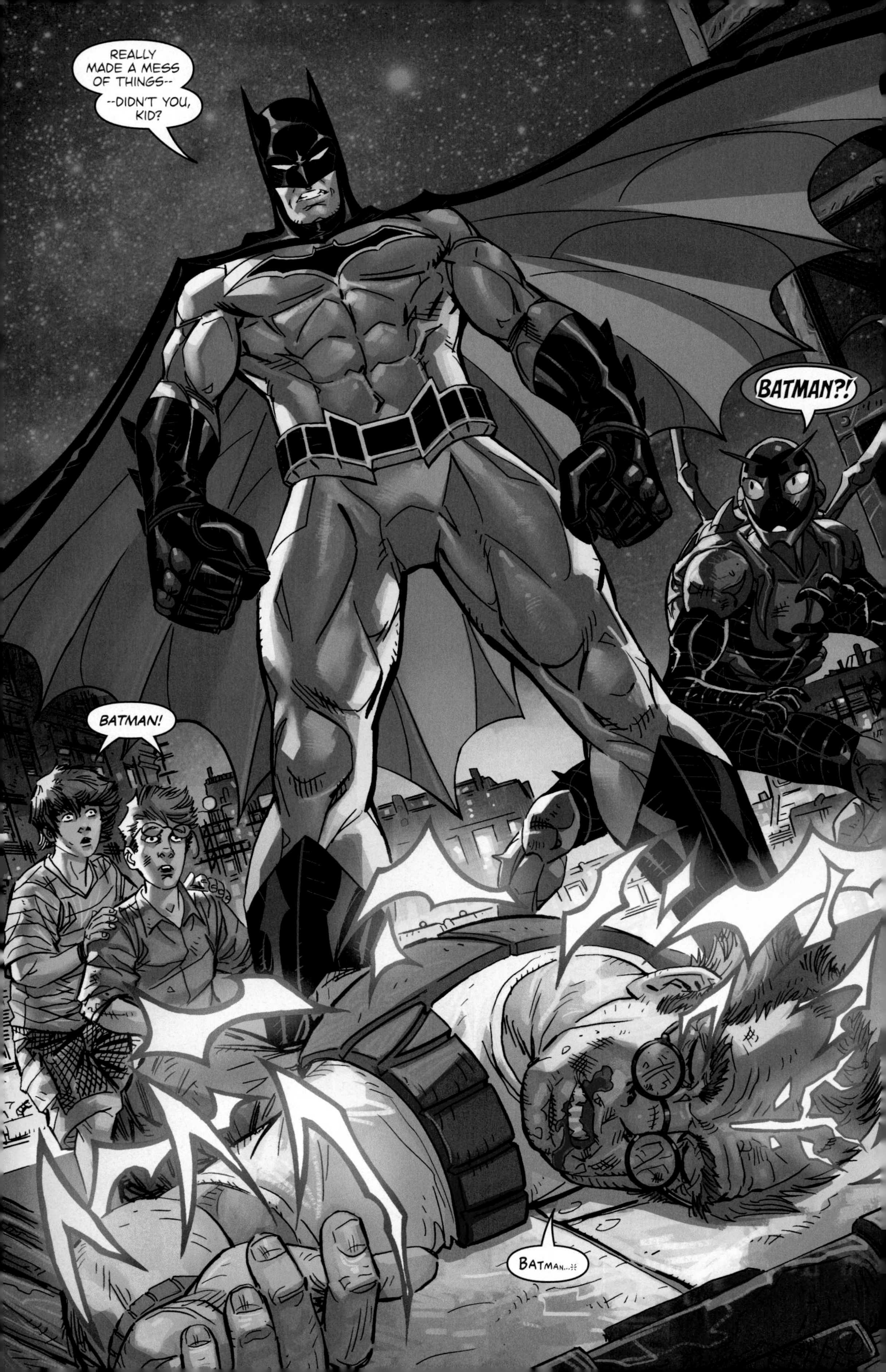
REALLY MADE A MESS OF THINGS--
--DIDN'T YOU, KID?
BATMAN?!
BATMAN!
BATMAN...

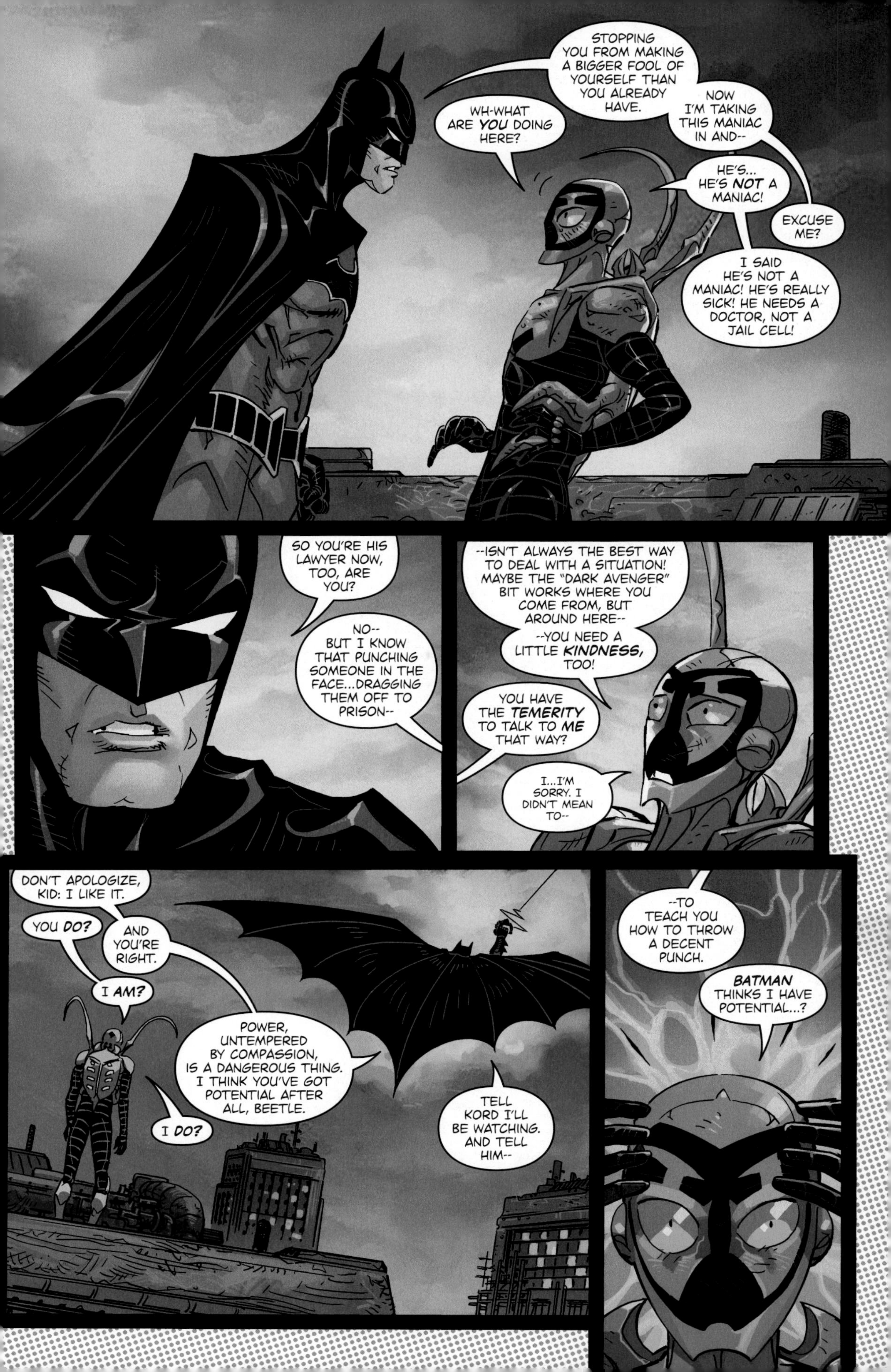
WH-WHAT ARE **YOU** DOING HERE?
STOPPING YOU FROM MAKING A BIGGER FOOL OF YOURSELF THAN YOU ALREADY HAVE.
NOW I'M TAKING THIS MANIAC IN AND--
HE'S... HE'S **NOT** A MANIAC!
EXCUSE ME?
I SAID HE'S NOT A MANIAC! HE'S REALLY SICK! HE NEEDS A DOCTOR, NOT A JAIL CELL!
SO YOU'RE HIS LAWYER NOW, TOO, ARE YOU?
NO-- BUT I KNOW THAT PUNCHING SOMEONE IN THE FACE...DRAGGING THEM OFF TO PRISON--
--ISN'T ALWAYS THE BEST WAY TO DEAL WITH A SITUATION! MAYBE THE "DARK AVENGER" BIT WORKS WHERE YOU COME FROM, BUT AROUND HERE--
--YOU NEED A LITTLE **KINDNESS,** TOO!
YOU HAVE THE ***TEMERITY*** TO TALK TO ***ME*** THAT WAY?
I...I'M SORRY. I DIDN'T MEAN TO--
DON'T APOLOGIZE, KID: I LIKE IT.
YOU ***DO?***
AND YOU'RE RIGHT.
I ***AM?***
POWER, UNTEMPERED BY COMPASSION, IS A DANGEROUS THING. I THINK YOU'VE GOT POTENTIAL AFTER ALL, BEETLE.
I ***DO?***
TELL KORD I'LL BE WATCHING. AND TELL HIM--
--TO TEACH YOU HOW TO THROW A DECENT PUNCH.
BATMAN THINKS I HAVE POTENTIAL...?

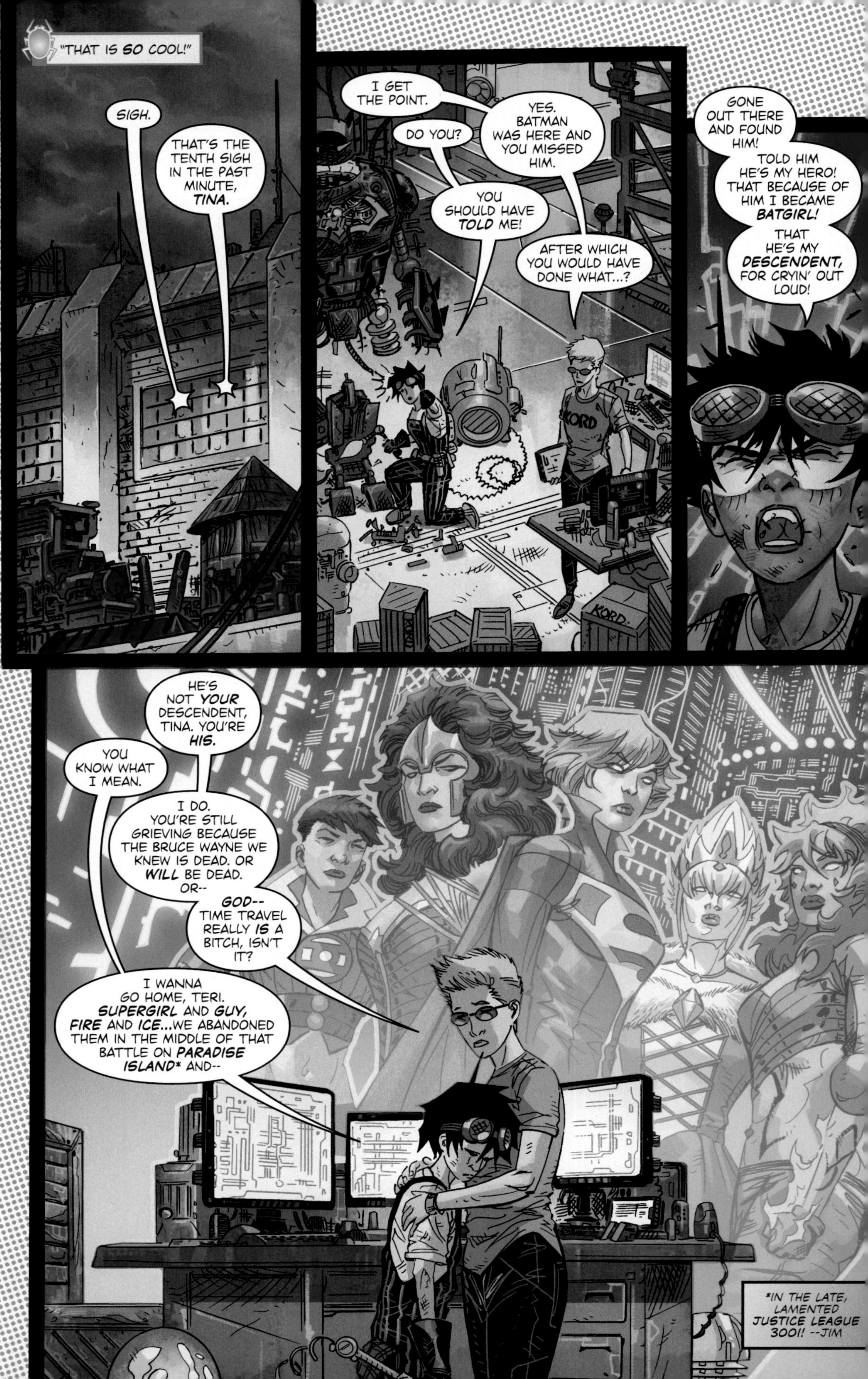
"THAT IS SO COOL!"
SIGH.
THAT'S THE TENTH SIGH IN THE PAST MINUTE, TINA.
I GET THE POINT.
YES. BATMAN WAS HERE AND YOU MISSED HIM.
DO YOU?
YOU SHOULD HAVE TOLD ME!
AFTER WHICH YOU WOULD HAVE DONE WHAT...?
KORD
KORD
GONE OUT THERE AND FOUND HIM!
TOLD HIM HE'S MY HERO! THAT BECAUSE OF HIM I BECAME BATGIRL!
THAT HE'S MY DESCENDENT, FOR CRYIN' OUT LOUD!
HE'S NOT YOUR DESCENDENT, TINA. YOU'RE HIS.
YOU KNOW WHAT I MEAN.
I DO. YOU'RE STILL GRIEVING BECAUSE THE BRUCE WAYNE WE KNEW IS DEAD. OR WILL BE DEAD. OR--
GOD-- TIME TRAVEL REALLY IS A BITCH, ISN'T IT?
I WANNA GO HOME, TERI. SUPERGIRL AND GUY, FIRE AND ICE...WE ABANDONED THEM IN THE MIDDLE OF THAT BATTLE ON PARADISE ISLAND* AND--
*IN THE LATE, LAMENTED JUSTICE LEAGUE 3001! --JIM

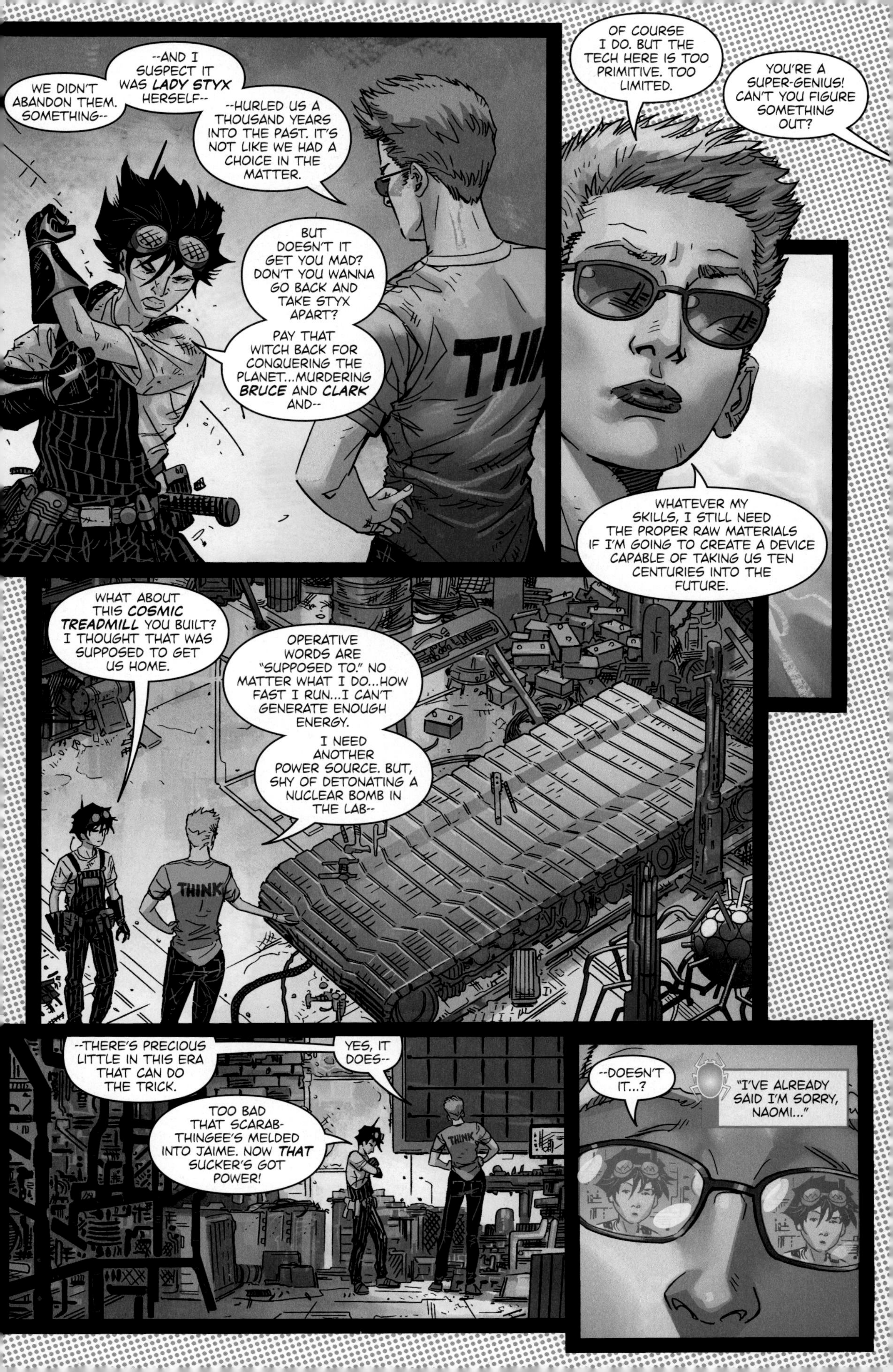
WE DIDN'T ABANDON THEM. SOMETHING--
--AND I SUSPECT IT WAS LADY STYX HERSELF--
--HURLED US A THOUSAND YEARS INTO THE PAST. IT'S NOT LIKE WE HAD A CHOICE IN THE MATTER.
BUT DOESN'T IT GET YOU MAD? DON'T YOU WANNA GO BACK AND TAKE STYX APART?
PAY THAT WITCH BACK FOR CONQUERING THE PLANET...MURDERING BRUCE AND CLARK AND--
THINK
YOU'RE A SUPER-GENIUS! CAN'T YOU FIGURE SOMETHING OUT?
OF COURSE I DO. BUT THE TECH HERE IS TOO PRIMITIVE. TOO LIMITED.
WHATEVER MY SKILLS, I STILL NEED THE PROPER RAW MATERIALS IF I'M GOING TO CREATE A DEVICE CAPABLE OF TAKING US TEN CENTURIES INTO THE FUTURE.
WHAT ABOUT THIS COSMIC TREADMILL YOU BUILT? I THOUGHT THAT WAS SUPPOSED TO GET US HOME.
OPERATIVE WORDS ARE "SUPPOSED TO." NO MATTER WHAT I DO...HOW FAST I RUN...I CAN'T GENERATE ENOUGH ENERGY.
I NEED ANOTHER POWER SOURCE. BUT, SHY OF DETONATING A NUCLEAR BOMB IN THE LAB--
THINK
--THERE'S PRECIOUS LITTLE IN THIS ERA THAT CAN DO THE TRICK.
YES, IT DOES--
TOO BAD THAT SCARAB-THINGEE'S MELDED INTO JAIME. NOW THAT SUCKER'S GOT POWER!
THINK
--DOESN'T IT...?
"I'VE ALREADY SAID I'M SORRY, NAOMI..."

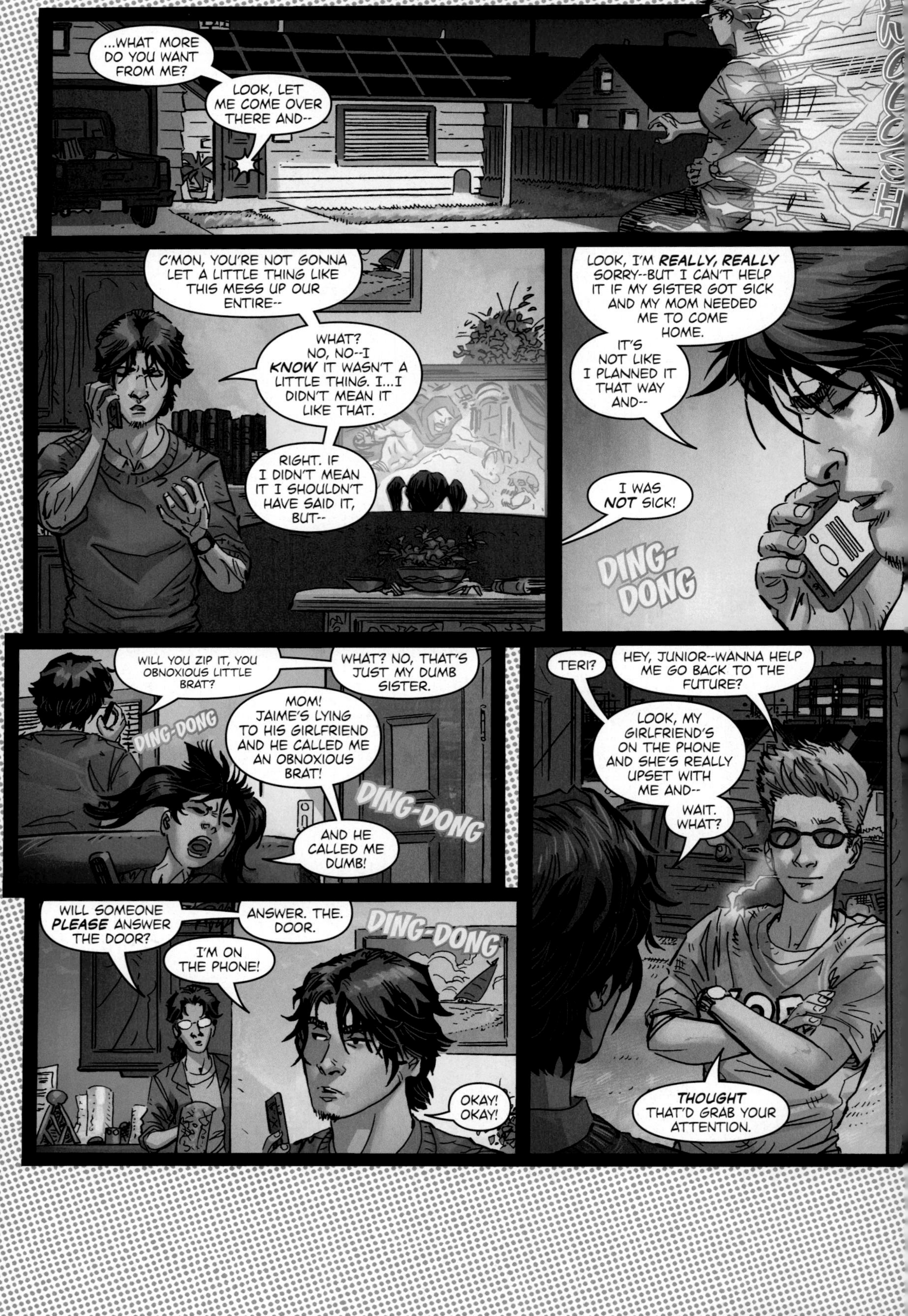

...WHAT MORE DO YOU WANT FROM ME?
LOOK, LET ME COME OVER THERE AND--
FRROOSH
C'MON, YOU'RE NOT GONNA LET A LITTLE THING LIKE THIS MESS UP OUR ENTIRE--
WHAT? NO, NO--I KNOW IT WASN'T A LITTLE THING. I...I DIDN'T MEAN IT LIKE THAT.
RIGHT. IF I DIDN'T MEAN IT I SHOULDN'T HAVE SAID IT, BUT--
LOOK, I'M REALLY, REALLY SORRY--BUT I CAN'T HELP IT IF MY SISTER GOT SICK AND MY MOM NEEDED ME TO COME HOME.
IT'S NOT LIKE I PLANNED IT THAT WAY AND--
I WAS NOT SICK!
DING-DONG
WILL YOU ZIP IT, YOU OBNOXIOUS LITTLE BRAT?
WHAT? NO, THAT'S JUST MY DUMB SISTER.
DING-DONG
MOM! JAIME'S LYING TO HIS GIRLFRIEND AND HE CALLED ME AN OBNOXIOUS BRAT!
DING-DONG
AND HE CALLED ME DUMB!
WILL SOMEONE PLEASE ANSWER THE DOOR?
ANSWER. THE. DOOR.
I'M ON THE PHONE!
DING-DONG
OKAY! OKAY!
TERI?
HEY, JUNIOR--WANNA HELP ME GO BACK TO THE FUTURE?
LOOK, MY GIRLFRIEND'S ON THE PHONE AND SHE'S REALLY UPSET WITH ME AND--
WAIT. WHAT?
THOUGHT THAT'D GRAB YOUR ATTENTION.

TO BE CONTINUED

blue beetle

VARIANT COVER GALLERY

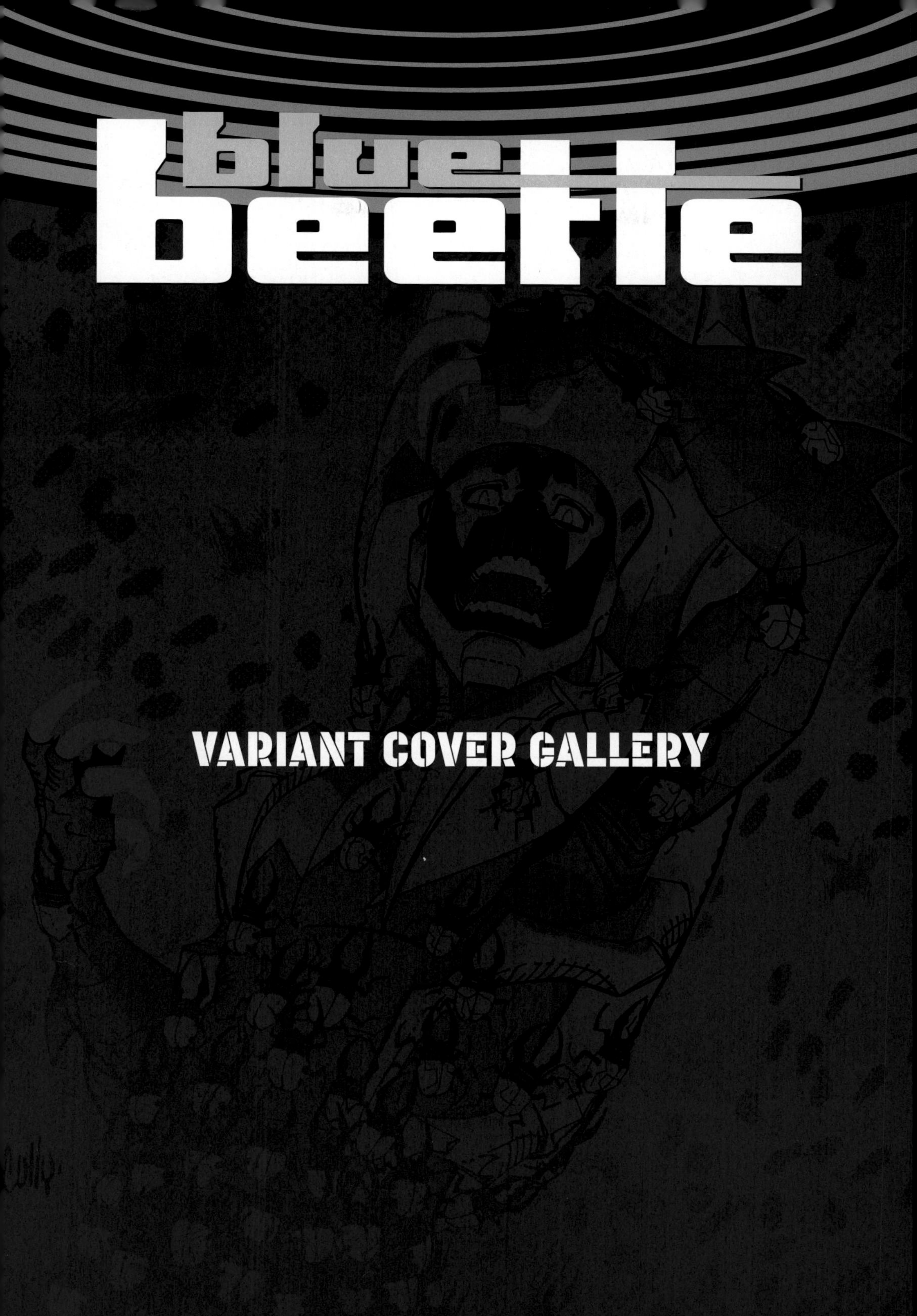

BLUE BEETLE #6 variant cover by CULLY HAMNER

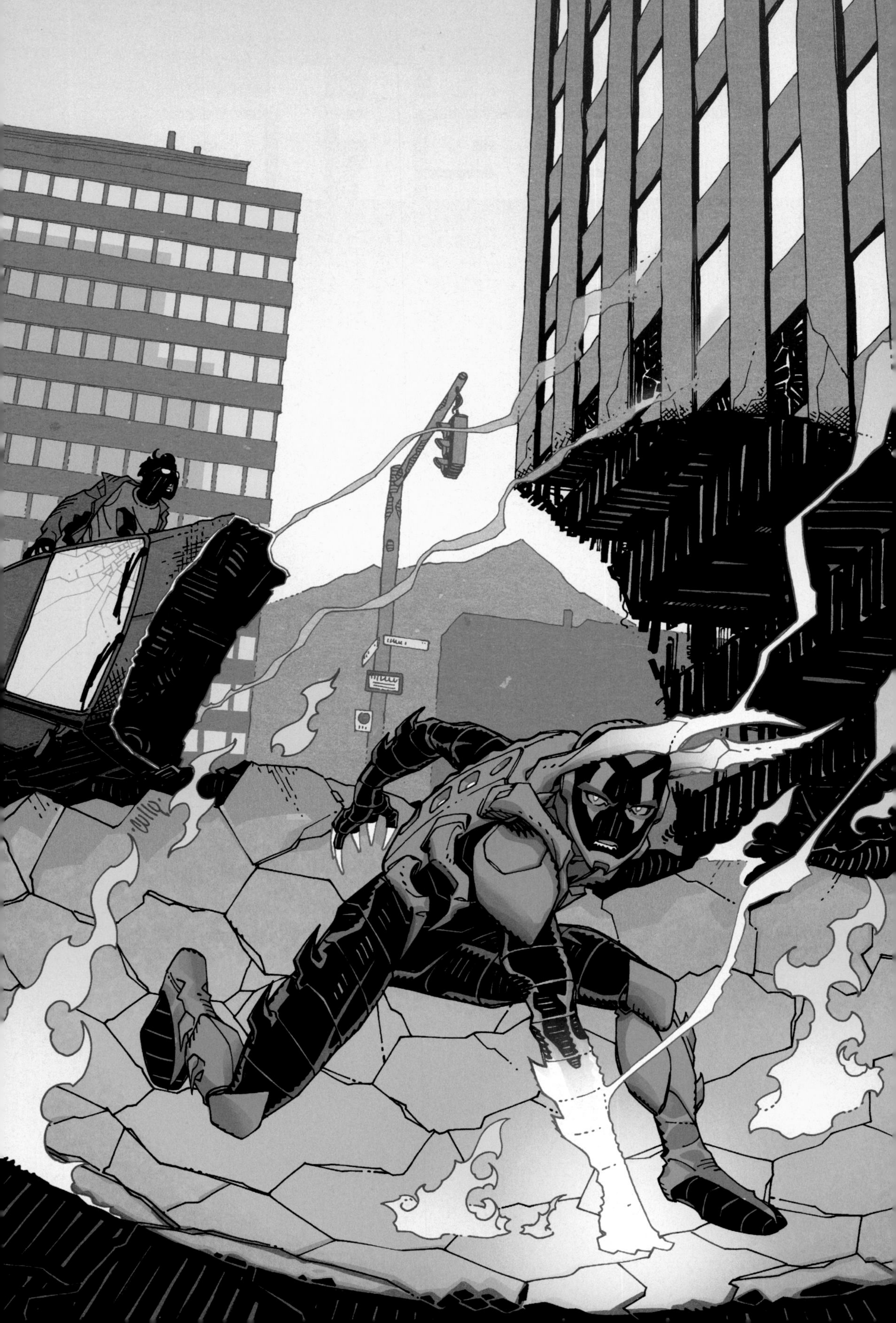

BLUE BEETLE #7 variant cover by CULLY HAMNER

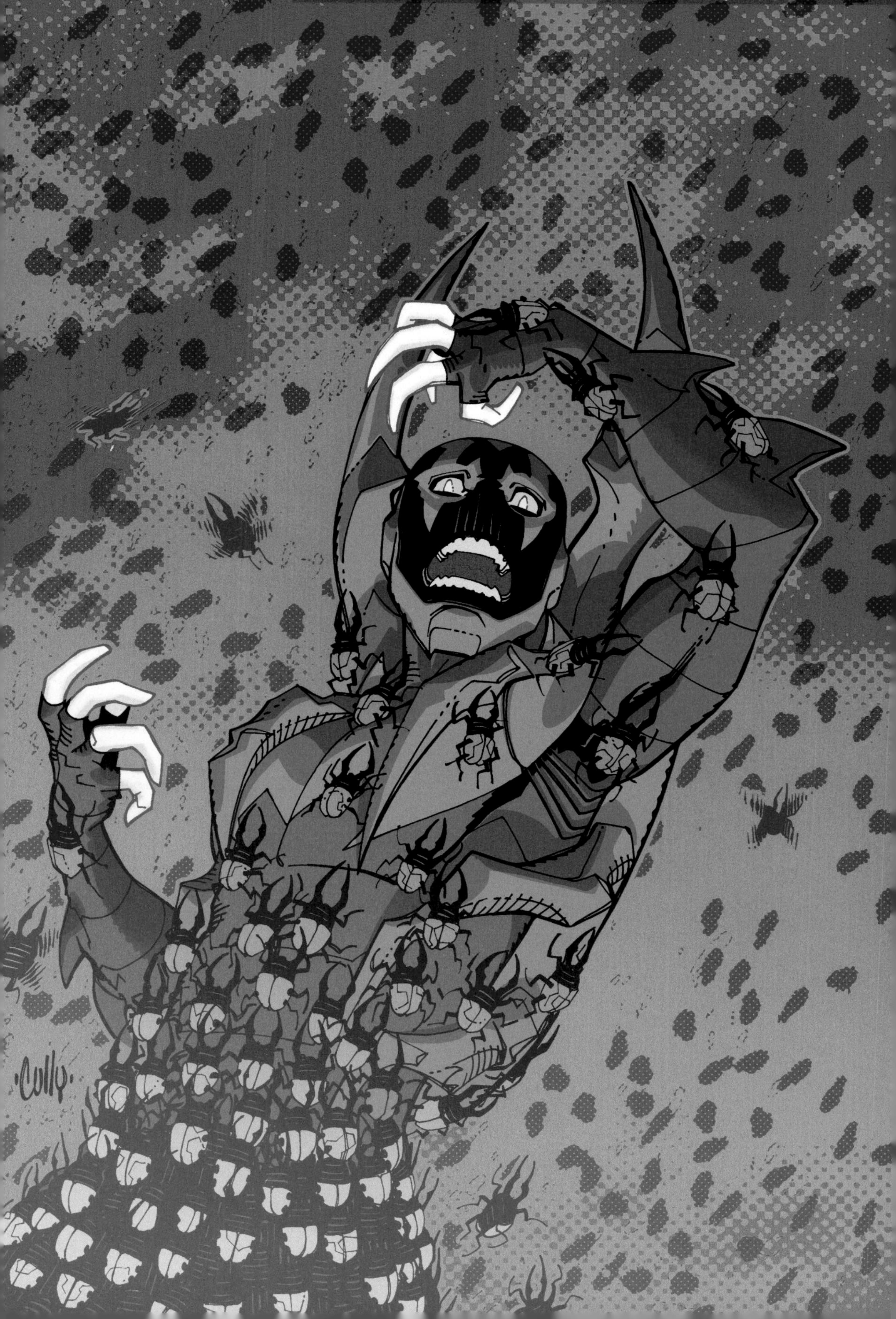
Cully

BLUE BEETLE #8 variant cover by TYLER KIRKHAM and TOMEU MOREY

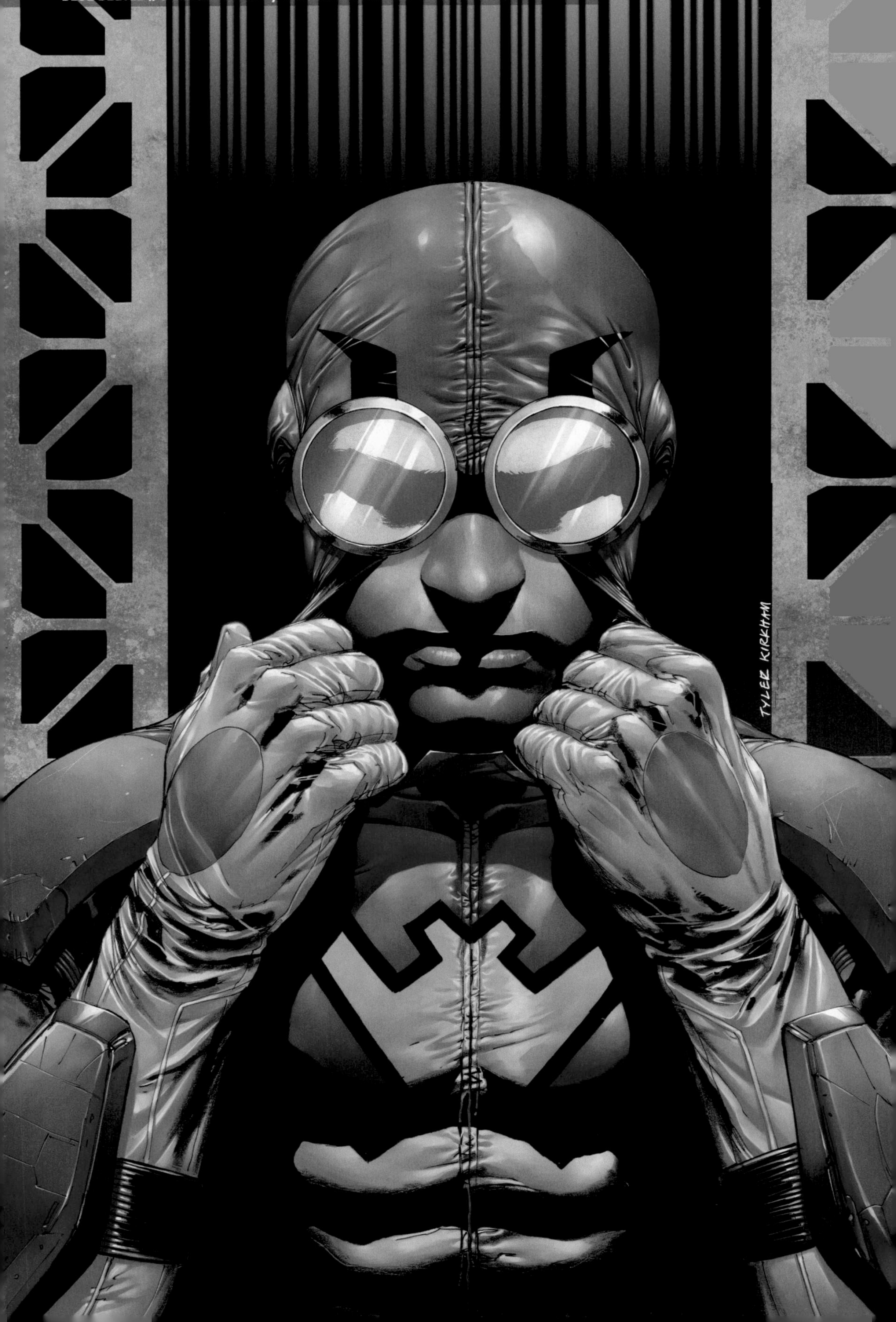
TYLER KIRKHAM

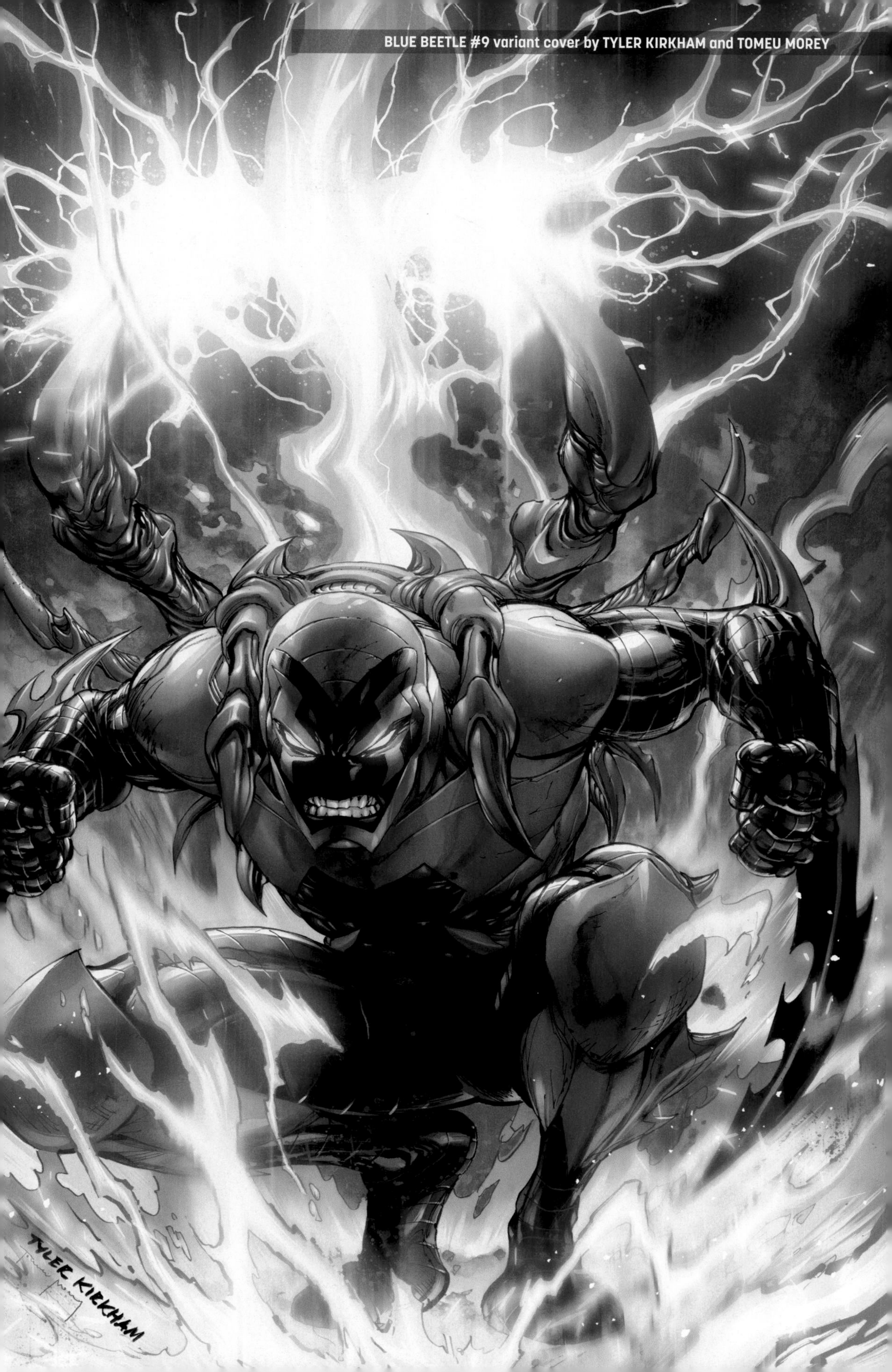
TYLER KIRKHAM

BLUE BEETLE #9 variant cover by TYLER KIRKHAM and TOMEU MOREY

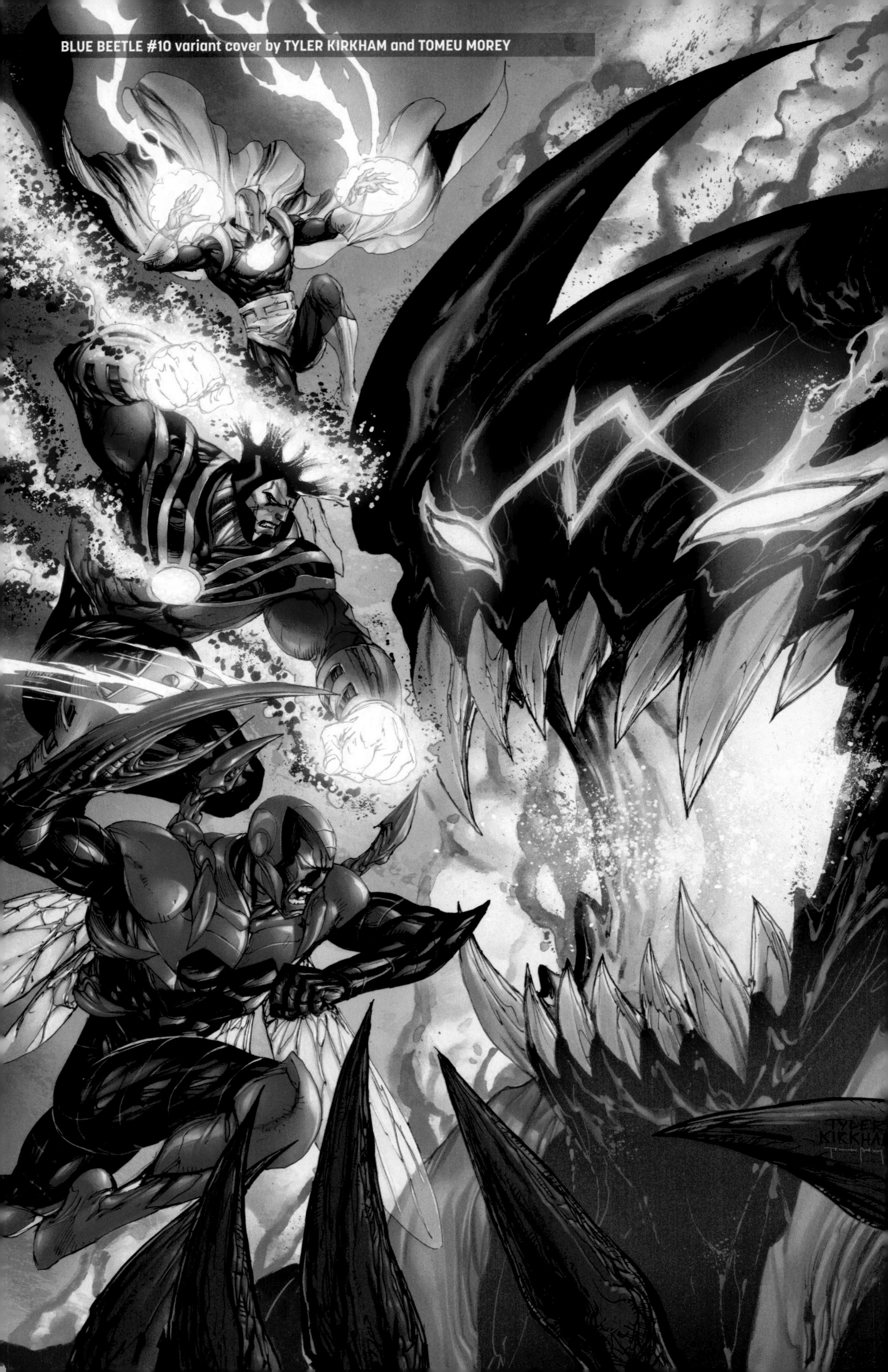
TYLER KIRKHAM

BLUE BEETLE #10 variant cover by TYLER KIRKHAM and TOMEU MOREY

BLUE BEETLE #11 variant cover BY TYLER KIRKHAM and TOMEU MOREY

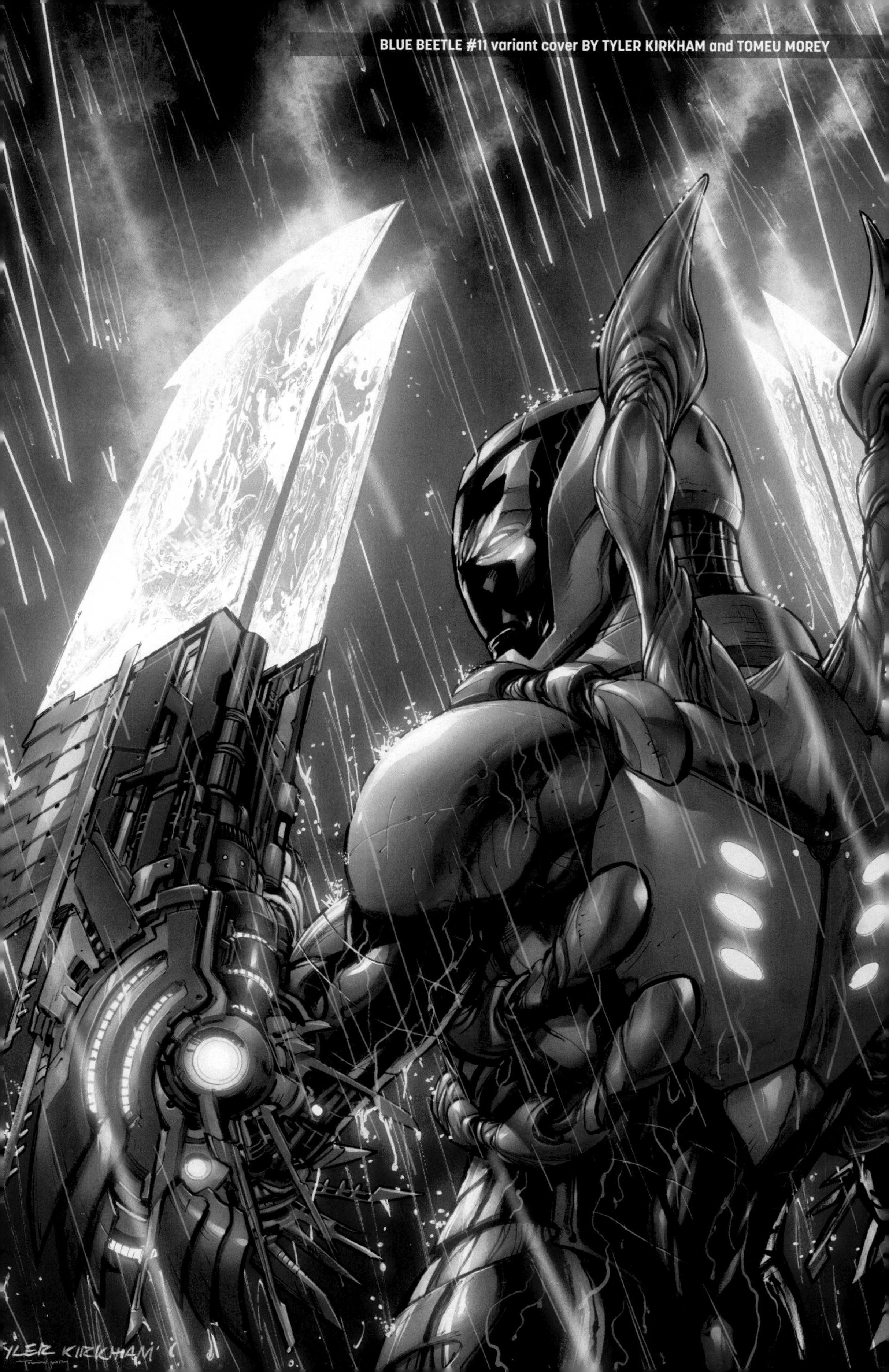
TYLER KIRKHAM

BLUE BEETLE #12 variant cover by TYLER KIRKHAM and TOMEU MOREY

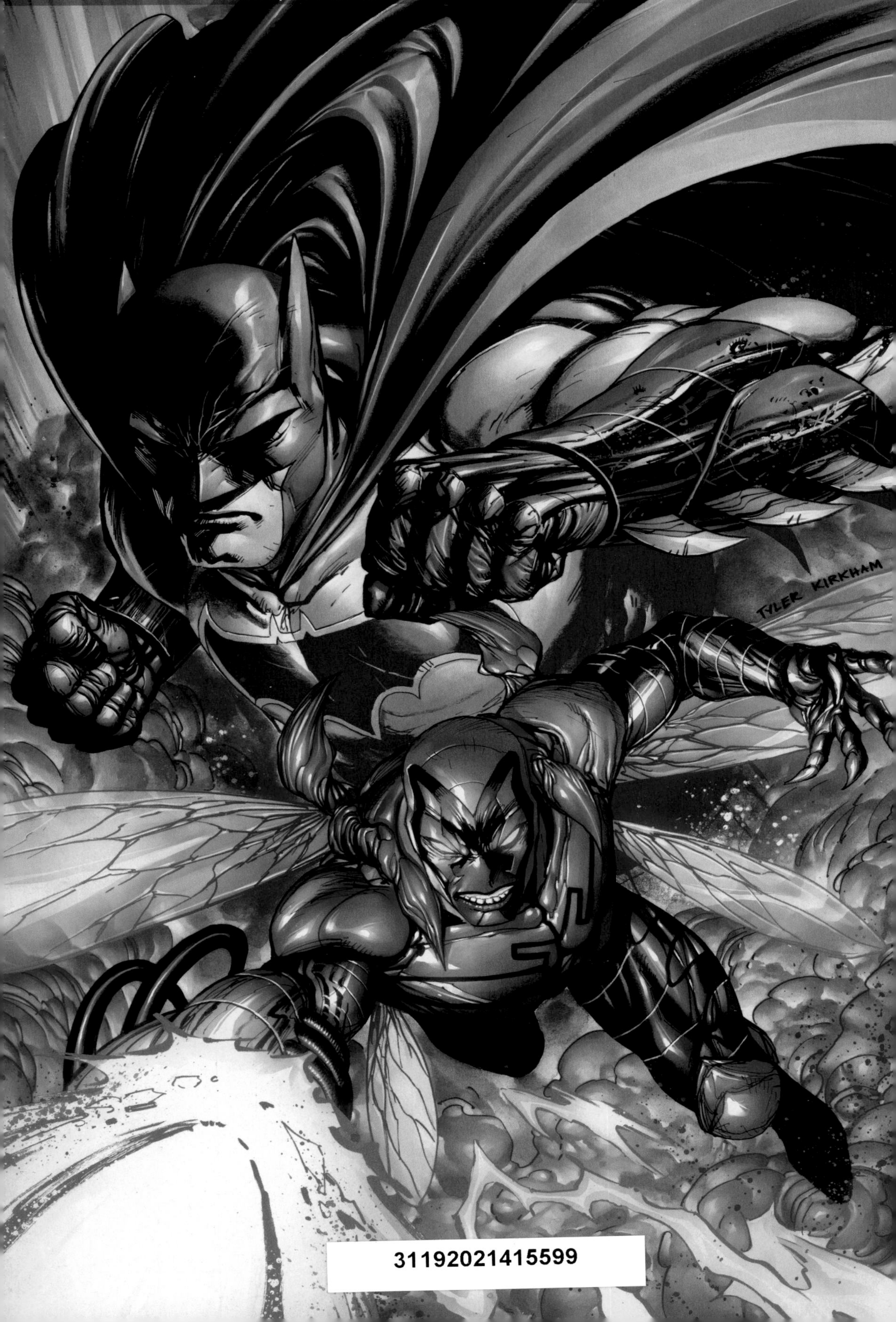
TYLER KIRKHAM